W9-BNV-777

VOICES
OF THE
WINDS

BY THE SAME AUTHORS

by Margot Edmonds and Ella E. Clark
Sacagawea of the Lewis and Clark Expedition

by Ella E. Clark
Poetry: An Interpretation of Life
Indian Legends of the Pacific Northwest
Indian Legends of Canada
Indian Legends of the Northern Rockies
Guardian Spirit Quest
In the Beginning

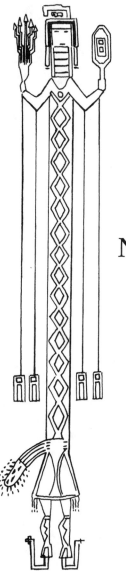

VOICES

OF THE

WINDS

NATIVE AMERICAN
LEGENDS

Margot Edmonds
Ella E. Clark

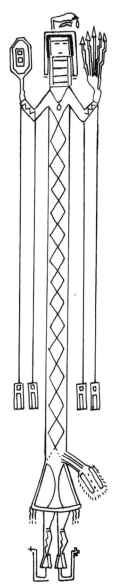

CASTLE BOOKS

This edition published in 2003 by

Castle Books ®

A division of Book Sales, Inc.
 276 Fifth Ave., Suite 206
 New York, NY 10001

Voices of the Winds by Margot Edmonds © 1989
Published under license from
Facts on File, Inc.
132 West 31st Street 17th Floor
New York, NY 10001

Edmonds, Margot.
  Voices of the winds: Native American legends/ Margot Edmonds, Ella E. Clark; illustrator, Molly Braun.
  p. cm.
Bibliography: p.
 I. Indians of North America—Legends. I. Clark, E. Elizabeth, 1896- . II. Title.
E98.F6E26   1989
396.2 08997—dc20

British and Australian CIP data available on request from Facts on File.

Text Design by Stein & Ehn
Composition by Facts on File

ISBN-13: 978-0-7858-1716-1
ISBN-10: 0-7858-1716-6

Printed in the United States of America

Contents

To the original North American Indians,
and to their descendants, who have preserved
Indian oral literature through the centuries,
since the last Ice Age, translating their wisdom
about this Universe for all its peoples.

Acknowledgments

The authors gratefully acknowledge the sources of assistance given in the preparation of this anthology of Indian legends:

The Bureau of American Ethnology, Smithsonian Institute, Washington, D.C.

The American Folklore Society, Washington, D.C., for its *Journal of American Folklore*.

The historical societies of Oregon, Washington, and Montana.

The U.S. Bureau of Indian Affairs, Washington, D.C.

AMS Reprints Press, Kraus Reprints, Gale Press Reprints, Johnson Corporation Reprints, and Reader's Digest Association.

The University of Washington State Libraries, Pullman. Mr. John Guido, Archival Head. The librarians at the University of California, San Diego, CA. The librarians at San Diego Central Library and its La Jolla Branch Library.

Grateful acknowledgment is also made to the original authors and publishers of these tales. Sources for legends appear in footnotes; see Bibliography for complete citation.

After diligently searching and using every effort to seek permissions from copyright proprietors, the authors regret any omissions.

Almis Okanagan
Makah Sanpoil Chelan
Salish Columbia Blackfeet
Wasco Piegan
Flathead Hidatsa
Shasta Yellowstone Mandan
Pomo Shoshone Arikara
Washo Dakota·Sioux
Miwak Cheyenne
Yosemite Paiute Pawnee
Mariposa Arapaho
Yokut Ute Wichi'z
Luiseno Hopi Apache
Diegueños Navaho Zuni Acoma
Papago Apache
Pima

Chipewyan

Chippewa
Ottawa
Winnebago
Iowa
Illini
Shawnee
Yuchi Cherokee
Tuskegee
Alabama Creek
Natchez
Seminole

Micmac
Wabanaki
Passamaquoddy
Penobscot
Abnaki
Seneca
Iroquois
Wampanoag

AS IT WAS

■

Long, long ago, as all good stories begin, man first appeared upon the North American continent from eastern Asia. He followed the trails of the caribou, elk, reindeer, camels, and bear who were seeking food, as was he. They crossed over the ice-covered Bering Strait land bridge long before the end of the last Ice Age disappeared, over 10,000 years ago. These early humans became the first inhabitants of the area, and along with their children and descendants became known as the North American Indians.

These Indians established colonies of tribes along the coastal region of what has now become Alaska. Eventually, still in search of food, they migrated eastward across what we today call Canada. They then moved southward along the West Coast and the East Coast. Later, they spread inland to the Central and the Great Plains regions of the present United States of America.

A few thousand years later the North American Indians were found in the southern areas of the continent from west to east, all of them descendants of those first Asians who crossed the Bering Strait land bridge, before the end of the last Ice Age.

Since the very beginning, North American Indians mostly communicated their beliefs through oral history, as well as through their paintings, carvings, the body movements in their expressive dances, and with rhythmic sounds produced on drumlike instruments.

Indians told their history using all of these methods. Most notable, of course, has been the oral transmission of myths and legends from one generation to the next, through tribal historians. From early childhood, these historians were trained by their elders to learn the tales and mimic the characters in the stories.

Traditionally, storytelling was reserved for the cold seasons, as people gathered around winter fires. Storytelling at any other season was taboo among the tribal ancients who maintained traditions for their people. During the other seasons more important activities for the tribal members were hunting, fishing, harvesting, and making clothes for all members in the tribal family. If violations of tribal rules occurred, offenders were certain to suffer great misfortune at the hands of evil spirits, according to tribal traditions.

To help us learn and understand more about the life of the North American Indians, their myths and legends are a rich source of their oral tradition, comparable to reading European folklore and fairy tales.

Classical Greek and Latin stories of giants, monsters, and other super-natural heroes provided a similar oral account of their time and people. So superbly trained were North American Indian tribal historians from generation to generation that their acting and the mimicry of sounds portraying human and animal characters were limited only by the imagination of the storytellers.

The Indian myths and legends collected in this volume represent most of the tribes of longtime North American Indian cultures in the six major regions of the United States of America: Northwest, Southwest, Great Plains, Central, Southeast, and Northeast. We hope to introduce these stories to the general reader, stories that were generally accessible only to the specialists in folklore.

American Indian legends originated from a variety of experience. Some describe the beauty and power of the landscape. Others reflect themes of natural phenomena, creation myths, the origin of fire, histori-cal events and customs, and the mystical beliefs of North American Indians.

We have chosen representative legends from various sources, preserved in government documents, old histories, periodicals, and reports from anthropologists in the field. Also included are a few tales from manuscripts treasured by early pioneers in the Northwest region.

Some of the legends from printed material have been rewritten slight-ly for clarity and grammatical expression, and to make them more suitable for the general reader.

Ella E. Clark spent many summers on fifteen North American Indian reservations, listening to elder tribal historians and recording their stories. Several of these are included in *Voices of the Winds*. You will find all of our sources for the material included in this book listed in the extensive bibliography.

We have considered as our underlying theme in this volume the way North American Indians believed that spirit life dwelled in all of nature. So very much of the North American Indian's way of life was related to their spiritual beliefs and to the rituals of daily life for each tribe. They believed that everything in nature possessed a life or spirit within, even the sky, earth, mountains, trees, waters, animals, birds—and man.

The North American Indian believed all rain or hail from the sky contained its own special spirit song for his sensitive ear, a challenge to him for further endeavor or perhaps a warning of things to come. Indians believed every wind breathed forth the spirit of the one who made the wind blow, however far away, and they had their own special names for the many spirit *Voices of the Winds*. "Indians heard them in every sigh, whisper, bluster, roar, moan, or whistle of the wind—each filled with spirit life and power for the one who listened," described Martin Sampson, an Indian grandfather.

The Indians believed the happenings in every river, waterfall, echo, thunder, and even the changing positions of stars in the sky resulted from actions by their indwelling spirits. They believed these spirits of nature controlled nature itself, the way good or bad spirits living in man seem to control much of his behavior.

North American Indians judged spirits as good or bad according to how they treated Indians, naturally favoring those that protected them from wrath or evil. Indians believed that angered spirits caused crop failures or caused fish and game to vanish, and were responsible for other catastrophies of nature that might endanger all life.

Evil spirits associated themselves with darkness in caves and deep underground caverns. From these they emerged periodically and performed horrendous deeds, or so thought the North American Indians. Spirits of swamplands and dark forests, inadvertently overheard by Indians, could cause them to lose their way home— forever. Indian children were taught *never* to listen to these kinds of misleading spirits for fear of kidnapping and separation from their tribes.

Enormous Thunderbird ruled over all as chief spirit of storms. North American Indian tales relate that his large flapping wings caused the frightening sounds of roaring thunder. His flashing eyes emitted lightning. Thunderbird lived in a black cloud high above the tallest mountain, or sometimes Thunderbird rested in an enormous cave of a mammoth mountain. When he became terribly hungry, he charged westward to the Pacific Ocean and devoured a whole whale. Thunderbird's homeward trip was accompanied by thunder and lightning, frightening Indians in his path.

Did the North American Indians think certain spirits in nature seemed more powerful than others? Many of their legends tell about the Great Spirit, probably meaning their most awesome spirit. Other Indians also speak of the Chief of the Sky Spirits. The coming of the white man to the Northwest followed the Lewis and Clark Expedition, from 1804 to 1806. Is it possible that both the Great Spirit and the Chief of the Sky Spirits was the Indians' interpretation of the white man's God or Supreme Being?

North American Indians believed that the mysterious power of spirits in nature was stronger than human power. Consequently, an Indian searched to discover for himself the strong spirit of a supernatural power to become his guardian spirit for life. For a young Indian, a Guardian Spirit Quest became the most important event of his life. To accomplish his feat, an Indian youth isolated himself from his family and tribe. He built a small shelter, then fasted and thirsted for many days and nights alone.

Usually in a dream, a strong animal spirit in human form appeared to the boy. The dream spirit taught him his own sacred song, his family duties, his tribal duties, and gave him a special gift to become a hunter, or a leader, or even a healer for his tribe. The young Indian was given a token, or talisman, usually by his father or his tribal Medicine Man to wear always. His newly acquired spirit power and his gifts became his "Medicine" for life.

He hid his "Medicine" in his own self-decorated animal skin bag. This became his power, or "sacred bundle," that he brought forth at ceremonials and for his meditation as long as he lived.

Medicine Men and Medicine Women of the tribes possessed phenomenal powers to help their people, and had a wide knowledge of medicinal herbs and potions. They also officiated at ceremonies and celebrations of their tribes. Their position in the tribe was equivalent to that of a high priest or high priestess.

Ella E. Clark wrote in her book, *Indian Legends of the Northern Rockies*, "My ideals of style have been simplicity, sincerity, a conversational tone or one of oral quality, and the variety of rhythms in everyday speech. In my opinion, these qualities are appropriate to the folk literature of any people." The authors of this volume have endeavored to use these ideals in *Voices of the Winds*.

You will discover here through Indian oral histories how tribal traditions and cultures have been preserved from generation to generation from their earliest beginnings in Alaska during the last Ice Age. Included in this collection of North American Indian myths and legends are some from the 1800s and early 1900s as well. From these, general readers can gain greater understanding of the long heritage of Indian tribal life.

Through these Indian legends from ancient times you can listen to the voices of the North American Indians. *Never* would they have opened their hearts to *strangers* in the past! Here, together, we are fortunate to hear an echo of these voices of the winds.

Margot Edmonds and
Ella E. Clark

VOICES
OF THE
WINDS

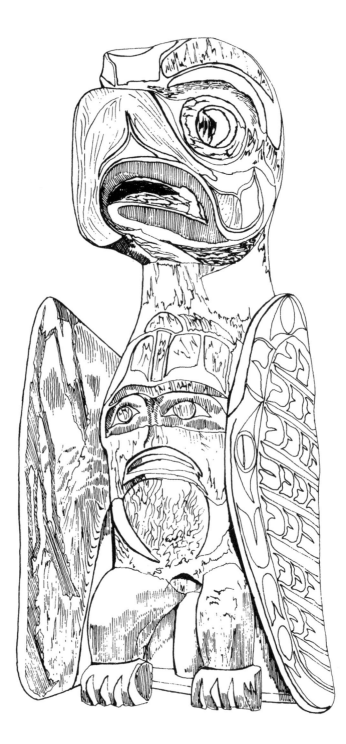

Thunderbird

PART ONE

FROM THE NORTHWEST

The saga of the Northwest Indians probably began millenniums ago when hunting families in search of food set out from Siberia, walked across a land bridge, the Bering Strait, to a new country that became known as Alaska.

Later, many Indian tribes lived south of the Arctic Circle and divided into two distinct language groups: the Algonquians extended eastward to below Hudson Bay, and the Athapascans stayed in northwest Canada. Gradually, some of each group moved southward into the United States.

The Lewis and Clark explorers of 1803 to 1806 probably were the first white men to be seen by some descendants of those ancient Athapascan tribes. Mainly they lived on the north side of the Columbia River; on the south side of the river tribes of the Salishan language family located. Salishan Indians derived their name from the Salish, another name for the Flathead tribes of Montana.

Hunting and fishing provided the chief occupation and food supply of the Northwest Indians. When trading posts developed, commerce increased with white emigrants. The traditions and ceremonies of the tribes, however, continued from one generation to the next.

■

THE CREATION OF THE FIRST INDIANS
Chelan

This story was told by the Chelan Indians, who used to live beside a long lake in the central part of the state of Washington. The lake is still called Lake Chelan (pronounced shȧ-lȁn), meaning "Beautiful Water."

■

Long, long ago, the Creator, the Great Chief Above, made the world. Then he made the animals and the birds and gave them their names— Coyote, Grizzly Bear, Deer, Fox, Eagle, the four Wolf Brothers, Magpie, Bluejay, Hummingbird, and all the others.

When he had finished his work, the Creator called the animal people to him. "I am going to leave you," he said. "But I will come back. When I come again, I will make human beings. They will be in charge of you."

The Great Chief returned to his home in the sky, and the animal people scattered to all parts of the world.

After twelve moons, the animal people gathered to meet the Creator as he had directed. Some of them had complaints. Bluejay, Meadowlark, and Coyote did not like their names. Each of them asked to be some other creature.

"No," said the Creator. "I have given you your names. There is no change. My word is law.

"Because you have tried to change my law, I will not make the human being this time. Because you have disobeyed me, you have soiled what I brought with me. I planned to change it into a human being. Instead, I will put it in water to be washed for many moons and many snows, until it is clean again."

Then he took something from his right side and put it in the river. It swam, and the Creator named it Beaver.

"Now I will give you another law," said the Great Chief Above. "The one of you who keeps strong and good will take Beaver from the water some day and make it into a human being. I will tell you now what to do. Divide Beaver into twelve parts. Take each part to a different place and breathe into it your own breath. Wake it up. It will be a human being with your breath. Give it half of your power and tell it what to do. Today I am giving my power to one of you. He will have it as long as he is good."

When the Creator had finished speaking, all the creatures started for their homes—all except Coyote. The Great Chief had a special word for Coyote.

"You are to be head of all the creatures, Coyote. You are a power just like me now, and I will help you do your work. Soon the creatures and all the other things I have made will become bad. They will fight and will eat each other. It is your duty to keep them as peaceful as you can.

"When you have finished your work, we will meet again, in this land toward the east. If you have been good, if you tell the truth and obey me, you can make the human being from Beaver. If you have done wrong, someone else will make him."

Then the Creator went away.

It happened as the Creator had foretold. Everywhere the things he had created did wrong. The mountains swallowed the creatures. The winds blew them away. Coyote stopped the mountains, stopped the winds, and rescued the creatures. One winter, after North Wind had killed many people, Coyote made a law for him: "Hereafter you can kill only those who make fun of you."

Everywhere Coyote went, he made the world better for the animal people and better for the human beings yet to be created. When he had finished his work, he knew that it was time to meet the Creator again. Coyote thought that he had been good, that he would be the one to make the first human being.

But he was mistaken. He thought that he had as much power as the Creator. So he tried, a second time, to change the laws of the Great Chief Above.

"Some other creature will make the human being," the Creator told Coyote. "I shall take you out into the ocean and give you a place to stay for all time."

So Coyote walked far out across the water to an island. There the Creator stood waiting for him, beside the house he had made. Inside the house on the west side stood a black suit of clothes. On the other side hung a white suit.

"Coyote, you are to wear this black suit for six months," said the Creator. "Then the weather will be cold and dreary. Take off the black suit and wear the white suit. Then there will be summer, and everything will grow.

"I will give you my power not to grow old. You will live here forever and forever."

Coyote stayed there, out in the ocean, and the four Wolf brothers took his place as the head of all the animal people. Youngest Wolf Brother was was strong and good and clever. Oldest Wolf Brother was worthless. So the Creator gave Youngest Brother the power to take Beaver from the water.

One morning Oldest Wolf Brother said to Youngest Brother, "I want you to kill Beaver. I want his tooth for a knife."

"Oh, no!" exclaimed Second and Third Brothers. "Beaver is too strong for Youngest Brother."

But Youngest Wolf said to his brothers, "Make four spears. For Oldest Brother, make a spear with four forks. For me, make a spear with one fork. Make a two-forked spear and a three-forked spear for yourselves. I will try my best to get Beaver, so that we can kill him."

All the animal persons had seen Beaver and his home. They knew where he lived. They knew what a big creature he was. His family of young beavers lived with him.

The animal persons were afraid that Youngest Wolf Brother would fail to capture Beaver and would fail to make the human being. Second and Third World Brothers also were afraid. "I fear we will lose Youngest Brother," they said to each other.

But they made the four spears he had asked for.

At dusk, the Wolf brothers tore down the dam at the beavers' home, and all the little beavers ran out. About midnight, the larger beavers ran out. They were so many, and they made so much noise, that they sounded like thunder. Then Big Beaver ran out, the one the Creator had put into the water to become clean.

"Let's quit!" said Oldest Wolf Brother, for he was afraid. "Let's not try to kill him."

"No!" said Youngest Brother. "I will not stop."

Oldest Wolf Brother fell down. Third Brother fell down. Second Brother fell down. Lightning flashed. The beavers still sounded like thunder. Youngest Brother took the four-forked spear and tried to strike Big Beaver with it. It broke. He used the three-forked spear. It broke. He used the two-forked spear. It broke. Then he took his own one-forked spear. It did not break.

It pierced the skin of Big Beaver and stayed there. Out of the lake, down the creek, and down Big River, Beaver swam, dragging Youngest Brother after it.

Youngest Wolf called to his brothers, "You stay here. If I do not return with Beaver in three days, you will know that I am dead."

Three days later, all the animal persons gathered on a level place at the foot of the mountain. Soon they saw Youngest Brother coming. He had killed Beaver and was carrying it. "You remember that the Creator told us to cut it into twelve pieces," said Youngest Brother to the animal people.

But he could divide it into only eleven pieces.

Then he gave directions. "Fox, you are a good runner. Hummingbird and Horsefly, you can fly fast. Take this piece of Beaver flesh over to that place and wake it up. Give it your breath."

Youngest Brother gave other pieces to other animal people and told them where to go. They took the liver to Clearwater River, and it became the Nez Perce Indians. They took the heart across the mountains, and it became the Methow Indians. Other parts became the Spokane people, the Lake people, the Flathead people. Each of the eleven pieces became a different tribe.

"There have to be twelve tribes," said Youngest Brother. "Maybe the Creator thinks that we should use the blood for the last one. Take the blood across the Shining Mountains and wake it up over there. It will become the Blackfeet. They will always look for blood."

When an animal person woke the piece of Beaver flesh and breathed into it, he told the new human being what to do and what to eat.

"Here are roots," and the animal people pointed to camas and kouse, and to bitterroot, "You will dig them, cook them, and save them to eat in the winter.

"Here are the berries that will ripen in the summer. You will eat them, and you will dry them for use in winter."

The animal people pointed to chokecherry trees, to serviceberry bushes, and to huckleberry bushes.

"There are salmon in all the rivers. You will cook them and eat them when they come up the streams. And you will dry them to eat in the winter."

When all the tribes had been created, the animal people said to them, "Some of you new people should go up Lake Chelan. Go up to the middle of the lake and look at the cliff beside the water. There you will see pictures on the rock. From the pictures you will learn how to make the things you will need."

The Creator had painted the pictures there, with red paint. From the beginning until long after the white people came, the Indians went to Lake Chelan and looked at the paintings. They saw pictures of bows and arrows and of salmon traps. From the paintings of the Creator they knew how to make the things they needed for getting their food.

Note: The paintings (or pictographs) on the lower rocks have been covered by water since a dam was built at the foot of the lake. Surprisingly high on the rocks that are almost perpendicular walls at the north end of the lake, the paintings remained for a long, long time. Then white people with guns and little respect for the past ruined them—for fun.

Clark, *In the Beginning*, 5.

■

COYOTE AND MULTNOMAH FALLS

Wasco

The Big River, or Great River, in the stories of the Northwest
Indians is the Columbia. The Big Shining Mountains are the Rockies.

■

"Long, long ago, when the world was young and people had not come
out yet," said an elderly Indian years ago, "the animals and the birds
were the *people* of this country. They talked to each other just as we do.
And they married, too."

Coyote (kĭ-o̓-tĭ) was the most powerful of the animal people, for he
had been given special power by the Spirit Chief. For one thing, he
changed the course of Big River, leaving Dry Falls behind. In some
stories, he was an animal; in others he was a man, sometimes a handsome
young man.

In that long ago time before this time, when all the people and all the
animals spoke the same language, Coyote made one of his frequent trips
along Great River. He stopped when he came to the place where the
water flowed under the Great Bridge that joined the mountains on one
side of the river with the mountains on the other side. There he changed
himself into a handsome young hunter.

When traveling up the river the last time, he had seen a beautiful girl
in a village not far from the bridge. He made up his mind that he would
ask the girl's father if he might have her for his wife. The girl's father
was a chief. When the handsome young man went to the chief's lodge,
he carried with him a choice gift for the father in return for his daughter.

The gift was a pile of the hides and furs of many animals, as many
skins as Coyote could carry. He made the gift large and handsome
because he had learned that the man who would become the husband
of the girl would one day become the chief of the tribe.

The chief knew nothing about the young man expect that he seemed
to be a great hunter. The gift was pleasing in the father's eyes, but he
wanted his daughter to be pleased.

"She is my only daughter," the chief said to the young hunter. "And
she is very dear to my heart. I shall not be like other fathers and trade
her for a pile of furs. You will have to win the heart of my daughter, for
I want her to be happy."

Plateau Indian carved skeleton figure
Wasco

So Coyote came to the chief's lodge every day, bringing with him some small gift that he thought would please the girl. But he never seemed to bring the right thing. She would shyly accept his gift and then run away to the place where the women sat in the sun doing their work with deerskins or to the place where the children were playing games.

Every day Coyote became more eager to win the beautiful girl. He thought and thought about what gifts to take to her. "Perhaps the prettiest flower hidden in the forest," he said to himself one day, "will be the gift that will make her want to marry me."

He went to the forest beside Great River and searched for one whole day. Then he took to the chief's lodge the most beautiful flower he had found. He asked to see the chief.

"I have looked all day for this flower for your daughter," said Coyote to the chief. "If this does not touch her heart, what will? What gift can I bring that will win her heart?"

The chief was the wisest of all the chiefs of a great tribe. He answered, "Why don't you ask my daughter? Ask her, today, what gift will make her heart the happiest of all hearts."

As the two finished talking, they saw the girl come out of the forest. Again Coyote was pleased and excited by her beauty and her youth. He stepped up to her and asked, "Oh, beautiful one, what does your heart want most of all? I will get for you anything that you name. This flower that I found for you in a hidden spot in the woods is my pledge."

Surprised, or seeming to be surprised, the girl looked at the young hunter and at the rare white flower he was offering her.

"I want a pool," she answered shyly. "A pool where I may bathe every day hidden from all eyes that might see."

Then, without accepting the flower that Coyote had searched for so many hours, she ran away. As before, she hurried to play with her young friends.

Coyote turned to her father. "It is well. In seven suns I will come for you and your daughter. I will take you to the pool she asked for. The pool will be for her alone."

For seven suns Coyote worked to build the pool that would win the heart of the girl he wished to marry. First he cut a great gash in the hills on the south side of Great River. Then he lined that gash with trees and shrubs and ferns to the very top of a high wall that looked toward the river.

Then he went to the bottom of the rock wall and slanted it back a long way, far enough to hollow out a wide pool. He climbed up the wall again and went far back into the hills. There he made a stream come out of the earth, and he sent it down the big gash he had made, to fall over the slanting rock wall. From the edge of that wall the water dropped with spray and mist. And so the water made, at the bottom, a big screen that hid the pool from all eyes.

When he had finished his work, Coyote went to the village to invite the chief and his daughter to see what he had made. When they had admired the new waterfall, he showed them the pool that lay behind it and the spray. He watched the eyes of the girl.

She looked with smiling eyes, first at the pool and the waterfall in front of it, and then at the young hunter who had made them for her. He could see that she was pleased. He could see that at last he had won her heart. She told her father that she was willing to become the wife of the young hunter.

In that long ago time before this time, two old grandmothers sat all day on top of the highest mountains. One sat on the top of the highest mountain north of Great River. The other sat on the highest mountain south of it. When the one on the north side talked, she could be heard eastward as far as the Big Shining Mountains, westward as far as the big water where the sun hides every night, and northward to the top of the world.

The grandmother on the south side of the river also could be heard as far west as the big water and as far south as anyone lived. The two old women saw everything that was done, and every day they told all the people on both sides of the river.

Now they saw the chief's daughter go every morning to bathe in the pool, and they saw Coyote wait for her outside the screen of waterfall and spray. The old grandmothers heard the two sing to each other and laugh together. The grandmothers laughed at the pair, raised their voices, and told all the people what they saw and heard.

Soon the chief's daughter knew that all the people were laughing at her—all the people from the big water to the Big Shining Mountains, all the people from the top of the world to as far south as anyone lived.

She was no longer happy. She no longer sang with joy. One day she asked Coyote to allow her to go alone to the pool. The old grandmothers watched her go behind the waterfall. Then they saw her walk from the pool and go down into Great River. Her people never saw her again.

Coyote, in a swift canoe, went down Great River in search of her. He saw her floating and swimming ahead of him, and he paddled as fast as he could. He reached her just before she was carried out into the big water where the sun hides at night.

There the two of them, Coyote and the girl, were turned into little ducks, little summer ducks, floating on the water.

That was a long, long time ago. But even today, when the sun takes its last look at the high cliff south of Great River, two summer ducks swim out to look back at the series of waterfalls that dash down the high mountain. They look longest at the lowest cascade and the spray that hides the tree-fringed pool behind them.

If those who want to understand will be silent and listen, they will hear the little song that the chief's daughter and Coyote used to sing to each other every morning after she had bathed in the pool. The song begins very soft and low, lifts sharply to a high note, and then fades gently away.

Ella E. Clark.

■

WHEN THE ANIMALS AND BIRDS WERE CREATED
Makah

The Indians who live on the farthest point of the northwest corner of Washington State used to tell stories, not about one Changer, but about the Two-Men-Who-Changed-Things. So did their close relatives, who lived on Vancouver Island, across the Strait of Juan de Fuca.

■

When the world was very young, there were no people on the earth. There were no birds or animals, either. There was nothing but grass and sand and creatures that were neither animals nor people but had some of the traits of people and some of the traits of animals.

Then the two brothers of the Sun and the Moon came to the earth. Their names were *Ho-ho-e-ap-bess*, which means "The Two-Men-Who-Changed-Things." They came to make the earth ready for a new race of people, the Indians. The Two-Men-Who-Changed-Things called all the creatures to them. Some they changed to animals and birds. Some they changed to trees and smaller plants.

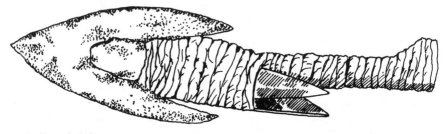

Indian whale harpoon
Makah

Among them was a bad thief. He was always stealing food from creatures who were fishermen and hunters. The Two-Men-Who-Changed-Things transformed him into Seal. They shortened his arms and tied his legs so that only his feet could move. Then they threw Seal into the Ocean and said to him, "Now you will have to catch your own fish if you are to have anything to eat."

One of the creatures was a great fisherman. He was always on the rocks or was wading with his long fishing spear. He kept it ready to thrust into some fish. He always wore a little cape, round and white, over his shoulders. The Two-Men-Who-Changed-Things transformed him into Great Blue Heron. The cape became the white feathers around the neck of Great Blue Heron. The long fishing spear became his sharp-pointed bill.

Another creature was both a fisherman and a thief. He had stolen a necklace of shells. The Two-Men-Who-Changed-Things transformed him into Kingfisher. The necklace of shells was turned into a ring of feathers around Kingfisher's neck. He is still a fisherman. He watches the water, and when he sees a fish, he dives headfirst with a splash into the water.

Two creatures had huge appetites. They devoured everything they could find. The Two-Men-Who-Changed-Things transformed one of them into Raven. They transformed his wife into Crow. Both Raven and Crow were given strong beaks so that they could tear their food. Raven croaks "Cr-r-ruck!" and Crow answers with a loud "Cah! Cah!"

The Two-Men-Who-Changed-Things called Bluejay's son to them and asked, "Which do you wish to be—a bird or a fish?"

"I don't want to be either," he answered.

"Then we will transform you into Mink. You will live on land. You will eat the fish you can catch from the water or can pick up on the shore."

Then the Two-Men-Who-Changed-Things remembered that the new people would need wood for many things.

They called one of the creatures to them and said "The Indians will want tough wood to make bows with. They will want tough wood to

Black raven mask
Makah

make wedges with, so that they can split logs. You are tough and strong. We will change you into the yew tree."

They called some little creatures to them. "The new people will need many slender, straight shoots for arrows. You will be the arrowwood. You will be white with many blossoms in early summer."

They called a big, fat creature to them. "The Indians will need big trunks with soft wood so that they can make canoes. You will be the cedar trees. The Indians will make many things from your bark and from your roots."

The Two-Men-Who-Changed-Things knew that the Indians would need wood for fuel. So they called an old creature to them. "You are old, and your heart is dry. You will make good kindling, for your grease has turned hard and will make pitch. You will be the spruce tree. When you grow old, you will always make dry wood that will be good for fires."

To another creature they said, "You shall be the hemlock. Your bark will be good for tanning hides. Your branches will be used in the sweat lodges."

A creature with a cross temper they changed into a crab apple tree, saying, "You shall always bear sour fruit."

Another creature they changed into the wild cherry tree, so that the new people would have fruit and could use the cherry bark for medicine.

A thin, tough creature they changed into the alder tree, so that the new people would have hard wood for their canoe paddles.

Thus the Two-Men-Who-Changed-Things got the world ready for the new people who were to come. They made the world *as it was* when the Indians lived in it.

Swan, *The Indians of Cape Flattery*, 64-65.

■

RAVEN'S GREAT ADVENTURE
Alaska

Early North American Indians living along the Alaska and North Pacific coast carved the stories of their people on trees, as they had no written language.

They carved strange and beautiful figures, representing people, animals, birds, fish, and supernatural characters, then painted them with bright colors. The tallest red cedar trees were selected for totem poles, and were used for landmarks as well as illustrating the legends told from generation to generation.

On one of these poles was carved a stunning Raven, but he had no beak!

The Raven in Alaska was no ordinary bird. He had remarkable powers and could change into whatever form he wished. He could change from a bird to a man, and could not only fly and walk, but could swim underwater as fast as any fish.

■

One day, Raven took the form of a little, bent-over old man to walk through a forest. He wore a long white beard and walked slowly. After a while, Raven felt hungry. As he thought about this, he came to the edge of the forest near a village on the beach. There, many people were fishing for halibut.

In a flash, Raven thought of a scheme. He dived into the sea and swam to the spot where the fishermen dangled their hooks. Raven gobbled their bait, swimming from one hook to another. Each time Raven stole bait, the fishermen felt a tug on their lines. When the lines were pulled in, there was neither fish nor bait.

But Raven worked his trick once too often. When Houskana, an expert fisherman, felt a tug, he jerked his line quickly, hooking something heavy. Raven's jaw had caught on the hook! While Houskana tugged on his line, Raven pulled in the opposite direction. Then Raven grabbed hold of some rocks at the bottom of the sea and called, "O rocks, 0please help me!" But the rocks paid no attention.

Because of his great pain, Raven said to his jaw, "Break off, O jaw, for I am too tired." His jaw obeyed, and it broke off.

Houskana pulled in his line immediately. On his hook was a man's jaw with a long white beard! It looked horrible enough to scare anyone. Houskana and the other fishermen were very frightened, because they thought the jaw might belong to some evil spirit. They picked up their feet and ran as fast as they could to the chief's house.

Raven came out of the water and followed the fishermen. Though he was in great pain for lack of his jaw, no one noticed anything wrong because he covered the lower part of his face with his blanket.

The chief and the people examined the jaw that was hanging on the halibut hook. It was handed from one to another, and finally to Raven, who said, "Oh, this is a wonder to behold!" as he threw back his blanket and replaced his jaw.

Raven performed his magic so quickly that no one had time to see what was happening. As soon as Raven's jaw was firmly in place again, he turned himself into a bird and flew out through the smoke hole of the chief's house. Only then did the people begin to realize it was the trickster Raven who had stolen their bait and been hooked on Houskana's fishing line.

On the totem pole, Raven was carved, not as the old man, but as himself without his beak, a reminder of how the old man lost his jaw.

Brindze, *The Totem Pole*, 43-44.

■

YELLOWSTONE VALLEY AND THE GREAT FLOOD

Yellowstone

"I have heard it told on the Cheyenne Reservation in Montana and the Seminole camps in the Florida Everglades, I have heard it from the Eskimos north of the Arctic Circle and the Indians south of the equator. The legend of the flood is the most universal of all legends. It is told in Asia, Africa, and Europe, in North America and the South Pacific." Professor Hap Gilliland of Eastern Montana College was the first to record this legend of the great flood.

This is one of the fifteen legends of the flood that he himself recorded in various parts of the world:

He was an old Indian. his face was weather beaten, but his eyes were still bright. I never knew what tribe he was from, though I could guess. Yet others from the tribe whom I talked to later had never heard his story.

We had been talking of the visions of the young men. He sat for a long time, looking out across the Yellowstone Valley through the pouring rain, before he spoke. "They are beginning to come back," he said.

"Who is coming back?" I asked.

"The animals," he said. "It has happened before."

"Tell me about it."

He thought for a long while before he lifted his hands and his eyes. "The Great Spirit smiled on this land when he made it. There were mountains and plains, forests and grasslands. There were animals of many kinds—and men."

■

The old man's hands moved smoothly, telling the story more clearly than his voice.

The Great Spirit told the people, "These animals are your brothers. Share the land with them. They will give you food and clothing. Live with them and protect them.

"Protect especially the buffalo, for the buffalo will give you food and shelter. The hide of the buffalo will keep you from the cold, from the heat, and from the rain. As long as you have the buffalo, you will never need to suffer."

For many winters the people lived at peace with the animals and with the land. When they killed a buffalo, they thanked the Great Spirit, and they used every part of the buffalo. It took care of every need.

Then other people came. They did not think of the animals as brothers. They killed, even when they did not need food. They burned and cut the forests, and the animals died. They shot the buffalo and called it sport. They killed the fish in the streams.

When the Great Spirit looked down, he was sad. He let the smoke of the fires lie in the valleys. The people coughed and choked. But still they burned and they killed.

So the Great Spirit sent rains to put out the fires and to destroy the people.

The rains fell, and the waters rose. The people moved from the flooded valleys to the higher land.

Spotted Bear, the medicine man, gathered together his people. He said to them, "The Great Spirit has told us that as long as we have the buffalo we will be safe from heat and cold and rain. But there are no longer any buffalo. Unless we can find buffalo and live at peace with nature, we will all die."

Still the rains fell, and the waters rose. The people moved from the flooded plains to the hills.

The young men went out and hunted for the buffalo. As they went, they put out the fires. They made friends with the animals once more. They cleaned out the streams.

Still the rains fell, and the waters rose. The people moved from the flooded hills to the mountains.

Two young men came to Spotted Bear. "We have found the buffalo," they said. "There was a cow, a calf, and a great white bull. The cow and the calf climbed up to the safety of the mountains. They should be back when the rain stops. But the bank gave way, and the bull was swept

Buffalo robe
Cheyenne

away by the floodwaters. We followed and got him to shore, but he had drowned. We have brought you his hide."

They unfolded a huge white buffalo skin.

Spotted Bear took the white buffalo hide. "Many people have been drowned," he said. "Our food has been carried away. But our young people are no longer destroying the world that was created for them. They have found the white buffalo. It will save those who are left."

Still the rains fell, and the waters rose. The people moved from the flooded mountains to the highest peaks.

Spotted Bear spread the white buffalo skin on the ground. He and the other medicine men scraped it and stretched it, and scraped it and stretched it.

Still the rains fell. Like all rawhide, the buffalo skin stretched when it was wet. Spotted Bear stretched it out over the village. All the people who were left crowded under it.

As the rains fell, the medicine men stretched the buffalo skin across the mountains. Each day they stretched it farther.

Then Spotted Bear tied one corner to the top of the Big Horn Mountains. That side, he fastened to the Pryors. The next corner he tied to the Bear Tooth Mountains. Crossing the Yellowstone Valley, he tied one corner to the Crazy Mountains, and the other to Signal Butte in the Bull Mountains.

The whole Yellowstone Valley was covered by the white buffalo skin. Though the rains still fell above, it did not fall in the Yellowstone Valley.

The waters sank away. Animals from the outside moved into the valley, under the white buffalo skin. The people shared the valley with them.

Still the rains fell above the buffalo skin. The skin stretched and began to sag.

Spotted Bear stood on the Bridger Mountains and raised the west end of the buffalo skin to catch the West Wind. The West Wind rushed in and was caught under the buffalo skin. The wind lifted the skin until it formed a great dome over the valley.

The Great Spirit saw that the people were living at peace with the earth. The rains stopped, and the sun shone. As the sun shone on the white buffalo skin, it gleamed with colors of red and yellow and blue.

As the sun shone on the rawhide, it began to shrink. The ends of the dome shrank away until all that was left was one great arch across the valley.

The old man's voice faded away; but his hands said "Look," and his arms moved toward the valley.

The rain had stopped and a rainbow arched across the Yellowstone Valley. A buffalo calf and its mother grazed beneath it.

Gilliland, *The Flood*, 1, 38-44.

■

COYOTE AND THE MONSTERS OF THE BITTERROOT VALLEY
Flathead or Salish

This story was recorded from a great-great-grandmother whose name means "Painted-Hem-of-the-Skirt." In the summer of 1955, she was the only person on the Flathead Reservation in western Montana that even an interested interpreter could find who knew the old stories of their people.

The Bitterroot Valley is in western Montana.

■

After Coyote had killed the monster near the mouth of the Jocko River, he turned south and went up the Bitterroot Valley. Soon he saw two huge monsters, one at each end of a ridge. Coyote killed them, changed them into tall rocks, and said, "You will always be there."

There the tall rocks still stand.

Then he went on. Someone had told him about another monster, an Elk monster, up on a mountain to the east. Coyote said to his wife, Mole, "Dig a tunnel clear to the place where that monster is. Dig several holes in the tunnel. Then move our camp to the other side."

Coyote went through the tunnel Mole had made, got out of it, and saw the Elk monster. The monster was surprised to see him.

"How did you get here?" he asked. "Where did you come from?" The monster was scared.

"I came across the prairie," lied Coyote. "Don't you see my trail? You must be blind if you didn't see me."

The monster became more scared. He thought that Coyote must have greater powers than he himself had.

Coyote's dog was Pine Squirrel, and the Elk monster's dog was Grizzly Bear. Grizzly Bear growled at Pine Squirrel, and Pine Squirrel barked back.

"You'd better stop your dog," said the monster. "If you don't, he'll lose his head."

The dogs wanted to fight. Grizzly Bear jumped at Coyote's dog. Pine Squirrel went under him and killed him with the flint he wore on his head. The flint ripped Grizzly Bear. Bones and flesh flew everywhere.

"Look down there," said Coyote to the Elk monster. "See those people coming along that trail? Let's go after them."

He knew that what he saw was Mole moving their camp, but the monster could not see clearly in the tunnel. Elk monster picked up his shield, his spear, and his knife. "I'm ready," he said.

After they had gone a short distance along the trail, the monster fell into the first hole. Coyote called loudly, as if he were calling to an enemy ahead of them. The monster climbed out of the hole, tried to run, but fell into one hole after another. At last Coyote said to him, "Let me carry your shield. Then you can run faster."

Coyote put the shield on his back, but the monster still had trouble. "Let me carry your spear," Coyote said. Soon he got the monster's knife, also—and all of his equipment. Then Coyote ran round and round, shouting, "This is how we charge the enemy."

Plateau Indian antler adze handle
Flathead

And he jabbed the monster with the monster's spear. "I have the enemy's warbonnet!" he yelled. He jabbed the monster four times, each time yelling that he had taken something from the enemy. The fifth time he jabbed the monster, he yelled, "I have stripped the enemy." Then he said to the Elk monster, "You can never kill anyone again."

Coyote went on up the Bitterroot Valley. He heard a baby crying, up on a hill. Coyote went up to the baby, not knowing it was a monster. He put his finger in the baby's mouth, to let it suck. The baby ate the flesh off Coyote's finger, then his hand, and then his arm. The monster-baby killed Coyote. Only his skeleton was left.

After a while, Coyote's good friend Fox came along. Fox stepped over the dead body, and Coyote came to life. He began to stretch as if he had been asleep. "I've slept a long time," he said to Fox.

You've been dead," Fox told him. "That baby is a monster, and he killed you."

Coyote looked around, but the baby was gone. He put some flint on his finger and waited for the baby to come back. When he heard it crying, he called out, "Hello, baby! You must be hungry."

Coyote let it have his flinted finger to suck. The baby cut himself and died.

Plateau Indian sheep horn bowl
Flathead or Salish

"That's the last of you," said Coyote. "This hill will forever be called Sleeping Child."

And that is what the Indians call it today.

After Coyote had left Sleeping Child, Fox joined him again and they traveled together. Soon Coyote grew tired of carrying his blanket, and so he laid it on a rock. After they had traveled farther, they saw a storm coming. They went back to the rock, Coyote picked up his blanket, and the two friends moved on. When the rain began to fall, he put the blanket over himself and Fox. While lying there, covered by the blanket, they looked out and saw the rock running toward them.

Fox went uphill, but Coyote ran downhill. The rock followed close on Coyote's trail. Coyote crossed the river, sure that he was safe. Spreading his clothes out on a rock, he thought he would rest while they dried. But the rock followed him across the river. When he saw it coming out of the water, Coyote began to run. He saw three women sitting nearby, with stone hammers in their hands.

"If that rock comes here," Coyote said to the women, "you break it with your hammers."

But the rock got away from the women. Coyote ran on to where a creek comes down from the mountains near Darby. There he took some vines—Indians call them "monkey ropes"—and placed them so that the rock would get tangled up in them. He set fire to the monkey ropes. The rock got tangled in the burning ropes and was killed by the heat.

Then Coyote said to the rock, "The Indians will come through here on their way to the buffalo country. They will play with you. They will find you slick and heavy, and they will lift you up."

In my childhood, the rock was still there, but it is gone now, no one knows where.

Coyote left the dead rock and went on farther. Soon he saw a mountain sheep. The sheep insulted Coyote and made him angry. Coyote grabbed him and threw him against a pine tree. The body went clear through the tree, but the head stayed on it. The horns stuck out from the trunk of the tree.

Coyote said to the tree, "When people go by, they will talk to you. They will say, 'I want to have good luck. So I will leave a gift here for you.' They will leave gifts and you will make them lucky—in hunting or in war or in anything they wish to do."

The tree became well known as the Medicine Tree. People from several tribes left gifts in it when they passed on their way to the buffalo country that is on the rising-sun side of the mountains.

In my childhood, the skull and face were still there. When I was a young girl, people told me to put some of my hair inside the sheep's horn, so that I would live a long time. I did. That's why I'm nearly ninety years old.

As the interpreter and I were leaving Painted-Hem- of-the-Skirt, she bent low and made a sweeping movement around her ankles and the hem of her long skirt. Then she said a few words and laughed heartily. The interpreter explained: "She says she hopes that she will not find a rattlesnake wrapped around her legs because she told some of the old stories in the summertime."

She had laughed often as she told the tales, but I feel sure that her mother would not have related them in the summertime. "It is good to tell stories in the wintertime," the Indians of the Northwest used to say. "There are long nights in the wintertime."

Ella E. Clark.

■

CREATION OF THE RED AND WHITE RACES

Flathead or Salish

The Salish or Flatheads, belonging to the Salishan language family, early in the 1800s were driven from the Plains into western Montana by the Blackfeet tribes, who had begun to use guns and horses. The Flathead name applied because they left their hair up-standing, flat on top. Other bands of Crow, Arapaho, Cheyenne, and Chippewa in the same area similarly "flattened their heads." Salish relations with whites were always friendly and they were missionized by Father De Smet. Most of these tribes and bands settled on the Flathead Reservation in Montana and still live there today.

■

Among the people of long, long ago, Old Man Coyote was the symbol of good. Mountain Sheep was the symbol of evil.

Old-Man-in-the-Sky created the world. Then he drained all the water off the earth and crowded it into the big salt holes now called the oceans. The land became dry except for the lakes and rivers.

Old Man Coyote often became lonely and went up to the Sky World just to talk. One time he was so unhappy that he was crying. Old-Man-in-the-Sky questioned him.

"Why are you so unhappy that you are crying? Have I not made much land for you to run around on? Are not Chief Beaver, Chief Otter, Chief Bear, and Chief Buffalo on the land to keep you company?

"Why do you not like Mountain Sheep? I placed him up in the hilly parts so that you two need not fight. Why do you come up here so often?"

Old Man Coyote sat down and cried more tears. Old-Man-in-the-Sky became cross and began to scold him.

"Foolish Old Man Coyote, you must not drop so much water down upon the land. Have I not worked many days to dry it? Soon you will have it all covered with water again. What is the trouble with you? What more do you want to make you happy?"

"I am very lonely because I have no one to talk to," he replied. "Chief Beaver, Chief Otter, Chief Bear, and Chief Buffalo are busy with their families. They do not have time to visit with me. I want people of my own, so that I may watch over them."

"Then stop this shedding of water," said Old-Man-in-the-Sky. "If you will stop annoying me with your visits, I will make people for you. Take this *parfleche*. It is a bag made of rawhide. Take it some place in the mountain where there is red earth. Fill it and bring it back up to me."

Old Man Coyote took the bag made of the skin of an animal and traveled many days and nights. At last he came to a mountain where there was much red soil. He was very weary after such a long journey, but he managed to fill the parfleche. Then he was sleepy.

"I will lie down to sleep for a while. When I waken, I will run swiftly back to Old-Man-in-the-Sky."

He slept very soundly.

After a while, Mountain Sheep came along. He saw the bag and looked to see what was in it.

"The poor fool has come a long distance to get such a big load of red soil," he said to himself. "I do not know what he wants it for, but I will have fun with him."

Mountain Sheep dumped all of the red soil out upon the mountain. He filled the lower part of the parfleche with white solid, and the upper part with red soil. Then laughing heartily, he ran to his hiding place.

Soon Old Man Coyote woke up. He tied the top of the bag and hurried with it to Old-Man-in-the-Sky. When he arrived with it, the sun was going to sleep. It was so dark that the two of them could hardly see the soil in the parfleche.

Old-Man-in-the-Sky took the dirt and said, "I will make this soil into the forms of two men and two women."

He did not see that half of the soil was red and the other half white. Then he said to Old Man Coyote, "Take these to the dry land below. They are your people. You can talk with them. So do not come up here to trouble me."

Then he finished shaping the two men and two women—in the darkness.

Old Man Coyote put them in the parfleche and carried them down to dry land. In the morning he took them out and put breath into them. He was surprised to see that one pair was red and the other was white.

"Now I know that Mountain Sheep came while I was asleep. I cannot keep these two colors together."

He thought a while. Then he carried the white ones to the land by the big salt hole. The red ones he kept in his own land so that he could visit with them. That is how Indians and white people came to the earth.

Clark, *In the Beginning*, 17.

■

THE WARM WIND BROTHERS VS. THE COLD WIND BROTHERS

Moses Band of Columbia River Indians

This story was recorded in 1961 at the request of George Nanamkin, who lived near the Grand Coulee Dam. In the early 1950s, he was not living on the Colville Reservation when I collected stories for *Indian Legends of the Pacific Northwest*. But he knew the book and several of the storytellers.

In his letter asking me for an interview, he wrote that the story he wanted recorded had been told by his people for many, many years. "It shows that we had an Ice Age." Scientists now believe that the last Ice Age ended over 10,000 years ago.

■

This is a story about two tribes that lived during the last Ice Age, many years ago. One of these tribes was called the Tribe of the Warm Wind. The people lived in the Dry Falls-Vantafe area. Wherever they camped, they were in warm country. The chief of the Warm Wind people had five sons.

The second tribe was the Tribe of the Cold Wind. The chief of this tribe also had five sons. Wherever the Cold Wind people settled, cold weather followed. All the lakes and rivers froze, and snow fell.

When the Tribe of the Cold Wind tried to move south, they were stopped by the Tribe of the Warm Wind. The Cold Wind people held council and decided that if they would kill the five brothers in the Warm Wind tribe, they could go south whenever they wished.

They asked Coyote to deliver a challenge for a duel between the five brothers in the Warm Wind tribe and the five brothers in the Cold Wind tribe. The challenge was accepted, and the date was set. Then Coyote traveled around to tell all the people in both tribes about the contest.

When the day arrived, both tribes gathered at the place for the duel. Two warriors fought at a time, one Warm Wind brother against one Cold Wind brother. The young warriors of the Cold Wind people were much stronger than their rivals. Soon all the Warm Wind brothers had been killed.

The Tribe of the Cold Wind now had the power to rule, and they ruled strongly and severely. The country became cold. The rivers and lakes froze solid, and snow fell until the lodges were nearly covered. As far south as Dry Falls, the ice was piled as high as mountains.

Coyote was cruelly treated, and his work was never done. The Warm Wind people were miserable. They were made the slaves of the Cold Wind people. Any food they found was taken from them. They had to eat the scraps of food the Cold Wind people did not want.

Not long before the struggles, the youngest son of the Warm Wind chief had married a girl from a tribe farther south. She decided to go back to her people. Before she left, she told her husband's people, "I am expecting a child. Pray that it will be a boy. If I have a son, I will train him to be the greatest warrior in the world. When he is grown, I will send him to you. Watch for him. He will avenge the defeat of his father and uncles."

A few moons later the woman gave birth to a son. When he was about three months old, he was given baths in cold water to make him strong. As soon as he was old enough, his mother and her brothers had him follow a training course that would make him a strong warrior.

For years he trained. He became so strong that he could uproot trees and throw them over hills. He could throw large boulders many miles. At this time he believed himself the strongest man in the world.

Then his mother told him about the duel between the Warm Wind brothers and the Cold Wind brothers. The young man felt that he was ready to avenge the death of his father and uncles, and to set their people free. But his mother insisted that he train for one more year.

By the end of that year he could move small mountains. Then his mother told him that he was ready to go north to help his people. She told him just what he should do and what he should ask his grandparents to do to help him.

The young warrior started north, and a warm south wind went with him. As he neared the home of his grandparents, the ice on their lodgepoles began to melt for the first time since they became slaves. They were glad and asked each other, "Do you think that our grandson is coming?"

Before the sun set that day, the young man reached them. They saw that he was strong, and they believed him when he said that he had come to free them and their people from the Cold Wind tribe. He was sorry that they had been treated unkindly.

Coyote was sent to the camp of the chief of the Cold Wind tribe to deliver a challenge from the grandson of the chief of the Warm Wind tribe. It was accepted. The day and the place were decided upon.

In the camp of the defeated people, the grandson asked them to follow his mother's instructions: "Boil some salmon, and put the broth in five containers."

On the morning of the duel, the people of both tribes gathered at the river at the chosen place. The grandson fought with the oldest brother from the Cold Wind tribe. The ice was very slick. But the grandson's people threw down a bucket of hot salmon broth, and the ice became rough. So the young warrior defeated the first of the five brothers.

Then the second brother stepped forth, and the grandson fought him. The Cold Wind people threw water on the ice, hoping to make it slick. Then the Warm Wind people threw another bucket of hot broth on the ice, and it became rough. So the young warrior defeated the second brother.

The third, fourth, and fifth brothers he struggled with, each in turn. Each time he was helped by the hot salmon broth. When he had defeated the youngest brother, the Warm Wind people were free. They drove the rest of the Cold Wind people so far north that they could never find their way back. Soon the warm wind came in and melted all the ice.

When the young grandson travels north in the spring, warm weather follows. If he had not defeated the five brothers of the Cold Wind tribe, we still would be living in the Ice Age.

Ella E. Clark.

Plateau Indian
Flathead

■

COYOTE'S ADVENTURES IN IDAHO

Flathead

North American Indians of the Flathead, Salish, Pend d'Oreilles (named by Europeans because they wore large shell earrings) or Kalispel tribes in Montana were all visited by Lewis and Clark in 1805. A Post was established in Pend d'Oreille Lake in 1809 by the North West Company and another Post at Clark Fort called Salish House. In 1844, these Indians were converted by the Roman Catholic church. By 1855, all of the tribes in the area had surrendered their lands, except those around Flathead Lake, which became the Jocko Reservation.

In 1700 the Indian population of that area ranged from 5,000 to 6,500. Lewis and Clark estimated about 1,600 when they visited in 1805. Tribal names have been preserved in countries, cities, banks, lakes, mountains, and rivers in the Northwest region.

■

Near Spokane one day, Coyote and Fox were traveling together on their way north. When they reached a river, Coyote said to Fox, "I believe I'll get married. I'd like to take one of those Pend d'Oreille women for my wife."

So they decided to go in search of the Chief of the Pend d'Oreilles. They soon located him with his tribe, and Coyote approached him with a gift of salmon.

"Chief, I would very much like to have one of your tribal women for my wife. Can we talk about which one you would choose for me?"

"Now Coyote, you know we do not approve that our women intermarry with other tribal members. So you cannot have one of our Pend d'Oreille women for your wife."

Coyote and Fox left the Chief. Coyote became so disappointed with the Chief's decision, he began to rage to his partner, Fox.

"Soon the Chief will be sorry for his refusal. I'll make a big waterfall here in his big river. Forevermore, salmon will not be able to get over the falls to feed the Pend d'Oreilles."

Since Coyote had the power for his wishes to be granted, the great falls immediately formed as he had proclaimed. That is how the Spokane Falls began.

From there, Coyote walked north to Ravalli. Soon he met an Old Indian Woman camped close by. Old Woman said to Coyote, "Where are you going?"

"I am on my way to travel all over the world."

"Well, you had better go back and not stay here," Old Woman said to Coyote.

"Why should I turn back and not stay here for a while? I am looking for a wife."

"Because there is a Giant here who kills everyone passing through this valley," replied Old Woman.

"But I am strong, I will fight him and kill him instead."

So Coyote did not heed Old Woman's warning and started walking on the trail again. He noticed a large tamarack tree nearby on a hillside.

"I'll put an end to the Giant with a hard blow from this tree. That's the way I'll kill him," Coyote said to himself. So he pulled the tamarack tree from the ground and swung it onto his shoulder and continued his search for the Giant.

Soon Coyote saw a woman who seemed nearly dead. He asked, "What is the matter, are you sick?"

"No, I am not sick," she replied.

"I am going to kill the Giant with this tamarack tree," said Coyote.

"You might as well throw the tree away. Don't you know the Giant already sees you and you are already a tasty bite in the Giant's belly?" said the woman.

Coyote took her advice and threw the tamarack tree up on a hillside where it is still growing near Arlee, a little station on the Northern Pacific Railroad. All of what was Jocko Valley now fills the Giant's belly.

As Coyote traveled on from there, he observed many people lying here and there. Some were already dead, others seemed about to die, or were nearly dead.

"Tell me what is the trouble with all of you people," asked Coyote of an Old Woman with her eyes open.

"We are all starving to death," she answered.

"How can that be, when I can see plenty to eat here, lots of meat and fat?" said Coyote.

Then Coyote attacked the Giant and cut away large chunks of grease and fat from the sides of the Giant and fed all of the people. Soon all became well again.

"All of you people prepare to run for your lives. I am going to cut out the Giant's heart. When I start cutting, you must all run to O'Keef's Canyon or to Ravalli," called out Coyote.

With his stone knife, Coyote cut out the Giant's heart. The Giant called out, "Please, Coyote, let me alone. Go away from here. Get Out!"

"No I won't go away. I'm going to stay right here until I kill you," said Coyote.

Then he cut out the Giant's heart. As he was dying, the Giant's jaws began to close tightly. Woodtick was the last one to escape from the Giant's belly when Giant's jaws closed. But Coyote caught hold of him, and with all his strength pulled Woodtick out of the Giant's mouth.

"We can't help it but you will always be flatheaded from your experience," said Coyote as he left and started again on his world trip.

From there the traveler continued on to what is today Missoula, Montana. Coyote walked along between Lolo and Fort Missoula when he thought he heard someone call his name. But he could not see anyone. He trotted forward again, and heard his name called again. He stopped and when he looked into the woods, he saw two women sitting down beside a river.

Coyote swam across the river, and went up the embankment to the women. They were very good-looking women, thought Coyote, maybe he could marry one of them. He sat down between them, but they stood up and danced down to the river.

"Wait for me," called Coyote. "I'll go swimming with you." He took off his jacket beaded with shells, denoting that he was a great Chief.

"We don't want to wait, we are having a good time dancing," replied the two women as they danced on into the river. When Coyote joined them, they pushed him down into the water and tried to drown him.

Later, Coyote's partner, Fox, appeared from around a bend in the river, looking for something to eat. When he looked into the river and saw something lying on the bottom, he said, "This must be my partner, Coyote!"

Fox pulled out the object, and when he was sure it was Coyote, he made a magical jump over him and brought Coyote back to life.

Coyote said, "Oh, I must have had a long sleep."

"You were not asleep, you were dead," replied Fox. "Why did you go near those women, you had no right to be near them, they are from the Shell tribe."

Coyote climbed partway up the hill and set the grass on fire. Later, it was discovered that the women could not escape, and died in the fire. Today some shells have a black side, because they had been burned at the same time.

McDermott, "Coyote's Adventures in Idaho."

■

THE ORIGIN OF CAMAS ROOTS
Okanagon

Camas (pronounced cắm-ás) is a flowering plant of the lily family, somewhat like the blue hyacinth in appearance. Its root was an important vegetable food for the Northwest Indians.

The Wishing Stone in the following story used to stand not far from Oroville, Washington, near the Canadian border. Whenever Indians passed it, they left gifts, believing that to do so would bring them good luck.

■

Long ago, a great sickness came upon the Indians who lived in the country near the Wishing Stone. So many people died that it seemed as if the whole nation would soon pass away. Every day the oldest and wisest of the medicine men talked to the Great Chief Above. One day the Great Chief Above said to him: "Tell your people that I will send a messenger to them. On the day after the moon is full, gather all the people together at the Wishing Stone. Tell them to bring all the sick ones."

The medicine man sent out runners, and on the morning after the moon was full, Indians for hundreds of miles came together at the Wishing Stone. All were dressed in their best robes. The sick people were with them.

Before the sun reached the middle of the sky, the medicine man pointed toward the highest mountain in sight. Hundreds of eyes looked where he pointed. They saw a white light, and then they saw a figure appear in the sky. As they watched, they saw that the figure was a woman, young and beautiful.

She floated toward them, came down slowly from the sky, and rested on the Wishing Stone. There she spoke to the people gathered round her.

"The Great Chief Above has heard your prayers and has sent me to help you. Come near and be healed of your sickness."

The people crowded round her, touched her, and soon all were well. They shouted with happiness. Lifting her hand to quiet them, the spirit woman spoke again.

"I will come again some time. But you must do what I tell you to do. You must plant the seed that I shall give you. It is camas seed. Plant it everywhere. In the spring it will have blue flowers. There will be so many that they will look like a blue lake. In the fall, gather the roots. If you eat the roots of the camas, the sickness will never return."

Then she gave them the seed. When she had put some in every hand, she was caught up by the breeze and carried back to the sky. The people watched until she could no longer be seen among the clouds. They called her the Spirit of the Camas.

Even after, when they drew near the Wishing Stone on which she had stood, they left gifts for the Spirit of the Camas.

Steele, *History of Northern Washington*, 529-530.

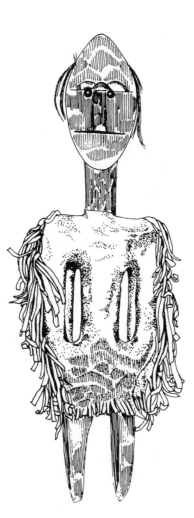

Shaman's wand
Flathead

■

COYOTE'S SALMON

Sanpoil

While *sanpoil* is a native American word meaning "unknown," the Sanpoil tribe has flourished since 1600 in Washington State with a large number of villages along the Sanpoil River, and the Columbia River below Big Bend, Oregon. Sanpoils belonged to the Salishan linguistic group. Later they lived on the Sanpoil and Colville Reservations in Washington State.

■

Long ago on the Sanpoil River that flows southward into the Columbia River, Old Man and old Woman lived with their tribe, the Sanpoils. They were so stooped that it appeared they were walking on their knees and their elbows. Their very pretty granddaughter lived with them.

One day Coyote came along and saw the old couple with the beautiful girl. Immediately, he decided that he wanted the girl for his wife. But he knew better than to ask for her then. He thought he would wait until evening. So during the day he sat around, becoming better acquainted with the family.

The old couple watched him, noting that his long hair was braided neatly and his forelocks were carefully combed back. They noticed too that he was tall and strong. Old Man and Old Woman talked between themselves about Coyote, wondering if he could be a Chief.

In the late afternoon, Coyote asked Old Man, "What is that thing down in the stream?"

"Why, that is my fish trap," Old Man replied.

"A fish trap? What is that? What do you do with it?" asked Coyote, pretending he did not know.

"Oh, occasionally I catch a few bullheads and sunfish," Old Man said.

"Is that what you eat? I never heard of them. Are they big enough for a meal?" asked Coyote.

"They are not much, but what else can we eat?" replied Old Man.

"I think I will go up the hill and look around," said Coyote. It was then about an hour before sunset.

On top of the hill, Coyote saw some grouse roosting in a tree. He threw some stones at them, killing five. He carried the grouse back to Old Man and said, "Let's eat these for supper."

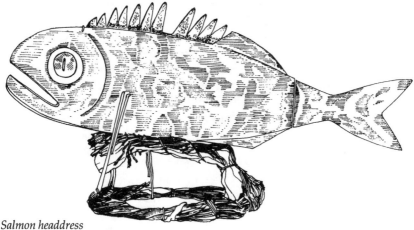

Salmon headdress
Sanpoil

After removing the feathers, Old Man roasted the game over the fire, and when they were done, everyone sat down to eat the wonderful meal. To Old Man and his family, it seemed like a feast.

"Is this the kind of food you eat every day?" the Old Man asked Coyote.

"Sometimes I eat berries, roots, and I catch some real big fish, as long as your arm," Coyote said.

Later, Coyote announced that he would like to stay there if they wanted him, otherwise he would move on.

"What do you mean?" asked Old Man.

"Well, it is like this. I would like to marry your granddaughter," said Coyote.

Old Man and Old Woman looked at each other but said nothing. Coyote went for a little walk to allow the old couple to talk privately.

While Coyote was gone Old Man said to his wife, "What do you think of this fellow? You saw what he did, bringing good food for our supper. If we let him marry our granddaughter, maybe they will stay here and we will have such good food always. Surely our girl will marry someone soon, perhaps some man not as good as this young fellow."

"Well, husband, I'll leave it entirely up to you."

Soon Coyote returned. He decided to let Old Man open the conversation. Old Man held his pipe in one hand and said, "How I wish I had a smoke. My tobacco ran out some time ago."

"Have some of mine," said Coyote, reaching into his jacket pocket. He pulled out a large bunch of tobacco and gave it to Old Man, who filled his pipe, feeling very much surprised that Coyote would have real tobacco.

After a while Old Man spoke, "My wife and I have talked over your proposal and she left the decision up to me. I have decided to let you marry our granddaughter and live here. If you go away, we want you to take her with you. How are we to know that you will do this?"

"You need not worry," said Coyote. "I am tired of traveling. I want to settle down here for the rest of my life, if you wish."

Old Man was pleased with Coyote and believed what he said. So Coyote took the pretty granddaughter for his wife.

Early that evening Coyote stayed with his wife and later said, "I am going out for a few minutes and when I return we will go to bed."

"All right," answered his wife.

Coyote went downstream to where Old Man had his fish trap. He changed it into a basket-type trap, piling rows of rocks to guide fish into the basket. When finished he called out, "Salmon, I want two of you in the basket trap tomorrow morning, one male and one female." Then he returned to his bride.

Next morning Coyote asked Old Man to go to his fish trap early. "I think I heard a noise in the night that sounded like fish caught in a trap," he said.

Old Man went downstream to see his fish trap. Sure enough, he saw two big fish in the trap. Old Man was so excited, he stumbled up the trail toward Coyote.

"You were right, there are two great fish in the trap—bigger than I have ever seen," reported Old Man.

"You must be dreaming," said Coyote.

"Come down with me and see for yourself," Old Man said.

When the two reached the trap, Coyote exclaimed, "You are so right. These are salmon, chief among all fish. Let us take them over to that flat place, and I will show you what to do with them."

When they reached the open field, Coyote sent Old Man up the hill to gather sunflower stems and leaves.

"Those are salmon plants," Coyote explained. "Salmon must always be laid on sunflower stems and leaves."

Old Man spread the sunflower plants upon the ground. Coyote placed the salmon on them, and proceeded to show Old Man how to prepare the salmon.

"First, put a stick in the salmon's mouth and bend it back to break off the head. Second, place long sharp poles inside the salmon lengthwise to hold for roasting over your campfire," said Coyote.

"Now remember this," he continued. "The first week go down to the trap and take out the salmon every day. But when fixing it, never use a knife to cut it in any way. Always roast the fish over the fire on sticks, the way I have shown you. Never boil salmon the first week. After the salmon is roasted, open it carefully and take out the backbone without breaking it. Also, save the back part of the head for the sacred bundle—never eat that.

"If you do not do these things as I have told you, either a big storm will come up and you will be drowned, or you will be bitten by a rattlesnake and you will die.

"After you have taken out the salmon's backbone, wrap it and the back of the head carefully in tules, the marsh grasses, to make a sacred bundle, then place it somewhere in a tree, where it will not be bothered. If you do as I tell you, you will always have plenty of salmon in your trap.

"I am telling you these sacred things about the salmon because I am going to die sometime. I want you and your tribe to know of the best way to care for and use your salmon. After this, your men will always place their fish traps up and down the river to catch salmon. The man having the first trap will be Chief of the Salmon, and the others should always do anything he tells them to do.

"After the first week of the salmon season, you can boil your salmon or cook it any way you wish. But remember to always take care of the bones, wrapping them in a sacred bundle—never leaving them where they can be stepped upon or stepped over."

For the next few days each time Old Man went down to his fish trap in the morning, he found twice as many salmon as on the day before. Coyote showed him how to dry fish to prepare them for winter use. Before long they had a large scaffold covered with drying fish.

People of the Sanpoil tribe saw the fish and noticed how well Old Man and Old Woman were doing. They went to their hogans and told others about the big red fish called salmon, and about the tall young stranger who taught Old Man about caring for the salmon.

Soon thereafter, all the people came to see for themselves. Old Man and Old Woman invited them to feast on their roasted salmon. The old couple explained how their new grandson-in-law had shown them how to trap the salmon and dry them for winter food.

To this day, the Sanpoils say their tribe harvests the salmon in exactly the way that Coyote taught their ancestors long, long ago.

Ray, "Coyote Introduces Salmon," 167.

■

WOODPECKER AND THE THEFT OF FIRE
Sanpoil

Probably every North American Indian tribe told a myth about the origin of fire, as did early people in all parts of the world.

The following story was a favorite among several tribes of the West. Woodpecker's part in it was sometimes taken by Chickadee, sometimes by Sapsucker, sometimes by Wren.

■

Long, long ago, in the days of the animal people, there was no fire on the earth. There was fire in the sky, but none on the earth.

One day the chief of the animal people said to those near him, "Let us go up to the sky country and try to get some fire. Tell all the people to gather here. Then I will tell you what to do."

When the animal people had gathered together, the chief said to them, "Each of you will make a bow and many arrows. Then come together again and shoot at the sky. We'll see if we can hit the sky. If we can, we'll make a chain of arrows down to the earth. Then we'll climb up to the sky country and steal some fire from the sky people."

The people obeyed the chief's orders—all except Woodpecker. They made long, strong bows, and they made many arrows. Then all the people came together again at one place. Everyone shot at the sky, but no one could hit it with his arrows.

Then Woodpecker decided to get busy. First he made a bow from the rib of Elk. Then he made some arrows from the stems of serviceberry bushes.

"Where can I get some feathers for my arrows?" Woodpecker asked himself.

He saw Golden Eagle, and then he saw Bald Eagle.

Woodpecker said to Bald Eagle, "Golden Eagle has been saying mean things about you."

Bald Eagle flew straight at Golden Eagle and began to fight him with his strong bill. That was just what Woodpecker wanted. Soon feathers were dropping from the two eagles fighting high in the air. Many feathers dropped.

Woodpecker spread out a mat and gathered all of them. He took all of the feathers home with him and fastened them to his arrows. Soon he had two big bags full of nice, feathered arrows.

"Now where can I get some points for my arrows?" Woodpecker asked his grandmother.

"Go to see Flint Rock and Hard Rock," his grandmother told him.

Woodpecker went. And he said to Flint Rock, "Hard Rock has been saying mean things about you."

Then Hard Rock and Flint Rock began to fight. That was just what Woodpecker wanted. Hard Rock broke Flint Rock into little pieces. Woodpecker took all the flint chips home with him and used them as arrowheads.

Plateau Indian warclub
Sanpoil

Woodpecker knew that in two days the animal people were going to have another meeting. They would try again to reach the sky with their arrows. So after two days Woodpecker went toward the shooting place with his two bags of arrows. When he got there, he saw Coyote.

"Why have you come?" asked Coyote. "You can't shoot."

"I came to look on."

Coyote looked at Woodpecker's bow and said, "That won't shoot anywhere."

All the people laughed at Woodpecker. "You can't shoot as far as the sky," they said.

The chief was a wise and kind chief. "Don't make fun of Woodpecker," he said. "He may shoot better than you think. I will call him when his time comes."

Then the chief called on each animal, one at a time, to shoot at the sky. But no one's arrow reached that far. At last Woodpecker's turn came. When the chief called him, Woodpecker dropped his two bags of arrows on the gound and put a string in his bow.

"Watch me," he said, and he shot an arrow toward the sky. It went so high it disappeared from sight. Everyone watched and waited. The arrow did not come down. Woodpecker shot another arrow. It disappeared from sight and did not come down. He kept on shooting until he had emptied one bag of arrows. By that time the animal people could see the end of the chain of arrows.

Then Woodpecker started to shoot the second bag of arrows. The people could see that each arrow stuck in the neck of the preceding arrow. When Woodpecker had emptied his second bag, the last arrow was still a long distance from the ground.

"Take some of the other people's arrows," said the chief.

Woodpecker shot from the other animals' bags until the chain reached the ground. Then, one by one, all the animals started up the arrow chain toward the sky. Golden Eagle was the first. The others followed him. Grizzly Bear was the last.

I'll take some food along with me," said Grizzly Bear. "We don't know what we are getting into."

So he filled a large bag with food and fastened it across his back. Then he took hold of the bottom arrow of the chain. He and his bag of food were so heavy that the arrow broke in two. He took hold of the second arrow. It broke in two. He broke the first five arrows that way. He could not reach the sixth one, so Grizzly Bear did not go up to the sky country.

By sunset all the other animal people were in the sky world.

"Let's all look around," said Woodpecker. "Let's not stay bunched together. If we go one by one, some of us will be sure to find fire."

So the animals separated, and each one got some fire. As they started back toward the arrow chain, they saw the sky people coming after them. And they found that the chain of arrows was broken.

"Quick!" said Eagle. "Each bird will take an animal on his back and fly down to earth with him."

That is the way the animals got down to earth again. Sapsucker was afraid to fly and so jumped instead. He hit the ground with his mouth. Ever since then, sapsuckers have had flat mouths and have to suck their food.

Fish slipped and fell down from Magpie's back. He was carrying his arrows with him, and when he hit the ground, the arrows went right through his body. Ever since then, fish have had many bones.

The animal people laid the fire down in front of their chief, "You can tell us what to do with it," they said.

The chief said to his people, "It is best to divide the fire, so that people all over the world can use it."

So he and Grizzly Bear gave pieces of the fire to Horsefly and Hummingbird. They carried the fire into all parts of the country.

People have had fire ever since.

Ray, "Sanpoil Folk Tales," 152-53.

Ella E. Clark.

■

Pah-To, the White Eagle
Wasco

When the first white people came to the Northwest, Indians of several tribes told them about a great bridge of rocks and earth that once spanned the lower Columbia River. When the bridge fell, they said, the rocks made numerous rapids and little waterfalls in the Columbia, near the present city of Hood River. Now the rocks and rapids are covered by the waters above Bonneville Dam.

Here is one of many stories that Indians used to tell about the fall of this natural bridge.

■

In the days of our grandfathers' grandfathers, the peaks now called Mount Hood and Mount Adams stood much closer to the Columbia River than they do today. Mount Hood, called Wy-east, stood on the south bank, facing Mount Adams, Pah-To, on the north bank.

Between the two peaks was a bridge, where big rocks formed an arch. One base of the bridge rested on Wy-east, the other on Pah-To. For many years the rock bridge stood there. Beneath it, the waters of the great river flowed peacefully. Canoes went up and down the river without danger from the rocks and rapids that have been there in our time.

Some people in the canoes admired the big arch over their heads and were proud of the Great Power Above that had made it. Other people were afraid. When they were traveling up or down the river, all except the oarsmen would get out of the canoes when they neared the spot. They would walk to the opposite side of the bridge and reenter the canoes there. All would pray for the oarsmen, because the medicine men of the tribe prophesied that some day the bridge would fall.

Our grandfathers and our great-uncles tell us about the long, dark journey under the bridge. They tell us that the river used to be peaceful where we now see rapids and waterfalls.

But mountains did not let the river remain at peace. Each peak was the home of a powerful spirit, and the spirits were jealous of each other. Each was proud of its beautiful home, and each envied the beauty and grandeur of the other. Sometimes they became so jealous and so angry that they threw hot rocks at each other.

The Great Power Above was made unhappy by their frequent quarrels. But he thought that he would let them fight until they grew weary

Wasco basket
Wasco

of fighting. Then they would become friends and would stay at peace with each other.

Instead, the mountain spirits became more and more quarrelsome. They became angry more and more often. They shook the earth. They sent forth fire and smoke, and they threw hot rocks across the river. At last the mountain peaks were set on fire, and a lake near the bridge was drained into the river.

Once more the fighting mountains made the earth tremble. This time they shook it so hard that the earth and the trees along the banks of the river slid into the water. The foundations of the bridge were loosened, the arch lost its balance, and the rocks fell into the river. There they made rapids and many waterfalls.

The Great Power Above was so angry that he determined to punish the mountain spirits. He came down from the sky and stood by the river. There he picked up Pah-To and hurled it as far as he could northeast of where he stood. Then he lifted Wy-east and hurled it as far as he could southwest of where he stood.

The mountain peaks stand there today, watching from a distance the Columbia River on its way to the sea.

McWhorter Papers.

■

THE BRIDGE OF THE GODS
Wasco

This story was told to McWhorter in 1914 by a Wasco Indian woman who was about 100 years old.

The Klickitat Indian custom was added in a note by McWhorter. He was a rancher in the Yakima Valley of Washington, and he employed native Americans for many summers. He recorded much of their history and folklore. Some of their history he had published.

■

In the days of the animal people, a great bird lived in the land of the setting sun. It was Thunderbird. All of the animal people were afraid of it. Thunderbird created five high mountains and then said to the animal people, "I made a law that no one is to pass over these five high mountains. If any one does, I will kill him. No one is to come where I live."

Wolf did not believe the law. "I will go," declared Wolf. "I will be the first to see what Thunderbird will do to me."

"I will go with you," said Wolf's four brothers.

So the five Wolf brothers went to the first mountain. They stood in a row, and each stepped with his right foot at the same time. Immediately the five wolf brothers were dead.

When the animal people heard that the five Wolf brothers were dead, Grizzly Bear, the strongest of the animals, decided that he would go.

"I will cross over the mountains," announced Grizzly Bear. "I will not die as the Wolf Brothers have died."

"We will go with you," said Grizzly Bear's four brothers.

So the five Grizzly Bear brothers went to the first mountain. They stood in a row, and each stepped with his right foot, all at the same time. Then each stepped with his left foot, all at the same time. Immediately the five Grizzly Bears were dead.

"I will go now," said Cougar. "I will take a long step and leap over the mountain."

Cougar's four brothers went with him. They made one leap together, and then all were dead.

"We will go next," said the five Beaver brothers. "We will go under the mountain. We will not be killed. We will not be like the Wolf brothers, the Grizzly brothers, and the Cougar brothers."

But as they tried to cross under the mountains, all five Beaver brothers were killed.

Then Coyote's oldest son said, "I will talk to the mountains. I will break down the law so that people may live and pass to the sunset."

His four brothers went with him, and two of them talked to the five mountains. They made the mountains move up and down; they made the mountains dance and shake. But the five sons of Coyote were killed. The five mountains still stood. No one could pass over or under them to the sunset.

Coyote's sons had not told their father their plans. He had told them that they must never stay away from home overnight. When they did not return, he knew that they had been killed by Thunderbird. Coyote was wiser than the others. He had been instructed in wisdom by the Spirit Chief.

After his sons had been gone five nights, Coyote was sure that they were dead. He cried loud and long. He went to a lonely place in the mountains and rolled on the ground, wailing and howling with grief.

Bear mask
Wasco

Then he prayed to the Spirit Chief for strength to bring his five sons back to life.

After Coyote had cried and prayed for a long time, he heard a voice. "You cannot break the law of the Thunderbrid. You cannot go over the five mountains. Thunderbird has made the law."

Coyote continued crying and praying, rolling on the ground in a lonely place in the mountains. After a time he heard the voice again.

"The only thing you can do is to go up to the Above-World. It will take you five days and five nights. There you will be told how you can bring your five sons to life again."

So for five days and five nights Coyote traveled to the Above- World. There he told his troubles to the Spirit Chief.

"Give me strength," he ended. "Give me so much strength that I can fight Thunderbird. Then the people can cross over the mountains to the sunset."

At last the Spirit Chief promised to help.

"I will blind the eyes of Thunderbird," he promised. "Then you can go over the five mountains and kill him.

"I will tell you what you must do," continued the Spirit Chief. "When you get back to the earth, find the big bird called Eagle. He has great strength. Ask him for a feather from his youngest son. Ask for a feather, a small feather from under his wing. This feather is downy and has great strength. It has power running out from the heart because it grows near the heart. Return now to the earth."

After five days and five nights, Coyote reached the earth again. He found Eagle and told him all that the Great Spirit had said. Then he asked, "Will you give me the feather that grows nearest the heart of your youngest son?"

"I will do as the Spirit Chief bids," replied Eagle. "If he told you to come to me, then I will give you my power to fight Thunderbird."

So Eagle picked a feather from under the wing of his youngest son. It was such a small downy feather that it could not be seen when it floated through the air. The coyote followed the next commandment the Spirit Chief had given him.

"Fast for ten days and ten nights," he had said. "If you will go without food and drink for ten days and nights, you will be changed to a feather. You will then be able to go anywhere."

So Coyote fasted. After ten days and ten nights, he was turned into a feather, like the one Eagle had given him. He floated through the air toward the five mountains. At a distance from them, he made a noise like thunder, as the Spirit Chief had told him to do. Three times he made a slow, deep rumbling, off toward the sunrise.

Thunderbird heard the rumble and asked, "Who is making this noise? I alone was given the power to make that rumbling sound. This noise must be coming from the Above-World. I am dead! I am dead! I am dead!"

A fourth time Coyote rumbled, this time closer to Thunderbird. Thunderbird became angry. "I will kill whomever this is that is making the noise. I will kill him! I will kill him!" he repeated angrily.

Thunderbird made a mighty noise, a greater thunder than Coyote had made. Coyote, in the form of a feather, went into the air, higher and higher and ever higher. He darted and whirled, but could not be seen.

Thunderbird was afraid. He knew that if a fifth rumble of thunder came he would be dead. He sought the deep water of Great River, to hide himself there. He heard Coyote far above him.

Coyote prayed to the Spirit Chief. "Help me one more time, just one more time. Help me kill Thunderbird so that the people may live, so that my sons will come to life again."

The Spirit Chief heard Coyote and helped him. Thunderbird sank deeper into the water, terrified. Coyote, still invisible above him, made a greater noise than ever, a noise like the bursting of the world. The five mountains crumbled and fell. Pieces of the mountain, floating down the Great River, formed islands along its course.

Thunderbird died, and his giant body formed a great bridge above the river. The five sons of Coyote and all the other animal people who had been killed by Thunderbird came back to life.

Though many hundreds of snows had passed, the great bridge formed from the rocks that had been made out of Thunderbird's body still stood above the river. It was there long after the first Indians came to the earth. The Indians always called it "the Bridge of the Gods." No one must look at the rocks of the bridge. People knew that some day it would fall. They must not anger the Spirit Chief by looking at it, their wise men told them.

The Klickitat Indians had a different law. Only a few men necessary to paddle the canoes would pass under the bridge. All the others would land when they approached the Bridge of the Gods, walk around to the opposite side of it, and there reenter the canoes. The oarsmen always bade their friends good-bye, fearing that the bridge would fall while they were passing under it.

After many snows, no one knows how many, the prophecy of the wise men came true. The Bridge of the Gods fell. The rocks that had once been the body of Thunderbird formed the rapids in the river that were long known as Cascades of the Columbia.

McWhorter Papers.

■

Raven and His Grandmother
Aleuts

These stories were obtained by F. A. Golder on Kodiak, Alaska, during his three year residence there at the end of the 1890s. They were told in the Russian language by Mrs. Reed, Nicoli Medvednikoff, and Corneil Panamaroff, all natives of Kodiak Island. The natives of Kodiak speak Russian as freely as they do their own tribal language. They call themselves "Aleuts," and that refers distinctly to them and not the "real Aleut" to the west on the Aleutian Islands.

■

In her *barrabara* (a native home) at the end of a large village, lived an old grandmother with her grandson, a raven. The two lived apart from the other villagers because they were disliked. When the men returned from fishing for cod, the raven would come and beg for food, but they would never give him any of their catch. But when all had left the beach, the raven would come and pick up any leftover refuse, even sick fish. On these, raven and his grandmother lived.

One winter was extremely cold. Hunting was impossible; food became so scarce the villages neared starvation. Even their chief had but little left. So the chief called all his people together and urged them to use every effort to obtain food enough for all, or they would starve.

The chief then announced that he wished for his son to take a bride, and she would be selected from the girls of the village. All the girls responded to the excitement of the occasion and dressed in their very best costumes and jewelry.

For a short time hunger was forgotten as the girls lined up for the contest and were judged by the critical eye of their chief, who selected the fairest of the fair for his son's bride. A feast was given by the chief following their marriage ceremony. But soon after hunger began again.

The raven perched on a pole outside his barrabara, observing and listening attentively to all that had happened. After the feast, he flew home and said to his grandmother, "I, too, want to marry." She made no reply, so he went about his work, gathering what food he could for his little home. Each day he flew to the beach and found dead fish or birds. He always gathered more than enough for two people. While he was in the village, he noted that the famine seemed worse. So he asked the chief, "What will you give me, if I bring you food?"

The chief looked at him in great surprise and said, "You shall have my oldest daughter for your wife." Nothing could have pleased raven more. He flew away in a joyful mood and said to his grandmother, "Let's clean out the barrabara. Make everything clean for my bride. I am going to give the chief some food, and he has promised to give me his oldest daughter."

"Ai, Ai, Y-a-h! You are going to marry? Our barrabara is too small and too dirty. Where will you put your wife?"

"Caw! Caw! Caw! Never mind. Do as I say," he screamed at his grandmother, and began pecking her to hurry.

Early next morning raven flew away, and later in the day returned with a bundle of *yukelah* (dried salmon) in his talons. "Come with me to the chief's house, grandmother," he called to her. Raven handed the fish to the chief and received the chief's oldest daughter for his bride.

Raven preceded his grandmother as she brought the bride to their little home. He cleared out the barrabara of old straw and bedding. When the two women arrived, they found the little home empty, and the grandmother began to scold him and said, "What are you doing? Why are you throwing out everything."

"I am cleaning house, as you can see," raven curtly said.

When night came, raven spread wide one wing, and asked his bride to lie on it, and then covered her with the other wing. She spent a miserable night, as raven's fish odor nearly smothered her. So she determined she would leave in the morning.

But by morning, she decided to stay and try to become accustomed to him. During the day she was cheerless and worried. When raven offered her food, she would not eat it. On the second night, raven invited her to lay her head on his chest and seek rest in his arms. Only after much persuasion did she comply with his wish. The second night was no better for her, so early the next morning she stole away from him and went back to her father's house, telling him everything.

Upon waking and finding his wife gone, raven inquired of his grandmother what she knew of his wife's whereabouts. She assured raven that she knew nothing. "Go then to the chief and bring her back to me," called raven. Grandmother feared him and left to do his bidding. When she came to the chief's house, she was pushed out of the door. This she promptly reported to her grandson.

The summer passed warm and pleasant, but a hard winter and another famine followed. As in the previous winter, the grandmother and the raven had plenty of food and wood, while others suffered greatly from lack of food. Raven's thoughts again turned to marriage. This time she was a young and beautiful girl who lived at the other end of the village. He told his grandmother about her and that he wanted to marry her. He asked, "Grandmother, will you go and bring the girl here, and I will marry her."

"Ai, Ai, Y-a-h! And you are going to marry her? Your first wife could not live with you because you smell strong. The girls do not wish to marry you.

"Caw! Caw! Caw! Never mind my smell! Never mind my smell! Go— do as I say."

To impress his commands and secure her obedience, he started pecking at her until she was glad to go. While his grandmother was gone, raven became restless and anxious. He hopped about the barrabara and nearby hillocks, straining his eyes for a sight of his expected bride.

Hurriedly he began cleaning out the barrabara, throwing out old straw, bedding, baskets, and all. The grandmother upon her return scolded raven, but he paid no attention to her.

The young bride, like her predecessor, was enfolded tightly in his wings, and likewise she had a wretched and sleepless night. But she was determined to endure his odor if possible. She thought at least with him she would have plenty of food to eat. The second night was as bad as the first, but she stayed on and secretly concluded she would do her best to stay until spring.

On the third day the raven, seeing that his wife was still with him, said, "Grandmother, tomorrow I will go and get a big, fat whale. While I am gone, make a belt and a pair of *torbarsars* (native shoes) for my wife."

"Ai, Ai, Y-a-h! How will you bring a big, fat whale? The hunters cannot kill one, how will you do it?"

"Caw! Caw! Caw! Be quiet and do what I tell you: make the belt and torbarsars while I go and get the whale," he angrily exclaimed, using his most effective method of silencing her.

Before dawn next morning the raven flew away to sea. In his absence the old woman was busily engaged making the things for the young bride, who watched and talked to her. About midday, they saw raven flying toward shore, carrying a whale.

The grandmother started a big fire, and the young woman tucked up her *parka* (native dress), belted it with her new belt, put on the new torbarsars, sharpened the stone knife, and went to the beach to meet her husband. As he drew near he called, "Grandmother, go into the village and tell all the people that I have brought home a big, fat whale."

She ran as hard as she could and told the joyful news. The half-dead people suddenly became alive. Some sharpened their knives, others dressed in their best clothes. But most of them just ran as they were and with such knives as they had with them to the beach to see the whale.

His sudden importance was not lost on the raven, who hopped up and down the whale's back, viewing the scene of carnage, as the people gorged themselves on the whale.

Every few moments raven would take a pebble out of his bag, then after some thought put it back. When the chief and his relatives came near, raven drove them away. They had to be content just watching the people enjoy their feasting, and carrying off blubber to their homes. Later, in the village, the people did share with the chief.

The raven's first wife, the chief's daughter, had a son by him, a little raven. She had it in her arms at the beach and walked in front of raven,

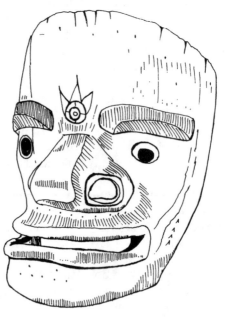

Wooden burial mask
Aleuts

where he could notice her. "Here is your child, look at it," she called. But he ignored her. She called to him several times and continued to show him the baby. At last he said, "Come closer—nearer still." But when she could not stand his odor any longer, she left him without a word.

Death occurred as a result of the feast. Many of the people ate so much fat on the spot that they died soon after. The rest of the people had eaten so much and filled their barrabaras so full, that during the night they all suffocated. Of the entire village, only three were left—the raven, his new wife, and the grandmother. There they lived on as their descendants do to this day.

Golder, "Raven and His Grandmother," 26.

———, "Kodiak Island Legends," 16-19, 26.

■

THE WHITE-FACED BEAR
Aleuts

■

In a tribal village there lived a mighty bear-hunter. For more than three years, he had been constantly successful in killing so many that his friend tried to persuade him to stop hunting.

"If you insist upon hunting one more bear, you will come across a huge bear who might kill you," he said. The hunter ignored his friend's advice and replied, "I will attack every bear I come across."

A few days later the hunter started out and saw a bear with two cubs. He decided this was not the huge bear he had been worried about, so he attacked the mother bear, and after some difficulty killed her. The cubs ran away. After the hunter dragged the bear home for his tribe, his friend continued to urge him to give up the bear hunt, but without success.

On another hunt, after a few days on the trail, the hunter met a stranger who informed him that near his village were a great many bears. "Every year many are killed by our hunters, but always there is an invincible one that has destroyed many of our hunters. Each time he kills a man, the bear tears him apart, examines him carefully as if searching for a special body mark. He is different because his feet and head are white."

They parted, and the hunter started out to look for that hunting ground. On his way, he stopped near a fish creek looking for game, but after a long night none appeared. Next morning he moved onward andcame to a high bluff; below it he saw many bears on the tundra. He waited until some separated and looked over the remainder.

Among those, he saw the white-faced bear with white feet and concluded that this must be the ferocious, huge bear he sought. First he would keep an eye on it and wait for a favorable opportunity to kill it.

Now it seems that at one time, the white-faced bear was a human being and a very successful bear-hunter, too successful for his own good. His friends were envious and plotted to kill him. So they went to a medicine-man deep in the woods, and begged him to transform the successful hunter into a beast.

"Shoot a bear, skin it and place the skin under the pillow of your successful hunter," advised the shaman.

After the bear-skin had been prepared, the shaman and his friends quietly went to the man's hut and placed the skin under the man's pillow. They hid themselves to see what would happen when the man went to bed. Upon waking, the man found that he had become a huge bear with a white face and white feet.

"The white marks will show you which bear he is," said the shaman, who disappeared into the woods.

Now our bear-hunter still sat at the edge of the bluff. Toward evening he saw the bears begin to leave, all except the white-faced bear. He was the last to get up, and he shook himself three times and acted as if he was deeply enraged. He moved toward the bluff where the hunter sat perfectly still. But the bear approached, and when he was almost face to face, asked, "What are you doing here?"

"I came out to hunt," he replied.

"Is it not enough that you have killed all my family, and recently killed my wife, and now you want to take my life? If you had injured my children the other day, I would now tear you to pieces. I will, however, spare your life this time on your promise that you will never hunt bears again. All the bears you saw today are my children and of my brother. Should I ever see you hunting bear, I will tear you apart."

Relieved to get away so easily, the hunter headed homeward. His friend met him and inquired about the white-faced bear, and when told what had happened, he urged the hunter to give up hunting. A whole week passed before the hunter set forth again, taking along six hunting friends.

For two days they hunted without luck, then came to the fish creek where they camped overnight. Next morning their leader took the six to the edge of the bluff where they could look down at the tundra and see many bears. But they could not see the white-faced bear and, encouraged, followed their leader toward the animals.

"Look at that strange-looking beast with white paws and a white face!" exclaimed one man.

The hunter-leader caught sight of that special bear and ordered his followers to retreat at once. So they went around another mountain where they saw many bears. They killed seven, one for each man.

Loaded with their spoil they took the homeward trail, but a short distance behind them they heard a commotion. They saw the white-faced bear rapidly approaching them. The hunter aimed, but his bowstring broke. The others shot and missed. The white-faced bear spoke up and said, "Why do you shoot at me? I never harm you. Your leader killed my wife and nearly all my family. I warned him that if I found him hunting again, I would tear him apart. And this I shall do now, piece by piece. The rest of you can go. I'll not harm you because you have not harmed me."

Hurriedly, as fast as possible, the six men fled. The white-faced bear turned to the bear-hunter.

"I had you in my power once and I let you go on your promise not to hunt bear again. Now you are back at it and brought more bear-hunters along. This time I will do to you as you have done to mine."

The hunter pleaded to be allowed to live one more night so he could go home. At first the bear refused outright. The white-faced bear then relented, and would even spare his life entirely, if the hunter would tell him who had transformed him from a man into a beast. The hunter agreed to meet him the next night and go to the home of the shaman.

When the bear-hunter reached home and found his six companions talking excitedly about the day's experience, they were surprised to see the hunter-leader alive.

The hunter told them his plan to meet the white-faced bear at the home of the shaman next evening and asked the six to go with him. They refused and tried to dissuade their leader. But the bear-hunter kept his word and met the white-faced bear at the appointed place. A light shone from every hut except that of the shaman.

"This is the place," said the man.

"I will remain here," ordered the bear. "You go inside and tell him there is a man outside wishing to speak with him."

The man advanced and found the skin-door tied, so he reported to the bear that the shaman must be out. The bear ordered him back to cut the door, then walk in. Upon entering, the man heard someone call, "Who dares come into my lodge?"

"It is I," said the bear-hunter.

"What do you wish?"

"There is a man outside who wishes to speak to you."

Had the shaman not been so sleepy, he might have been suspicious. Under the circumstances, his mind was not clear and he fell into the trap.

When the shaman came near the white-faced bear, the old man became frightened and was ready to run away. But the bear blocked his way and said, "For years you have tortured me and made my life a burden in this condition. I demand you give me back my human form immediately, otherwise I shall tear you to pieces."

The shaman promised to do so if the bear would follow him into his hut. Before going in, the bear said to the hunter, "Meet me here when I come out."

All night the shaman worked hard with the bear, and by next morning succeeded in pulling off the bear-skin, and a human form appeared. The shaman asked to keep the white-faced bear's skin, but the man kept the white-face and the white claws, which he cut off at once, giving the rest of the skin to the shaman.

"If you ever again try to transform a man into a beast, I will be back and kill you dead, dead, dead," said the man.

The next day when the bear-man met the bear-hunter he said, "I caution you against ever going out to hunt bear. You may even hear people say I've become a bear again, and they will hunt me. Don't you joint them. If I find you in their company, I will kill you dead, dead, dead."

For about four weeks the hunter remained at home with every intention of keeping his promise to the transformed man. But one day two young men from the neighboring tribal village came to beg his assistance. They asked his help to kill a ferocious bear with a white face and four white feet.

Of course the hunter knew the bear they feared, but decided to disguise himself and go help them. They gathered all of the village warriors and set out to find the white-faced bear. The bear saw them coming. He rose and shook himself three times, giving the impression of great anger, which frightened the warriors. Their chief said, "We are in great danger, so we must stand and fight."

Madly, the white-faced bear jumped, landed in front of the hunter and tore him to pieces. Then it pawed a hole in the ground and covered up the parts. The terrified warriors tried to escape, but the white-faced bear chased them back to their village, tearing them apart, killing all of them, including the old shaman. Finished, the white-faced bear turned back into the woods to rest undisturbed forever.

Golder, "The White-Faced Bear," 296–299.

■

THE TWO INQUISITIVE MEN

Aleuts

■

There were two men in the old days by the names of Acha-yuongch and Ach-goyan. They lived together, but spoke and looked at each other only when they were compelled to do so. They were curious about anything happening nearby and they usually went to investigate.

One day, as they were sitting in their barrabara around the fire, their backs toward each other, eating shellfish, Ach-goyan pulled out a feather from his hair, threw it in front of him and said, "Acha-yuongch, what shall we do? There is a man living over there on the other side of the village. He hunts every day with his sling."

Acha-yuongch was silent for a while, then he scratched his ear and said, "I do not know what is the matter with me. There is much whistling in my ear."

Silence followed for some time, then Ach-goyan pulled out another feather from his hair and threw it up in front of him and said, "Acha-yuongch, what shall we do? There is a man living over there who hunts every day with his sling."

Acha-yuongch again replied, "There is very much whistling in my ear." A third time Ach-goyan threw a feather into the air and said, "There is a man living on the other side whose name is Ploch-goyuli. He hunts every day with his *plochgo* (sling). Let's go and see him." So they prepared for the trip, piling their barrabara and all their other possessions on their canoe, including the grave with the remains of their wife.

But on launching, they discovered that the load was too heavy on one side. So they dug up a small hillock and placed it on top to equalize their load. They filled hollow reeds with fresh water and started on their trip. When they arrived on the other shore they saw Ploch-goyuli hunting ducks with his sling. He saw them, too, and knew the nature of their visit, so he threw rocks at them. The first rock hit close to the canoe. Ach-goyan exclaimed, "Ka! Ka! Ka! It nearly hit me."

The second rock hit closer, and he exclaimed louder, "Ka! Ka! Ka!" Rocks kept coming, and they turned their damaged canoe around and headed homeward, where they replaced their barrabara and all of their things.

A few days later, sitting around the fire in their barrabara, Ach-goyan pulled out a feather from his hair, tossing it in the air and said, "Let's visit the man on the island who heats a bath and catches codfish every day."

"My ear is still whistling," replied Acha-yuongch. After tossing another feather into the air, Ach-goyan said, "Let's visit the man living on an island in the middle of the sea, who heats his bath and catches codfish every day. His name is Peting-yuwock."

Again they loaded the canoe with all of their things and started off. They reached the island, beached their canoe, and went to the old man's barrabara. He cried out, "Where is the man-smell coming from?"

"We came to visit you because we heard you heat your bath and catch codfish every day."

"The hot bath is ready," said Peting-yuwock and directed the two inquisitive men to it. While they were bathing, the old man tied together a lot of thin, dried kelp, which he had kept to make clothes. Out of it, he made a long rope and fastened one end of it to the canoe. He then roasted a codfish and gave it to the two men after their bath.

"There is a strong wind blowing. You had better hasten to your barrabara before it becomes too strong," suggested the old man.

Kayak
Aleuts

The two men heeded his warning and shoved off into the sea. When they were about halfway across, the old man pulled the rope and brought the two men back to his shore. He came out and called to them, "Why have you come back. I warned you how strong the wind was."

Again the two men started off, and again were halfway home when the old man pulled on the rope and hauled them back to the beach. "Why are you back here? Get on with you or you will never make it," he shouted at them against the wind.

The third time when the old man pulled on the rope, it broke, and the canoe upset and the two men were lost with all of their belongings.

The grave of their wife became a beautiful porpoise. Acha-yuongch and Ach-goyan were cast upon the shore, where they became two capes of land, jutting into the sea like two peninsulas.

They had been so inquisitive about everything that they became prominent landmarks, two safe harbors for fishermen and others at sea, forever.

Golder, "The Inquisitive Men," 19-21.

■

THE GIRL WHO SEARCHED FOR HER LOVER

Aleuts

■

A terrible misfortune befell the people of a very large tribe. Of all the hunters that left the village, not one came back alive, nor was it known what had happened to them. In that tribe lived a beautiful young girl, who loved and was beloved by a brave hunter. She had joyfully consented to be his wife, but her parents objected.

The disappointed hunter had decided to drown his grief by going with the warriors to hunt. Older men cautioned against his hunting, but the young lover departed with the warriors. A month passed, but he did not return and was given up for lost by his tribe. Not so the young girl, who could not believe him dead. She felt she must go and search for him.

Secretly she made preparations, and one night she stole away quietly, taking her father's one-hatch kayak and a waterproof elk skin shirt. After some distance from her village, she ceased paddling, closed her eyes, and began singing. After a verse, she opened her eyes. Noticing the kayak drifting with the current, she closed her eyes again and sang some more. At the end of the second verse, she looked again and found the kayak drifting faster than before. Then she closed her eyes and sang for a long time.

When she looked again, the kayak was going so fast that she became alarmed but could not change her course. Her speed increased by the moment, then she heard the mighty roar of waterfalls. Since life without her lover was not worth living, she closed her eyes to await her fate.

Very swiftly the boat rushed forward. The roaring waters became powerful. Her heart nearly stopped beating from fright when she felt herself going down, down, down, then come suddenly to a standstill.

She was not hurt, but could neither get out of the kayak nor move it. The boat was stuck fast. Dawn approached as she lay there, wondering what would become of her and what had happened to her lover. At sunrise, she saw a kayak coming toward her with one man paddling.

The man exclaimed aloud, "Ha! Ha! I have another victim," as he placed a bow and arrow beside him with a two-edged knife attached to the tip. But as he drew nearer, he put away his weapons, thinking, "That is a woman." Then he called out, "If you are a woman, speak up, and I will not kill you, for I never kill women." She assured him that she was a woman, and he came and helped her out of her boat and seated her in his kayak. He paddled off with her.

They reached his own barrabara where he lived alone. She noticed many human heads scattered about. One she recognized as her lover's. She said nothing, but to herself she pledged vengeance. The man asked her to be his wife, and ordered her to cook deer and seal meat for them to eat. At bedtime, he pointed to a corner for her to sleep, while he slept in an opposite corner. She obeyed without questioning him.

Next morning, he led her to a smaller barrabara and showed her a number of headless bodies. He said, "These I do not eat; but I have three sisters living some distance from here, who eat human flesh only. It is for them I have killed these people. Each day I take one body to a different sister." He then picked up a corpse and his bow and arrow and walked away.

The young girl followed him to the place where the road forked. One path led to the right, one led to the left, and one led straight ahead. She noticed which one he took, then returned to his barrabara, where she busied herself, removing two posts from one of the walls. She dug out an underground passage for escape.

All of the extra dirt she carried to the sea, then cunningly concealed the passage. Toward evening, she cooked a good supper for him when he returned, eating in silence, then they retired, each to their own corner.

After breakfast next morning, he carried away another corpse. She took the bow and arrow, which he left behind, following him secretly. He took the left fork while she took the middle one. She hurried on, then cut across to the left fork and managed to reach the home of his sister before he arrived, killing her with the bow and arrow.

From there she ran to the homes of the other two sisters, killing them, before running back to the barrabara. He found all three sisters dead and was suspicious.

She was sitting on the barrabara when he returned. "You killed my sisters, now I will kill you," he cried out angrily, rushing for his bow and arrow. They were not in their usual place and he discovered them in her hands. He begged her to give them to him, promising to do her no harm. At first she refused, but he pleaded and promised until she trusted him and gave them to him.

As soon as they were his again, he shouted, "Now you shall die," and shot at her. She suddenly dropped through the smoke hole, out of sight, before the arrow could reach her. While he looked for the arrow, she

Wood hat
Aleuts

crawled out through the underground passage and perched herself anew on top of the barrabara.

Her disappearance and sudden reappearance was a mystery to him. he shot at her again and again, but she disappeared each time mysteriously. At least, since he could not kill her, he said, "Take this bow and arrow and kill me."

"I do not want to kill you," she told him. "But I'm afraid you will kill me someday."

He swore never to hurt her, and she came down from the roof. Together they ate their supper and retired in the usual manner. But as he was about to fall asleep, she moved closer to him and began talking to him, keeping him awake the entire night.

For five days and five nights she tormented him in this way, giving him no time to sleep. On the sixth day, in spite of all she could do, he fell into a deep, deep sleep. Although she pinched him and pulled at him, she could not arouse him. She brought a block of wood from outside and placed it under his neck. Then, with a knife she had stolen from one of his sisters, she beheaded him.

In his kayak, she put his bow, arrow, and knife, then seated herself and paddled homeward by way of the falls. But there were no falls, as they had existed only through the evil of that man. When he died, the river flowed smoothly and steadily in its own original channel. She found her kayak, which had drifted onto the beach, and she tied it to his and paddled to her home.

Her people learned of her adventures and the evil man. The older men decreed his weapons be burned on the trash pile. Then the people rejoiced in the young girl's safe return and the safety of their tribe.

Golder, "Girl Searches for Her Lover," 26-28.

■

THE GIRL WHO MARRIED THE MOON
Aleuts

■

Long ago there were two girl cousins who lived in a large tribal village. Those evenings when the moon was out, they liked to go to the beach and play. Claiming the moon as their husband, they spend the night gazing and making love to the man in the moon.

For shelter they had propped up a *bidarka* (large skin boat), and during the night they changed positions several times, so they could always face the moon. In the morning, upon returning home, their parents always questioned them about their whereabouts. The girls told them how they had watched the moon until it passed from sight. Many of their family heard them tell how much they loved the moon, always wishing they were moons.

One evening, with other young people of their tribe, they amused themselves on the beach. Night came and the others returned to their homes, but the two girls remained. When the moon went away out of their sight, one complained, "Why does the moon hide so suddenly? I like to play with him and enjoy his moonlight." "I, too," said the other. It was not yet midnight, and the moon was already behind the clouds.

Up to now they had not noticed how disheveled their appearance was from playing. They became startled when they heard the voice of a young man as he approached them. "You have been professing your love for me," he said. "I have observed you and know you love me, therefore, I have come for you. But since my work is very hard, I can only take one of you—the more patient one."

Each begged to be chosen. He said, "I have decided to take both of you. Now close your eyes and keep them closed." So he grabbed each by the hair, and the next moment they were rushing through the air. The patience of one wore thin. As she opened her eyes, she felt herself drop down, down, down, leaving her hair behind in his hands. She found herself beside the bidarka where she had left it.

The patient cousin kept her eyes closed the entire time, and in the morning found herself in a comfortable barrabara, the home of the moon. There she lived as the wife of the moon, happy in loving him. Generally he slept during the day, as he worked all night.

Frequently he went away in the morning and returned in the evening. Sometimes he was gone from mid-day until midnight. His irregular schedule puzzled his wife. But he never offered an explanation to her of what he did in his absence.

His silence and indifference piqued the young bride. She waited as long as she could, until one day she said, "You go out every day, every evening, every night, and you never tell me what you do. What kinds of people do you associate with, while I am left behind?"

"I am not with other people, for there are not my kind of people here," he said. "I have important work to do, and I cannot be with you all the time."

"If your work is so hard, can you take me with you to help you sometimes?" she asked.

"My work is too hard for you," he replied. "I brought you up here, because I had no rest when you were down there. You and your lovely cousin were constantly staring at me and teasing me. Now stop your foolishness, you cannot help me. Stay home and be happy for me when I do return."

"Surely, you don't expect me to stay home all the time." She began to weep. "If I cannot go with you, can I go out by myself occasionally?"

"Of course, go anywhere you like, except in the two homes you see yonder. In the corner of each there is a curtain, under which you must never look." After this warning, he left his barrabara, and that night he looked paler than usual.

Later, she went out for a walk. Although she went far and in different directions, she saw no people. She tried several short trails, and on each saw a man lying face down. It gave her pleasure to kick them to disturb them. Each would turn and look at her with his one bright, sparkling eye and cry out, "Why do that to me? I am working and busy." She kicked all of them until she tired and ran home.

On her way she saw the two forbidden barrabaras, and she just had to look inside. A curtain hid a corner in the first. She couldn't resist the desire to look under the curtain. There she beheld a half-moon, a quarter-moon, and a small piece of moon. In the second barrabara, she found a full moon, one almost full, and another more than half-full.

Thinking about the beautiful pieces, she decided it would be such fun and no harm to try on one to see how she would feel. The one almost full pleased her most, so she placed it on one side of her face and there it stuck. She cried, "Ai, Ai, Y-a-h, Ai, Ai, Yah!" She tugged and pulled but the moon would not come off. For fear her husband would soon arrive, she hastened home, threw herself on the bed, and covered that side of her face.

There he found her, complaining that her face pained her. He suspected the real cause and went out to investigate. Upon his return he asked her about the missing moon. "Yes," she admitted. "I tried it on for fun, and now I cannot take it off." He laughed and laughed at her. Gently he pulled it off for her.

Seeing his good humor, she told him of her eventful day, especially the sport she had with the one-eyed people scattered about the sky.

"They are stars," he said reprovingly. "Since of your own free will you put on this moon, you can wear it from now on and help me in my hard work. I will finish my rounds with the full moon, and after that you can start in and finish out the month while I rest."

To this happy arrangement she consented gladly. Since that time the two have shared the hard work between them—the man in the moon and his lady in the moon.

Golder, "The Girl Who Married the Moon," 28-31.

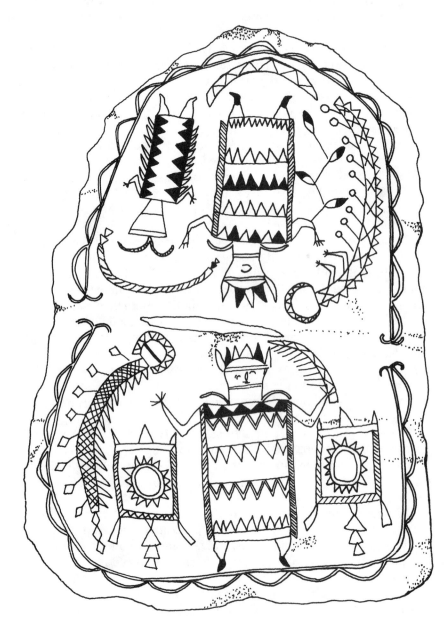

Painted Cape
Apache

PART TWO

FROM THE SOUTHWEST

In early times, the states of this area nurtured great Indian tribes who gave us these stories from the Southwest.

The Apache, a name that means "enemy," is an extensive Athapascan language family located mostly in New Mexico, Arizona, Texas, and southeast Colorado. Coming from the north in prehistoric times, the Apache traveled along the east side of the Rocky Mountains. Francisco Vasquez de Coronado, with his Spanish explorers, met them in 1540 in eastern New Mexico, where they became cliffdwellers. These Indians did not reach Arizona until 100 years later. The Jicarilla (whose name means "little basket" because of their expert women basket makers), became a strong band of the Apache, one group extending west into Colorado permanently and another east into Texas.

Frequent skirmishes occurred between the Navaho, Pueblo, Apache, and Zuñi over territorial rights, and later against the whites. The name Pueblo ("town") indicated those tribes who lived in community stone cliff-houses perched along the canyon walls of New Mexico. These Indians descended from the prehistoric Anasazi culture.

The Hopi, the "peaceful ones," a group from the north and east, became a Pueblo culture living on the Three Mesas in northern Arizona. When the gold rush began in 1849, these tribes guided and protected prospectors on their way to California.

The Yuma and Maricopa tribes were related closely to each other and lived along the Gila River and on both sides of the Colorado River. The Ute, Paiute, and Arapaho spread over Colorado, Nevada, and Utah, and the Pima, Papago, Navaho, and Chipewyan, tribes expanded and extended mostly throughout New Mexico and Arizona.

The many tribes of California mainly followed their sources of water. Several landscape myths and legends are included here.

■

THE FLOOD ON SUPERSTITION MOUNTAIN
Pima

In the state of Arizona, the Pima Indian tribe declares that the
father of all men and animals was Great Butterfly—Cherwit Maké,
meaning the Earth-Maker.

■

One day long ago, Great Butterfly fluttered down from the clouds to
the Blue Cliffs, where two rivers met, later called the Verde and Salt
rivers. There he made man from his own sweat.

From that day on the people multiplied, but in time they grew selfish
and quarrelsome. Earth-Maker became annoyed with their behavior
and decided it might be best to drown all of them.

But first, he thought to warn them through the *voices of the winds.*

"People of the Pima tribe," called North Wind. "Sky Spirit warns you
to be honest with one another and to live in peace from now on."

Suha, Shaman of the Pimas, interpreted to the people what North
Wind had warned them about.

"What a fool you are, Suha, to listen to the voices of the winds,"
taunted his tribesmen.

On the next night, the same warning from Earth-Maker was repeated
by East Wind, who added, "Chief Sky Spirit warns that all of you will
be destroyed by floods if you do not live nobler lives."

Again, the Pimas mocked the winds and ignored their warnings.
Next night, West Wind spoke, "Reform, people of the Pimas, or your evil
ways will destroy you."

Then South Wind breathed into Suha's ear, "Suha, you and your good
wife are the only people worth saving. Go and make a large, hollow ball
of spruce gum in which you and your wife can live a long as the coming
flood will last."

Because Suha and his wife believed the warnings and were obedient,
they set to work immediately on a high hill, gathering spruce gum and
shaping it into a large hollow ball. They stocked it with plenty of nuts,
acorns, water, and bear and deer meats.

Near the appointed time, Suha and his good wife looked down sadly
upon the lovely green valley. They heard the songs of the harvesters.
They sighed to think of the beauty about them that would be destroyed
when the flood came because of the people's selfishness. Suddenly, a

bright lightning flash and loud thunder rocked the Blue Cliffs. It was a signal for the flood to begin.

Suha and his wife went into the gum-ball ark and closed the door tightly. Swirling, dark clouds surrounded them. Torrents of rain poured down everywhere. For many days, the ark rolled and tossed about on the deepening sea.

After many, many moons, the downpour of rain stopped. The ark settled upon the land again, high on a mountaintop. Suha opened the door and stepped forth to see a tuna cactus growing near his feet. He and his wife ate some of the red fruit of the cactus plant. Below them, they saw water everywhere.

Basket
Pima

That night they retired again to the ark. They must have slept a very long time, because when they awoke the water had disappeared, the valleys were green, and the bird songs rang forth again.

Suha and his wife descended from Superstition Mountain, a name later given to the mountain upon which the ark had landed. They went down into the fertile valley and lived there for a thousand years. The forthcoming people prospered, becoming known as the Pima tribe.

These Pimas later believed a story that an evil one named Hauk lived behind Superstition Mountain. He was also called the "Devil of Superstition Mountain" because he tried to steal daughters from the Pimas.

One day, Hauk secretly descended into Pima valley, where the women were busy weaving. He stole one of Suha's daughters. Suha followed Hauk to his home behind Superstition Mountain, where he observed his daughter treated as a servant-girl by Hauk.

Suha poisoned the cactus wine that his daughter served Hauk. When he drank it, Hauk died instantly. After that the world seemed less wicked, but always the Pimas feared that Hauk's evil spirit still lurked behind Superstition Mountain.

Suha, Shaman and inspired leader of the Pima tribe, taught his people to build adobe houses, to dig gardens with bones and stones, to irrigate their lands from the rivers; to raise sheep, horses, and cattle, and, above all, to live in peace with one another.

On his dying day, Suha gathered his people and foretold:

"If you ever grow arrogant with wealth, if you ever become covetous of others' lands, if you ever make war for gain, if you ever disgrace yourselves before Chief of the Sky Spirits—another flood will come upon you.

"If that happens again, bad persons will never be saved; only good persons will eventually live with the Sun-God."

Since that time, Pimas have believed Suha's prophecies; and they never, never go onto Superstition Mountain.

But their people love to tell the story of why and how the gum-ball ark landed on Superstition Mountain, saving Suha and his good wife, who became the beloved ancestors of their large and important Pima Tribe.

Skinner, *Myths and Legends of Our Own Land*, vol. II, 215-218.

■

HOW THE HOPI INDIANS REACHED THEIR WORLD

Hopi

Hapitu or Hopi meaning the "peaceful ones" were the only Shoshones to adopt a pueblo culture, located on the Three Mesas in Northeastern Arizona.

Their first European contact was with the Spanish explorer Coronado in 1540. In 1598, the Governor of New Mexico territory made them swear allegiance to the King of Spain. In 1529, a Franciscan Mission was established at several Hopi settlements, however they were destroyed in 1680 at the general Pueblo uprising. The present Hopi Reservation became a reality by presidential order on December 16, 1882.

The performance of their spectacular Snake Dance attracts a huge public, and they remain one of the largest and best known of the North American tribes.

■

When the world was new, the ancient people and the ancient creatures did not live on the top of the earth. They lived under it. All was darkness, all was blackness, above the earth as well as below it.

There were four worlds: this one on top of the earth, and below it three cave worlds, one below the other. None of the cave worlds was large enough for all the people and the creatures.

They increased so fast in the lowest cave world that they crowded it. They were poor and did not know where to turn in the blackness. When they moved, they jostled one another. The cave was filled with the filth of the people who lived in it. No one could turn to spit without spitting on another. No one could cast slime from his nose without its falling on someone else. The people filled the place with their complaints and with their expressions of disgust.

Some people said, "It is not good for us to live in this way."

"How can it be made better?" one man asked.

"Let it be tried and seen!" answered another.

Two Brothers, one older and one younger, spoke to the priest-chiefs of the people in the cave world, "Yes, let it be tried and seen. Then it shall be well. By our wills it shall be well."

The Two Brothers pierced the roofs of the caves and descended to the lowest world, where people lived. The Two Brothers sowed one plant after another, hoping that one of them would grow up to the opening through which they themselves had descended and yet would have the strength to bear the weight of men and creatures. These, the Two Brothers hoped, might climb up the plant into the second cave world. One of these plants was a cane.

At last, after many trials, the cane became so tall that it grew through the opening in the roof, and it was so strong that men could climb to its top. It jointed so that it was like a ladder, easily ascended. Ever since then, the cane has grown in joints as we see it today along the Colorado River.

Up this cane many people and beings climbed to the second cave world. When a part of them had climbed out, they feared that that cave also would be too small. It was so dark that they could not see how large it was. So they shook the ladder and caused those who were coming up it to fall back. Then they pulled the ladder out. It is said that those who were left came out of the lowest cave later. They are our brothers west of us.

After a long time the second cave became filled with men and beings, as the first had been. Complaining and wrangling were heard as in the beginning. Again the cane was placed under the roof vent, and once more men and beings entered the upper cave world. Again, those who were slow to climb out were shaken back or left behind. Though larger, the third cave was as dark as the first and second. The Two Brothers found fire. Torches were set ablaze, and by their light men built their huts and kivas, or traveled from place to place.

While people and the beings lived in this third cave world, times of evil came to them. Women became so crazed that they neglected all things for the dance. They even forgot their babies. Wives became mixed with wives, so that husbands did not know their own from others. At that time there was no day, only night, black night. Throughout this night, women danced in the kivas (men's "clubhouses"), ceasing only to sleep. So the fathers had to be the mothers of the little ones. When these little ones cried from hunger, the fathers carried them to the kivas, where the women were dancing. Hearing their cries, the mothers came and nursed them, and then went back to their dancing. Again the fathers took care of the children.

These troubles caused people to long for the light and to seek again an escape from darkness. They climbed to the fourth world, which was this world. But it too was in darkness, for the earth was closed in by the sky, just as the cave worlds had been closed in by their roofs. Men went from their lodges and worked by the light of torches and fires. They found the tracks of only one being, the single ruler of the unpeopled world, the tracks of Corpse Demon or Death. The people tried to follow these tracks, which led eastward. But the world was damp and dark, and people did not know what to do in the darkness. The waters seemed to surround them, and the tracks seemed to lead out into the waters.

With the people were five beings that had come forth with them from the cave worlds: Spider, Vulture, Swallow, Coyote, and Locust. The people and these beings consulted together, trying to think of some way of making light. Many, many attempts were made, but without success. Spider was asked to try first. She spun a mantle of pure white cotton. It gave some light but not enough. Spider therefore became our grandmother.

Then the people obtained and prepared a very white deerskin that had not been pierced in any spot. From this they made a shield case, which they painted with turquoise paint. It shed forth such brilliant light that it lighted the whole world. It made the light from the cotton

Tabilita
Hopi

mantle look faded. So the people sent the shield-light to the east, where
it became the moon.

Down in the cave world Coyote had stolen a jar that was very heavy,
so very heavy that he grew weary of carrying it. He decided to leave it
behind, but he was curious to see what it contained. Now that light had
taken the place of darkness, he opened the jar. From it many shining
fragments and sparks flew out and upward, singeing his face as they
passed him. That is why the coyote has a black face to this day. The
shining fragments and sparks flew up to the sky and became stars.

By these lights the people found that the world was indeed very small
and surrounded by waters, which made it damp. The people appealed
to Vulture for help. He spread his wings and fanned the waters, which
flowed away to the east and to the west until mountains began to appear.

Across the mountains the Two Brothers cut channels. Water rushed
through the channels, and wore their courses deeper and deeper. Thus
the great canyons and valleys of the world were formed. The waters
have kept on flowing and flowing for ages. The world has grown drier,
and continues to grow drier and drier.

Now that there was light, the people easily followed the tracks of Death eastward over the new land that was appearing. Hence Death is our greatest father and master. We followed his tracks when we left the cave worlds, and he was the only being that awaited us on the great world of waters where this world is now.

Although all the water had flowed away, the people found the earth soft and damp. That is why we can see today the tracks of men and of many strange creatures between the place toward the west and the place where we came from the cave world.

Since the days of the first people, the earth has been changed to stone, and all the tracks have been preserved as they were when they were first made.

When people had followed in the tracks of Corpse Demon but a short distance, they overtook him. Among them were two little girls. One was the beautiful daughter of a great priest. The other was the child of somebody-or-other. She was not beautiful, and she was jealous of the little beauty. With the aid of Corpse Demon the jealous girl caused the death of the other child. This was the first death.

When people saw that the girl slept and could not be awakened, that she grew cold and that her heart had stopped beating, her father, the great priest, grew angry.

"Who has caused my daughter to die?" he cried loudly.

But the people only looked at each other.

"I will make a ball of sacred meal," said the priest. "I will throw it into the air, and when it falls it will strike someone on the head. The one it will strike I shall know as the one whose magic and evil art have brought my tragedy upon me."

The priest made a ball of sacred flour and pollen and threw it into the air. When it fell, it struck the head of the jealous little girl, the daughter of somebody-or-other. Then the priest exclaimed, "So *you* have caused this thing! You have caused the death of my daughter."

He called a council of the people, and they tried the girl. They would have killed her if she had not cried for mercy and a little time. Then she begged the priest and his people to return to the hole they had all come out of and look down it.

"If you still wish to destroy me, after you have looked into the hole," she said, "I will die willingly."

So the people were persuaded to return to the hole leading from the cave world. When they looked down, they saw plains of beautiful flowers in a land of everlasting summer and fruitfulness. And they saw the beautiful little girl, the priest's daughter, wandering among the flowers. She was so happy that she paid no attention to the people. She seemed to have no desire to return to this world.

"Look!" said the girl who had caused her death. "Thus it shall be with all the children of men."

"When we die," the people said to each other, "we will return to the world we have come from. There we shall be happy. Why should we fear to die? Why should we resent death?"

So they did not kill the little girl. Her children became the powerful wizards and witches of the world, who increased in numbers as people increased. Her children still live and still have wonderful and dreadful powers.

Then the people journeyed still farther eastward. As they went, they discovered Locust in their midst.

"Where did you come from?" they asked.

"I came out with you and the other beings," he replied.

"Why did you come with us on our journey?" they asked.

"So that I might be useful," replied Locust.

But the people, thinking that he could not be useful, said to him, "You must return to the place you came from."

But Locust would not obey them. Then the people became so angry at him that they ran arrows through him, even through his heart. All the blood oozed out of his body and he died. After a long time he came to life again and ran about, looking as he had looked before, except that he was black.

The people said to one another, "Locust lives again, although we have pierced him through and through. Now he shall indeed be useful and shall journey with us. Who besides Locust has this wonderful power of renewing his life? He must possess the medicine for the renewal of the lives of others. He shall become the medicine of mortal wounds and of war."

So today the locust is at first white, as was the first locust that came forth with the ancients. Like him, the locust dies, and after he has been dead a long time, he comes to life again—black. He is our father, too. Having his medicine, we are the greatest of men. The locust medicine still heals mortal wounds.

After the ancient people had journeyed a long distance, they became very hungry. In their hurry to get away from the lower cave world, they had forgotten to bring seed. After they had done much lamenting, the Spirit of Dew sent the Swallow back to bring the seed of corn and of other foods. When Swallow returned, the Spirit of Dew planted the seed in the ground and chanted prayers to it. Through the power of these prayers, the corn grew and ripened in a single day.

So for a long time, as the people continued their journey, they carried only enough seed for a day's planting. They depended upon the Spirit of Dew to raise for them in a single day an abundance of corn and other foods. To the Corn Clan, he gave this seed, and for a long time they were able to raise enough corn for their needs in a very short time.

But the powers of the witches and wizards made the time for raising foods grow longer and longer. Now, sometimes, our corn does not have time to grow old and ripen in the ear, and our other foods do not ripen. If it had not been for the children of the little girl whom the ancient people let live, even now we would not need to watch our cornfields whole summers through, and we would not have to carry heavy packs of food on our journeys.

As the ancient people traveled on, the children of the little girl tried their powers and caused other troubles. These mischief-makers stirred up people who had come out of the cave worlds before our ancients had come. They made war upon our ancients. The wars made it necessary for the people to build houses whenever they stopped traveling. They built their houses on high mountains reached by only one trail, or in caves with but one path leading to them, or in the sides of deep canyons. Only in such places could they sleep in peace.

Only a small number of people were able to climb up from their secret hiding places and emerge into the Fourth World. Legends reveal the Grand Canyon is where these people emerged. From there they began their search for the homes the Two Brothers intended for them.

These few were the Hopi Indians that now live on the Three Mesas of northeastern Arizona.

Cushing, "Origin Myth from Oraibi," 163-169.
James, "How the Hopi Indians Reached Their Country," 12.

■

HOW THE GREAT CHIEFS MADE THE MOON AND THE SUN
Hopi

"Haliksai" was the usual beginning when a Hopi told a story in his own language. "Once upon a time" was his beginning when he told it in English.

■

Once upon a time, when our people first came up from the villages of the underworld, there was no sun. There was no moon. They saw only dreary darkness and felt the coldness. They looked hard for firewood, but in the darkness they found little.

One day as they stumbled around, they saw a light in the distance. The Chief sent a messenger to see what caused the light. As the messenger approached it, he saw a small field containing corn, beans, squash, watermelons, and other foods. All around the field a great fire was burning. Nearby stood a straight, handsome man wearing around his neck a turquoise necklace of four strands. Turquoise pendants hung from his ears.

"Who are you?" the owner of the field asked the messenger.

"My people and I have come from the cave world below," the messenger replied. "And we suffer from the lack of light and the lack of food."

"My name is Skeleton," said the owner of the field. He showed the stranger the terrible mask he often wore and then gave him some food. "Now return to your people and guide them to my field."

When all the people had arrived, Skeleton began to give them food from his field. They marveled that, although the crops seemed so small, there was enough food for everyone. He gave them ears of corn for roasting; he gave them beans, squashes, and watermelons. The people built fires for themselves and were happy.

Later, Skeleton helped them prepare fields of their own and to make fires around them. There they planted corn and soon harvested a good crop.

"Now we should move on," the people said. "We want to find the place where we will live always."

Away from the fires it was still dark. The Great Chiefs, at a council with Skeleton, decided to make a moon like the one they had enjoyed in the underworld.

They took a piece of well-prepared buffalo hide and cut from it a great circle. They stretched the circle tightly over a wooden hoop and then painted it carefully with white paint. When it was entirely dry, they mixed some black paint and painted, all around its edge, completing the picture of the moon. When all of this was done, they attached a stick to the disk and placed it on a large square of white cloth. Thus they made a symbol of the moon.

Then the Great Chiefs selected one of the young men and bade him stand on top of the moon symbol. They took up the cloth by its corners and began to swing it back and forth, higher and higher. As they were swinging it, they sang a magic song. Finally, with a mighty heave, they threw the moon disk upward. It continued to fly swiftly, upward and eastward.

As the people watched, they suddenly saw light in the eastern sky. The light became brighter and brighter. Surely something was burning

Eagle kachina
Hopi

there, they thought. Then something bright with light rose in the east. That was the moon!

Although the moon made it possible for the people to move around with less stumbling, its light was so dim that frequently the workers in the fields would cut up their food plants instead of the weeds. It was so cold that fires had to be kept burning around the fields all the time.

Again the Great Chiefs held a council with Skeleton, and again they decided that something better must be done.

This time, instead of taking a piece of buffalo hide, they took a piece of warm cloth that they themselves had woven while they were still in the underworld. They fashioned this as they had fashioned the disk of buffalo hide, except that this time they painted the face of the circle with a copper-colored paint.

They painted eyes and a mouth on the disk and decorated the forehead with colors that the Great Chiefs decided upon according to their desires. Around the circle, they then wove a ring of corn husks, arranged in a zig zag design. Around the circle of corn husks, they threaded a string of red hair from some animal. To the back of the disk, they fastened a small ring of corn husks. Through that ring they poked a circle of eagle feathers.

To the top of each eagle feather, the old Chief tied a few little red feathers taken from the top of the head of a small bird. On the forehead of the circle, he attached an abalone shell. Then the sun disk was completed.

Again the Great Chiefs chose a young man to stand on top of the disk, which they had placed on a large sheet. As they had done with the moon disk, they raised the cloth by holding its corners. Then they swung the sun disk back and forth, back and forth, again and again. With a mighty thrust, they threw the man and the disk far into the air. It traveled fast into the eastern sky and disappeared.

All the people watched it carefully. In a short time, they saw light in the east as if a great fire were burning. Soon the new sun rose and warmed the earth with its kindly rays.

Now with the moon to light the earth at night and the sun to light and warm it by day, all the people decided to pick up their provisions and go on. As they started, the White people took a trail that led them far to the south. The Hopis took one to the north, and the Pueblos took one midway between the two. Thus they wandered on to the places where they were to live.

The Hopis wandered a long time, building houses and planting crops until they reached the mesas where they now live. The ruins of the ancient villages are scattered to the very beginnings of the great river of the canyon—the Colorado.

James, *Haliksai* 10-11.

■

First Journey through Grand Canyon
Hopi

Long ago, on the enormous far rim of the Grand Canyon in Arizona, lived the ancestors of the Snake Clan, who belonged to the Hopi Indian tribe.

■

Chief of the Hopis had a very wise son, who liked to sit and meditate on the edge of the canyon rim. He tried many times to imagine where the powerful river far below finally ended.

Experienced ancient men of their tribe did not know the answer for Wise Son. Their council leaders had different ideas among themselves. One thought the river took a secret course through enormous underground passages. Another thought it entered the middle of the world and there it nurtured large and dangerous reptiles.

Impatient, Wise Son said to his father, the Chief, "Is it not time for me to seek my quest? I wish to go down the great river and find the place where it ends."

Proud of his son's desire for accomplishment, the Chief gladly granted him permission to follow his quest. Wise Son, overjoyed with his coming venture, planned specifically for every need. His family and tribal friends helped him to design and to build a waterproof boat that could be closed entirely, like a cocoon.

He constructed a long pushing-pole to help him navigate the waters. The Shaman tied prayer sticks at the top of the pole, with special blessings for a safe journey.

Finally, the day arrived for Wise Son to launch his special canoe. The Chief and his braves arrived with supplies of food, good wishes, and more prayer sticks.

Week after week, Wise Son drifted with the river. He was happy. He learned to keep his boat in the main current, though it carried him through several turbulent side routes, including rapids and tunnel-like caves. He victoriously came though these experiences with joy in his heart.

On and on Wise Son traveled, winding his way out of steep canyons and through flat meadowlands. He caught fresh fish for his main food supply. One day, Wise Son noticed a change in the taste of the water. It was salty and he knew that he should not drink it. Then to his surprise, he suddenly floated into a great body of water that extended as far as he could see. He had discovered the place where the mighty river ended, in the ocean where the sun sleeps!

He saw an island and guided his boat to its shore. There was a house nearby. Upon investigation, he found only a very small entrance door. He knocked and asked, "Please, will you let me come in and see you?"

Spider Woman, who possessed supernatural power, lived there and answered, "Please make the hole large enough and enter." This, Wise Son did and sat down inside. He presented to Spider Woman one of his prayer sticks and told her of his adventure to find the place where the river ended.

"When I return to my tribe, I wish to take with me a gift that might be helpful to my people," he said.

"There is a neighboring house where there are many beautiful ornament-like beads and rocks. These might be gifts that you can take to your people," she replied. "But I must caution you to be careful of the vicious animals on the path. I will give you some of my magic lotion to protect you."

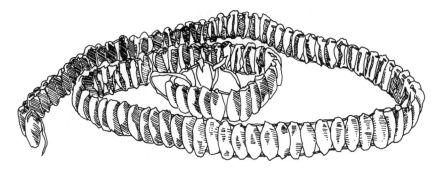

Cocoon sash
Hopi

Together they started for the treasure house. To guide him, Spider Woman sat upon Wise Son's ear, where she could whisper to him.

Immediately, Wise Son sprinkled some magic lotion on the marshy path. A colorful bridge appeared instantly, guiding them across the marsh to the treasure house.

First, they encountered an enormous lionlike animal showing its fangs. Wise Son tossed him a prayer stick and sprinkled magic lotion, which calmed the creature.

Second, they met a bearlike animal; third, a mad catlike creature; fourth, a ferocious wolf-like beast; fifth, a huge angry-looking snake with rattles on its tail. Wise Son quieted all of them with Spider Woman's magic lotion.

The treasure house had steps leading to the roof, and from there steps took them down into a large room. Men squatted around the inside walls. The braves wore handsome, bright-colored beads hanging about their necks. They had painted their faces tribal fashion.

Wise Son squatted by the fire. All remained quiet for some time. The men gazed at Wise Son constantly. Finally, their Chief arose and lighted his pipe. After smoking four times, he passed the pipe to the stranger. Wise Son smoked the magic number of times that seemed to please the Chief and the others. They then greeted him in a friendly manner, as if he were one of their own.

In return for their warm welcome, Wise Son gave to each man a prayer stick tipped with special feathers made by ancient Hopi tribesmen.

"Now it is time to put on our snake costumes," announced the Chief.

Wise Son observed that skins of enormous serpents were suspended from the ceiling, around all four walls. He was asked to face about, so that he would not see how the braves got into their snakeskin costumes.

When Wise Son was asked to turn back, he saw snakes of many sizes and colors, hissing and writhing over the dirt floor. Spider Woman remained on Wise Son's ear.

"Be strong," she whispered to him. "The snakes will not hurt you, only frighten you. Do whatever I tell you." The Chief of the Snake People had made his daughter become a yellow-snake-with-rattles. Wise Son did not know this, and he was asked to choose the Chief's daughter. If he could choose correctly, the Snake People would show him their ceremonial dance. They also would give him many beads and gem-rocks to take to his tribe.

Wise Son tried very hard to guess which snake was the Chief's daughter. Spider Woman whispered in his ear, "Choose the yellow one with rattles." Wise Son did, and yellow-snake-with-rattles suddenly became the loveliest and fairest of Indian maidens. He knew immediately that he could easily fall in love with her.

That evening the Chief and his braves gave to Wise Son all the secrets of the Snake Ceremony. They taught him the words of praise and thanksgiving, which they sang for him. They showed him the ceremonial steps, which they danced for him. They showed him how they put on their snake costumes. Finally, they showed him their religious altar.

After Wise Son learned all that he should know, he and Spider Woman re-crossed the bridge and returned to her house. He presented her with another prayer stick, as he thanked her for her help. In return, she gave him a beautiful bead of turquoise from her north room. She gave him a white shell from her east room. From her south room, she gave him a red bead, and from her west room a larger turquoise. She then gave him a bag of special beads for his tribe, but she warned him not to open it on the way home.

Next morning, Wise Son went back to the house of the Snake People to say farewell. Their Chief welcomed him and declared, "You have gained our friendship and my beautiful daughter. Take her for your wife. We wish you happiness and a pleasant journey back to your tribe."

The tribe gave them many presents of good clothing and much food to send the happy couple on their way to Hopiland.

They took the overland route following the great river. Each day Wise Son found the treasure bag heavier and heavier. He and his wife could hardly carry it between them. One day out of extreme curiosity, they opened the bag and looked inside.

Regardless of Spider Woman's caution, the two rolled out the beads and made strands for each to wear around their necks. By the following morning, all of the gift beads had vanished. Only remaining were the gems from the four rooms in Spider Woman's house.

Many moons later, the young couple reached Hopiland on the far rim of the Grand Canyon. Wise Son was delighted to be home again after his great adventure. The entire Hopi tribe rejoiced over his safe return and welcomed his new young wife to their tribe.

Wise Son told where the great river ended. He told them about the Snake Clan, and that he and his wife brought them a special ceremony from the Snake People, living where the sun sleeps.

Wise Son and his wife taught the Hopis all the songs and dances of the Snake Ceremony. This was the beginning of the Snake Clan of the Hopi Tribe.

Today, visitors are welcomed by the Hopis when their Snake Clan performs at its annual Snake Ceremony. This is their traditional praise and thanksgiving offering for the blessings of rain to the Hopi Tribe.

James, *Haliksai*, 14-15.

■

ORIGIN OF THE CLANS
Hopi

■

A long time ago, when the Hopi Tribe was emerging from the First World, their people started to hunt for the land of the rising sun. Moving in related groups, they thought it fun to play a name game.

When the first band came upon a dead bear, immediately they thought it a sign for them to become the Bear Clan. Another Hopi band came upon the same skeleton but saw little gopher holes surrounding the carcass. They agreed among themselves to become the Gopher Clan.

In the same way, other Hopis found a nest of spiders and they named themselves the Spider Clan. Far ahead the Bear Clan traveled with Chief Bahana leading. Always, the Bear Clan seemed to move faster in many ways.

Spider Clan trailed all the clans because they had so many children. One day they came upon a friendly spider sitting near her large web. The Spider Clan encircled her as she spoke to their Chief, "I am Spider Woman, possessed of Supernatural Power. Since you are named for my people, I will help you in any way I can."

"Thank you, Spider Woman," replied the Chief. "We are traveling to find the land of the rising sun. Other clans of our Hopi Tribe are much farther ahead of us. We wish we could travel faster, but we have much to pack on our backs as we have so many children."

"Perhaps I can make something to ease your travel," said Spider Woman.

"What do you have in mind?" asked the Chief.

"First, I need something of yourself," said Spider Woman. "You must go into my secret room where you will find a large water jug. You must wash yourself all over and save the dust and skin that rolls off and fetch it to me."

Because of many travel days, the Chief was so hot and dusty that he made a sizeable ball of dirt, which he gave to Spider Woman. With this she began her magic creation. She spread a white, fleecy cloth in front of her, placing the ball in the Center. Then she rolled it up carefully into a white ball.

Spider Woman sang her ceremonial creation song four times, while the Spider Clan sat in a circle and waited expectantly. Now and then, she touched the fleecy ball with her magic web and looked to see if any signs of life were evident within the ball. Again, Spider Woman sang

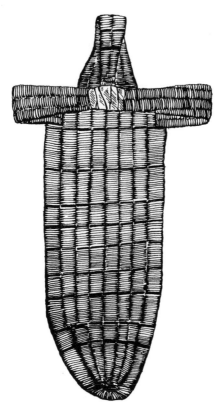

Wicker cradleboard
Hopi

another magic song four times and behold!—the fleecy, white ball moved back and forth and rolled about. To everyone's surprise, through the fleecy cover emerged a tiny gray animal stretching forth four tiny legs.

Spider Woman called it a burro. At the sight of it, the Spider Clan knew that it needed to grow much stronger before it could be of any help to them. Spider Woman kept the young animal warm and gave it some of her magic food. She spent much time massaging its tiny legs with her magic salve to make them grow faster.

After only four days, the burro was ready to travel with the Spider Clan. They packed the sides of the burrow with their excess supplies and started on their way to the land of the rising sun.

Later, Spider Woman decided to create a man who should know more about caring for the burro than the Hopis. This she did and sent the man to catch up with the Spider Clan, to teach them how better to care for the burro.

But that man was selfish. Instead of helping the people, he ran away one dark night, taking the burro with him. Even though saddened over the loss of their helpful burro, Spider Clan continued their trek to the land of the rising sun, shouldering their heavy packs as before.

Of course, the Bear Clan arrived at their destination first. They set about establishing their village. Gradually the other Hopi Clans joined them, making their villages nearby. There the Hopi Tribe grew and prospered.

But the Spider Clan, which arrived last in the land of the rising sun, became the largest and most prosperous of all the Hopi Clans, because they had so many children during the following years.

■

THE WIND GOD

Hopi

Long, long ago, the Hopis were greatly troubled by the wind. It blew and blew and blew and blew—all the time. The Hopis planted their crops, but before the seeds could begin to sprout, the wind blew the soil and seeds away. Unhappy and worried, all the people made prayer offerings of many kinds. But they accomplished nothing.

The old men held councils in their kivas. They smoked their pipes prayerfully and asked one another, "Why do the gods turn such strong winds upon us?" After a while, they decided to ask for help from the "Little Fellows" who were the two little War Gods, two of the five grandsons of Spider Woman.

"Why did you ask us to come?" was their first question.

"We need your help," answered the old men. "Something must be done to the Wind."

"We will see what we can do for you," said the Little Fellows. "You stay here and make many more prayer offerings."

The Hopis make many kinds of prayer offerings—as many as there are prayers, and there are prayers for every occasion in life and death. They are reverently fashioned of various types of feathers, carved and painted sticks, and hand-spun cotton yarn.

The Little Fellows went first to their wise old grandmother, Spider Woman. They asked her to make some sweet cornmeal mush for them to take along on a journey. Of course they knew who the Wind God was and knew that he lived over near Sunset Mountain in the big crack of the black rock.

When Spider Woman had the cornmeal mush ready, the Little Fellows came back to the kiva where the men were holding their council. The prayer offerings were ready and also the ball that the Little Fellows like to take with them wherever they went. They liked to play catch with it.

The men made bows and arrows for them to take on their journey, which seemed much like going on a war party. The arrows were tipped with bluebird feathers, thought to be more powerful than any other kinds of feathers.

Kiva and pueblo
Hopi

The two Little Fellows started toward the San Francisco Peaks. The old men went along until they reached the Little Colorado River, and there they sat down and smoked their pipes. The smoking of tobacco among the Hopis, as among many other tribes, is strictly ceremonial. The sacred smoke carried the prayers of the Hopis to their Gods.

Continuing their journey, the two Little Fellows played catch-ball from time to time. On the fourth day they reached the home of the Wind

God who lived at the foot of Sunset Crater, in a big crack in the black rock. There he breathed through the crack, as he does to this day. The Little Fellows threw the prayer offerings into the crack and hastily put their old grandmother's sticky cornmeal mush into and over the crack, and thus sealed the Wind God's door. Phew—he became very angry, so angry that he blew and blew and blew, but could not get out. The Little Fellows laughed and laughed and then went home, feeling very proud of themselves and of what they had done.

But after a while, the people in the villages began to feel very hot. Every day the weather became hotter and hotter. People came out of their homes and stood on housetops to look toward the San Francisco Peaks, to see if any clouds were coming their way. But they did not see even a wisp of a cloud, and they seemed not to feel a breath of air. They thought they would suffocate.

"We must do something right away," everyone said or thought. So the men made some more prayer offerings and called the two Little Fellows again. "Please go back to the House of the Wind God at once and tell him that there must be peace between us. Then give him these prayer offerings and let him out. This heat is much worse than the wind."

The Little Fellows replied, "We will go and see what we can do with the Wind God to make life more comfortable for you."

After four days, they arrived at the House of Yaponcha—the House of the Wind God. The Little Fellows decided that the wisest thing to do would be to let the Wind God have a small hole open—just enough to let him breathe through but not enough for him to come out of the crack in the black rock.

So they took a little of the cornmeal mush out of the crack. Immediately, a nice cool breeze came out and a small white cloud appeared. It floated over across the desert toward the Hopi villages.

When the Little Fellows reached home, everyone was pleased. The Hopis have been grateful to the Little Fellows ever since. The winds have been perfect—just strong enough to keep the people happy but not strong enough to blow everything away.

Every since then, every year in the windy month of March, the chiefs and the high priests of the three villages on the Second Mesa give prayer offerings to the Wind God, Yaponcha.

Nequatewa, *Truth of a Hopi*, 103-104, 125-126.

■

AT THE RAINBOW'S END
Navaho

The Navaho, together with the Apache, constitute the southern branch of the Athapascan linguistic family, living in New Mexico, Arizona, western Texas, southeastern Colorado, Utah, and in northern Mexico. The earliest recorded mention of the Navaho is in 1629, when white settlers from Mexico moved among them. A revolution in the Navaho economy occurred with the introduction of sheep, raised for food, clothing, and commerce. Peace treaties with the white man in 1846 and 1849 were not observed and Colonel Kit Carson invaded Navaho territory in 1863 to stop Navaho incursions. He killed large numbers of their sheep and also captured the greater part of the tribe as prisoners and sent them to Fort Sumner and Redondo on the Rio Pecos in New Mexico. In 1867, after the Civil War, the Navaho nation was restored to its homeland. They continue to live in peace and prosperity with the growth of their flocks and income from the sale of their famous Navaho blankets. In addition, the Navaho tribe has attracted great attention from writers, artists, sculptors and choreographers because of their colorful culture.

■

Long, long ago when First Woman the Goddess was created, she became fully grown in four days. It seemed that every Navaho Indian tribesman wanted her for his wife.

She did not love any of them, but she did like the handsome ones. Of all the men, however, she thought the most attractive was the Sun-God. Of course, she thought he could never be her husband.

To her surprise, one day Sun-God came up behind her and gently tickled her neck with a feathery plume. She was engulfed with warm sunshine, and in a magical way the Goddess became the wife of Sun-God. He fathered her firstborn, a son.

Not long thereafter, the Goddess was resting beneath an overhanging cliff when some drops of water fell upon her. Soon the Goddess gave birth to a second son, fathered by Water-God. Because the two boys were so close in age, they became known as the Twins of the Goddess.

They lived in a beautiful canyon that later became a part of Navaholand. About that time, a Great Giant roamed over the country

Navaho hogan

and ate every human he could catch. He discovered the Goddess but did not want to kill her, because at first sight he fell in love with her beauty.

The Goddess knew of the Great Giant's evil ways and would have nothing to do with him. He became very jealous of her when he saw footprints of the Twins outside her Hogan.

She saw Great Giant approaching, so she quickly dug a hole in the center of her floor and there hid her two children, whom she dearly loved. She covered the opening with a flat sandstone rock, spreading dirt over it to prevent the Great Giant from finding her Twins.

Another day, Great Giant saw the children's tracks.

"Where did these children come from?" he asked the Goddess.

"I have no children," she replied, because she knew that he would try to kill them if he found the Twins.

"You are not telling me the truth," he said. "I see children's footprints in the dirt, right here."

The Goddess laughed heartily and said "Those are only my hand-prints. I am very lonesome for children, so I only pretend by making tracks with the heels of my hand and the tips of my fingers, like this. These are the tracks of my children."

"Now I believe you," he replied.

As the Twins grew larger, their mother could not hide them any longer. She was alarmed for their safety because of the Great Giant, who saw them one day and tried to catch them. But the Twins were too quick and got away.

The Spirit who made the Goddess appeared with a bow made of cedar wood for Sun-Child.

"It is time for you to learn to hunt," she said to him.

"We must now make some arrows and another bow for your brother," said the Goddess to Sun-Child.

"Mostly, we want to hunt for our father," said Sun-Child. "Mother, who is our father and where does he live?"

"Your father is the Sun-God, but he lives far away in the East," replied the Goddess.

Another bow was made for Water-Child and many arrows for both Twins. They began their journey to the East and traveled as far as they could, but without success in finding Sun-God. When they returned they asked, "Mother, have you lied to us? In the East, we looked everywhere and we could not find our father, the Sun-God."

"He must have gone to the South," she said. Again the Twins set out on another journey, this time to the South, returning without success.

"Please try the West and then the North, if at first you do not find your father in the West," said the Goddess.

She sent the Twins again on their hunting journey, anxious to keep them away and out of sight of the Great Giant. Many moons later, the Twins came back and said, "Mother, have you lied to us four times? Our father was neither in the North nor the West."

"Now I will tell you the truth, my sons," said the Goddess. "Your fathers, the Sun-God and Water-God, live far away in the middle of the great Western Water. Between here and there are great canyons where the walls of the cliffs clap together and would crush you.

"Even if you should succeed in getting through the canyons, there are the terrible reeds that you must cross. Their long knife-like sharp leaves will cut you into pieces.

"If you should escape the reeds, you can never cross the Grand Canyon, which comes first before you can reach the Great Water. You can never, never cross the water where your father's house is in the middle of the Great Water, the Western Ocean."

"But, Mother, we want to go and try to find our fathers," said the Twins.

The Goddess taught the Twins a song of protection for their next journey:

"We are traveling in an Invisible Way to seek our fathers, the Sun-God and the Water-God."

This song she taught them to sing four times, the magic number. Day after day as they traveled along, they sang their song for protection.

One day, as they passed a little spider hole in the ground, they heard a voice say, "Ssh!" four times. The Twins looked into the hole and saw Spider Woman.

"Do not be afraid of me, I am your Grandmother. Come down into my lodge," she said four times.

"We cannot enter your lodge, because your doorway is too small," said the Twins.

"Please blow toward the Eastwind, Southwind, Westwind, and Northwind," Spider Woman called out.

The Twins blew in the four directions and the entrance enlarged enough for them to go through. Inside and to their amazement, they saw the lodge walls covered with bundles of bones wrapped in spider webs, exactly the way spiders wrap flies in a web.

"Do not be afraid, my grandsons," said Spider Woman. "These are the bones of bad men whom I killed."

Spider Woman talked with the Twins about encounters they might have on their trip. She taught them songs for their protection and explained what they could do to overcome obstacles they might meet on their way. "I will give each of you a magic Feather-Plume. Hold it before you as you travel, straight up or sideways to carry you safely forward," she said to the Twins.

"Be on the look out for a little man with a red head and a striped back. He will resemble a sand-scorpion, only a little larger—about the size of a Jerusalem cricket," she explained.

"Thank you, Grandmother, we'll be on our way," said the Twins.

Many days later, the Twins heard a voice from the ground. It was from the little man with the red head.

"Do not scorn me because I am so small," he said. "I can and want to help you. Put your hands down on the ground and spit into them four times. Now close your fists, saving the spit until you come to the Big Water. There you can wash off the spit."

The Twins did exactly as they were told, and after thanking the little man with the red head, they again began their travel. Soon the canyon walls that smashed together loomed ahead of them.

They repeated Spider Woman's prayers, holding the Feather-Plumes sideways. As they moved forward the clapping walls stopped long enough to allow the Twins to walk through safely.

When they came to the jungle of sharp reeds, again they sang the song Spider Woman taught them, touching the tops of the reeds with their magical Feather-Plumes. Behold! The reeds turned into cattails, which pleased the reeds so much that they quickly opened a wide path for the Twins to pass through. A puzzling encounter for the Twins was the giant cliff. They walked around and around its rim, making a complete circle and finally returning to their starting place.

They were making no forward progress, so they sang songs taught them by their mother and Spider Woman. They prayed over and over again. When they opened their eyes, a beautiful Rainbow appeared, creating a large bridge for them to cross over the Grand Canyon of the Colorado River.

After this spectacular adventure, the Twins continued West for a long time, until they saw the Great Water before them. The Water spread so far, they wondered, "How can we ever reach the Turquoise House of Sun-God, which we know is in the middle of the Great Water?"

The Twins walked down to the beach to the edge of the water and washed the spit off their hands, singing and praying at the same time.

Behold! The Rainbow appeared again! A long Rainbow Bridge stretched before them from the beach to the Turquoise House.

Onto the Rainbow Bridge the Twins raced happily, find their two fathers, the Sun-God and the Water-God, who welcomed them in the Turquoise House at the end of the Rainbow Bridge.

Coolidge, *The Rain Makers.*

■

LEGEND OF THE NIGHT CHANT
Navaho

"Like all primitive people, the Navahos are intensely religious," wrote Edward S. Curtis, whose twenty-volume study of *The North American Indian* was published between 1907 and 1930. Colorful expressions of their religious life were found in the many ceremonies performed by their medicine men.

Medicine men were believed to be powerful not only in curing disease of body and mind, but also in preventing disease by their ceremonies. These were referred to as "medicine ceremonies," but they were really "ritualistic prayers," of their tradition.

There were many of these ceremonies, each of them having many ritual prayers. Some of the ceremonies lasted only a day. Some lasted four days, each with its own sand paintings, as they are usually called today. The principal ceremonies lasted nine consecutive days and nights. Each of these was based on a mythical story or legend.

The Navahos considered the *Kieje Hatal* (Night Chant) one of the most important chants. It was based on this legend.

■

Long, long ago, three brothers lived among their people, who were known as the *Dine* or *Dinneh*, meaning "people." The oldest brother was

Mask
Navaho

rich. The second was a wayward, roving gambler. The youngest was a growing boy. Their only sister was married and lived with her husband a little distance from her brothers.

The second brother often took property belonging to his brothers and then went to distant corners of th earth to gamble. Upon his return, he never failed to relate a story about the wonders he had seen and the Holy People who had revealed many interesting things to him. His brothers never believed him. They called him *Bith Ahatini*, "The Dreamer."

One day they wished to go hunting, but did not want The Dreamer to go with them. Without telling him, they asked their brother-in-law to accompany them. Near the end of their fourth day away from home, The Dreamer suddenly realized that he had been tricked. Immediately he started in search of the hunters. He hoped to meet them and to help them carry their game—and also to be rewarded by a pelt or two.

He traveled far, but he had not seen them when the sun passed behind the hills in the distance. Near him was a deep, rock-walled canyon, from the depths of which came the sound of many voices. The Dreamer walked to its edge and peered over. Back and forth, from one side to the other, flew countless crows. They passed in and out of holes in opposite walls.

When darkness had covered everything, The Dreamer heard a human voice call from below in loud tones, "They say! They say! They say!"

From the far side came the answer: "Yes, yes! What's the matter now?

"Two people were killed today," the voice replied.

"Who were they? Who were they?"

The first voice answered, "*Ana-hail-ihi*, killed at sunrise; and *Igak-izhi*, killed at dusk, by the People of the Earth. They went in search of meat, and hunters shot arrows into them. We are sorry, but they were told to be careful and did not heed. It is too late to help them now; let us go on with the chant."

In the darkness, The Dreamer had become very frightened, but he stayed to listen and to watch. Muffled strains of song came from deep recesses in each canyon wall—the gods were singing! And just within the openings, visible in the glow of a fire, many dancers were performing in unison as they kept time with rattles.

Throughout the night, firelight flickered from wall to wall, and singing and dancing continued. At daylight, the dancers departed, and The Dreamer began again his search for the hunters.

After a short time, he reached his brothers. They were resting from their journey with heavy packs of game.

"Here comes The Dreamer," said his older brother. "I will wager that he has something marvelous to tell us!"

The Dreamer was greeted first by his brother-in-law. "You must have slept near here last night, for you are too far from home to have traveled this distance since daylight."

"I slept near a canyon that is surely holy," replied The Dreamer. "Many people had gathered to dance, the gods sang, and—"

"There! I told you that he'd have some lie to tell," interrupted the oldest brother. He picked up his pack and started on.

"Go ahead," urged the brother-in-law. "Tell me the rest."

The younger brother, also not believing, took up his pack and walked on. As the brother-in-law looked interested, The Dreamer related all that he had seen and heard. "You or my brothers must have killed the people they spoke about," said The Dreamer, as he ended the story.

"Oh, no! It was none of us,' his brother-in-law protested. "We have killed no people. Yesterday morning one of us shot a crow and last night we killed a magpie. But there was no harm done."

"I fear there was," said The Dreamer. "They were hunters like you, in search of meat for the Holy People. At the time, they were disguised as birds," The Dreamer explained.

When the two men overtook the others, the youngest brother asked his brother-in-law, "Did you hear a fine story?"

"It was not a lie," he retorted. "We killed a crow and a magpie yesterday, and the Holy People talked about it in the canyon last night. Look! Here come four mountain sheep. Hurry!" he said to The Dreamer. "Hurry and head them off!"

They had reached the canyon where strange voices had been heard. Four sheep, along large boulders, were carefully threading their way out of the canyon. As the three hunters dropped back, The Dreamer ran ahead and hid himself near the top of the trail.

As the sheep approached, he drew his bow and aimed for the leader's heart. But his fingers would not release their grip upon the arrow, and the sheep passed unharmed. He scrambled up over the rim of the canyon and ran to get ahead of them again. But when the sheep were passing him, the bowstring would not leave his fingers. A third effort to kill them failed, and a fourth effort failed.

He cursed himself and the sheep, but suddenly became quiet. Whom did he see but four gods, the four who had transformed themselves into sheep!

The man in the lead ran up to him and dropped his *balil*—a rectangular, four-piece, folding wand—over The Dreamer as he sat. Then the man in the lead uttered a peculiar cry. Immediately three other gods appeared behind him. All wore masks.

"Whence came you?" The Dreamer asked them.

"From Kinni-nikai," the Leader replied.

"Whither are you going?"

"To Taegyil, to hold another chant four days from now. Won't you come along?"

"No, I couldn't travel so far in four days."

But after a little persuasion, The Dreamer agreed to go. He was told to disrobe. While he was obeying the order, the Leader breathed upon him, and his raiment became the same as that of the four gods. Then all took four steps eastward, changed into sheep, and bounded away along the canyon's rim.

The hunters in hiding became restless because The Dreamer did not return. So they ventured out to where they could see the trail on which they had last seen him. No one was in sight. One of them went to the rock where The Dreamer first hid near the sheep. He followed the tracks from hiding place to hiding place until he reached the fourth and last one.

There he found his brother's clothes, with his bow and arrows upon them. He traced the four human footsteps to the east and found that they merged into the trail of five mountain sheep. The oldest brother

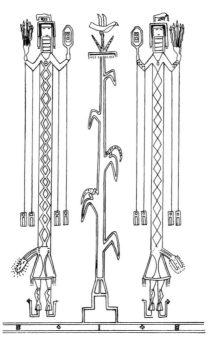

Sand painting with detail of corn
Navaho

cried in his remorse. He had always treated The Dreamer with scorn, but he now realized that he had been wrong.

The gods and The Dreamer, transformed into mountain sheep, traveled very far during their four days' journey. On the fourth day they came to a large hogan, which is an earth-covered lodge of the Navahos. Inside were numerous Holy People, both gods and men.

When The Dreamer entered the hogan with his four holy companions, a complaint at once arose from those inside—a complaint about an earthly odor. The Leader of the five who had just arrived took The Dreamer outside and had him washed with yucca-root suds.

Inside the hogan stood four large jewel posts, upon which the gods hung their masks. The eastern post was of white shell, the southern of turquoise, the western of abalone, and the northern of jet. Two jewel pipes lay beside a god sitting on the western side of the hogan. He filled both pipes with tobacco and lighted them, passing one to his right and one to his left.

All in the hogan smoked, the last to receive the pipes being two large Owls sitting on each side of the entrance at the east. Each smoker drew in deep draughts of smoke and puffed them out violently. While the smoking continued, people came in from all directions.

At midnight, lightning flashed, followed by heavy thunder and rain. All were sent by Water Sprinkler, who was angered because he had not been told about the dance before it began. But a smoke with the Holy People quickly appeased him. In a short time, the chant began and lasted until morning.

Some of the gods had beautiful paintings on white deerskins, resembling those the Navahos now make with colored sands. These paintings they unfolded on the floor of the hogan during the successive days of the chant.

The last day of the dance was well attended, with people coming from all directions. Throughout the performance, The Dreamer paid careful attention to all the songs, prayers, paintings, and dance movements. He studied closely every sacred apparatus used in the dance—its form, its color, its size. When the chant was over, he had learned all the details of the ceremony—of *Kieje Hatal*, the "Night Chant."

The gods permitted him to return to his people long enough to perform the chant with his younger brother and to conduct it for people afflicted with illness or with wickedness. They spent nine days in its performance.

Then he returned to the gods at Taegyil, where he now lives. His younger brother taught the ceremony to his earthly brothers, the Navahos. They conduct it under the name *Kieje Hatal*, "Night Chant," or *Yebichai Hatal*, "The Chant of Paternal Gods."

Curtis, *The North American Indian*, vol. I, 77-80, 111-116.

■

SPIDER ROCK

Navaho

Spider Rock stands with awesome dignity and beauty over 800 feet high in Arizona's colorful Canyon de Chelly National Park (pronounced dà Shāy). Geologists of the National Park Service say that "the formation began 230 million years ago."

Windblown sand swirled and compressed with time created the spectacular red sandstone monolith. Long ago, the Navaho Indian tribe named it Spider Rock.

Stratified, multicolored cliff walls surround the canyon. For many, many centuries the Navahos built caves and lived in these cliffs. Most of the caves were located high above the canyon floor, protecting them from enemies and flash floods.

■

Spider Woman possessed supernatural power at the time of creation, when Navahos emerged from the third world into this fourth world.

At that time, monsters roamed the land and killed many people. Since Spider Woman loved the people, she gave power for Monster-Slayer and Child-Born-of-Water to search for the Sun-God who was their father. When they found him, Sun-God showed them how to destroy all the monsters on land and in the water.

Because she preserved their people, Navahos established Spider Woman among their most important and honored Deities.

She chose the top of Spider Rock for her home. It was Spider Woman who taught Navaho ancestors of long ago the art of weaving upon a loom. She told them, "My husband, Spider Man, constructed the weaving loom making the crosspoles of sky and earth cords to support the structure; the warp sticks of sunrays, lengthwise to cross the woof; the healds of rock crystal and sheet lightning, to maintain original condition of fibers. For the batten, he chose a sun halo to seal joints, and for the comb he chose a white shell to clean strands in a combing manner." Through many generations, the Navahos have always been accomplished weavers.

The ruins at Canyon de Chelly
Navaho

From their elders, Navaho children heard warnings that if they did not behave themselves, Spider Woman would let down her web-ladder and carry them up to her home and devour them!

The children also heard that the top of Spider Rock was white from the sun-bleached bones of Navaho children who did not behave themselves!

One day, a peaceful cave-dwelling Navaho youth was hunting in Dead Man's Canyon, a branch of Canyon de Chelly. Suddenly, he saw an enemy tribesman who chased him deeper into the canyon. As the peaceful Navaho ran, he looked quickly from side to side, searching for a place to hide or to escape.

Directly in front of him stood the giant obelisk-like Spider Rock. What could he do? He knew it was too difficult for him to climb. He was near exhaustion. Suddenly, before his eyes he saw a silken cord hanging down from the top of the rock tower.

The Navaho youth grasped the magic cord, which seemed strong enough, and quickly tied it around his waist. With its help he climbed the tall tower, escaping from his enemy who then gave up the chase.

When the peaceful Navaho reached the top, he stretched out to rest. There he discovered a most pleasant place with eagle's eggs to eat and the night's dew to drink.

Imagine his surprise when he learned that his rescuer was Spider Woman! She told him how she had seen him and his predicament. She showed him how she made her strong web-cord and anchored one end of it to a point of rock. She showed him how she let down the rest of her web-cord to help him to climb the rugged Spider Rock.

Later, when the peaceful Navaho youth felt assured his enemy was gone, he thanked Spider Woman warmly and he safely descended to the canyon floor by using her magic cord. He ran home as fast as he could run, reporting to his tribe how his life was saved by Spider Woman!

Skinner, *Myths and Legends of Our Lands*, vol. II, 235.

■

SONG OF THE HORSES

Navaho

■

Before the Spaniards brought horses to the Navahos, they told about the Sun-God's walking across the heavens, carrying the sun on his back. When he reached the west, he hung the sun on a peg, so that it could cool off. He spent the evening with his family, resting after his long journey.

After he was rested, he removed the sun from its peg, apparently hid it in some way as he retraced his steps, and returned in the darkness. In the morning, he started on his westward trip again.

Of course, the ancient story continued to be told long after the following one was created.

■

The Sun-God, Johano-ai, starts each morning from his home in the east and rides across the skies to his home in the west. He carries with him his shining gold disk, the sun. He has five horses—a horse of turquoise, one of white shell, one of pearly shell, one of red shell, and one of coal.

Traditional chief's blanket
Navaho

When the skies are blue and the weather is fair, the Sun-God rides his horse of turquoise, or the one of white shell, or the one of pearly shell. But when the heavens are dark with storm, he mounts the red horse or the horse of coal.

Beneath the hoofs of the horses are spread precious hides of all kinds and also beautiful blankets, carefully woven and richly decorated. In the days gone by, the Navahos wove rich blankets, said to have been found first in the home of the Sun-God.

He lets his horses graze on flower blossoms, and drink from mingled waters. These are holy waters of all kinds—spring water, snow water, hail water, water from the four corners of the world. The Navahos use such waters in their ceremonies.

When any horse of the Sun-God trots or runs, he raises not dust, but *pitistchi*. It is glittering grains of mineral, such as are used in religious ceremonies. When a horse rolls and shakes himself, shining grains of sand fly from him. When he runs, not dust, but the sacred pollen offered to the Sun-God is all about him. Then he looks like a mist. The Navahos say that the mist on the horizon is the pollen that has been offered to the gods.

A Navaho man sings about the horses of the Sun-God in order that he, too, may have beautiful horses. Standing among his herd, he scatters holy pollen and sings this song for the blessing and the protection of his animals:

> How joyous his neigh!
> Lo, the Turquoise Horse of Johano-ai,
> How joyous his neigh,
> There on precious hides outspread, standeth he;
> How joyous his neigh,
> There of mingled waters holy, drinketh he;
> How joyous his neigh,
> There in mist of sacred pollen hidden, all hidden he;
> How joyous his neigh,
> These his offspring may grow and thrive forevermore;
> How joyous his neigh!

Burlin, *The Indians' Book*, 360-362.

■

THE STORY OF THE TWO BROTHER-COUSINS
Navaho

■

Of all the Divine Ones, none is more revered by the Navahos than She-Who Changeth. Highly honored, also, is her younger sister, White-Shell-Woman. She-Who-Changeth was made of the turquoise of the land. White-Shell-Woman was made of the white shell of the ocean. Each of these sisters gave birth to a son. Their father was a god.

At the time they were in the world, many *Anaye* (Ahn-ah-yee) were unfriendly to our people. The Anaye were evil beings and giants and monsters, all of whom desired to kill the people. When the two young gods were grown, they wanted to slay Anaye in order that their tribesmen might be saved.

The brothers often asked the mothers, "Who is our father?" The mother always answered, "You have none." At last, the two young men set out to learn the answer to their question. They took a holy trail and journeyed on the sunbeams. It was the Wind that guided them, whispering his counsel in their ears.

Their father was Johano-ai, the Sun-God. His beautiful house was in the East. It was made of turquoise and stood on the shore of Great Waters. There the Sun lived with his wife, White-Shell-Woman, his daughters, and his sons, the Black Thunder and the Blue Thunder. Until the coming of the strange brother-cousins, the wife had not known that her husband had visited goddesses on the earth. Nor would Johano-ai believe that the two gods were his sons until he had proved their powers by making them go through all kinds of trials.

The young men came through each test unharmed. Then the Sun rejoiced that these two handsome youths were indeed his children, and he promised to give them what they asked. They said immediately, "We need weapons with which to slay the Anaye."

So their father, the Sun, gave them helmets, shirts, leggings, and moccasins, all made of black flint (the power of flint came from Morning Star). When the young men put this armor on, the four lightnings flashed from their different joints. For weapons, the Sun gave each a mighty knife of stone and also arrows of rainbow, of sunbeam, and of lightning.

Necklace
Navaho

So after they returned home, the brother-cousins slew the Anaye.
After every victory, the mothers rejoiced with them.

Then Johano-ai came to She-Who-Changeth and asked her to make
for him a home in the West, where he might rest at evening after his long
day's journey by foot across the skies. He pleaded long with her. At
least she yielded and said to him, "I will go and make a home for you if
you will do what I ask. You have a beautiful house in the East, I have
heard. I must have just such a beautiful house in the West. It must be
beyond the shore and floating amid the waters. Around the house all
kinds of gems must be planted, so that they may grow and become
numerous."

Johano-ai granted every wish expressed by She-Who-Changeth, and
now the Sun-God rests in the evening in the gem-surrounded floating
house of Estsan-Natlehi, She-Who-Changeth.

Burlin, *The Indians' Book*, 359-360.

■

CREATION
Apache

Apache, meaning "enemy," was the Zuñi name for Navaho, who were also called *Apachis de Nabaju* by the earliest Spaniards exploring New Mexico. Apaches had come down from the north during prehistoric times, along the eastern flanks of the Rocky Mountains. When they confronted Coronado in 1540, they lived in eastern New Mexico, and reached Arizona in the 1600s. Continuous wars among other tribes and invaders from Mexico followed the Apaches' growing reputation of warlike character.

Apaches have always been inherently aware of earth and sky spirits. From their early morning prayers to the Sun-God, through their hours, days, and their entire lives—for them every act has sacred significance.

Animals, elements, the solar system, and natural phenomena are revered by the Apaches. That which is beyond their understanding is always ascribed to the supernatural.

■

In the beginning nothing existed—no earth, no sky, no sun, no moon, only darkness was everywhere.

Suddenly from the darkness emerged a thin disc, one side yellow and the other side white, appearing suspended in midair. Within the disc sat a small bearded man, Creator, the One Who Lives Above. As if waking from a long nap, he rubbed his eyes and face with both hands.

When he looked into the endless darkness, light appeared above. He looked down and it became a sea of light. To the east, he created yellow streaks of dawn. To the west, tints of many colors appeared everywhere. There were also clouds of different colors.

Creator wiped his sweating face and rubbed his hands together, thrusting them downward. Behold! A shining cloud upon which sat a little girl.

"Stand up and tell me where are you going," said Creator. But she did not reply. He rubbed his eyes again and offered his right hand to the Girl-Without-Parents.

"Where did you come from?" she asked, grasping his hand.

"From the east where it is now light," he replied, stepping upon her cloud.

"Where is the earth?" she asked.

"Where is the sky?" he asked, and sang, "I am thinking, thinking, thinking what I shall create next." He sang four times, which was the magic number.

Creator brushed his face with his hands, rubbed them together, then flung them wide open! Before them stood Sun-God. Again Creator rubbed his sweaty brow and from his hands dropped Small-Boy.

All four gods sat in deep thought upon the small cloud.

"What shall we make next?" asked Creator. "This cloud is much too small for us to live upon."

Then he created Tarantula, Big Dipper, Wind, Lightning-Maker, and some western clouds in which to house Lightning-Rumbler, which he just finished.

Creator sang, "Let us make earth. I am thinking of the earth, earth, earth; I am thinking of the earth," he sang four times.

All four gods shook hands. In doing so, their sweat mixed together and Creator rubbed his palms, from which fell a small round, brown ball, not much larger than a bean.

Creator kicked it, and it expanded. Girl-Without-Parents kicked the ball, and it enlarged more. Sun-God and Small-Boy took turns giving it hard kicks, and each time the ball expanded. Creator told Wind to go inside the ball and to blow it up.

Tarantula spun a black cord and, attaching it to the ball, crawled away fast to the east, pulling on the cord with all his strength. Tarantula repeated with a blue cord to the south, a yellow cord to the west, and a white cord to the north. With mighty pulls in each direction, the brown ball stretched to immeasurable size—it became the earth! No hills, mountains, or rivers were visible; only smooth, treeless, brown plains appeared.

Creator scratched his chest and rubbed his fingers together and there appeared Hummingbird.

"Fly north, south, east, and west and tell us what you see," said Creator.

"All is well," reported Hummingbird upon his return. "The earth is most beautiful, with water on the west side."

But the earth kept rolling and dancing up and down. So Creator made four giant posts—black, blue, yellow, and white—to support the earth. Wind carried the four posts, placing them beneath the four cardinal points of the earth. The earth sat still.

Creator sang, "World is now made and now sits still," which he repeated four times.

Then he began a song about the sky. None existed, but he thought there should be one. After singing about it four times, twenty-eight

Headdress
Apache

people appeared to help make a sky above the earth. Creator chanted about making chiefs for the earth and sky.

He sent Lightning-Maker to encircle the world, and he returned with three uncouth creatures, two girls and a boy found in a turquoise shell. They had no eyes, ears, hair, mouths, noses, or teeth. They had arms and legs, but no fingers or toes.

Sun-God sent for Fly to come and build a sweathouse. Girl-Without-Parents covered it with four heavy clouds. In front of the east doorway, she placed a soft, red cloud for a foot-blanket to be used after the sweat.

Four stones were heated by the fire inside the sweathouse. The three uncouth creatures were placed inside. The others sang songs of healing on the outside, until it was time for the sweat to be finished. Out came the three strangers who stood upon the magic red cloud-blanket. Creator then shook his hands toward them, giving each one fingers, toes, mouths, eyes, ears, noses and hair.

Creator named the boy, Sky-Boy, to be chief of the Sky-People. One girl he named Earth-Daughter, to take charge of the earth and its crops. The other girl he named Pollen-Girl, and gave her charge of health care for all Earth-People.

Since the earth was flat and barren, Creator thought it fun to create animals, birds, trees, and a hill. He sent Pigeon to see how the world looked. Four days later, he returned and reported, "All is beautiful around the world. But four days from now, the water on the other side of the earth will rise and cause a mighty flood."

Creator made a very tall piñon tree. Girl-Without-Parents covered the tree framework with piñon gum, creating a large, tight ball.

In four days, the flood occurred. Creator went up on a cloud, taking his twenty-eight helpers with him. Girl-Without-Parents put the others into the large, hollow ball, closing it tight at the top.

In twelve days, the water receded, leaving the float-ball high on a hilltop. The rushing floodwater changed the plains into mountains, hills, valleys, and rivers. Girl-Without-Parents led the gods out from the float-ball onto the new earth. She took them upon her cloud, drifting upward until they met Creator with his helpers, who had completed their work making the sky during the flood time on earth.

Together the two clouds descended to a valley below. There, Girl-Without-Parents gathered everyone together to listen to Creator.

"I am planning to leave you," he said. "I wish each of you to do your best toward making a perfect, happy world.

"You, Lightning-Rumbler, shall have charge of clouds and water.

"You, Sky-Boy, look after all Sky-People.

"You, Earth-Daughter, take charge of all crops and Earth-People.

"You, Pollen-Girl, care for their health and guide them.

"You, Girl-Without-Parents, I leave you in charge over all."

Creator then turned toward Girl-Without-Parents and together they rubbed their legs with their hands and quickly cast them forcefully downward. Immediately between them arose a great pile of wood, over which Creator waved a hand, creating fire.

Great billowy clouds of smoke at once drifted skyward. Into this cloud, Creator disappeared. The other gods followed him in other clouds of smoke, leaving the twenty-eight workers to people the earth.

Sun-God went east to live and travel with the Sun. Girl-Without-Parents departed westward to live on the far horizon. Small-Boy and Pollen-Girl made cloud homes in the south. Big Dipper can still be seen in the northern sky at night, a reliable guide to all.

Curtis, *The North American Indian*, vol. I, 23-35.

■

ORIGIN OF FIRE
Jicarilla-Apache

The Jicarilla were part of the Apache people. The name Jicarilla means "little basket," deriving from the expertise of their tribal women in making baskets of all sizes, shapes, and colors. Within historic times, they made their homes in southeastern Colorado and northern New Mexico, though a few groups roamed into Kansas, Oklahoma, and Texas. Originally they came from northwestern Canada among the migration of Athapascan language tribes, then along the eastern flank of the Rocky Mountains. When first met by explorers in the 1540s, they were called the Vaqueros by the Spanish. Though the Spanish established a mission for Jicarillas in 1733 near Taos, New Mexico, it did not succeed as general hostility existed between them until they were defeated by the U. S. Army in 1854. Later, in 1880, the government set aside a reservation for the Jicarillas in the Tierra Amarilla region of New Mexico. Today they live on their reservations in Arizona and in Rio Arriba and Sandoval Counties, New Mexico.

■

Long, long ago, animals and trees talked with each other, but there was no fire at that time.

Fox was most clever and he tried to think of a way to create fire for the world. One day, he decided to visit the Geese, *tĕ-tl*, whose cry he wished to learn how to imitate. They promised to teach him if he would fly with them. So they contrived a way to attach wings to Fox, but cautioned him never to open his eyes while flying.

Whenever the Geese arose in flight, Fox also flew along with them to practice their cry. On one such adventure, darkness descended suddenly as they flew over the village of the fireflies, *kō-nă-tcic-â*. In midflight, the glare from the flickering fireflies caused Fox to forget and he opened his eyes—instantly his wings collapsed! His fall was uncontrollable. He landed within the walled area of the firefly village, where a fire constantly burned in the center.

Two kind fireflies came to see fallen Fox, who gave each one a necklace of juniper berries, *kătl-te-i-tsé*.

Fox hoped to persuade the two fireflies to tell him where he could find a way over the wall to the outside. They led him to a cedar tree, which they explained would bend down upon command and catapult him over the wall if he so desired.

That evening, Fox found the spring where fireflies obtained their water. There also, he discovered colored earth, which when mixed with water made paint. He decided to give himself a coat of white. Upon returning to the village, Fox suggested to the fireflies, "Let's have a festival where we can dance and I will produce the music."

They all agreed that would be fun and helped to gather wood to build up a greater fire. Secretly, Fox tied a piece of cedar bark to his tail. Then he made a drum, probably the first one ever constructed, and beat it vigorously with a stick for the dancing fireflies. Gradually, he moved closer and closer to the fire.

Fox pretended to tire from beating the drum. He gave it to some fireflies who wanted to help make the music. Fox quickly thrust his tail into the fire, lighting the bark, and exclaimed, "It is too warm here for me, I must find a cooler place."

Straight to the cedar tree Fox ran, calling, "Bend down to me, my cedar tree, bend down!"

Down bent the cedar tree for Fox to catch hold, then up it carried him far over the wall. On and on he ran, with the fireflies in pursuit.

As Fox ran along, brush and wood on either side of his path were ignited from the sparks dropping from the burning bark tied to his tail.

Fox finally tired and gave the burning bark to Hawk, *i-tsàrl-tsü-i*, who carried it to brown Crane, *tsi-nes-tso-l*. He flew far southward, scattering fire sparks everywhere. This is how fire first spread over the earth.

Fireflies continued chasing Fox all the way to his burrow and declared, "Forever after, Wily Fox, your punishment for stealing our fire will be that you can never make use of it for yourself."

For the Apache tribe, this too was the beginning of fire for them. Soon they learned to use it for cooking their food and to keep themselves warm in cold weather.

Russell, "The Origin of Fire," 261-262.

■

ORIGIN OF THE ANIMALS
Jicarilla-Apache

■

When Apaches emerged from the underworld, they traveled south-ward for four days. They had no other food than two kinds of seeds, which they ground between two stones.

Near where they camped on the fourth night, one tepee stood apart from the others. While the owner and his wife were absent for a short time, a Raven brought a quiver of arrows and a bow, hanging them on the lodgepole. When the children came out of the lodge, they took down the quiver and found some meat inside. They ate it and instantly became very fat.

Upon her return, the mother noticed grease on the hands and faces of her children, who told her what had happened. The woman hurried to tell her husband the tale. All the tribe marveled at the wonderful food that made the children so fat. How they hoped the Raven might soon return with more of his good food.

When Raven discovered that his meat had been stolen, he flew eastward to his mountain home beyond the normal range of man. A bat followed Raven and later informed the Apaches where Raven lived. That night the Apache Chief called a council meeting. They decided to send a delegation to try and obtain some of Raven's special kind of meat.

In four days the Apache delegation reached the camp of the ravens, but could not obtain the information they desired. They discovered, however, a great circle of ashes where the ravens ate their meals. The Apaches decided to spy upon the ravens. That night the Medicine Man changed an Apache boy into a puppy to spy from a nearby bush. The main delegation broke camp and started homeward, leaving behind the puppy.

Next morning the ravens examined the abandoned camp of the Apaches. One of the young ravens found the puppy and was so pleased, he asked for permission to keep it under his blanket. Toward sunset, the puppy peaked out and saw an old raven brush aside some ashes from the fireplace. He then removed a large flat stone. Beneath was an opening through which the old raven disappeared. But when he returned he led a buffalo, which was then killed and eaten by all the ravens.

For four days the puppy spied upon the ravens, and each evening a buffalo was brought up from the depths and devoured. Now that he

Violin and bow
Apache

was certain where the ravens obtained their good food, the puppy resumed his normal shape.

Early on the fifth morning, with a white feather in one hand and a black one in the other, he descended through the opening beneath the fireplace.

In the underworld, he saw four buffaloes and placed the white feather in the mouth of the nearest one. He commanded it to follow him. But the first buffalo told him to take the feather to the last buffalo. This he did, but the fourth buffalo sent him again to the first one, into whose mouth the boy thrust the white feather.

"You are now the King of the Animals," declared the boy.

Upon returning to the above-world, the boy was followed by all the animals present upon the earth at that time. As the large herd passed through the opening, one of the ravens awoke, hurrying to close the lid. Upon seeing that all the animals willingly followed the Apache boy, the raven exclaimed, "When you kill any of the animals, remember to save the eyes for me."

For four days the boy followed the tracks of the Apaches and overtook them with his giant herd of animals. Soon they all returned to the camp of the Apaches, where the Chief slew the first buffalo for a feast that followed. The boy remembered and saved the eyes for the ravens.

One old grandmother who lived in a brush lodge was annoyed with one of the deer that ate some of her lodge covering. Snatching a stick from the fire, she struck the deer's nose and the white ash stuck there, leaving a white mark that can still be seen on the descendents of that deer.

"Hereafter, you shall avoid mankind," she pronounced. "Your nose will tell you when you are too close to them."

Thus ended the short period of harmony between man and the animals. Each day the animals wandered farther and farther from the tribes. Apaches prayed that the animals would return so they could enjoy the good meat again. It is mostly at night when the deer appear, but not too close, because the old grandmother told them to be guided by their noses!

Apaches developed skill in using the bows and arrows to hunt the good animal meat they liked so much, especially the buffalo.

Russell, "The Origin of Animals," 259-260.

■

An Apache Medicine Dance
Jicarilla-Apache

This published story was found by his daughter, Kay F. Nordquist, in the effects of the late Dr. E. R. Fouts, M.D. It was a reminiscence of his 1898 internship among the Jicarilla-Apache tribes. While stationed as an intern in Santa Fe, New Mexico, he met the white anthropologist/writer Frank Russell who published this legend in December 1898. At that time white men were not allowed to witness tribal ceremonies, but an Apache friend, Gunsi, arranged to smuggle the two white men into the celebration. Gunsi, a powerful leader, provided a hiding place and explained that as long as they "played a pretend game of not being seen," they would be overlooked. Besides, Gunsi had great confidence in the doctor of white man's medicine.

■

At present there are no men or women among the Jicarillas who have the power to heal the sick and perform other miracles that entitle them to rank as medicine men or medicine women—at least none who are in active practice and are popular. This being the case, medicine feasts have not been held for several years on the reservation. But in August and September 1898, two such feasts were conducted by the old Apache woman, Sotli, who now lives in Pueblo of San Ildefonso. Sotli made the journey of nearly a hundred miles to the Jicarillas on a burro. She was delayed for some time on the way by the high waters of Chama Creek, so rumors of her arrival were repeatedly spread for some weeks, before she actually appeared.

For festive dances, the U.S. Indian Agent or his representative, the clerk at Dulce, issue extra rations of beef and flour, and the Indians themselves buy all the supplies from the traders that their scanty funds will permit. Edible supplies do not keep well in Indian camps, and successive postponements threatened to terminate a feast without adequate provisions. But fortunately Sotli arrived in time.

The preliminary arrangements were made by Satl, the husband of the invalid Kes-nos'-un-da, in whose behalf the ceremonies were to be performed. Satl presented Sotli with a pipe of ancient pattern, a short cylinder of clay; a few eagle feathers and a new basket as well.

As the Jicarilla Apaches live in scattered tipis and cabins about the reservation, there is no specified place, such as the plaza of a pueblo tribe, where religious ceremonies are performed. Sotli chose a spot in La Jara Cañon where Satl and his friends built a medicine lodge with an enclosure surrounded by a pine brush fence. The lodge was begun on the morning of August 22 and the fence was completed by noonday. The builders were served food by the women of Satl's family.

At noon of the 22nd, the first day, about a dozen of the older men gathered in the medicine lodge. According to Gunsi, these men were selected by Sotli because of their ability in outlining the dry paintings, which they made in the lodge under her direction. No one but Apaches are admitted to the medicine lodge, so that I have depended upon the account of it given by Gunsi in the following description:

"The ground was cleared at the back of the lodge—between the fire and the western wall—over a space about six feet in diameter, and covered with a layer of clean gray sand. The sand painting the first day contained the figures of snakes only, having their heads directed toward the west, with the exception of the sun symbol, which was drawn each day during the ceremony around a shallow hole six or eight inches in diameter at the center of the painting.

"The sun was represented by a ring of white sand around the margin of the hole; next came a circle of black, and then a ring of red with white rays. After the painting had been completed, the invalid woman, in an ordinary gown not especially prepared for the occasion, entered the enclosure, laid aside her blanket, and passed into the lodge, on the floor

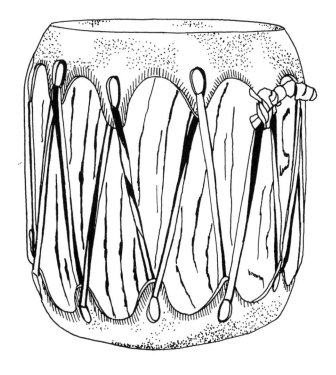

Drum
Apache

of which four "bear tracks" had been made, leading to the dry painting. (Presumably because she had the snake and bear disease.)

"The patient stepped upon the footprints in going to the sand painting, on which she spread pollen *(kat-u-tin)* from the cattail flag, and sacred meal. She then sat down upon the painting, facing the east. Songs were sung and prayers were offered to the sun, after which the women brought food from the camps into the enclosure. Those within the lodge seated themselves around the wall and were served by the doorkeeper, who began at the left and carried food to each in turn. After all were served, the doorkeeper gathered a morsel of food from each and threw it outside the enclosure, as a sacrifice to the sun, followed by prayers to the sun. Then the doorkeeper joined the others in the lodge and ate his food, as did the invalid. All others dined within the enclosure. The remaining food was gathered for the next meal. The men carried the food vessels from the lodge into the enclosure, later removed by the women.

"When darkness fell in the evening, the men again painted snakes in the medicine lodge, where a fire had been built. A young pine tree was placed at the right and another at the left of the sand painting. The children were then expelled from the enclosure.

"The patient entered as in the morning, offering pollen and meal, then seated herself upon the painting. A terrifying figure rushed into the semidarkness of the lodge, lunged toward the invalid, but seemed unable to reach her, gave forth two or three cries similar to those uttered by the bear, and then made his exit.

"Gunsi admitted 'I was frightened, although I knew it was only one of the men in disguise, who had been painted black with charcoal and covered with pine branches. He wore no mask. Since the invalid suffered from snake and bear disease, the painting with prayer meal and pollen offerings represented snakes and the bear was called upon to drive away the disease.'

"While the bear was in the lodge the singing men yelled at the tops of their voices to scare the bear. The invalid fell shaking to the ground. An eagle feather was waved rapidly to and fro above her head as she continued to rise, fall, shake, and cry out. I thought she was dying.

"Sotli then placed a live coal in a dish of blue corn meal and allowed the invalid to inhale the smoke. This quieted her somewhat as she sat upright but staring just like a drunk. Sotli then handed her the medicine pipe filled with 'Mexican' tobacco. After smoking this, the patient seemed to recover her senses. Two or three songs concluded the day's serious part of the ceremony. The ex-patient then moved to the north side of the lodge and remained there for the rest of the evening. An old buffalo hide was spread over the sand painting, and the sacred basket given to Sotli was inverted with the hide over the hole in the center of the painted area. The hide was then doubled over the basket, and the margin of the hide was held down by the feet of the men sitting around it.

"The white basket was ornamented with conventional red butterflies. The ex-patient removed her moccasins from a tight bundle and used them as drumsticks, striking four times upon the basket drum as a signal for the whole encampment to gather inside for the dance.

"Two notched sticks were placed upon the basket drum, a black one on the east, a white one on the west side. The sticks were laid with one end resting upon the drum and the other end upon the ground. A tarsal bone of a deer was rubbed across the notches, at the sound of which the young women began to dance.

"The women occupied the southern portion of the enclosure and the men arranged themselves along the wall opposite them. The lodge was brilliantly lighted by a circle of fires around the inside wall. The women's dance was ended by repetition of the same drum signal by which it had begun—four strokes upon the basket drum.

"When again the drum sounded, those afflicted with ailments of any kind placed their hands upon the affected part of their bodies and made a hand gesture of casting off the disease. When the sticks were scraped again, the women chose partners from the men and boys and all danced together. This became the lighter aspect of the ceremonies: serious thoughts, the desire to propitiate the gods, and the awe inspired by the priestess and the deity symbolized by the bear, all gave way to light-hearted, merrymaking spirit, which by no means exhausted itself before the sound of the drum ceased, about midnight, and the voice of one of the old men within the lodge was heard, directing the assembly to disperse.

"Second day ceremonies resembled those of the first, except the figures outlined upon the sand were of bears, foxes, and other animals, with here and there a snake. The same patient was not induced into a trance, nor was the general ceremony of casting off diseases performed.

"The third day differed only in the character of the sand painting. Animals differed from those of the previous days. Sotli forbade representation of the horse or elk at any time.

"On the fourth day, the figures of two deities were drawn in the dry painting, along with all kinds of animals. A black circle outside the painting symbolized the ocean. The program of the evening consisted of two groups of men, painted and dressed in the manner prescribed by the rites in the tradition of Jicarillas.

"One party of six men were the clowns with bodies and limbs painted with white and black horizontal rings. Ragged remnants of old blankets served as loincloths. On necks and shoulders appeared necklaces and festoons of bread, which had been baked in small fantastic shapes. Four wore old buffalo-skin caps, with the skin sewed to look like buffalo horns, projecting laterally and downward; to one horn was attached an eagle feather, to the other a turkey feather. Two men dressed their hair in the shape of horns.

"The other group of twelve men, painted white with oblique black stripes extending downward from the inner corners of their eyes, wore necklaces and an eagle feather in their hair. Bands of pine brush were wrapped around their waists, arms, and ankles.

"As on the other evenings, the women began the dance; then the general dance followed in which the women selected their partners from among the men. Then the two deities entered the enclosure and marched directly to the medicine lodge, around which four circuits were made in a sunwise direction. The twelve then took positions on the south side of the pathway from the gate to the lodge. Clowns ran about among the crowd. Two men led the singing and also took the lead during the exit back through the medicine lodge. Clowns created much amusement for everyone. The dance continued until sunrise."

As the disc of the sun rose above the mountaintops, every man, woman, and child present joined in the dance. The ceremony again took on a serious nature, as the sun's rays clear and bright in that rare and arid atmosphere lit up the valley and the whole band of Jicarilla-Apaches marched in line out of the enclosure toward the sun.

Sotli led the way, carrying the two young pines from the ends of the dry sand painting, along with the sacred basket containing the meal. Each person marched past the old medicine woman, took a pinch of the meal from the basket, and cast it upon the pine trees. The line was re-formed, facing the lodge, then one of the older men stepped forward and shook his blanket four times. At this signal, all shook their blankets to frighten away diseases and then ran into the enclosure.

The ceremonies ended. Every tipi in that vicinity must be moved at once. The invalid was cured, but Sotli warned her not to sleep on a rope or string or the disease would return. No one should sing the medicine songs for some time or a bear would kill the offender. Severe illness would overtake the twelve should they forget and sleep with their heads toward any clay vessel.

Sotli accepted food only as remuneration for her services. Her terms were known in advance, so a considerable quantity of provisions were laid aside for her. The only article of food that was taboo during the four-day celebration was bread baked in ashes.

I did not see the invalid after the feast, but when I left the reservation three weeks later, the Indian of whom I inquired all insisted that she was then in perfect health.

Russell, "An Apache Medicine Dance," 367-372.

■

LEGEND OF THE BIG BIRD

Chipewyan

Chipewyan Indians were known caribou eaters as early as 1600, coming down from northern Canada as far south as Lake Superior and Minnesota. They spread into numerous tribes, separated mainly by physical boundaries, such as lakes, rivers, and mountains.

Their distinctive language of the Athapascan family is heard far and wide between the West and East Coasts, and even southward among the Apaches and Navahos. Chipewyans seem to be an extremely imaginative people, and nature is interpreted by them in a pleasing and poetic manner. For instance, the Chipewyans might describe two trees, as "two trees growing side by side, so neither will tire of living alone."

■

Big Bird was a widow of the tribe's most famous Chief, Peace River. She lived with her son and beautiful daughter on the bank of a large stream. Her great ambition seemed to be to secure a rich husband for her daughter, suitable to her birth position.

So she asked her son to go to the riverbank and watch unceasingly to see if he could discover a stranger passing through suitable to be her son-in-law. One day the boy came running home to his mother with a beaming face and reported, "There is somebody passing by whom I would like to have for a brother-in-law."

Big Bird seemed delighted with the news, and took an armload of bark and went down to the river to meet the expected bridegroom. On her way, she placed the bark on the path for him to walk upon. She saw how magnificently dressed he was in a white skin costume covered with shell-beads. At their camp, she and her daughter had prepared a meal of unusual splendor and set it before their handsome guest.

Now it happened there was an old dog in the camp, which the young man objected to, and he would not eat until the dog was removed. Big Bird, wishing to show her guest every courtesy, complied with his request, took the dog out, and had him killed and left in the bush. The invited guest then enjoyed his supper, and they all went to sleep.

Next morning when Big Bird arose to make a fire, no wood was in the tepee. She went out to fetch some, and became startled to see the dog lying with his eyes removed, with his flesh pecked all over, and with the footprints of a three-toed animal all around the dog.

When she returned, she asked everyone to take off their shoes. they all did so, except the stranger, who said he never removed his shoes. However, Big Bird kept insisting, telling him she had a beautiful pair of new moccasins for him that would match his handsome costume. At last, she appealed to his vanity and he consented.

While quickly removing his shoes he said, "Kinno, kinno," meaning "Look, look!" but just as quickly put them on again. The boy saw his feet and called out, "He has three toes!" The stranger denied this statement and said, "I did it so quickly that you just imagined I have only three toes. You are mistaken."

After breakfast, he told his new wife that he wanted to go for his clothes, which were some distance upstream at his camp. He wished for her to accompany him. She thought her husband's conduct rather strange and not according to their tradition. At first she objected, but when he told of the many gew-gaws he wished to show her, she decided to go with him.

They got into their canoe and started off, the man sitting in the bow and the woman in the stern. In a short time, rain began to fall heavily. She noticed the rain washing off the shining white stuff from her husband's back and black feathers began to appear!

"Oh, I have married a crow!" she thought to herself. When he was not looking, she tied his long tail to the crossbar of the canoe. He turned and asked, "What are you doing?" "Your coat is so fine, I'm working with the beads to lay them straight." "I see I have married an industrious wife," he said as he resumed his paddling.

She then wondered how she could escape. So she said, "This point we are passing is famous for wild duck eggs. I'd like to go ashore and get us some for our supper." He consented, but as soon as she was out of the canoe, she ran up the bank and disappeared into the forest.

The crow tried to get out quickly to follow her, but because his tail was tied to the canoe, it was impossible. So he had to content himself with calling after her, "Caw! Caw! Once again I have tricked your people." He leisurely proceeded to untie his tail, and in his original black crow feathers flew away in search of another mischievous episode.

Big Bird welcomed her daughter home, grateful to be rid of the three-toed stranger. "We can all be more selective in the future when it comes to choosing in-laws," she advised her two younger children.

Bell, "Legend of the Big Bird," 73, 77-78.

■

THE LEGEND OF THE WHITE BEAR
Chipewyan

This legend gives an explanation of the reason for the extreme ferocity of the White Bear, and explains why his usual habitat is more hostile than others of his own species.

■

Once upon a time there was a White Bear whose nephew, Black Bear, lived with him along with several other animals, including Fox. Because Fox was always up to mischief, the White Bear took away Fox's right shoulder. Consequently Fox became ill. White Bear tied Fox's right shoulder to a bunch of claws that he always carried with him.

Now Fox became very sick and unable to get along very well without his right shoulder. He sent for Crow, who seemed always full of cunning, to devise some scheme to get back Fox's right shoulder. After a long talk, Crow left to visit White Bear, who was old and infirm and troubled with rheumatism. He found White Bear sitting by his fire warming himself, and saw the bunch of claws and Fox's shoulder hanging from the cave top. Crow began to talk with White Bear who nodded now and then. Crow touched the bag of claws, explaining he was only curious to see what they were made of.

At last, White Bear took no notice of what Crow was doing, as he was half-asleep. Crow saw his chance, and pulled down Fox's shoulder and ran out of the camp. White Bear waked and asked his nephew Black Bear, "What has happened?" Black Bear stuttered and took so long to tell White Bear that Crow had run away with Fox's right shoulder that White Bear became ferociously angry with Black Bear.

He told Black Bear to go away and find himself a new home and never come back again. White Bear in his rage took down the Sun and put it alongside of the claws. Outside, everything was in darkness. Animals could not hunt and were starving. So they appealed to Crow to get them out of their present trouble, caused by White Bear.

In the meantime, White Bear's daughter went for water. She took a drink and saw something black; but it was too late. She had swallowed

Cloth design
Chipewyan

the black speck. Sometime later a child was born to her, and the infant grew so fast he could walk about. When he noticed the bright Sun hanging beside the bunch of claws, the child began to cry for it.

After much frustration and begging, White Bear gave the Sun to the child to play with inside their cave. Soon he wished to play outside with the Sun, but at first White Bear would not allow it. Because the child continually begged, White Bear relented and said yes, but only close to their home. If the child saw anyone coming, he was to run inside at once and bring the Sun with him.

All of these commandments the child promised to do as White Bear directed. But as soon as the boy ran outside, he threw the Sun up into the sky, for the child was the scheming Crow in yet another disguise. When White Bear discovered how he was cheated again by Crow, he was doubly furious, driving away everyone.

Ever since then, White Bears always have been more ferocious and bad-tempered toward other species, as well as man.

Bell, "The Legend of the White Bear," 78-79.

■

THE HUMMINGBIRD
Zuñi

Long ago, the Zuñi tribe of North American Indians lived in the area of the present states of New Mexico and Arizona. A large, thriving Zuñi Pueblo was discovered in 1500 by Franciscans from Mexico, who returned with glowing reports of the Zuñi "Kingdom of Cibola" on the Zuñi River. Concerned about attacks, Zuñi leaders moved their women, children, and property to their stronghold Mesa, to which they escaped when Corondo tried to subjugate the tribe. In 1629, about 10,000 Zuñis were accounted for when the first mission was established in Hawikuh by the Franciscans. Today, they remain a strong tribe, active on the Zuñi Reservation in New Mexico.

■

Not far from Rainbow Cave on the Sacred Mountain in what is now New Mexico, Hummingbird Hoya lived with his beloved grandmother long ago.

Hummingbird pin
Zuñi

"I think I will go to Kiakima to see what their clansmen are doing," Hoya said one day to his beloved grandmother.

Because he was so small and wanted to be sure that people could see him, Hoya dressed himself in his colorful hummingbird coat and flew far away. Below him, he saw a lovely spring and decided to stop, taking off his beautifully feathered coat.

Before long, Kia, the daughter of Chief Kya-ki-massi, arrived to fill her jar with the cool spring water. Many young men of the Zuñi Indian tribe longed to marry Kia, but were afraid to ask her father, the Chief.

Kia began to fill her water jar without speaking to the attractive young man nearby.

"May I have some of your water to drink?" Hoya asked.

Kia handed him a cupful. When he returned the cup to her, a small amount of water remained. Playfully, she tossed it to him and giggled.

Some young Zuñis watching from the brush wondered why she laughed. They also wondered about the stranger. Then they heard the princess say, "Let's go to my home."

Hoya followed Kia to her house, and they talked for some time at the bottom of her ladder, which led to the lodge roof. Then Hoya said, "I think it is time for me to start home."

"I hope to see you at the spring tomorrow," Kia said. She then climbed to the roof of her lodge. Hoya put on his magic feathered coat, flying away invisibly. The young men of the village did not see Hoya vanish, which aroused their curiosity.

When Hoya arrived back at his beloved grandmother's house, she met him with a bowl of honey combined with sunflower pollen. The next day, he carried some of the delicacy to the spring as a gift for the princess. Again, he walked Kia home and they conversed at the bottom of her ladder. He gave her the honey and pollen to share with her family.

"Um-m-m good, we like this kind of food," her parents said. "You should marry this young man."

Next day, when Hoya walked Kia home from the spring, she invited him to come into her lodge to meet her family.

"No, thank you, Kia, I cannot marry you yet," said Hoya. "I do not have deerskins, blankets, or beads for you."

"But I do not need these things," she replied. "I like the good food you brought to me, that is enough."

"Then, if I may, I will come to your lodge tomorrow evening," said Hoya. He then put on his magic coat and flew away instantly as Kia ascended the ladder to her roof.

Hoya reported to his beloved grandmother all that had taken place. He told her the Chief's daughter wanted him for her husband.

"No, not now," she replied. "You do not have enough things to give her; you cannot marry her yet."

"But, Grandmother, the daughter of the Chief wants nothing except our delicious honey food."

"If you are sure of her parents' approval, then I give you my permission to marry Kia."

At dawn next day, Hoya and his beloved grandmother, dressed in their hummingbird coats, zoomed away southward to the land of the sunflowers.

All that day, they gathered pollen and honey. Later, when they returned, they placed a deerskin on the floor. Onto this, they shook the pollen from their feathers. Into a large shell, they deposited the honey. Hoya's beloved grandmother mixed the pollen and honey together, much the same way as kneading bread dough. She then wrapped a large ball of the mixture in a deerskin, which Hoya took to Kia that very evening.

Village youths gathered and watched from a distance as Hoya climbed Kia's ladder to her lodge roof. There Hoya secretly hid his magic coat under a rock before lowering himself into Kia's lodge.

"How sad for us that Kia will marry a stranger," the youths repeated among themselves.

The young men of Zuñi village gathered in a Kiva, a ceremonial lodge, saying to the Bow Chief, "Please announce that in four days we will go on a parrot hunt. Say, also, that anyone who does not join us will lose his wife."

Later, Kia's brother returned home and reported, "In the village, they are saying that on the hunt for young parrots, the young hunters will throw my new brother-in-law from the mesa and kill him. they will then claim his wife."

"They are just loud-mouth talking," said Chief Kya-ki-massi.

But Hoya believed that whe he heard from younger brother. He quickly put on his hummingbird coat and flew away to Parrot Woman's Cave.

"What have you to say?" she asked.

"I wish to warn you to protect your young parrots from harm. I also ask your help for myself," Hoya said, telling her of the plot to kill him. In a few minutes, he returned to Kia's home.

Next day, the parrot hunt began, with Hoya bringing up the rear. He secretly wore his magic coat beneath his buckskin shirt. At the high mesa, a yucca rope was let down toward the parrot's cave.

Hoya was instructed by the group to go down the rope to the nest of the young parrots. When he was halfway down, the village hunters let go of the rope. Parrot Woman was waiting for him, spreading her large fanlike tail outside her cave entrance. She caught Hoya in time.

Upon returning to the village, the young men reported that the rope broke, letting hoya fall to his death. In Kia's lodge, there was much sadness at the loss of Kia's new husband.

Parrot Woman took her two young birds and, with Hoya in his magic coat, flew up to the mesa.

"Please keep my two children with you," she said. "But bring them back to me in four days."

Hoya took the two young parrots to his new home and, from the roof, he heard Kia crying inside.

"I hear someone on our roof," her father said. "Perhaps, it is your new husband."

"Impossible," said his son. "Hoya is dead. But Kia ran up the ladder and to her great joy, she discovered her husband with the two parrots.

At dawn, Hoya placed the two young parrots on the tips of the ladder poles. A village youth came out of the Kiva and saw the birds. He ran back inside calling, "Wake up everyone! Hoya is not dead. He has come back to his home with two young parrots!"

When the Zuñi villagers saw the two parrots, they decided to make another plan to rid themselves of Hoya.

"Please, Bow Chief, give us permission to hunt the Bear's children. If anyone does not come along with us, he will lose his wife."

Hoya heard the terrible news, so he went to the cave of the Bear Mother.

"What do you wish of me?" she asked Hoya.

"The young hunters of Zuñi village are going on a hunt for your children. I have come to warn you and to ask you for your help in protecting me," replied Hoya. Then he told her of the plot to kill him.

Four days later, the young hunters charged toward Bear Mother's cave. Hoya again secretly wore his magic hummingbird coat beneath his buckskin shirt. He was forced by the young men to lead the attack at the cave entrance. Then the others pushed him inside the Bear's cave!

Mother Bear grabbed him but she shoved him behind her. She chased the young Zuñi hunters, killing a few of the young tribesmen. Later, Hoya flew home with two bear cubs and at dawn he placed them on the roof. When the villagers discovered the bears on Kia's roof, they knew that Hoya was sitll alive.

Hoya decided to fly to his beloved grandmother's home near Rainbow Cave to seek her wisdom about a new plan of his. She helped him paint a bird cage with many colors and they filled it with birds of matching colors. Back to Zuñi village he flew, carrying the cage, which he placed in the center of the plaza. Around it, he planted magic corn, bean, squash, and sunflower seeds.

That very evening welcome rains came down gently. Next morning the sun shone brightly and warmly. When the Zuñi villagers came out of their hogans, they were amazed at the sight before them! In the plaza center, growing plants surrounded the beautiful cage of colorful, singing birds!

From that moment on, all of the happy, dancing Zuñi tribe accepted Hoya and his gifts. They learned to love him as one of their own. His wife they called Mother, and they called him Father of their tribe for many contented years.

Curtis, *The North American Indians*, vol. 17, 179-81.

■

THE FOUR FLUTES
Zuñi

■

How the Zuñis wished for new music and new dances for their people when they participated in ceremonials! But they knew not how to create their wishes into realities.

Their Chief and his counselors decided to ask their Old Grandfathers for help. They journeyed to the Elder Priests of the Bow and asked, "Grandfathers, we are tired of the same old music and the old dances. Can you please show us how to make new music and new dances for our people?"

After much conferring, the Elder Priests arranged to send our Wise Ones to visit the God of Dew. Next day the four Wise Ones set out upon their mission.

Slowly climbing a steep trail, they were pleased to hear music coming from the high Sacred Mountain. Near the top, they discovered that the music came from the Cave of the Rainbow. At the cave's entrance, vapors floated about, a sign that within was the god Paíyatuma.

When the four Wise Ones asked permission to go in, the music stopped; however, they were welcomed warmly by Paíyatuma, who said, "Our musicians will now rest while we learn why you have come."

"Our Elders, the Priests of the Bow, directed us to you. We wish for you to show us your secret in making new sounds of music. Also with the new music, we wish to learn how to create new ceremonial dances.

"As gifts, our Elders have prepared these prayer sticks and special plume-offerings for you and your people."

"Come sit with me," responded Paíyatuma. "You shall now see and hear."

Before them appeared many musicians with beautifully decorated long shirts. Their faces were painted with the signs of the gods. Each held a lengthy tapered flute. In the center of the group was a large drum, beside which stood its drum-beater. Another musician held the conductor's wand. These were men of age and experience, graced with dignity.

Paíyatuma stood and spread some magic pollen at the feet of the visiting Wise Ones. With crossed arms, he then strode the length of the cave, turning and walking back again. Seven beautiful young girls, tall and slender, followed him. Their garments were similar to the musicians, but were of various colors. They held hollow cottonwood shafts from which bubbled dainty clouds when the maidens blew into them.

"These are not the maidens of corn," Paíyatuma said. "They are our dancers, the young sisters from the House of Stars."

Paíyatuma placed a flute to his lips and joined the circle of dancers. From the drum came a thunderous beat, shaking the entire Cave of the Rainbow, signaling the performance to begin.

Beautiful music from the flutes seemed to sing and sigh like the gentle blowing of the winds. Bubbles of vapor arose from the girls' reeds. In rhythm, the Butterflies of Summerland flew about the cave, creating their own dance forms with the dancers and the musicians. Mysteriously, over all the scene flooded the colors of the Rainbow throughout the cave. All of this harmony seemed like a dream to the four Wise Ones, as they thanked the God of Dew and prepared to leave.

Paíyatuma came forward with a benevolent smile and symbolically breathed upon the four Wise Ones. He summoned four musicians, asking them to give each one a flute as a gift.

"Now depart to your Elders," said Paíyatuma. "Tell them what you have seen and heard. Give them our flutes. May your people the Zuñis learn to sing like the birds through these woodwinds and these reeds."

In gratitude the Wise Ones bowed deeply and accepted the gifts, expressing their appreciation and farewell to all of the performers and Paíyatuma.

Upon the return of the four Wise Ones to their own ceremonial court, they placed the four flutes before the Priests of the Bow. The Wise Ones

Dance mask
Zuñi

described and demonstrated all that they had seen and heard in the Cave of the Rainbow.

Chief of the Zuñi tribe and his counselors were happy with their new knowledge, returning to their tribe with the gift of the flutes and the reeds. Before their next ceremonial, many of their tribesmen learned to make new music and to create new dances for all their people to enjoy.

Nusbaum, *Zuñi Indian Tales*, 125-132.

■

THE YELLOW HAND
Papago

The Papago tribe's native word *papáh*, beans, is the source for being called the "bean people." They belong to the Piman branch of the Uto-Aztecan linquistic family, and are closely related to the Pima tribe southeast of the Gila River and south of Tucson, Arizona, and extending west and southwest across the desert Papaguería on into Sonora, Mexico. In 1694, Father Kino became the first white man to visit the Papago nation, finding a very large population into the thousands. Census figures in 1937 listed 6,305 members of the Papago tribe. They have their own Papago printed alphabet and language studies.

■

Years ago, but not nearly so many years ago as in most of our stories, said an old Papago Indian, a man who lived in this village owned much land and worked very hard. He was always getting fields from someone who did not work so hard.

Sometimes his wife scolded him. "Both of us do nothing but work," she would say to him. "We already have more than we need and more than our daughter needs." Their daughter was their only child.

Her husband kept on working and trading until he had the very best land in all this valley. He had the best horses. He had the greatest number of cattle.

Then he began to collect yellow stones.

And his wife began to scold more and more. "It is time to choose a husband for our daughter," she told him, "but you do not know anyone. You are always too busy to go with other men on hunts or to feasts. The people of the village do not like you and are afraid of you." But her scolding had no effect.

One day a Stranger appeared from the south, riding a burro. He went to the place where the man I am telling you about was working. There Stranger emptied a sack of rocks. Then the two men pounded some of these rocks, pounded them, and burned them. After doing this a long time, the man brought Stranger to his home for food. His wife and daughter served them. The mother was very cross and scolded a great deal. Stranger watched the girl closely.

When Stranger left, the wife asked her husband, "What did you trade this time?"

Her husband only laughed and showed her a pile of stones.

When the woman had decided upon a husband for her daughter, the father would not lsiten to her. He paid no attention to anything that she said. She was very sad and quiet and worried.

But one morning, everything seemed to change. When the woman looked far south, she saw several burros with baskets on their sides. The burros came to the house. Driving them was the Stranger who had been there before. He asked the woman for her husband, who soon came from his fields. He helped Stranger unload the baskets. When they finished, the girl's father came to the house and said to his wife, "I have found a husband for our daughter. Tell her to get her things together, so that she can go with Stranger."

The mother wept and begged her husband not to give up her daughter to a stranger from a strange land. But her husband paid no attention to her. He was pounding the rocks that Stranger had brought. He paid no attention to his wife or to his daughter.

Next day the girl started south with her husband. Her father pounded the rocks that Stranger had brought to him. Her mother grumbled while she did her work, feeling very heavy and queer inside.

Time passed. The man no longer worked in his fields. He spent all of his time pounding his rocks and washing them and burning them. Again Stranger came with his burros loaded with baskets of rocks. After the baskets had been emptied, he went away.

Now all the people in the village knew that the man had traded his daughter for a pile of rocks. They laughed at him and ignored him. The woman was alone too much and became very sad. She complained that her husband was changing to rock.

When he had almost finished with one pile of rocks, Stranger would appear from the south with more rocks. This would make the man work harder than ever. His wife did not know what he did with the small yellow stones that he got out of the rocks. She thought that he put them in a hole in the ground.

Often she had to carry his meals out to him, where he was working. All day long he pounded, pounded, and pounded the rocks. The pile that he had crushed became larger than three houses. And the man's hands, his wife noticed, were always covered with yellow dust.

After a few years, she became old and very tired all the time. She refused to work in the fields; the man did nothing but pound rocks. So other people plowed and planted his fields and gave the man and his wife a certain portion of the crops.

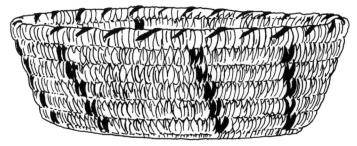

Basket
Papago

When the summer rains fell, the man refused to leave the rocks. He worked all day and worked at night by the light of a big fire. Many times he became wet from the rains. Soon he began to cough—very hard. His wife begged him to stop and rest. "If you do not rest, the deer will come," she reminded him.

A certain sickness, the Desert People used to believe, was brought by a deer. When people got sick in that way, there was no hope that they would ever get well. The deer that brings that sickness has a black tail. So when the Desert People eat meat from a deer with a black tail, they are still very careful. If they cough while eating the meat from that kind of deer, some of them believe they will cough until they die.

But the man who pounded rocks all day was not kept from his work by fear that the deer would come. Day after day he sat in the rain and pounded the rocks for which he had traded his only daughter. And his wife noticed that the rain did not wash the yellow from one of his hands.

One morning when the woman looked out, her husband was not pounding rocks. She went to him and found that he was dead.

She called the people living nearest her, and they began to prepare for the burial ceremony. She brought out all the blankets and the other things needed. While the dead man was being wrapped in the blankets, his right hand fell off. Picking it up, his wife found that it was very yellow and heavy and hard—just like a rock.

When everything was ready, the body was taken to the burial hill. The hand was placed beside the body and, according to custom, everything was covered with brush and stones.

That night, some kind women stayed with the widow in her home because she was now all alone. After they had been sleeping for a few hours, they heard a sound of pounding near the house! The dead man's wife was very tired and very sleepy. Hardly half-awake, she said to her friends, "It is only my husband at his rocks." And then she went to sleep again.

But the other women were frightened and could not sleep. The pounding continued until morning. Then the widow realized that her husband could not be working at his rocks. So she went out to find who had made the sound of pounding but came back puzzled, still wondering.

The next night the sounds were heard again. The third night the pounding seemed to be growing louder. The people of the village began to whisper, and they began to keep away from the widow and her home.

Then the woman became so angry that she determined to find out who was making the noise. When night came and she heard the pounding, she went out to the rocks that her husband had been breaking up when he died. As she drew near the pile of rocks, the sound became fainter.

Then she decided to visit her husband's grave. The night was dark. As she drew nearer the burial mound, the sound of the pounding became louder and louder. But everything was so dark that she decided to go home and wait until morning. Then she and some other women went to the place where Man-Who-Pounded-Rocks was buried.

They heard no noise, but they knew that a very restless spirit was there. The widow could not understand. She walked all around the mound of brush and rocks, looking at it keenly and wondering.

Suddenly she saw something bright. She stooped and looked carefully. It was the yellow hand of her husband that had broken off!

Her friends who were with her said that Coyote had tried to take the hand. But the widow felt sure she had a better idea. When they took the yellow hand to the house, one woman kept watching it. When she picked it up, several little pieces of yellow rock fell out. She quickly picked them up and slipped them out of sight. She thought that no one saw her, but the widow of the dead man had noticed her and the tiny bits of yellow rock.

After a long talk about what they should do with the yellow hand, the widow decided to put it in the ground. She and her friends wrapped it, dug a hole near the house, put the hand in it, and covered it with dirt. Then her neighbors went to their homes.

That night the widow was so very tired that she went to sleep early. But she was soon wakened by a tap, tap, tap. When she opened the door, she found no one there. She went back to bed thinking that she had been mistaken. A few minutes later she heard again the tap, tap, tap.

This time she felt sure that the sound came from the yellow hand, and so she started toward the place where they had buried it. In a few minutes she stumbled over something. Feeling around in the dark, she soon found it—the yellow hand!

She sat down to think. She did not know what to do or whom to ask for help. Soon some Little People, who work night and day in the summer, passed by her. She called to them. Quickly the message was passed to all the Little People that a human being needed their help.

The woman remained sitting on the ground, in the dark, waiting for the message that she knew would come from the Little People. They will not always help, but when they are willing, the advice they give is always good. After a time, still in the darkness, the woman heard, or felt, or understood, what she was to do.

She knew now that her dead husband's yellow hand had come back for the little pieces of yellow rock that a woman had taken. Her husband had loved them very much. The sound of pounding in the night had come from the yellow hand working at the rocks as the man was working when he died.

"If the yellow hand is left where others can find it," the woman was made to realize, "those who find it will feel that same intense love for the little pieces of yellow rock that the dead man felt for years. You must hide the yellow hand far away, where no one can ever find it. And you must find all the pieces of yellow rock that the yellow hand wanted, so that it will never come back again."

This was the advice that the woman received, in some way, from the Little People.

When morning came, she went to the home of the friend who, she knew, had kept those pieces of yellow rock. At first, the woman said that she had not taken them, but later she gave them up.

At the place where he had broken many, many rocks, she searched and searched until she had picked up all the little yellow pieces. Late in the day, she put them and those that her friend had picked up—put them all, with the yellow hand, in a blanket. Then she started up the steep side of the mountain, alone. It was a rough, hard climb for an old woman.

She became so tired that she sat down to rest in the twilight. As she sat there, she considered just throwing the yellow hand and the pieces of rock far from her and then going back to her house and her supper. Just as she was feeling sorry for herself, Taw-tawn-ye, Ant, ran over her hand. And Taw-tawn-ye stopped. "Does Taw-tawn-ye have a message for me?" the old woman thought to herself. She sat very still and listened hard, with her inside ears.

"Remember the advice the Little People gave you," Ant reminded her. "And remember what troubles would happend if you left the yellow hand where people could find it."

The woman thought of her lonely years. She thought of her daughter who had been traded for rocks. And she knew that she would never let anyone else live in this way. So she wrapped her blanket around her and slept until the morning light made eveything clear.

Then she picked up the yellow hand and all the pieces of yellow rock and hid them in different places on the mountain.

When she had finished, she returned to her home and lived in peace and happiness ever after, with all her people. Not once did she ever hear the sound of the yellow hand pounding rocks.

The mountain where the woman hid the yellow hand and the pieces of yellow rock is called *Schook Toahk*, which means "Black Mountain." Many people have searched for the place where this gold is hidden, but they have never found it. If the Desert People should learn where gold is, they would not tell anyone. Gold has always brought trouble to Indians, the Desert People of today believe. The gold hand held the beginning of all their troubles.

Wright, *Legends of the Papago Indians*, 277-290.

■

WHY THE NORTH STAR STANDS STILL
Paiute

The North American Indians told many stories about the stars—individual stars and groups of stars. Often in these legends, the stars are referred to as "the People of the Sky World."

■

Long, long ago, when the world was young, the People of the Sky were so restless and traveled so much that they made trails in the heavens. Now, if we watch the sky all through the night, we can see which way they go.

But one star does not travel. That is the North Star. He cannot travel. He cannot move. When he was on the earth long, long ago, he was known as Na-gah, the mountain sheep, the son of Shinoh. He was brave, daring, sure-footed, and courageous. His father was so proud of him and loved him so much that he put large earrings on the sides of his head and made him look dignified, important, and commanding.

Every day, Na-gah was climbing, climbing, climbing. He hunted for the roughest and the highest mountains, climbed them, lived among them, and was happy. Once in the very long ago, he found a very high peak. Its sides were steep and smooth, and its sharp peak reached up into the clouds. Na-gah looked up and said, "I wonder what is up there. I will climb to the very highest point."

Around and around the mountain he traveled, looking for a trail. But he could find no trail. There was nothing but sheer cliffs all the way around. This was the first mountain Na-gah had ever seen that he could not climb.

He wondered and wondered what he should do. He felt sure that his father would feel ashamed of him if he knew that there was a mountain that his son could not climb. Na-gah determined that he would find a way up to its top. His father would be proud to see him standing on the top of such a peak.

Again and again he walked around the mountain, stopping now and then to peer up the steep cliff, hoping to see a crevice on which he could find footing. Again and again, he went up as far as he could, but always had to turn around and come down. At last he found a big crack in a rock that went down, not up. Down he went into it and soon found a hole that turned upward. His heart was made glad. Up and up he climbed.

Soon it became so dark that he could not see, and the cave was full of loose rocks that slipped under his feet and rolled down. Soon he heard a big, fearsome noise coming up through the shaft at the same time the rolling rocks were dashed to pieces at the bottom. In the darkness he slipped often and skinned his knees. His courage and determination began to fail. He had never before seen a place so dark and dangerous. He was afraid, and he was also very tired.

"I will go back and look again for a better place to climb," he said to himself. "I am not afraid out on the open cliffs, but this dark hole fills me with fear. I'm scared! I want to get out of here!"

But when Na-gah turned to go down, he found that the rolling rocks had closed the cave below him. He could not get down. He saw only one thing now that he could do: He must go on climbing until he came out somewhere.

After a long climb, he saw a little light, and he knew that he was coming out of the hole. "Now I am happy," he said aloud. "I am glad that I really came up through that dark hole."

Looking around him, he became almost breathless, for he found that he was on the top of a very high peak! There was scarcely room for him

Wickiup
Paiute

to turn around, and looking down from this height made him dizzy. He saw great cliffs below him, in every direction, and saw only a small place in which he could move. Nowhere on the outside could he get down, and the cave was closed on the inside.

"Here I must stay until I die," he said. "But I have climbed my mountain! I have climbed my mountain at last!

He ate a little grass and drank a little water that he found in the holes in the rocks. Then he felt better. He was higher than any mountain he could see and he could look down on the earth, far below him.

About this time, his father was out walking over the sky. He looked everywhere for his son, but could not find him. He called loudly, "Na-gah! Na-gah!" And his son answered him from the top of the highest cliffs. When Shinoh saw him there, he felt sorrowful, to himself, "My brave son can never come down. Always he must stay on the top of the highest mountain. He can travel and climb no more.

"I will not let my brave son die. I will turn him into a star, and he can stand there and shine where everyone can see him. He shall be a guide mark for all the living things on the earth or in the sky."

And so Na-gah became a star that every living thing can see. It is the only star that will always be found at the same place. Always he stands still. Directions are set by him. Travelers, looking up at him, can always find their way. He does not move around as the other stars do, and so he is called "the Fixed Star." And because he is in the true north all the time, our people call him *Qui-am-i Wintook Poot-see*. These words mean "the North Star."

Besides Na-gah, other mountain sheep are in the sky. They are called "Big Dipper" and "Little Dipper." They too have found the great mountain and have been challenged by it. They have seen Na-gah standing on its top, and they want to go on up to him.

Shinoh, the father of North Star, turned them into stars, and you may see them in the sky at the foot of the big mountain. Always they are traveling. They go around and around the mountain, seeking the trail that leads upward to Na-gah, who stands on the top. He is still the North Star.

Palmer, *Pahute Indian Legends*, 79-81.

■

A California Creation Myth
Yokut

Yokuts were originally thought to be a distinct linguistic family but are now considered a part of the large Penutian family. They occupy the entire floor of San Joaquin Valley of central California from the mouth of the San Joaquin River to the foot of the Tehachapi Mountains and adjacent to the foothills of the Sierra Nevada range, up to an altitude of a few thousand feet. Their environment lends itself to agriculture and forestry. In 1770 the estimated population of the Yokuts was 18,000 and in 1910 only 600. Today dozens of small bands and villages are spread over a wide area.

■

A Great Flood had occurred upon Earth long, long ago. While Earth was still covered with water, there were no living creatures upon the land.

Then out of the sky one day glided an enormous Eagle with a black Crow riding upon its back, searching for a place to light.

Around and around Eagle flew until he discovered a projecting tree stump, or what appeared to be a stump, upon which he landed to rest. There was a home at last upon the flat surface, which was amply large enough for Eagle and Crow to roost upon.

From here, they surveyed the greenish gray water as far as they could see. The sky was a gorgeous bright blue with a few white drifting clouds, occasionally swirled by a passing breeze. All seemed serene to Eagle and Crow.

Small fish were visible below the water, sometimes leaping out of the sea playfully. Hunger caused Eagle and Crow to swoop down, catching a meal for themselves from time to time. Soon a game developed between the two birds to see which one would be the winner in the fish-catching contest. Upon their return to the stump, however, they always shared the reward.

Because of Eagle's great size and wingspan, he soared to great heights and surveyed widely, as the two birds often flew in opposite directions exploring for land. But no land did they find. No other flying creatures did they see. But they always returned to their home base on the tree stump.

Between them, they wondered "How can we possibly think of a way to make land?"

"We know we cannot dive deep enough to find dirt, and the fish are of no help except to provide food."

Day after day these scenes were repeated, exploring in search of land or wondering how to create land, only to return to their stump and catch more fish.

One morning soon thereafter and much to their surprise, a Duck was swimming around and around their stump. Occasionally, it dived deep in the water, rose to the surface chewing small fish, twisting its head from side to side trying to swallow its meal. One time, Duck emerged with more mud than fish in its mouth.

Eagle and Crow birdtalked excitedly about this! "Can Duck possibly bring up enough mud for us to build land?" they wondered.

How could they let Duck know that mud was what they needed most?

An idea occurred to Eagle, which he birdtalked to Crow, "If we supply fish for Duck, maybe he will bring up more mud than fish."

By trial and error, the two birds caught fish for Duck, placing them at the edge of the stump, until Duck learned that the fish were for him in exchange for mud!

When Duck appeared on the surface after a deep dive, Eagle and Crow brushed off the mud from Duck's bill and his body with their wings. Progress was slow but steady.

Gradually, Eagle had a pile of mud on his side of the stump and Crow had a similar pile on his side. Each placed fish on his own side for Duck, who now responded by carrying more and more mud to Eagle and Crow. This became a great game of fish-and-mud exchange.

Duck worked very hard, consequently he was always hungry. The birds were surprised at how large each one's mud pile grew every day. In birdtalk they said, "Duck is helping us to make a new world. This we will share equally."

Occasionally, Eagle and Crow flew toward the horizon, exploring for any new signs of land. But they returned with nothing new to report; however, they noticed a slight lowering of water around the tree stump.

"Surely, the flood must be coming to an end," Crow and Eagle birdtalked.

Each day they watched for a change in the waterline. Each day their piles of mud seemed higher and higher. Faithful Duck kept up his good work as Eagle and Crow caught fish for him and scraped off mud from him for each side of the new world.

Another time, Eagle flew high and far in search of dry land, not returning until late. The sun set and darkness enveloped his world on the stump. Next morning, to Eagle's surprise, he saw how much more mud he had acquired, and he was pleased. But after looking across at Crow's mud pile, Eagle was astounded to see that Crow had given himself twice as much mud while Eagle was away.

"Was this Crow's idea of sharing the new world equally?" accused Eagle.

Of course, they quarreled all that day and the next over Crow's unfairness. But the following day, they went back to work making their new land. Eagle decided that he must catch up. He caught two fish for Duck and put them in his usual place. Duck responded by bringing up mud twice to Eagle in exchange for his two fish. All three worked very hard for many, many moons.

Gradually, Eagle's half of the new world became taller and taller than Crow's half, even though Crow seemed to work just as hard as Eagle. Duck was faithful to his task, never tiring in his effort to supply mud. Of course, Duck continued to give Eagle twice as much mud for his two fish. Crow never seemed to notice why Eagle's half became higher and higher than his half.

One morning, as the sun rose brightly, the two birds looked down through the water and saw what appeared to be land!

"So that is where Duck finds the mud," they birdtalked. They were pleased to see that the water was subsiding. How they hoped that soon they would be high and dry on their new world.

But all was not so easy, for that very night lightning flashed across the waters and thunder rolled and rolled from one horizon to the other, followed by a heavy, drenching rain. Eagle and Crow sought shelter in holes they dug into the sides of their mud piles. All night long the rain continued to fall, washing away much of the new world into the sea.

As the rain stopped and the sun rose, Eagle and Duck looked out upon the waters and saw an arc of many colors reaching from one edge of the horizon across the sky to the other horizon. This brilliant display held their eyes in wonderment. What did it mean? They marveled at how long the colors lingered in the sky. Eagle flew toward the scene for a closer look, returning when the arc disappeared.

In birdtalk, Eagle and Crow decided that the storm of the night before must have been a clearing shower. They began their land-building project again, hoping that Duck would resume his work as mud-carrier. Soon the sun's rays burned strong and hot, packing the mud until it was hard. Duck appeared and the team of three continued to build the two halves of the new world.

Day by day, the waters subsided and new land began to show above the waterline but far, far below the new creation by Eagle and Crow. Eagle's half became taller and taller and hard packed by the hot sun. Crow's share of the new world was still great, but never could become as large as Eagle's half of the new world.

> In retelling this creation story, Yokut tribal historians always claim that Eagle's half became the mighty Sierra Nevada Mountains. They also tell how Crow's half became known as the Coast Mountain Range.
>
> Yokut historians end their tale by saying that people everywhere honor the brave and strong Eagle, while Crow is accorded a lesser place because of his unfair disposition displayed during the creation of the new world by Eagle and Crow.

Potts, "A California Creation Myth," 73-74.

Reed boat
Yokut

■

WHY MOUNT SHASTA ERUPTED

Shasta

The Shasta tribe probably acquired its name from a long ago chief named Sasti. They are located in California and Oregon, on the Klamath River from Indian and Thompson Creeks to the mouth of Fall Creek; in the drainage areas of two Klamath River tributaries, the Scott and Shasta rivers; and on the north side of the Siskiyou Mountains in Oregon on affluents of the Rogue River. All of these waterways proved rich sources of fish for many tribes through the centuries. Mount Shasta and Shasta County perpetuate the name of the Shasta Indians.

■

Coyote, a universal and mischievous spirit, lived near Mount Shasta in what is now California. Coyote's village had little fish and no salmon. His neighboring village of Shasta Indians always had more than they could use.

Shasta Indians had built a dam that served as a trap for fish, especially the wonderful salmon. They ate it raw, baked it over hot coals, and dried large quantities for their winter food supply. Other tribes came to Shasta Village to trade for salmon, which created wealth and respect for the Shasta tribe.

One day Coyote was dreaming of a delicious meal of salmon. His mouth watered at the thought of a nice freshly cooked, juicy salmon.

"I am so terribly hungry," he said to himself upon waking. "If I visit the Shasteans, maybe I can have a salmon dinner."

Coyote washed and brushed himself to look neat and clean, then started for Shasta Village with visions of fresh salmon swimming behind his eyes. He found the Shasteans at the dam hauling in big catches of salmon. They welcomed him and said that he could have all the fish he could catch and carry.

Hunger and greed caused Coyote to take more fish than was good for him. Finally, he lifted his big load onto his back and began his homeward journey, after thanking the Shasta Indians for their generosity.

Because his load was extra heavy and he still had a long way to go, Coyote soon tired.

"I think I had better rest for a while," he thought. "A short nap will do me good."

He stretched himself full length upon the ground, lying on his stomach, with his pack still on his back. While Coyote slept, swarms and swarms of Yellow Jackets dived down and scooped up his salmon. What was left were bare salmon bones.

Coyote waked very hungry. His first thought was how good a bite of salmon would taste at that moment. Still half-asleep, he turned his head and took a large bite. To his great surprise and anger, his mouth was full of fish bones! His salmon meat was gone. Coyote jumped up and down in a rage shouting, "Who has stolen my salmon? Who has stolen my salmon?"

Coyote searched the ground around him but could not locate any visible tracks. He decided to return to Shasta Village and ask his good friends there if he could have more salmon.

"Whatever happened to you?" they asked when they saw his pack of bare salmon bones.

"I was tired and decided to take a nap," replied Coyote. "While I slept, someone slightly stole all of the good salmon meat that you gave me. I feel very foolish to ask, but may I catch more fish at your dam?"

All of the friendly Shasteans invited him to spend the night and to fish with them in the morning. Again, Coyote caught salmon and made a second pack for his back and started homeward.

Strangely, Coyote tired at about the same place as he had on the day before. Again he stopped to rest, but he decided that he would not sleep today. With his eyes wide open, he saw swarms of hornets approaching. Because he never imagined they were the culprits who stole his salmon, he did nothing.

Quicker than he could blink his eyes, the Yellow Jackets again stripped the salmon meat from the bones and in a flash they disappeared!

Furious with himself, Coyote raged at the Yellow Jackets. Helpless, he ran back to Shasta Village, relating to his friends what he had seen with his own eyes. They listened to his story and they felt sorry for Coyote, losing his second batch of salmon.

"Please take a third pack of fish and go to the same place and rest. We will follow and hide in the bushes beside you and keep the Yellow Jackets from stealing your fish," responded the Shasta Indians.

Coyote departed carrying this third pack of salmon. The Shasteans followed and hid according to plan. While all were waiting, who should come along but Grandfather Turtle.

"Whoever asked you to come here?" said Coyote, annoyed at Grandfather Turtle's intrusion.

Turtle said nothing but just sat there by himself.

"Why did you come here to bother us," taunted Coyote. "We are waiting for the robber Yellow Jackets who stole two packs of salmon. We'll scare them away this time with all my Shasta friends surrounding this place. Why don't you go on your way?"

But Turtle was not bothered by Coyote; he continued to sit there and rest himself. Coyote again mocked Grandfather Turtle and became so involved with him that he was completely unaware when the Yellow Jackets returned. In a flash, they stripped the salmon bones of the delicious meat and flew away!

Coyote and the Shasta Indians were stunned for a moment. But in the next instant, they took off in hot pursuit of the Yellow Jackets. They ran and ran as fast as they could, soon exhausting themselves and dropping out of the race. Not Grandfather Turtle, who plodded steadily along, seeming to know exactly how and where to trail them.

Yellow Jackets, too, knew where they were going, as they flew in a straight line for the top of Mount Shasta. There they took the salmon into the center of the mountain through a hole in the top. Turtle saw where they went, and waited patiently for Coyote and the other stragglers to catch up to him. Finally, they all reached the top, where turtle showed them the hole through which the Yellow Jackets had disappeared.

Coyote directed all the good people to start a big fire on the top of Mount Shasta. They fanned the smoke into the top hole, thinking to smoke out the yellow jackets. But the culprits did not come out, because the smoke found other holes in the side of the mountain.

Frantically, Coyote and the Shasta Indians ran here, there, and everywhere, closing up the smaller smoke holes. They hoped to suffocate the Yellow Jackets within the mountain.

Furiously, they worked at their task while Grandfather Turtle crawled up to the very top of Mount Shasta. Gradually, he lifted himself onto the top hole and sat down, covering it completely with his massive shell, like a Mother Turtle sits on her nest. He succeeded in completely closing the top hole, so that no more smoke escaped.

Coyote and his friends closed all of the smaller holes.

"Surely the Yellow Jackets will soon be dead," said Coyote as he sat down to rest.

What is that rumbling noise, everyone questioned? Louder and louder the noise rumbled from deep within Mount Shasta. Closer and closer to the top came the rumble. Grandfather Turtle decided it was time for him to move from his hot seat.

Suddenly, a terrific explosion occurred within the mountain, spewing smoke, fire, and gravel everywhere!

Then to Coyote's delight, he saw his salmon miraculously pop out from the top hole of Mount Shasta—cooked and smoked, ready to eat!

Coyote, the Shasta Indians, and Grandfather Turtle sat down to a well-deserved meal of delicious salmon.

To this day, the Shasta Indian tribe likes to conclude this tale saying, "This is how volcanic eruptions began long, long ago on Mount Shasta."

Dixon, "The Origin of the Mount Shasta Eruptions," 27-29.

■

LAND OF THE GHOST DANCE
Shasta

■

Eagle, the supreme spirit of all flying creatures, wanted to create people. So he sent two children to earth, a boy and a girl. They created more children, and in time there were many, many people everywhere on earth. It seems that no one ever died. More and more people were created, and soon the world was becoming much too crowded.

Everyone pondered the question of what could be done about the crowded conditions on earth? Then a boy died! His people were very sad to lose him, and friends gathered to comfort the family of the lost boy. They said to each other, "Let us not die, let us not die!"

Buy Coyote replied, "People must die, people must die!"

Soon thereafter the parents buried the little boy. But in their hearts, they were disturbed about what Coyote kept saying. Now they secretly wished that Coyote's child might die. Perhaps then he would understand somewhat of how they felt about losing their son.

A few moons passed, when Coyote's child became ill and he died. Coyote wanted so much to bring him back to life. He even followed his child's spirit to the land where the Ghosts danced about a fire. There he watched the spectacular cavortings of the Ghosts dancing continuously, enjoying their frolic.

Coyote built his own fire of wild parsnips to attract his child's ghost. When the Ghost clan smelled the burning parsnips, they could not stand the aroma and gave Coyote's child back to him. They returned happily to their homeland.

On their way, Coyote was so very delighted to have his child with him. Coyote asked, "What wish would you like to have me grant you?"

"Father, for ten years you must never scold me," replied the child.

All was happiness for five years, no one scolded Coyote's child. Then someone forgot and scolded him, and he died a second time. Again

California Indian point
Shasta

Coyote went to the Land of the Ghost Dance. Again the Ghosts saw Coyote return and said, "Go back, go back to your home and return the day after tomorrow to see your child."

Joyous at the future prospect of seeing his child again, Coyote practically danced all the way home. Because he was tired from the excitement of his journey, Coyote lay down to rest when he reached his home. The very next day, his friends found Coyote dead in his own bed. Coyote's spirit returned for the third time to the Land of the Ghost Dance, and for the third time was welcomed by his child and the other dancing Ghosts.

Shasta Indians used to say that no one should follow the dead to the Land of the Ghost Dance, or soon they, too, would become a new Ghost in the Land of the Ghost Dance!

Gifford, *California Indian Nights' Entertainment.*

■

A SAN JOAQUIN VALLEY TALE
Mariposa

In the central part of California is a wide level plain about 300 miles long, extending southward from the Sacramento River. This area of about 20,000 square miles is walled in on three sides by the Sierra Nevada and the Coast Ranges.

At one time, the Mariposa Indian tribe occupied a large portion of this land. Today, only remnants of the tribe live along the western slope of the Sierras.

■

Long ago, a Mariposa tribesman named Soho lived in a pleasant canyon with his beautiful wife, Ule, whom he loved very, very much.

They made a comfortable home in a hillside cave with a thatched cover over their doorway. Soho covered the thatch and the doorway with animal hides to keep them warm in stormy weather.

Nearby, their fenced garden provided them with bountiful supplies of fresh fruits and vegetables. Beyond the fencing, their domestic animals roamed freely on good grazing land. Besides horses and a few cows, they had goats, rabbits, and even wild deer joined the herd occasionally, probably for protection from wild coyotes and foxes. Toward evening, the domestic animals gathered beneath the thatched shelter Soho had built for them. He was continually enlarging the sheds as the numbers of his stock increased.

The animals gave them a plentiful supply of meat and hides for their food and clothing. Members of other tribes stopped by to trade with Soho on their migrations north and south. Consequently, Soho and Ule were content with their home location and with the success they experienced with their crops, stock production, and trading. They agreed that they could not have been happier with their lives.

Suddenly, Soho's beautiful Ule became ill. Without any warning, she died. Soho's grief overwhelmed him. He felt very, very sad, crying aloud and wailing to himself. He could find little comfort in his daily living—even his friendly animals were neglected at the end of the day. He could neither eat nor sleep.

In despair, Soho walked to his wife's grave and lay there beside her mound for three days and three nights. During the fourth night while he was crying for his wife to come back to him, he noticed a very bright star directly overhead that spread light everywhere. What did it mean?

Then suddenly Soho felt the ground shake like an earthquake. The earth on top of his wife's grave moved! His wife arose from the grave! She stood and brushed sand and dirt from her clothing!

Soho stared at Ule in silence, because a Mariposa superstition claimed that one who speaks with a ghost will soon die. As Soho continued to stare speechless, Ule floated swiftly away toward Toxil, the place of the setting-sun. Soho ran in pursuit of her with tears of joy overflowing his eyes at seeing his wife again.

Ule turned and motioned Soho to go back, go back! She told him that she was going to Tib-ik-nict, the home of the dead—he must not follow her.

But for four days and four nights Solo pursued Ule, until they reached a large roaring river. She stepped onto a light bridge, fragile as a spider's web, and started to cross over.

Soho cried aloud and beckoned frantically for Ule to come back! She turned, stretching her hand toward him as a sign of comfort. He sprang forward onto the bridge, but she would not let him touch her. Together they crossed the long bridge where good spirits can cross easily. Bad spirits somehow unbalance the bridge and fall off into the water. Later, they turn into pike fish that must swim back to feed the living people.

At the far end of the bridge, Soho saw a warm, fruitful land with happy people from all parts of the world. They seemed to live peacefully together and there seemed to be plenty for everyone.

Ule told Soho to observe everything closely, because he must return to the Mariposa tribe and tell them all that he had experienced before he died on the fourth day.

She guided him back over the bridge and said good-bye, until his return. Soho ran fast to his home and reported to his tribe all that he had seen and heard. At the fourth sunrise, Soho's friends came to find him dead, as Ule had foretold. They wrapped his body in a cowhide and carried him to the sacred burial ground, placing him beside the mound where Ule had once lain.

Hudson, "Legend of the San Joaquin Valley," 104-105.

■

THE QUEEN OF DEATH VALLEY
Shoshone

"Ground Afire" is the meaning of the Indians' name for what is now known as Death Valley. "And in the height of summer there is no better name for this sun-tortured trench between blistered ranges. But when a group of forty-niners [1849] blundered into it, they renamed it Death Valley."

The valley and the high mountain ranges west and east of it are now called Death Valley National Monument. It is located in southeastern California and southwestern Nevada. Many square miles of the valley are below sea level—the lowest level in the Western Hemisphere.

More than 600 kinds of plants thrive in the valley. Its rocks make it a geologists' paradise. And for everyone, "the great charm of the area lies in its magnificent range of color, which varies from hour to hour."

■

Long, long ago, Indians used to say, this valley was beautiful and fertile. The people who lived there were ruled by a beautiful but capri-

Bear claw necklace
Shoshone

cious queen. One time she ordered them to build a mansion for her, one that would surpass any mansion ever built by their neighbors, the Aztecs.

For years, her people worked to make a palace that would please her. From places many miles away they dragged stones and logs. The queen, fearing that her age or an accident or an illness might prevent her from seeing her dream come true, ordered many of her people to assist in the work. Gradually, her tribe became a tribe of slaves.

The queen commanded even her own daughter to join those dragging logs and stones. When the noonday heat caused the workers to drag along slowly, with heads bowed, the queen strode angrily among them and lashed their naked backs.

Because royalty was sacred, the people did not complain. But when she struck her daughter, the girl turned, threw down her load of stone, and solemnly cursed her mother and her mother's kingdom. Then, overcome by heat and weariness, the girl sank to the ground and died.

In vain, the queen lamented and regretted. All nature seemed to punish her. The sun came out with blinding heat and light. Vegetation withered. Animals disappeared. Streams and wells dried up. At last the queen had to give up her life; she died with high fever. There was no one to soothe her last moments, for her people, too, were dead.

The mansion, half-completed, stands in the midst of this desolation. Sometimes it seems to rise into view of people at a distance, in the shifting mirage that plays along the horizon.

Skinner, *Myths and Legends of Our Own Lands*, vol. II, 259-260.

■

THE STORY OF CREATION

Diegueños

The Mission Indians of San Diego County, California, include the Diegueños of Yuman heritage and fragments of Shoshonean tribes related to people of Mexican Baja California. The Diegueños therefore have Aztec influences in their culture.

Though Mission Indians were converted long ago and civilized by Spanish friars, those teachings were not evident in the continuance of their early folklore, passed down from generation to generation. Cinon Duro, the last of long-ago chiefs of the Diegueños, related their traditions of very primitive people in the following legends to Constance Goddard Du Bois in the late 1890s.

■

When Tu-chai-pai made the world, the earth was the woman, the sky was the man. The sky came down upon the earth. The world in the beginning was a pure lake covered with tules. Tu-chai-pai and his younger brother, Yo-ko-mat-is, sat together, stooping far over, bowed down by the weight of the sky. The Maker said to his brother, "What am I going to do?"

"I do not know," said Yo-ko-mat-is.

"Let us go a little farther," said the Maker.

So they went a little farther and sat down to rest. "Now what am I going to do?" said Tu-chai-pai.

"I do not know, my brother."

All of this time the Maker knew what he was about to do, but he was asking his brother's help. Then he said, "We-hicht, we-hicht, we-hicht," three times. He took tobacco in his hand, and rubbed it fine and blew upon it three times. Every time he blew, the heavens rose higher above their heads.

Yonger brother did the same thing because the Maker asked him to do it. The heavens went higher and higher and so did the sky. Then they did it both together, "We-hicht, we-hicht, we-hicht," and both took tobacco, rubbed it, and puffed hard upon it, sending the sky so high it formed a concave arch.

Then they placed North, South, East, and West. Tu-chai-pai made a line upon the ground.

"Why do you make that line?" asked younger brother.

"I am making the line from East to West and name them so. Now you make a line from North to South."

Yo-ko-mat-is thought very hard. How would he arrange it? Then he drew a crossline from top to bottom. He named the top line North, and the bottom line South. Then he asked, "Why are we doing this?"

The Maker said, "I will tell you. Three or four men are coming from the East, and from the West three or four Indians are coming."

The brother asked, "Do four men come from the North, and two or three men come from the South?"

Tu-chai-pai said, "Yes. Now I am going to make hills and valleys and little hollows of water."

"Why are you making all of these things?"

The Maker explained, "After a while when men come and are walking back and forth in the world, they will need to drink water or they will die." He had already made the ocean, but he needed little water places for the people.

Then he made the forests and said, "After a while men will die of cold unless I make wood for them to burn. What are we going to do now?"

"I do not know," replied younger brother.

"We are going to dig in the ground and find mud to make the first people, the Indians." So he dug in the ground and took mud to make the first men, and after that the first women. He made the men easily, but he had much trouble making women. It took him a long time.

After the Indians, he made the Mexicans and finished all his making. He then called out very loudly, "People, you can never die and you can never get tired, so you can walk all the time." But then he made them sleep at night, to keep them from walking in the darkness. At last he told them that they must travel toward the East, where the sun's light was coming out for the first time.

The Indians then came out and searched for the light, and at last they found light and were exceedingly glad to see the Sun. The Maker called out to his brother, "It's time to make the Moon. You call out and make the Moon to shine, as I have made the Sun. Sometime the Moon will die. When it grows smaller and smaller, men will know it is going to die, and they must run races to try and keep up with the dying moon."

The villagers talked about the matter and they understood their part, and that Tu-chai-pai would be watching to see that they did what he wanted them to do. When the Maker completed all of this, he created nothing more. But he was always thinking how to make Earth and Sky better for all the Indians.

Du Bois, "The Story of Creation," 181-183.

Basket bowl
Diegueños

■

THE FLY AT THE COUNCIL

Diegueños

■

Another time, Tu-chai-pai thought to himself, "If all my sons do not have enough food and drink, what will become of them?" He thought about this for a long, long time and said, "Then they will surely die." He then thought, "What do my men want to do? I will give them three choices: to die now forever, or to live for a long time and then return to the heavens or to live forever."

When the Maker had finished his thinking, he called all men together, but none of the women. He said to the men, "I have been thinking, since there is not much food and water now, I want to know what you wish to do? Here are your three choices: to die forever, to live for a long time on Earth, or to live forever."

Some Indians replied, "We want to die forever"; some said, "We want to live for a time and then die"; others said, "We want to live forever." So they talked and talked in a Council meeting, for they did not know how to decide for everyone.

Then the fly arrived and said, "Oh, you men, what are you talking so much about? Tell the Maker you want to die forever." So the people talked and talked a long time and decided upon their choice: to die and be done with life forever.

This is the reason the fly rubs his hands together constantly, because he is begging forgiveness of the Indians for these fateful words of his.

Du Bois, "The Fly at the Council," 183.

■

THE IMPIETY OF FROG
Diegueños

■

When the moon had grown very little, all the Indian people were running races to keep up with the moon. At the end, the rabbit and the frog agreed to run a race together. The people watched and laughed loudly at the frog, because he had the shape of a man but wore no clothes. Frog became very angry at the Maker and said, "Because you did not make me well, you shall have to pay for my disgrace."

Now Tu-chai-pai had gone away to a very high place and fell asleep. Frog was down in a deep place shaking his fists in defiance of the Maker.

Suddenly the Sun appeared, and the maker came with it. He had a long stick pointed at both ends, which he held over his head. He reached down with it around the deep place and touched the back of the frog, where it left a long white mark.

By this time Frog had become so angry that he thought of a wrong deed to commit. He decided to spit poison into the water where Tu-chai-pai would drink. Thoughts of this evil deed by now had magically entered the Maker's heart, who said to himself, "I shall die." Some boys then came and told the Maker what the frog had done.

Tu-chai-pai told them, "I shall die with the Moon. Watch the Moon and when it becomes very small, then I will die." The boys watched and watched as the Moon grew smaller, and in six large stars, the Maker finished his life.

At that time, since all of the things on this Earth were the children of Tu-chai-pai, they too will die, sometime when the Moon seems right, according to the Maker of long, long ago.

Du Bois, "The Impiety of Frog," 183-184.

■

FIESTA TU-CHAI-PAI
Diegueños

■

As soon as the Indian villagers found that Tu-chai-pai was dead, all living things came together from the mountains and the valleys—all men and all animals—to mourn for him. The dove that lives here went away to seek her mate upon a high white mountain, and when she came back there was blood on her wings, the blood of her Maker.

Then the people went up on a high mountain and set two stone tablets—one facing East and one facing West. On these tablets were marked the number of days of the fiesta for Tu-chai-pai.

The men wished to bury him, and they made a great funeral pyre. They were about to set fire to it when Coyote appeared and would not agree to this, and the men gave in to him, because they were afraid of him. The villagers sent Coyote far to the East on an errand. He was far away when he saw a plume of smoke rising above the hills, and he came rushing back.

"What are you burning?" he asked.

"We are burning nothing," they told him.

Again the villagers sent Coyote far away toward the sunset. When he looked back, again he saw smoke. By then the people had finished burning the body—all but the heart. Coyote returned and found the Indian warriors standing shoulder to shoulder about the heart of their beloved Tu-chai-pai.

"I see what you are doing," said Coyote. "You are burning the heart." Suddenly, he sprang over the heads of the Indian men and seized the heart and fled to the mountains, where he devoured it. Ever since the Indians have hated Coyote for this dreadful trick he played upon them.

Yo-ko-mat-is, the younger brother, went far away to the West, but when the Indians pray to him for rain, he comes back every time, and their prayers are answered by the great spirits of himself and Tu-chai-pai.

Du Bois, "Fiesta Tu-Chai-Pai," 184-185.

■

THE ORIGIN OF YOSEMITE
Yosemite
(Miwok)

Long, long ago before the white man came to the West, a large happy tribe of peaceful Indians lived among the trees of beautiful Oak Canyon. This spectacular place is now known as Yosemite Valley, situated in Yosemite National Park, California.

In the beginning these peaceful Indians were called Ah-wah-nees, meaning "Deep Grass Valley," which was the first name given to Yosemite Valley.

It is of interest to note that because of a printer's error at a later date, the spelling of the tribe's name was inadvertently changed to Yosemite. Now Yosemite National Park identifies the original home of the Ah-wah-nee band (Yosemite), southern division of the Miwok Tribe.

Today, the California State flag carries a picture of the grizzly bear as a reminder of the State's official animal, Yo Semitee.

■

Ah-wah-nees were proud of their Chief, a tall and young athletic man. Early one spring morning, he started off with his spears in hand to hunt for trout in the nearby lake known as Sleeping Water.

Imagine his astonishment when he rounded a large boulder and came face to face with an enormous grizzly bear, probably just out of its winter hibernation!

Such an unexpected meeting caused both of them to rear back in stunned surprise. Immediately, however, all of the fighting spirit within each arose. They attacked one another furiously! The Chief realized his fighting power was not equal to the great strength of the grizzly.

"What can I do to help myself?" he wondered.

At that moment, he saw an oak limb within reach and grabbed it for a weapon.

"I must do everything possible to subdue this bear, even if it means my own death," he thought while he fought. "I am determined that future Ah-wah-nee children will always remember the proud and brave blood that flowed in the veins of their ancestors."

Mush paddle
Miwok

He pounded heavy blows, one after another, upon the head of the grizzly bear. In return, the young Chief received innumerable cuts from the bear's teeth and claws. They exchanged blows that could have been death blows to either one, if each had not been determined to survive. The grizzly bear's hunger drove him to attack; the Chief's pride, courage, and great height strengthened his defense.

On and on they fought. Then when the Chief saw the eyes of the bear glaze with a cold stare, he knew his great moment had come. With his club raised overhead, the Chief brought down a whopping smash upon the head of the bear, who then slowly slumped to the ground. The Chief charged in to finish the task, making sure the grizzly bear was dead.

Exhausted, the young Chief withdrew a short way to rest, but kept his eyes upon the grizzly bear in case it revived. After some time, when he was certain of the bear's death, the Chief stepped forward and skinned the animal.

Later, dragging the bearskin behind him, the Chief returned to his village and proclaimed his victory. Young and old braves gathered to welcome him and to praise his success. The young braves took off, following the trail where the bearskin dragged upon the ground. They found the grizzly bear before any other wild animal had a chance to claim it. Immediately, they set to work and butchered the bear and then carried the parts back to their camp.

In the meantime, the braves prepared a huge fire and sent young runners to the outlying camps, inviting all the people to an evening of feasting.

The victory of their young Chief over the enormous grizzly bear astounded all of the Ah-wah-nees. They cheered and cheered their admiration for their great Chief. They renamed their hero, Chief Yo Semitee, which means "Grizzly Bear."

Following the feast, the entire tribe gathered for a victory dance, attired in all their fine beads and fine feathers. Chief Yo Semitee sat and overlooked the celebration, smoking the peace pipe with his tribal council. More feasting and dancing continued most of the night, as Ah-wah-nees showed their affection for their young and strong Chief.

Yo Semitee's children, and finally all of the tribe, became known as Yo Semitees in honor of their brave Chief.

Hutchings, *In the Heart of the Sierras, the Yosemite Valley*, 58.

■

THE ORIGIN OF TU-TOK-A-NU-LA

Yosemite

(Miwok)

■

Two young and curious Indian boys, long ago, lived in Yosemite Valley. They were always exploring faraway places, climbing ledges where later they needed rescue, yet they continued their adventures.

One day, they came upon a new lake and decided to swim across to a large rock. When they reached the opposite shore, they climbed to the top of the huge rock to rest in the sunshine, but soon they fell asleep. On and on they slept through that night, the next, and the next night, until many moons had come and gone.

Can you imagine what happened to that rock? It kept right on growing and growing, rising higher and higher, until the faces of the two Indian boys brushed the sky.

Of course their families were distraught in the beginning, but finally gave up hope of ever seeing their two lost sons again.

Now it happened that many animals had heard from their ancestors about what had happened to the two lost Indian boys. At a council gathering of the animals, they were wondering how they could help bring the boys down as the huge rock had grown into a giant granite mountain.

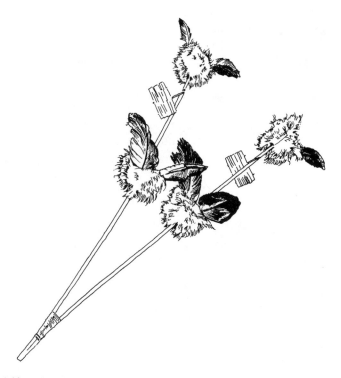

Ceremonial hairpins
Miwok

All of the animals decided to have a contest. Every creature would try to jump up to the mountain top. Poor little mouse only jumped a foot, larger rat leaped two feet, strong racoon much higher, grizzly bear made a mighty leap, but he was too heavy, mountain lion took a long run and jumped, but he fell down flat on his back. None could jump high enough.

Insignificant little measuring-worm came late to the contest. Everyone explained to him their predicament. None could leap high enough to the top of the mountain to rescue the two boys.

Measuring-worm decided to try. Step by step, inch by inch, little by little he began measuring his way up the granite wall that reached to the sky. He went so high that he was out of sight!

Up and up he crawled through many sleeps and through many moons, almost through a whole snow. Measuring-worm kept on crawling and at last reached the top of the giant mountain, whose magic somehow allowed the boys to remain boys!

What fun they experienced on the way down! Measuring-worm led them on a continuous, circuitous slide around and around the slippery snowy sides of the mighty mountain. They laughed and screamed with delight at the adventure they were having.

At last, measuring-worm and the two Indian boys were safe on the ground again. Their animal friends gathered to welcome them down from the sky, as well as the elders and braves of the Yosemite tribe.

From that day on to this, the great granite mountain has been called by the Indians *Tu-tok-a-nu-la*, which means "measuring-worm." Later, the Spaniards named the mountain El Capitan, a name that now appears on most maps of the Yosemite National Park.

Powers, *Tribes of California*, 366-367.

■

HOW HALF DOME WAS FORMED
Yosemite
(Miwok)

■

Tu-tok, Yosemite Spirit Chief, lived in his castle atop this highest mountain. He was the giver of all creature comforts to his people. He was giver of future enjoyment in the happy hunting grounds of Indian heaven. Tu-tok lived for all the Indians surrounded by the granite range of mountains. He kept vigilant watch that no foreign enemy should invade their homeland.

Long, long ago, when the children of the Sun lived in Yosemite Valley, all was happiness. Tu-tok sat high on his rocky throne overlooking the peaceful people and animals below.

He herded the wild deer and roused the sleeping bear so that the brave Yosemites might have a good hunt. He prayed to the Sky Chief for soft rain and warm sunshine to make the corn grow. He prayed that the harvest be rich for their womenfolk to gather.

When Tu-tok laughed, the winding river rippled with smiles. When he sighed, the wind swept sadly through the pines. When he spoke, the sound was like the deep voice of a roaring waterfall. When he smote the bear, his triumphant whoop rang out and echoed from mountaintop to mountaintop. His feet were swift. His eyes were strong and bright like the rising sun.

One morning a shining vision of the maiden Tis-sa appeared before the eyes of Tu-tok. She was the guardian angel of Yosemite Valley. He saw her sitting on the southern granite Dome, among the highest mountains. She was beautiful. On her shoulders rested two filmy, cloudlike wings.

"Tu-tok," she whispered. Then she vanished over the rounded granite Dome. With his eyes alert, his ears quick, his feet swift, he ran in pursuit. She had left a soft, downlike mist behind. His vision was blurred by it. He could not find her.

"Tis-sa! Tis-sa!" he called every morning as he leaped the stony crests in search of her. Every day he placed acorns and wild flowers upon her granite Dome. Sometimes he seemed to have a vision of her and saw her beautiful eyes. But never did he hear her voice. Never did he speak to her.

Tu-tok's love for Tis-sa grew so strong that he forgot the crops of the Yosemites. The rain did not fall. The corn drooped their heads. The wind whistled mournfully through the wild crops. The flowers lost their blooms. The bees stored no honey in the hollow trees. Green leaves turned brown.

Tu-tok saw none of these changes in the valley, because he was blinded by his love for Tis-sa. But she looked down with sad eyes upon the neglected valley below. Kneeling upon the gray granite Dome, she prayed to the Chief of the Sky spirits. She prayed that the flowers might be bright again; that the grasses and trees might be green again; that the corn might be ripe again.

Then a thundering sound like a giant earthquake split the Dome beneath her. Half the Dome disappeared. Melting snow from the High Sierra Mountains gushed through an opening made by the split. Rushing water, tumbling over rocks, formed a waterfall into Mirror Lake below. The lake overflowed into the beautiful Merced River winding through Yosemite Valley. All was changed!

Birds dipped their bodies into small pools. Fluttering from the water, they burst into songs of delight again. Moisture seeped silently into the parched earth. Flowers lifted their heads with fragrant gratitude. Corn gracefully stood upright. Sap ran upward into all the trees. But the maid, Tis-sa, vanished as strangely as she had first appeared. In memory of her, she left in the hearts of the Yosemites the beautiful falls, the quiet lake, the winding river, the Half Dome. The Yosemite tribe called it Tis-sa-ack.

When Tis-sa flew away, small downy feathers drifted from her shiny wings. Where they fell on the edge of the lake and in the meadows, you can see thousands of little white violets growing today. Some people say they hear whispers that he who sees a white violet and lovingly picks it with a kiss will have happy thoughts and pleasant dreams.

When Tu-tok was certain that Tis-sa was gone, he left his rocky mountain castle. He wandered everywhere in search of the one he loved. Before he left, however, he carved a bold outline of his head upon the rock, El Capitan, which bears his nobel tribal name, Tu-tok-ah-nu-lah.

There in stone, Tu-tok still guards the entrance to Yosemite Valley, which once he cared for tenderly. There the Yosemites remember him, though he wandered for many years. His search for Tis-sa ended without success. He returned alone to his mountaintop home, always looking expectantly toward Half Dome for Tis-sa.

Hutchings, *In the Heart of the Sierras, the Yosemite Valley*, 387.

■

BRIDAL VEIL FALL
Yosemite
(Miwok)

"Bridal Veil Fall's plume of mist seems to drop out of a lost world. The 620-foot cataract...wears a triple crown: Cathedral Rocks." The base of the fall is surrounded by trees and shrubs.

"The vast ravine of Yo Semitee, formed by tearing apart the solid Sierras, is graced by many waterfalls raining down the mile-high cliffs." The Indians used to tell this legend about the one called Bridal Veil Fall.

■

Hundreds of years ago, in the shelter of this valley, lived Tu-tok-a-nu-la and his tribe. He was a wise chief, trusted and loved by his people, always setting a good example by saving crops and game for winter.

While he was hunting one day, he saw the lovely guardian spirit of the valley for the first time. His people called her Ti-sa-yac. He thought her beautiful beyond his imagination. Her skin was white, her hair was golden, and her eyes were like heaven. Her voice, as sweet as the song of a thrush, led him to her. But when he stretched his arms toward her, she rose, lighter than a bird, and soon vanished in the sky.

From that moment, the Chief knew no peace, and he no longer cared for the well-being of his people.

Without his directions, Yo Semite became a desert. When Ti-sa-yac came again, after a long time, she wept because bushes were growing where corn had grown before, and bears rooted where the huts had been. On a mighty dome of rock, she knelt and prayed to the Great Spirit Above, asking him to restore its virtue to the land.

He granted her plea. Stooping from the sky, the Great Spirit Above spread new life of green on all the valley floor. And smiting the mountains, he broke a channel for the pent-up snow that soon melted. The water ran and leaped far down, pooling in a lake below and flowing off to gladden other land.

The birds returned with their songs, the flowering plants returned with their blossoms, and the corn soon swayed in the breeze. When the Yo Semitee people came back to their valley, they gave the name of Ti-sa-yac to what is now called South Dome. That is where she had knelt.

Then the Chief came home again. When he heard what the beautiful spirit maiden had done, his love for her became stronger than ever. Climbing to the crest of a rock that rises three thousand feet above the valley, he carved his likeness there with his hunting knife. He wanted his tribe to remember him after he departed from the earth.

Tired from his work, he sat at the foot of Bridal Veil Fall. Suddenly he saw a rainbow arching over the figure of Ti-sa-yac, who was shining

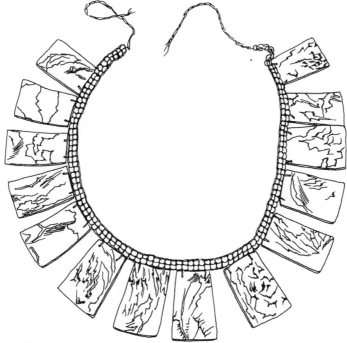

Abalone necklace
Miwok

from the water. She smiled at him and beckoned to him. With a cry of joy, he sprang into the waterfall and disappeared with his beloved.

The rainbow quivered on the falling water, and the sun went down.

Skinner, *Myths and Legends of Our Own Lands*, vol. II, 259-260.

■

LEAPING FROG ROCKS
Yosemite
(Miwok)

Long ago, the Yosemites named the three peaks outlined against the north ridge the Leaping Frog Rocks. Yosemites called them Kom-po-pai-ses, because they look like three frogs sitting on their haunches, ready to spring. Today in Yosemite National Park you can still see the same formation.

■

The last great chief of the Yosemites was Chief Ten-a-ya. Constantly he watched from his hideaway mountain lodge, and saw strange white horsemen riding from across the plains to the West.

Often he remembered what the Old Chief his father had said, "Obey my word, Ten-a-ya, and your people shall be as many as the blades of grass. No enemy tribe shall ever dare to bring war into Yosemite Valley.

"But beware, my son, of the white horsemen coming from across the plains beyond. If once they cross the western mountains, your tribe will scatter as the dust before the desert wind. Then the Yosemites will never be the same again.

"Guard your stronghold, Ten-a-ya my son, lest you be the last of the great Chiefs of the Yosemites."

The Old Chief, trembling, had raised his peace pipe above his head and prayed, "Great Spirit Above, be good to my son, Ten-a-ya, Young Chief of the Yosemites."

To the four points of the compass, he turned and prayed:

"To the pines of the north, cold Wind treat him kindly.

"To the rising Sun of the east, Great Sun shine upon his lodge early in the morning.

"To the place where the Sun goes in winter, south wind bless my son, Ten-a-ya.

Cane whistle
Miwok

"To the land of the Setting Sun in the west, tenderly carry on the breezes a gentle sleep for him.

"Lowering my pipe I say to you, kind Mother Earth, when you receive my son into your warm bosom, hold him gently forever.

"Let the howl of the coyote, the roar of the bear and the mountain lion, and the sound of the wind swaying the tops of the tall pine trees, be to him a sweet lullaby."

As he remembered the Old Chief's words, Ten-a-ya guarded his mountain retreat like a mother-bear protects her young cub. With great anxiety day after day, he saw the white horsemen coming nearer and nearer from across the plains.

Ten-a-ya watched them take the land that the Great Spirit had made for the Yosemites and the other tribes. Ten-a-ya watched the white men burrow into the earth like moles. He watched them wash the sands and rocks of the rivers, searching for something yellow and shiny. They pastured their cattle upon the sacred hunting grounds of the Yosemites.

Ten-a-ya heard of the strangers stealing Yosemite women and girls for their wives. Nearer and nearer they made their camps, stealing Yosemite supplies.

Because Ten-a-ya was young and strong, he did not fear the white men. In his heart, he hated them for their disregard of what the Great Spirit had created for the Yosemites. Sometimes at night, Ten-a-ya and his braves drove away the white men's horses or killed them for food in place of their own natural game which supply was stolen by the white men.

A feeling of defiance against the white man's encroachment grew among the Yosemite braves. Ten-a-ya grew older with time. White horsemen increased in numbers, arriving at the very walls of Yosemite Valley. Again Ten-a-ya recalled his dying father's words, and Ten-a-ya knew the evil day was drawing near.

The white men climbed the western mountains. They offered gifts in the name of their White Father in Washington, and then made Ten-a-ya their captive. Young Yosemite braves fled from their camps, crossing the North Dome to the camp of the Mono Indians. They were young and could hunt far for food to supply their families. They refused to be herded like cattle in the white man's camp.

Though a captive, in spirit Chief Ten-a-ya remained strong. With native cunning, he watched for a chance and escaped to his mountain stronghold. More and more in his heart, he was growing a strong hatred for the white man.

The children of the Yosemites scattered. They were unable to rally again around Chief Ten-a-ya, because the white horsemen pursued him into his mountain retreat. Day and night, signal fires burned upon the mountaintops.

When messengers from the White Father entered Yosemite Valley, they found it deserted. But five dark figures darted from trees to rocks at the base of the jagged spur of the northern rock wall of Yosemite Valley.

A swollen river lay between the enemy and the five Indian scouts. With this protection, the scouts came into the open and taunted the white strangers. Then the scouts disappeared up the mountain, leaving no trail visible for white men to follow. Later, however, false promises induced the five scouts to come again to the white men's camp. Three of the scouts were sons of Ten-a-ya.

One brother was killed when he became a hostage. Another brother escaped only because of the bad aim of a white stranger.

When Ten-a-ya realized that it was useless to resist further, he surrendered to the messengers of the White Father in Washington. They had stolen his lands and his families, and they would not let the Yosemites live in peace in their homeland.

Ten-a-ya came down the mountain by his secret path from Le-ham-i-te, the canyon of the Arrowwood. His first sight was that of his oldest son's dead body. He spoke no word. That night he secretly carried the young chief's body to a sacred burial place.

Angered at the loss of his son, once more Ten-a-ya tried to escape and gather his tribe together, but he was captured a second time. In grief, he turned his bare chest toward his captors and cried:

"Kill me, White Chief, kill me as you have killed my sons and my people. You have brought sorrow to my heart and to the Yosemites. Kill me—and when I am dead, my spirit will rise up and call the spirits of our dead Yosemites to avenge the deaths you have caused. Our spirits will follow your footsteps forever.

"You will not see me or other Yosemites, but we will follow you wherever you go. You will know it is the spirit of Ten-a-ya and his people. You will come to fear us. Someday you will be sorry. This message is from our Great Spirit Above."

Ten-a-ya's prophecy came true. When the white men crossed the western mountains they encountered many problems and hardships because they had not made friends with the native people in the beginning. Yosemites scattered and never came together again as a tribe. Ten-a-ya was the last great Chief of the Yosemites.

Because the three sons of Ten-a-ya were captured at the base of the northern mountain wall, the three peaks were named to honor the "Three Brothers." Because their posture still resembles the "Three Leaping Frogs," they are also called Kom-po-pai-ses.

Smith, *Yosemite Legends*, 57-64.

■

THE LEGEND OF THE GEYSERS
Ashochimi
(Pomo-Wappo)

Long, long ago, the peaceful Ashochimi Indian tribe inhabited a rich and luxuriant valley on both sides of a river, now known as the Russian River north of San Francisco.

With ample hunting and fishing, with crops of wild clover, wild oats, acorns, roots, and berries, they lived a happy and contented life of abundance—until Spaniards and Mexicans arrived, establishing their settlements.

The Ashochimis were compelled to hunt for adequate game farther and farther away from their homeland, because their traditional hunting grounds were overtaken by the intruders.

■

One day, Guavo and Kolo, two young Ashochimi hunters, caught sight of an unusually large grizzly bear. They shot their barbed arrows into the monstrous animal's side. The bear dropped instantly as if dead. But the hunters knew the tricks of the grizzly, that he would fall to the ground at the slightest wound, pretending he was dead.

Again the young hunters fired their flint-headed arrows and struck the bear. With four arrows in him, the grizzly got to his feet and staggered into the underbrush, leaving a trail of blood.

Guavo and Kolo pursued at a safe distance, with their arrows ready. They knew it would be only a matter of time until they could claim their prize.

Up the canyon, the grizzly bear led the two young hunters, pausing occasionally to rest. Guavo and Kolo were amazed at its strength, as mile after mile the bear struggled on, never wavering from its direct course through the canyon.

Most of the way was timbered with low chaparral, but, suddenly, ahead the hunters saw an open grassy spot where the grizzly bear came to a halt. To Guavo and Kolo the animal seemed to writhe in pain. They let out a victory whoop at the sight of their dying quarry. But the startled grizzly bear gave forth one more life-effort as he plunged forward into a ravine below.

Elkhorn dagger
Pomo

Guavo and Kolo ran to the edge of the cliff, where they saw the lifeless body of the grizzly at the bottom of the gorge. At first in their excitement, they did not notice hundreds of minute jets of steam coming out of the hillside. They did not at first hear the hoarse rushing sound that filled the canyon with a continuous noise.

Guavo and Kolo ran to the dead grizzly. They halted in amazement when they suddenly realized they were on the brink of a "witches' cauldron" in the midst of seething steam spouts. They wondered if the geysers had been there before the grizzly bear died.

They took one horrified look at the steaming hillsides, they took one breath of the sulfurous vapor, they took one terrified glance at the trembling earth beneath them. Scared, Guavo and Kolo ran as fast as they could back to their village.

Chief Asho and his council listened skeptically as the two young hunters told their story:

"After the grizzly bear died, the ground began to smoke," said Guavo.

"Water boiled and bubbled without fire," said Kolo.

"Everywhere steam came out of holes in the ground," said Guavo.

"Choking smells came from the steam," said Kolo.

"Where we stood, the ground shook and trembled," said Guavo.

Because the two young hunters were known among their tribe to be truthful, Chief Asho said, "Take twenty young braves with you and show them the way to the place you have told us about."

All was true. There lay the dead grizzly bear beside the black, bubbling, steaming water.

"The grizzly's evil spirit brought forth the strange hot steam to heal his wounds," declared the tribal Medicine Man. "Before he died, the bear must have known this to be his healing place."

They skinned the bear and cut up parts of the meat for all of the braves to carry back to their tribe. Guavo and Kolo were awarded the skin as their prize, and the tribe prepared a huge fire to roast the bear meat for a feast.

Medicine Man thought the healing steam jets might help their sick people. He led the tribal men and built platforms over the steaming area, then placed their invalids upon them.

But that night, strange sounds arose in the darkness and the earth trembled violently. Medicine Man remembered stories of evil spirits within grizzly bears, and became concerned that those evil spirits were trying to take charge of the geysers.

"All is not good," he warned his people. "Go back to your village and stay there."

Soon thereafter, a strange plague appeared among the tribal men.

"We must help the sick and dying," said Medicine Man. "But I am afraid for you to return to the medicinal springs, because the angry bear's spirit has caused this pestilence."

Finally, a gray-haired, beloved Ashochimi sculptor appeared before Chief Asho.

"With my special tools, I can carve a stone guardian high above the canyon, whose good spirit will appease any angry spirits below," he said as he pleaded for permission.

"Go ahead. We anxiously await the completion of your stone guardian," replied Chief Asho.

Day after day the old sculptor worked alone. He chiseled at the hard rock until it resembled a human face. Each day he carved from dawn until the light of day was nearly gone. The people watched from a distance, eagerly awaiting the time when they could return for healing at the geysers.

"Only one more day of work on the rocky head," announced the old sculptor. But that evening he did not return to the village. A terrible earthquake occurred, toppling many cliffs, and it continued shaking throughout the night.   .

When the sun arose the next morning, the old sculptor had disappeared; however, the stone face on the great rock was finished and stood alone above the geysers. New springs jetted forth everywere farther down the river. Medicine Man led the men of the tribe to examine the new springs.

"It is safe now," Medicine Man announced bowing reverently toward the stone guardian of the canyon. "Let us build new platforms of willow boughs and bring the sick."

This they did. Steam vapors encircled and healed the invalids of the Ashochimi tribe miraculously. All the people rejoiced at the blessing of good health.

There above them, they were always mindful of the sculptured stone face that guarded all Indians from the wrathful spirit of the dead grizzly bear. They also were mindful of their loving sculptor who gave his life in sacrifice.

Guavo and Kolo were accorded special places of honor among the young braves of their tribe for their discovery of the geysers.

Powers, *Tribes of California*, 200-203.

■

BEFORE THIS LAND

Luiseño

Another tribe of Mission Indians in San Diego County of California are the Luiseños, who derive their name from the San Luis Rey Mission established in about 1770 by the Franciscan Junipero Serra. Many cultural similarities existed between them and the Dieguenos. Under American rule in 1846, the Indians were driven deeper into desert and mountain country, far back from the ocean.

Today, descendants of those first Luiseños still thrive on their reservation in San Diego County.

■

Long, long ago, the Luiseño Indian tribe lived at the ocean side, by the setting-sun. They loved their life there, feeding on the many seafood available with little effort. Their life was leisurely, crops were plentiful, all seemed serene and their tribe prospered.

The Luiseños worshiped their Great Spirit, the Sun-God. Always they did what was commanded of them by the Great Spirit. Their tribal leader and war-god, Uu-yot, was responsible to the Sun-God for the

Basket
Luiseño

welfare of his people. Luiseños were loyal and obedient to both Uu-yot and the Sun-God.

One day, Sun-God willed the Luiseños to move eastward and settle in the land of the rising-sun. Many boats were made by the young braves, and the Luiseño tribe began their voyage to find a new home. Uu-yot led the fleet eastward through heavy mist and fog up the San Luis River.

To help keep the boats together, the Luiseños sang their sacred songs to each other while they traveled. At last they reached a beautiful canyon area with wide meadows and woods on either side of the river. They camped and rested, finding the land good. Plenty of acorns from the nearby oak trees were on the ground, providing their favorite dish of *weewish*, a kind of mush made by grinding acorn pulp in a stone metate. Weewish made delicious patty-cakes cooked over a fire or on hot rocks. Besides, the tribal children were kept busy collecting acorns for storage, a good winter food supply.

After several days of rest at this natural homelike campground, Uu-yot declared this to be a good homeland for them to settle upon permanently. All the Luiseños were happy, and agreed. Immediately, the people set to work establishing their family homes, creating a village.

That very evening the entire tribe gathered around a large campfire and participated in a tribal thanksgiving ceremonial led by Uu-yot. A large feast followed, which was prepared by the women of the tribe in gratitude for their new land. Much dancing and singing continued into the night, a "home-warming" affair.

On the following days, garden land was prepared by young braves. Corn and root seeds were planted by all the families for a community garden. Others hunted for wild rabbits, deer, and other small game, as well as fishing the river for food supplies. Uu-yot gave thanks each day to sun-God for the many blessings bestowed upon his tribe, the Luiseños.

Later and without warning, a period of darkness and storms descended upon the area, with sharp lightning flashes and roaring crashes of thunder. Torrential rains fell upon the land. The river overflowed, creating a dangerous situation for the tribe. Uu-yot led his people to higher ground and all were saved. They prayed to the Great Spirit to quiet the forces of nature that again they might live in peace and safety.

Uu-yot gathered his tribesmen to smoke the sacred tobacco in the ceremonial circle, appeasing the Great Spirit and his gods of wrath.

Soon thereafter, a thin line of light broke overhead through the black ominous sky and moved eastward. Next morning, out of the east, the Sun arose again, spreading widely its light, life, and warmth. The Luiseños were grateful and returned to their homes to clean up the debris left by the storm.

Jones, *So Say the Indians*, 26-27.

■

TALES OF LAKE TAHOE
Washo

Tah-hoe (Tä'-ho') is some Indians' pronunciation of their name for the beautiful lake that forms twenty-one miles of the boundary between California and Nevada. Mark Twain wrote of it when he was there: "We plodded on, and at last the lake burst upon us, a noble sheet of blue water...walled in by a rim of snow-clad peaks that towered aloft full 3,000 feet higher still."

The cave mentioned in the second story is on the shore near present-day Glenbrook, Nevada.

■

Long, long ago, our people used to say, Lake Tahoe was the home of the water babies. If they wanted to cross the lake or fish in the lake, they had to prepare by making a basket sealed well with pitch. In it, they put corn, bread, and pine nuts. After each basket was full, the owners would put the cover on it and sink it in the lake.

By doing this, they believed that the water babies helped them to get across safely and to have luck while fishing. But if they didn't take a basket of food, they believed that the water babies would become very angry. Sometimes people did not return from their trips because they were drowned by the will of the water babies.

In Lake Tahoe stood a tall pine tree with a mass of large branches at its top. In these branches was the nest of an enormous bird that ate human beings. The bird's winter home was a cave on the east shore of the lake.

One day it carried a man into its nest and left him sitting there while it ate. The man covered his head with his blanket made of rabbit skin and peered out through the holes in it. Each time the giant bird took a bite, the man could see into its huge mouth and down into its gullet. He threw an arrowpoint into the bird's mouth, and the bird swallowed it along with the meat it was chewing The arrowpoint was made from some kind of volcanic rock that is poisonous.

Repeatedly, the man threw an arrowpoint into the bird's mouth. Soon it began to tremble, and in a short time it died from the poison of the arrowpoints.

Then the man cut off the bird's wings and tied them together. He climbed down the tree, placed the huge wings on the water like a boat, and sat on them. The wind soon after carried him to the other shore of Lake Tahoe.

Powers, *Tribes of California*, 388.

Curtis, *The North American Indian*, vol. XV, 150-151.

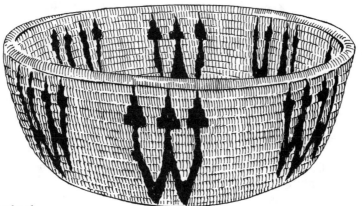

Basket bowl
Washo

■

THE LEGEND OF THE FIRST PEARL FISH HOOK
Hawaii

Grandmothers of long ago passed along stories of the old ways of the Hawaiian Islands. As with other people living close to the earth and relying upon the resources of land and sea, Hawaiians were continually aware of the creative forces, including gods and goddesses, in their daily living. To these they turned for blessings and ceremonials of thanksgiving.

■

Here is one of these legends, as recited by a wise storyteller:

Ka'eha was a fisherman of Kona on Hawaii. He stood beside his dying father, his heart heavy with sorrow. The old man opened his eyes and spoke: "Do not be sad, my son. I have lived long, and my time has come to die. Throw my bones into the sea, and the gods will give you a good gift."

Ka'eha obeyed his father's dying words. When he returned to the place where he had thrown the bones, he found them gone. He looked carefully for the gift his father had promised and found a shell of pearl. He took it up and looked long at its beauty. Then he separated the halves and tossed one to the sea. From the other he carved an *aku* hook.

That was the first pearl *aku* hook and it proved a good gift indeed. It was a sacred hook which seemed to call these fish. With it Ka'eha became a great fisherman, and his fame went all about these islands.

One day when he was fishing, a great *aku* leaped from the sea. It took the hook, and Ka'eha pulled with all his strength, eager to land that great fish. But his line broke, and the *aku* swam away carrying the sacred hook.

For days Ka'eha was filled with sadness. Then hope came. Perhaps some other fisherman had caught that fish and found the hook! He journeyed all about Hawaii, but heard nothing of the hook that he had lost.

Finally he went to other islands, but had no news until he came to windward Oahu. There, as he paddled near the shore, he saw white-capped terns dipping and circling over a house just as they dip and circle over a school of *aku*. "My hook is there!" he thought, and beached his canoe.

"These are the houses of a chief," he was told.

"Then I shall visit him," Ka'eha thought, for he too was of chiefly family.

He was made welcome and stayed for many days. Always the white-capped birds circled and dipped above the house where fishing gear was kept. But nothing was said of *aku* fishing. Ka'eha heard nothing of a sacred hook. "Perhaps the chief does not know its powers," he thought. "If only he would go *aku* fishing!"

But something very different happened. Ka'eha married the chief's daughter and settled down as son-in-law of the chief. Had he forgotten the pearl hook? Much time passed.

Then one day the chief said, "Tomorrow, O Ka'eha, my men go *aku* fishing with Kaneiki, my son. I have heard that you too are a fisherman. Will you go?"

All the young man's longing for his sacred hook returned, but he answered quietly, "Yes, I will go."

"Good!" said the chief. "Then tomorrow you shall be head fisherman. Be ready at the rising of the morning star."

But Ka'eha thought, "I must make sure that we take the sacred hook. He did not rise before dawn, but lay upon his mats, waiting.

"Ka'eha!" He heard the voice of Kaneiki outside his sleeping house. His brother-in-law was ready to start. He had a hook. That Ka'eha knew. Ka'eha knew also that this was not the sacred hook, so he lay as if still sleeping.

"Ka'eha!" The call came again. Kaneiki was angry that the young man was not ready and chanted:

> The paddles make a rattling sound
> And the bails of the fishermen too,
> O Crab Claws!

The name Crab Claws angered Ka'eha, for it meant one who talks much and does nothing. However, he did not show his anger, but chanted quietly:

> A white shell is the hook of Kaneiki,
> A lifeless thing, a lifeless thing to use.
> Where is the many-colored hook?
> Take that worthless hook back to your father.
>   Kaneiki.

The brother-in-law looked at the white shell in his hand. "Ka'eha lies in his sleeping house," he thought. How does he know what shell I have? He must be very wise." And Kaneiki went to get another hook.

"Come now!" Ka'eha heard the call once more. "I have a good hook for you."

But Ka'eha knew that this still was not his sacred hook. "It is useless!" he called in answer. "Only the many-colored hook will catch *aku* today."

Again and again this happened. Kaneiki could find no hook that pleased his brother-in-law, and at last the chief's hook bowl was empty. What should he do? Suddenly he remembered a hook found some time ago in the stomach of a big fish. The chief had stuck that hook in the thatch of the house where fishing gear was kept. "It is an old and useless hook," he had said.

"That is the only hook left," Kaneiki thought. "I shall take it."

Ka'eha met him at the door of his sleeping house. "That is the one!" he cried, taking the hook. Tears came to his eyes as he looked at this gift from his father and the gods. He put it carefully into a small gourd box which he wore on a cord about his neck. "Today we shall have good fortune in our fishing," he said. "Let us go."

They reached the landing place. "Remember, I am head fisherman," Ka'eha said. "We shall take this double canoe, and the paddlers must be strong men able to save it if it swamps."

The men listened with wonder. Of course they were good paddlers! But the sky was clear, and there was no sign of storm. Soon the canoe was launched, and the men paddled fast. Others had gone *aku*-fishing when first the morning star arose. Those early ones must not get all the fish!

"Look!" someone cried. "There are the other canoes! There the birds circle and dip. Let us paddle swiftly! Any moment the great fish may sound!" They paddled with all their might.

"Here!" called Kaneiki. "We are among the *aku*."

"Paddle farther," Ka'eha commanded, and the men turned to stare at him.

"The fish are here," repeated Kaneiki.

"Today, I am head fisherman," Ka'eha reminded him. "Paddle farther out."

Wondering greatly, the men obeyed. On and on they paddled until Oahu was only a dim gray line upon the ocean. "This is the place," Ka'eha said at last.

The others looked about. No white-capped birds! No *aku*! Again they stared at Ka'eha. What was he thinking of?

"Listen to my commands," the young man said. "Turn the canoe and paddle toward the shore. Paddle with all your might. Do not once look back. When I shout, leap into the sea."

Wondering greatly, the men obeyed. They did not see Ka'eha take the sacred fishhook from his gourd, but they heard the rush of *aku* following the canoe. They felt them splash into it. They felt the canoe sinking beneath the weight of fish. "Leap overboard!" They heard Ka'eha's shout, and leaped into the ocean, just as the canoe filled and swamped.

The paddlers were strong men, at home in the sea. They splashed the water from the canoe and bailed. Wondering greatly, they scrambled in once more. They had no fish, for Ka'eha had put the sacred hook back into its box, and the *aku* had all swum away. Silently the men paddled toward the shore.

As they came near Oahu and could see the breaking surf, Ka'eha repeated his commands: "Paddle toward shore with all your strength. Do not once look back. When I shout, be ready to leap into the sea." Again the rush and splash of *aku*! Again, the men leaped from the swamping boat. Again they emptied the canoe, then paddled toward the reef.

When they were over the reef, Ka'eha spoke once more. "Paddle steadily," he said. "Here I shall fish."

Again the men stared in wonder, and Kaneiki said, "It is useless to fish here. It is true that small fish swim over the reef, but not the great *aku*. To fish for *aku* here is useless, O Ka'eha!"

"Today I am head fisherman," the young man told them once again. "Paddle over the reef without looking back. Be ready to leap when I call to you." He took out his sacred hook and watched as the *aku* came rushing through the shallow water to splash into the canoe. "Leap quickly!" he shouted to the men as he put away his hook.

The paddlers leaped into the water just in time to prevent their boat's sinking to the coral. They waded to the beach, pushing the full canoe. The chief came, and a great crowd of servants and common people. All stared in wonder at the huge, silvery fish. "Never have I seen such a catch!" the chief exclaimed.

"Let these fish be shared," Ka'eha said. "This is my last command. Let the chief feast, and let common men feast also. This is a great day, for my sacred *aku* hook has returned to me." He took just two fish—one for his wife and one to offer in the *heiau* to the spirit of his father.

A long moment of silence told the master the deep interest of those who listened. At last Malu took out the pearl hook which Aukai had given him. He took it from an inner fold of his *malo* where he had kept it close to his body and very safe. "What of this, O master?" he asked.

"Ka'eha found a pearl shell. Do you remember? One part he returned to the sea. From that came many hooks, and this is one. This hook has been in my family for years. It brings good fortune in *aku* fishing. I have no son and give the hook to you, O Malu. Some day you will be head fisherman."

Malu could not speak, but Aukai knew his joy in the gift.

The good time went on—hula, riddles, games. When at last the guests went home, no one was empty-handed. Each had a bundle of food as well as some other gift. This had been a day of sharing, a happy memory for everyone, and for Keao and Malu a time never to be forgotten.

Caroline Curtis, *Life in Old Hawaii.*

■

THE HULA SCHOOL
Hawaii

Much of the information and customs of the ancient Hawaiian people have been absorbed by more modern influences. However, through their stories told from one generation to the next, we are able to glimpse the interests of boys and girls growing up in those times. This story of the Hula School is a good example of learning that brought happiness to the participants, and enjoyment to others, as Hula Teams displayed their skills and talents to larger groups.

■

Laka, Goddess of the Hula

Keao and 'Ilima were watching children playing in the sand. Suddently 'Ilima spoke. "I was playing in the sand that way when I heard the call of drums. It was long ago, and I was very small, but the call of the drums drew me as a fisherman draws in the fish. I ran. People were crowded together watching something. I slipped through the crowd to see. You know how a child can slip in where there seems to be no room.

"It was a hula. Men and women were dancing to the beat of drums. There was my grandmother—my own dear grandmother. Perhaps I had seen the hula before. I do not know. But this one I remember; the dancers with moving arms and swirling *pa'u*, the shine of sunlight on leis and bracelets, the tinkle of anklets, and Grandmother softly tapping the drum with her finger tips.

"That night I crawled into her lap. 'Teach me, Grandmother,' I said. 'I want to be a dancer.'

"She did teach me in the years that followed. There is much a child can learn. She said, 'I am too old and heavy to dance and gesture,' but she was not. To me she was beautiful.

"'What are you seeing, Grandmother?' I asked one day. She was looking beyond me, and I turned to look. Only breadfruit trees touched by the wind. "What are you seeing!' I asked again.

"'Laka, my goddess.'

"'Where!' My eyes searched the breadfruit grove.

"'In my mind, Grandchild. I see her as I once saw her in the forest.' Then Grandmother told me about Laka, godess of the hula. 'She is also the goddess of the wild plants which grow in the forest.'

"'She is my goddess,' I said. Every day I prayed to her. Whenever women went to the forest I went with them. I looked for Laka everywhere.

"'Some day you will see her.' Grandmother told me.

"One day I was in the lower forest helping women who were gathering berries to make dye. Rain came, and the women ran into a cave, but I stayed to watch the rain. It was only a light, misty rain. Sunshine sparkled on it and made a rainbow. Then I saw her!" 'Ilima's voice was almost a whisper, and Keao leaned close to listen. "Her *pa'u* was swirling mist. Her anklets were shiny raindrops. She was dancing a hula I did not know. Oh, Keao, I cannot tell you how lovely she was, how graceful!

"Then the misty rain was gone, and the women called me to gather berries. Laka was gone too, but the memory of her is still clear in my mind.

"That night I told Grandmother. 'She has chosen you, 'Ilima, Grandmother said earnestly. You are to be a hula dancer.' After that I worked harder than ever to learn the chants and gestures.

"'When can I train with a hula group?' I asked.

"'We shall ask Wahi.'

"But Wahi, the hula master, said I was too young. 'The training of the *halau* is very hard. You know that,' he said to Grandmother. 'Wait until your grandchild is older and stronger.'

"We have waited. It is three years since Wahi taught the hula in this district. Grandmother has heard that he will come this year. If only he will take me!" Keao saw the longing in her friend's eyes. She heard the longing in her voice. She did not answer, but in her heart she prayed.

A few days passed. Then 'Ilima found Keao making ready to beat *kapa*. Keao jumped up when she saw her friend, for "Ilima's eyes were shining. "Wahi has chosen you!" she cried. "I knew he would. I prayed."

"Can you come, Keao? I have something for you to see."

Keao looked at the bark and *kapa* beater. She did not like to leave her work. But Ana, her mother, said, "Go, Keao. This is a great day for 'Ilima. When she enters the *halau* you two cannot be together. Go with her today."

'Ilima took her friend's hand and urged her along the beach to the place where an old woman sitting under a *hau* tree was braiding sennit. Her hair was white and her face wrinkled, but shining with happiness. "'Ilima has told you," she said.

"I didn't have to tell," 'Ilima answered. "She knew by just looking at me. May I show her—you know what, Grandmother?"

The old woman took a *kapa*-wrapped bundle from the top of her *pa'u*. The girls were on their knees beside her as 'Ilima unwrapped the bundle. "Shells!" Keao exclaimed. "Such beautiful red-striped shells and all the same size! I have never seen shells like those, 'Ilima."

"They are anklets. See. They are strung on coconut fiber. Tell Keao about them, Grandmother."

"You know that I was a hula dancer, Keao," the old woman began. "Once the troupe I was in danced before a visiting chiefess. I danced one hula alone to the rhythm of sharkskin drums. When I had finished, the chiefess said, 'That is a hula dear to my heart, for it is like sunshine on rippling water. Here is something for you to wear next time you dance,' and she gave me these rare shells.

"They were my dearest treasure, and I wore them many times. When I was too old and heavy to dance and gesture I learned to play the instruments. Now I am very old.

"Yesterday Wahi said, 'The grandchild should have bracelets or anklets that have been used before. Have you something you have worn, something that will give her the blessing of our goddess?'

"So I brought out these shells. They are 'Ilima's now for she is my dearest treasure."

The two young women looked thoughtfully at the anklets and Keao said, "The sunlight shines on them as it shines on a lei of feathers. The color glows."

Grandmother put the shells away. "Until tomorrow," 'Ilima whispered. Then she added, "Tell us about the *halau* Grandmother. Tell us what Kanoe is doing."

"An altar will be built in the *halau*," the grandmother explained, "an altar to Laka. Kanoe was the one chosen to get branches for the altar as well as vines and flowers to trim it. He went into the forest at dawn and as he went he prayed. His work is sacred. It must be done in silence and with prayer. Tell Keao what he must gather, Grandchild."

"He is getting *koa* branches." 'Ilima was speaking now. Her eyes seemed to be looking into the dark *kao* forest as she went on. "'*Koa*' means 'unafraid.' The *koa* branches are a prayer that we shall never be afraid even when we dance before a crowd."

"What else must he gather?" the grandmother asked.

"*Lehua* in the lower forest, sweet smelling *maile*, *'ie'ie*, *palai* fern and *halapepe*," 'Ilima answered. "He must repeat a special prayer for each.

And *pili* grass," she added quickly. "That is very important for *'pili'*
means to 'cling.' The *pili* grass is a prayer that chants and gestures may
cling to us through all our lives.

"You tell what happens next, Grandmother."

"When Kanoe comes back to the *halau* Wahi will sprinkle the vines
and branches with purifying water. He and Kanoe will build an altar to
Laka, an altar made of the sacred branches and trimmed with vines and
flowers. They will pray Laka to send her spirit into that altar. If you and
the others try earnestly Laka will be pleased. Her spirit will stay in the
altar, and vines and branches will be green and full of life."

There was a long silence. Keao was thinking, "Tomorrow 'Ilima will
be there. She will see. O Laka," she prayed silently, "bless my friend.
Help her to be a good hula dancer."

Then 'Ilima spoke, "And tonight, Grandmother? Tell Keao about
that."

"Tonight Wahi will stay alone in the *halau*. He will pray Laka to bless
his teaching. He will pray that he may remember every chant and
gesture, that he may teach with patience and with wisdom. He will pray
for all his pupils; that you may work earnestly and remember, that your
voices may be rich and true, your bodies graceful, your hearts unafraid
and reverent.

"Wahi will also pray for new wisdom. He will ask the goddess to
come to him in a dream and teach him a hula he did not know or call to
mind one he had forgotten."

Again the three were silent, thinking. Perhaps all three were praying.
There was no movement but the sunlight dancing through *hau* leaves.

At last the old woman picked up the coconut fibers which had fallen
in her lap. Keao watched her quick fingers as she braided. Though she
was old, her hands were not stiff, but beautiful in movement. "Her voice
too is strong and sweet," the young woman thought. "It is because of
her hula training."

Aloud she said, "I think our district has the best dancers on this
island."

"That is something we must never think," the old woman told her.
"Chants and gestures taught in one hula school are different, sometimes
different only in little ways. But each is good. I still remember the words
of my master, 'Never find fault with the teaching of another school. All
knowledge does not come from one.'"

"That is what my mother said about *kapa* making," Keao remembered.
"'Patterns and dyes may be different, but all work done with prayer and
skill is good.'"

Then she asked, "Do you know any stories about the hula?"

"I think the art was brought from far Kahiki by our ancestors," the
old woman told her. "Girls of Hawaii taught it to Hi'iaka, and she and

other sisters of Pele danced in the fire pit. Then La'a came. Do you know that story, Keao?"

"I have heard it, but tell it once more so we shall be sure to remember it."

"La'a was a son of Moikeha, the voyager," Grandmother began. "He came from far Kahiki. As his canoe sailed along the coast of Hawaii by night La'a softly beat his drum.

"The sound was new and beautiful.

"'What is it?' people asked, and others answered, 'It is the great god, Ku.' At daybreak they paddled out with offerings of food for the god.

"Sometimes La'a stopped at a landing place. Then hula teachers gathered, for they had heard the voice of La's drum. He taught them hulas. Though he beat the drum, he kept it hidden. 'What is it?' they asked each other. 'Its tone is rich and beautiful. If only we could make drums like that!'

"A hula master on Oahu followed the canoe. 'That drum's voice is most beautiful!' he thought. 'I have nothing with such a deep tone. I must see the drum!' So he ran, following the canoe. Sometimes he ran along the beach. Sometimes the trail was on the cliff above.

"As the hula teacher ran, he listened to the rhythms of the drum. They were new to him, and he must learn them. So he beat each one with his hands on his chest until it was fixed in his mind.

"When at last the canoe landed the hula master was there to greet La'a. 'I heard your drum,' he said. 'It sounds like one of mine. I wonder whether they are the same.'

"La'a brought out his drum. The man saw it was larger than any he had known before. It was made from a section of a breadfruit log, hollowed and covered with sharkskin. The sharkskin was laced on with sennit. 'Yes,' said the hula master, 'as I thought, it is much like mine.'

"Soon these words came true for the hula teacher made a drum like that of La'a. On it he played the rhythms he had learned. Since that day the sharkskin drum has been used through all Hawaii."

As 'Ilima came to the *halau*, the house where the hula dancers were to be trained, she felt cold with excitement. She joined others who were chosen for the training. Some were older men and women who had been dancers and would now be trained to play the rhythm instruments. Some were young men and women of 'Ilima's own age. All were people she knew, but today they seemed strange.

At the door of the *halau*, Wahi, the hula master, sprinkled them with purifying water. Once inside, 'Ilima looked about. The *halau* was larger than a sleeping house, but smaller than she had expected.

On the east side was the altar. 'Ilima knew it must be on the side of the rising sun. Placing the altar on the east was a prayer for life, health, and for growth in dancing.

There was time for short rests and for food, but not for games and idleness. The pupils could never forget that they were in the presence of their goddess. They could never be careless in speech or act.

Food was brought to the door by relatives. These people did not enter the *halau*, for it was sacred. Certain kinds of food were *kapu* to those who learned the hula, and these were never brought. The name of one *limu* meant "to hide." It was *kapu*, for eating it might make the memory of chant or gesture hide from those who tried to learn.

One morning as the pupils came from the bathing pool they noticed the master's face. "It is shining," 'Ilima thought.

"Wahi has had a dream," someone whispered. And it was so. The master told them that he had tried for many months to remember a certain hula learned in childhood. "But it had flown," he said. "Last night, as I slept, I saw our goddess, Laka. She danced the hula I longed for. Every gesture, every word was clear."

As 'Ilima learned the hula she seemed to see the goddess dancing. "Laka is in me," the young woman thought again, and danced and chanted easily. That hula was indeed a sacred thing.

One morning Wahi said, "Soon our district chief will send for this hula troupe to dance before his household. That is your graduation. I have asked Ka-ipo, a great hula master, to watch your work and tell us how it can be made better. Yesterday a message came from him. I think he will be with us today."

Many had heard of Ka-ipo. It would be an honor to have him watch their work. There was excitement in the *halau* and in 'Ilima's heart a little fear.

Just as the pupils were taking their places for a dance they heard a voice chanting the password. Wahi's face lighted with joy. The drums were hushed, and everyone listened eagerly as Wahi chanted the reply giving permission to enter.

Ka-ipo was old and white-haired, but straight and handsome. Wahi sprinkled him with purifying water. The old man went to the altar and lifted his voice in prayer. How strong and rich his tones!

> Thy blessing, O Laka,
> On me, the stranger,
> And on these within the *halau*.
> Teacher and pupils.
> O Laka, bless the dancers
> When they come before the people.

Then Wahi took Ka-ipo in his arms. Their faces touched, and their eyes filled with tears of joy. But they did not wail aloud, for they were in the presence of the goddess.

Wahi seated the old master on a mat to watch. Ka-ipo did not interrupt a dance, but after each told how it could be improved. "In this place your breathing was not right," he might say. "Fill your lungs and do not stop for breath until the phrase is finished." After another chant, "Your tone is not that of the bamboo rattles. Listen!" He struck a rattle. "Do you hear the light song of wind blowing through reeds in a marshy place? The music of your voices must be as light as the note of the bamboo."

That night 'Ilima went to her mats tired with the effort of the day, yet happy. The old man's words had made the hula even more full of beauty and worship than before.

Ka-ipo stayed for several days while pupils worked their hardest on dance and chant. At last he said, "It is well." That was all, but coming from the master it was praise enough. 'Ilima knew—everyone knew— the troupe was ready for graduation. A few days later came the chief's command to dance before his household. The time had come!

Just after midnight, when no one was about, the pupils went to the ocean to bathe. Oh, how good to feel its waves once more! At the door of the *halau* Wahi sprinkled each one with purifying water as he had done every time they entered. Then he himself went to bathe. When he returned they danced and chanted, then slept a little while.

At daybreak the pupils were wakened by their teacher's tapping on the sharkskin drum. 'Ilima was wide awake at once. This was the day!

All bathed in the pool just as they had each morning. They chanted as they dressed, but the *pa'u* each put on was new and beautiful. They gathered about the altar and chanted prayers to Laka.

A long ceremony of prayers and chants followed the morning meal. The pupils watched as vines and branches were taken from the altar and replaced with fresh ones. They listened as Wahi talked to them. "Be true to what you have learned in this *halau*," he said. "Then the chants will be yours through all your lives."

And now, for the first time since entering the *halau*, the pupils visited their homes. The men might shave. Everyone might trim hair and nails. They were given fresh leis made by their families. For a moment 'Ilima held her grandmother in her arms. Each knew that understanding and love had grown between them.

The time at home was short. Soon all returned to the *halau* to be sprinkled once more with purifying water and to chant reverently:

Laka sits in her shady grove.
An offering we give to you.
O Laka, let it be well,
Well with us all,
O giver of all things.

As the chant ended the pupils crowded to the altar and heaped their leis upon the block of *lama* wood where the spirit of Laka rested.

The many prayers were answered. Quietly the hula troupe went to the chief's home. The audience was there, sitting or lying about the large mat made ready for the dancers. The program was long. Chants and instruments changed, but always the voices carried the tone of instruments used—drums, gourd rattles, sticks, small stones. It seemed to 'Ilima that the spirit of Laka had driven fear from eveyone. The praise which followed the program was not praise for the dancers and musicians. It was not praise for Wahi, but for Laka, their goddess.

That night when graduation was over Wahi took all the sacred things to Kanoe's canoe. He took the branches which had made the altar, the vines and every *pa'u* and lei worn by a dancer, even bits of food from the feast shared with the goddess. Wahi and Kanoe paddled to deep ocean and reverently dropped everything into the starlit waves. Wahi prayed, and the two watched the sacred things disappear. They were safe. No careless hands could touch them, no careless feet step on them.

As she lay in the sleeping house 'Ilima heard the dip of a paddle. "Perhaps it is Wahi and Kanoe returning," she told herself. "Our training is finished." There was a bit of sadness in the thought. Then came another, "Soon *Makahiki* will begin. Our hula troupe will dance in this district and in others." With a thankful prayer to Laka the young woman fell asleep.

Caroline Curtis, *Life in Old Hawaii.*

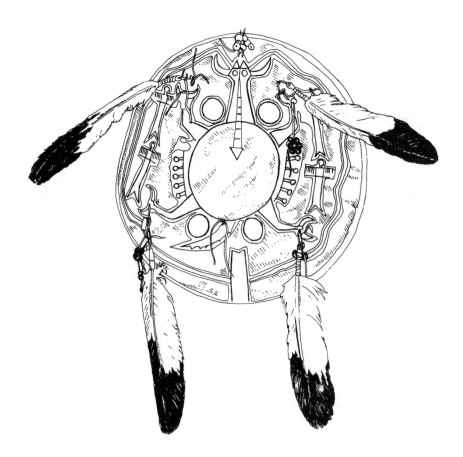

Buffalo-hide shield
Arapaho

PART THREE

FROM THE GREAT PLAINS

"Westward Ho!" applied equally to the movement of North American Indians as well as to white settlers of the western Great Plains.

Into North and South Dakota, Nebraska, Wyoming, Montana and Colorado they spread. Many tribes followed the hunt for wild horses and buffaloes and gave up their agricultural pursuits for a period. With horses and guns, certain tribes became warlike in defense of their territories against the whites.

Smallpox epidemics killed thousands of Indians, wiping out villages and almost whole tribes in the middle 1800s. Several tribes united to strengthen their numbers, and lived together on reservations assigned to them by the government of the United States.

Tribes repesented by these stories became part of this western migration. The Hidatsa, Mandan, and Arikara, reduced in numbers, moved to Fort Berthold, North Dakota, which later became their reservation in 1880. In 1900 they became "American Citizens."

Cheyenne, meaning "people of alien speech," of the Algonquian language group, left Minnesota and adopted a nomadic life. They, too, joined the westward movement as far as the North Platte and Yellowstone rivers. At the treaty signing of 1851 in Fort Laramie, Wyoming, the tribe separated into two parts: the Northern Cheyenne settled in Montana, the Southern Cheyenne in Oklahoma.

Western migration enlarged many tribes: Ute, Acoma, Arapaho, Blackfeet, Piegan, and the powerful Dakota-Sioux who practiced the Ghost Dance Religion and became involved in wars with the U.S. military.

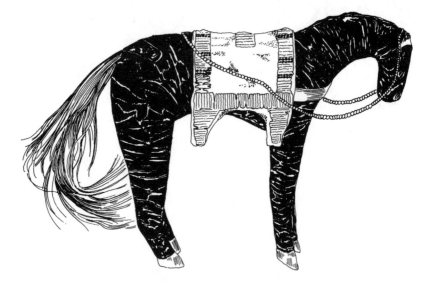

Plains Indian toy horse with beaded leather saddle
Cheyenne

■

ORIGIN OF THE BUFFALO
Cheyenne

The Cheyenne tribe moved frequently: In South Dakota they lived along the Cheyenne River and in the Black Hills. But bands of their tribe were known in every western state. Before 1700 a large group settled on the Minnesota River, and some Cheyennes visited LaSalle's Fort in Illinois in 1680. Between 1780 and 1790, their settlements were attacked by Chippewas while Cheyenne men were away hunting. Escapees settled on the Missouri River near other Cheyennes.

■

Long ago, a tribe of Cheyenne hunters lived at the head of a rushing stream, which eventually emptied into a large cave.

Because of the great need for a new food supply for his people, the Chief called a council meeting.

"We should explore the large cave," he told his people. "How many brave hunters will offer to go on this venture? Of course, it may be very dangerous, but we have brave hunters." No one responded to the Chief's request.

Finally, one young brave painted himself for hunting and stepped forth, replying to the Chief, "I will go and sacrifice myself for our people."

He arrived at the cave, and to his surprise, First Brave found two other Cheyenne hunters near the opening, where the stream rushed underground.

"Are they here to taunt me," First Brave wondered? "Will they only pretend to jump when I do?"

But the other two braves assured him they would go.

"No, you are mistaken about us. We really do want to enter the cave with you," they said.

First Brave then joined hands with them and together they jumped into the huge opening of the cave. Because of the darkness, it took some time for their eyes to adjust. They then discovered what looked like a door. First Brave knocked, but there was no response. He knocked again, louder.

"What do you want, my brave ones?" asked an old Indian grandmother as she opened her door.

"Grandmother, we are searching for a new food supply for our tribe," First Brave replied. "Our people never seem to have enough food to eat."

"Are you hungry now?" she asked.

"Oh, yes, kind Grandmother, we are very hungry," all three braves answered.

The old grandmother opened her door wide, inviting the young braves to enter.

"Look out there!" she pointed for them to look through her window.

A beautiful wide prairie stretched before their eyes. Great herds of buffalo were grazing contentedly. The young hunters could hardly believe what they saw!

The old grandmother brought each of them a stone pan full of buffalo meat. How good it tasted, as they ate and ate until they were filled. To their surprise, more buffalo meat remained in their stone pans!

"I want you to take your stone pans of buffalo meat back to your people at your camp," said the old grandmother. "Tell them that soon I will send some live buffalo."

"Thank you, thank you, thank you, kind Grandmother," said the three young Cheyenne braves.

When the young hunters returned to their tribe with the gifts of buffalo meat, their people rejoiced over the new, good food. Their entire tribe ate heartily from the old grandmother's three magic pans, and were grateful.

When the Cheyennes waked at dawn the next day, herds of buffalo had mysteriously appeared, surrounding their village! They were truly thankful to the old Indian grandmother and to the Sky Spirits for their good fortune.

Voth, "Origin of Buffalo," 45.

■

How the Buffalo Hunt Began
Cheyenne

The following tales were collected at the Cheyenne Agency in Oklahoma in 1899, a task undertaken by the American Museum of Natural History. Oral and written recordings were made in English from translations and writings of the Cheyenne Indians. These versions are only slightly altered to retain the character and flavor of the original.

■

The buffalo formerly ate man. The magpie and the hawk were on the side of the people, for neither ate the other or the people. These two birds flew away from a council between animals and men. They determined that a race would be held, the winners to eat the losers.

The course was long, around a mountain. The swiftest buffalo was a cow called Neika, "swift head." She believed she would win and entered the race. On the other hand, the people were afraid because of the long distance. They were trying to get medicine to prevent fatigue.

All the birds and animals painted themselves for the race, and since that time they have all been brightly colored. Even the water turtle put red paint around his eyes. The magpie painted himself white on head, shoulders, and tail. At last all were ready for the race, and stood in a row for the start.

They ran and ran, making some loud noises inplace of singing to help themselves to run faster. All small birds, turtles, rabbits, coyotes, wolves, flies, ants, insects, and snakes were soon left far behind. When they approached the mountain the buffalo-cow was ahead; then came the magpie, hawk, and the people; the rest were strung out along the way. The dust rose so quickly that nothing could be seen.

All around the mountain the buffalo-cow led the race, but the two birds knew they could win, and merely kept up with her until they neared the finish line, which was back to the starting place. Then both birds whooshed by her and won the race for man. As they flew the course, they had seen fallen animals and birds all over the place, who had run themselves to death, turning the ground and rocks red from the blood.

The buffalo then told their young to hide from the people, who were going out to hunt them; and also told them to take some human flesh with them for the last time. The young buffaloes did this, and stuck that meat in front of their chests, beneath the throat. Therefore, the people do not eat that part of the buffalo, saying it is part human flesh.

From that day forward the Cheyennes began to hunt buffalo. Since all the friendly animals and birds were on the people's side, they are not eaten by people, but they do wear and use their beautiful feathers for ornaments.

Another version adds that when coyote, who was on the side of buffalo, finished the race, the magpie who even beat the hawk, said to coyote, "We will not eat you, but only use your skin."

Grinnell, "How the Buffalo Hunt Began," 161-162.

■

EAGLE WAR FEATHERS

Cheyenne

■

A long, long time ago the Cheyenne warriors had not learned yet how to use eagle for their war ornaments. One of their men climbed a high mountain; there he lay for five days, crying, without food. Some powerful being, he hoped, would see him and come to him, to teach him something great for his people.

He was glad when he heard a voice say, "Try to be brave, no matter what comes, even if it might kill you. If you remember these words, you will bring great news to your people, and help them." After a time he heard voices, and seven eagles came down, as if to fly away with him. But he was brave, as he had been told, though he continued to cry and keep his eyes closed. Now the great eagles surrounded him. One said, "Look at me. I am powerful, and I have wonderfully strong feathers. I am greater than all other animals and birds in the world."

This powerful eagle showed the man his wings and his tail, and he spread all his feathers as wide as possible. He shows him how to make war headdresses and ornaments out of eagle feathers.

"Your people must use only eagle feathers, and it would be a great help to them in war and bring them victories," eagle said.

Since no loose feathers were about, the seven eagles shook themselves, and plenty of feathers fell to the ground. The Cheyenne picked them up and gratefully took them home to his tribe. On that day, eagle feathers were seen for the first time by the Cheyenne and they knew where they came from.

Eagle-feathered warbonnet
Cheyenne

The man showed his people how to make war ornaments from the eagle feathers, as he had been told. From that day onward, the man became a great warrior in his tribe, and their leader in war parties.

He became so successful his people named him Chief Eagle Feather and he wore his Eagle Feather Warbonnet, as he led the Cheyennes with dignity and pride.

Grinnell, "Eagle War Feathers," 163-164.

■

ENOUGH IS ENOUGH
Cheyenne

■

One Cheyenne man of long ago had a pointed leg. By running and jumping against trees he made his leg stick in them. When he said the magic word, he dropped again to the ground. Sometimes on a hot day he would stick himself high on the tree trunk for greater shade. However, he knew he could not do this trick more than four times in one day.

A white man came along, saw him perform, and cried out, "Brother, sharpen my leg!" Cheyenne man said, "That's not too hard. I can sharpen your leg." So the white man stood on a large log, and with an axe the Cheyenne sharpened his leg. "But you must remember never to perform your trick more than four times in one day, and keep exact count."

White man then went down toward the river and saw a large tree growing on the bank. Toward this he ran, jumped, and thrust his leg into the tree, where it stuck. He called himself back to the ground. Again he jumped against another tree, but only counted one. The third time he only counted two. The fourth time, birds and animals stood by and watched as the white man jumped high and pushed his leg on the tree, up to his knee. But he only counted three.

Then coyotes, wolves, and other animals came to see him. Some asked, "How did the white man learn the trick?" They begged him to show them, so they could stick themselves to trees at night. The white man became even prouder from all of this admiration, and the fifth time he ran harder, jumped higher, and half his thigh entered the tree and there he stuck fast. Then he counted four.

He called and called to bring himself down to the ground again, but he still stuck fast. He called out all night and the next day—but nothing helped him. He asked his animal friends to find the Cheyenne who had taught him the trick, but no one knew whom to look for. The white man had forgotten the secret of freeing himself, and after many days stuck in the tree, he starved to death.

Grinnell, "Enough Is Enough," 169.

■

FALLING-STAR

Northern Cheyenne

More than fifty versions of a story about a Star-Husband have
been recorded from many Indian tribes across the United States.

■

One day in the long ago, two young Indian girls were lying on the
grass outside their tepee on a warm summer evening. They were
looking up into the sky, describing star-pictures formed by their imag-
inations.

"That is a pretty star. I like that one," said First Girl.

"I like that one best of all—over there," Second Girl pointed.

First Girl pointed to the brightest star in the sky and said, "I like the
brightest one best of all. That is the one I want to marry."

That evening they agreed to go out the next day to gather wood. Next
morning they started for the timbered area. On their way they saw a
porcupine climb a tree.

"I'll climb the tree and pull him down," said First Girl. She climbed
but could not reach the porcupine.

Every time she stretched her hand for him, the porcupine climbed a
little higher. Then the tree started growing taller. Second Girl below
called to her friend, "Please come down, the tree is growing taller!"

"No," said First Girl as the porcupine climbed higher and the tree
grew taller. Second Girl could see what was happening, so she ran back
to the camp and told her people. They rushed to the tree, but First Girl
had completely disappeared!

The tree continued to grow higher and higher. Finally, First Girl
reached another land. She stepped off the tree branch and walked upon
the sky! Before long she met a kindly looking middle-aged man who
spoke to her. First Girl began to cry.

"Whatever is the matter? Only last night I heard you wish that you
could marry me. I am the Brightest-Star," he said.

First Girl was pleased to meet Brightest-Star and became happy again
when she got her wish and married him. He told her that she could dig
roots with the other star-women, but to beware of a certain kind of white
turnip with a great green top. This kind she must never dig. To do so
was "against the medicine"—against the rules of the Sky-Chief.

Pipe
Cheyenne

Every day First Girl dug roots. Her curiosity about the strange white turnip became so intense that she decided to dig up one of them. It took her a long, long time. When she finally pulled out the root, a huge hole was left. She looked into the hole and far, far below she saw the camp of her own people.

Everything and everyone was very small, but she could see lodges and people walking. Instantly she became homesick to see her own people again. How could she ever get down from the sky? She realized it was a long, long way down to earth. Then her eyes fell upon the long tough grass growing near her. Could she braid it into a long rope? She decided to try, every day pulling more long grass and braiding more rope.

One time her husband Brightest-Star asked, "What is it that keeps you outdoors so much of the time?"

"I walk a great distance and that makes me tired. I need to sit down and rest before I can start back home."

At last she finished making her strong rope, thinking by now it must be long enough. She tied one end of the rope to a log that she rolled across the top of the hole as an anchor. She let down the rope. It looked as though it touched the ground.

She lowered herself into the hole, holding onto the braided rope. It seemed to take a long time as she slowly lowered herself until she came to the end of the rope. But it did not touch the earth! For a long while she hung on dangling in midair and calling uselessly for help. When she could hold on no longer, she fell to the ground and broke into many pieces. Although she died, her unborn son did not die, because he was made of star-stone and did not break.

A meadowlark saw what happened and took the falling-star baby to her nest. There the lark kept him with her own baby birds. When they were older, Falling-Star crept out of the nest with the little birds. The stronger the birds grew, the stronger grew Falling-Star. Soon all of them could crawl and run. The young birds practiced their flying while Falling-Star ran after them. Then the young birds could fly anywhere they wished, while Falling-Star ran faster and faster to keep up with them.

"Son, you had better go home to your own people," said Mother Meadowlark. "It is time for us to fly south for the winter. Before long, the weather here will be very cold."

"Mother Meadowlark," asked Falling-Star. "Why do you want me to leave you? I want to go with you."

"No, Son," she replied. "You must go home now."

"I will go if Father Meadowlark will make me a bow and some arrows."

Father Meadowlark made a bow and pulled some of his own quills to feather the arrows. He made four arrows and a bow for Falling- Star. Then he started Falling-Star in the right direction toward his home, downstream.

Falling-Star traveled a long time before he reached the camp of his people. He went into the nearest lodge owned by an old grandmother.

"Grandmother," he said. "I need a drink of water."

"My grandson," she said to him, "only the young men who are the fastest runners can go for water. There is a water-monster who sucks up any people who go too close to it."

"Grandmother, if you will give me your buffalo-pouch and your buffalo-horn ladle, I will bring you water."

"Grandson, I warn you that many of our finest young men have been destroyed by the water-monster. I fear that you will be killed, too." But

Pipe bowl
Cheyenne

she gave him the things he asked for. He went upstream and dipped water, at the same time keeping watch for the monster.

At the very moment Falling-Star filled his bucket, the Water- monster raised its head above the water. His mouth was enormous. He sucked in his breath and drew in Falling-Star, the bucket, water, and the ladle. When Falling-Star found himself inside the monster's stomach, he saw all the other people who had ever been swallowed. With his Star-stone, he cut a hole in the animal's side. Out crawled all the people, and Falling-Star rescued his pouch and ladle for his grandmother, taking her some cool, fresh water.

"My grandson, who are you?" she asked, marveling at his survival.

"Grandmother, I am Falling-Star. I killed the monster who has caused our people much suffering, and I rescued all the people who had been swallowed."

The old woman told the village crier to spread the good news that the monster was dead. Now that Falling-Star had saved the camp people there, he asked the grandmother, "Are there other camps of our people nearby?"

"Yes, there is one farther downstream," she said.

Falling-Star took his bow and arrows and left camp. The fall of the year had now arrived. After traveling many days, he reached the other camp. Again he went into an old woman's lodge where she sat near her fire.

"Grandmother, I am very hungry," he said.

"My son, my son, we have no food. We cannot get any buffalo meat. Whenever our hunters go out for buffalo, a great white crow warns the buffalo, which drives them away.

"How sad," he said. "I will try to help. Go out and look for a worn-out buffalo robe with little hair. Tell your chief to choose two of his fastest runners and send them to me."

Later, the old woman returned with the robe and the two swift runners. Falling-Star told them his plan. "I will go to a certain place and wait for the buffalo. When the herd runs, I will follow, disguised as a buffalo in the worn-out robe. You two runners chase me and the buffalo for a long distance. When you overtake me, you must shoot at me. I will pretend to be dead. You pretend to cut me open and leave me there on the ground."

When the real buffalo arrived, the white crow flew over them screaming, "They are coming! They are after you! Run, run!" The buffalo herd ran, followed by a shabby-looking bull.

The two swift runners chased the old bull according to plan. All kinds of birds, wolves, and coyotes came toward the carcass from all directions. Among them was the white crow. As he flew over Falling-Star in disguise, he called out shrilly, "I wonder if this is Falling-Star?"

Time after time the crow flew over the carcass, still calling, "I wonder if this is Falling-Star?" He came closer and closer with each pass. When he was close enough, Falling-Star sprang and grabbed the legs of the white crow. All of the other birds and animals scattered in every direction.

When Falling-Star brought the captive white crow home to the grandmother, she sent word for the chief.

"I will take the white crow to my lodge. I will tie him to the smoke hole and smoke him dead," said the chief.

From that moment on, the good Cheyennes were able to kill many buffalo and they had plenty of buffalo meat for all their needs.

The people in gratitude gave Falling-Star a lovely lodge-home and a pretty Indian maiden waiting there to become his wife. They remained all of their lives with the Northern Cheyenne Indian tribe.

Grinnell, "Falling-Star," 308-312.

■

Buffalo and Eagle Wing

Unknown

This story was written years ago by a pupil at the Haskell Institute, a school for Indian boys and girls. He had heard his grandfather tell it. The boy's exact tribe is unknown, although it was one from the Great Plains.

■

A long time ago there were no stones on the earth. The mountains, hills, and valleys were not rough, and it was easy to walk on the ground swiftly. There were no small trees at that time either. All the bushes and trees were tall and straight and were at equal distances. So a man could travel through a forest without having to make a path.

At that time, a large buffalo roamed over the land. From the water, he had obtained his spirit power—the power to change anything into some other form. He would have that power as long as he only drank from a certain pool.

In his wanderings, Buffalo often traveled across a high mountain. He liked this mountain so much that one day he asked it, "Would you like to be changed into something else?"

"Yes," replied the mountain. "I would like to be changed into something nobody would want to climb over."

"All right," said Buffalo. "I will change you into something hard that I will call 'stone.' You will be so hard that no one will want to break you, and so smooth that no one will want to climb you."

So Buffalo changed the mountain into a large stone. "And I give you the power to change yourself into anything else as long as you do not break yourself."

Only buffaloes lived in this part of the land. No people lived here. On the other side of the mountain lived men who were cruel and killed animals. The buffaloes knew about them and stayed as far away from them as possible. But one day Buffalo thought he would like to see these men. He hoped to make friends with them and persuade them not to kill buffaloes.

Parfleche
Sioux

So he went over the mountain and traveled along a stream until he came to a lodge. There lived an old woman and her grandson. The little boy liked Buffalo, and Buffalo liked the little boy and his grandmother. He said to them, "I have the power to change you into any form you wish. What would you like most to be?"

"I want always to be with my grandson. I want to be changed into anything that will make it possible for me to be with him, wherever he goes."

"I will take you to the home of the buffaloes," said their guest. "I will ask them to teach the boy to become a swift runner. I will ask the water to change the grandmother into something, so that you two can always be together."

So Buffalo, the grandmother, and the little boy went over the mountain to the land of the buffaloes.

"We will teach you to run swiftly," they told the boy, "if you will promise to keep your people from hunting and killing buffaloes."

"I promise," said the boy.

The buffaloes taught him to run so fast that not one of them could keep up with him. The old grandmother could follow him wherever he went, for she had been changed into Wind.

The boy stayed with the buffaloes until he became a man. Then they let him go back to his people, reminding him of his promise. Because he was such a swift runner, he became a leader of the hunters. They called him Eagle Wing.

One day the chief called Eagle Wing to him and said to him, "My son, I want you to take the hunters to the buffalo country. We have never been able to kill buffaloes because they run so very fast. But you too can run fast. If you will kill some buffaloes and bring home the meat and the skins, I will adopt you as my son. And when I die, you will become chief of the tribe."

Eagle Wing wanted so much to become chief that he pushed from his mind his promise to the buffaloes. He started out with the hunters, but he climbed the mountain so fast that they were soon left far behind. On the other side of the mountain, he saw a herd of buffaloes. They started to run in fright, but Eagle Wing followed them and killed most of them.

Buffalo, the great one who got his power from the water, was away from home at the time of the hunt. On his way back he grew so thirsty that he drank from some water on the other side of the mountain not from his special pool. When he reached home and saw what the hunter had done, he became very angry. He tried to turn the men into grass, but he could not. Because he had drunk from another pool, he had lost his power to transform.

Buffalo went to the big stone that had once been a mountain.

"What can you do to punish the hunter for what he has done?" he asked Stone.

"I will ask the trees to tangle themselves so that it will be difficult for men to travel through them," answered Stone. "I will break myself into many pieces and scatter myself all over the land. Then the swift runner and his followers cannot run over me without hurting their feet."

"That will punish them," agreed Buffalo.

So Stone broke itself into many pieces and scattered itself all over the land. Whenever the swift runner, Eagle Wing, and his followers tried to run over the mountain, stones cut their feet. Bushes scratched and bruised their bodies.

That is how Eagle Wing was punished for not keeping his promise to Buffalo.

Clark, "Buffalo and Eagle Wing."

■

THE SUN DANCE
Hidatsa

The Hidatsa Tribe were a part of the Siouan family, also related to the Crow Indians, who lived in Montana on the Missouri River. The Sun Dance of the Hidatsa is similar to that of other tribes. Primarily, it is a prayer to the Sun-God for a Dancer's secret wishes: for his deliverance from his troubles, for supernatural aid, and for beneficent blessings upon all of his people.

■

For many moons this particular Dancer had dreamed of the Chief's daughter becoming his wife. He had a vision of himself performing the Sun Dance in supplication for his secret wish. The vision prompted him to call his tribe together for a Sun Dance. Then the Dancer went to a high place alone, declaring to the Sun-God:

"In the coming summer, I shall build your lodge. I shall stand in the holy place. I shall kill buffalo and take the hides for you. I shall dance for you to be worthy of my beloved that I may have her for my wife. I shall dance for you so that I may have visions to help protect me from my enemies, so that my people may grow strong, so that no disease may come, so that the buffalo may be plentiful, so there will be an abundance of rain throughout the year."

The young Dancer called upon his Mother and his Grandmother, saying, "Please tell all of your relatives that I shall perform the Sun Dance." They spread the news and the tribal men gathered buffalo hides. These they brought to the tribal women for curing. The Dancer provided the feasts for all who came to the celebration of his Sun Dance.

When everything was in readiness, the Dancer took a buffalo robe to the Priest, one of his Father's clansman who was experienced in presiding over the Sun Dance Ceremony. The Priest represented the Sun-God. Before him the Dancer placed his buffalo robe and offered his pipe,

Elk horn rake
Hidatsa

saying, "Wise One, I have come to you for guidance. I wish to obtain the blessings of the Sun-God."

The Priest accepted the pipe and replied, "I am glad, my son, that you have come to me. I will aid you in this ceremony."

When the public announcement was made that the Sun Dance was to be given, the clansmen of the Dancer's Father asked for a scalp and left hand taken from an enemy. Sometimes both of these items were offered freely by a relative or purchased for a high price.

Before raising the sun-pole, a fresh buffalo head with a broad center strip of the back hide and tail were fastened with strong thongs to the top crotch of the sun-pole. Then the pole was raised and set firmly in the ground, with the buffalo head facing toward the setting-sun.

The sacred lodge was built by the Dancer and his clansmen. Men who owned medicine bundles brought them into the lodge of the Priest. The Dancer furnished each man with a buffalo robe upon which to lay his sacred bundle. The Dancer selected a favorite bundle that might be a red fox skin, for example, and for which the owner might ask the Dancer for a token.

The tribal Singer took the red fox skin and held it toward the burning incense. Then he touched it to the body of the Dancer and to that of his mother and Grandmother. Then he replaced it in front of its former owner. In this manner, the Dancer bought many of the medicine bundles and paid what the owners asked, in addition to his gifts of buffalo robes upon which rests each medicine bundle.

By this time, the Singer had learned the sacred songs and the manner of painting that each medicine required. The Singer taught the Dancer the secrets of each medicine that the Dancer bought. Some protect against enemies, some are good luck in contests, and some are for success in love and in hunting. When the Dancer had bought what he desired, the men went out, carrying his gift of the buffalo robe.

After construction of the Sun-Lodge, the Priest took the enemy scalp and left hand and raised them to the North Wind, South Wind, East Wind, and West Wind, saying, "I have often taken these in combat. May you have protection against your enemy always," giving them to the Dancer.

Young men, who are the Fasters and have their flesh pierced, arrived and went into the Sun-Lodge. Each carried his medicine bundle and an armful of sage. They crossed to the south side of the lodge, and each chose a place for his sage. They hung their medicine bundles on short sticks stuck in the ground in front of their sage.

The Dancer took the bundles that he brought and piled them on a buffalo skull. The Singer began the chants of mystery in a slow, measured rhythm. The incense was then burned. The Dancer trembled from excitement. The Priest took white paint, holding it in the incense smoke for a moment and smeared it over the body of the Dancer and drew a white circle around his face.

To complete dressing the Dancer, the Priest hung a medicine hoop on his back, held by a cord around his neck. On his head, the Priest placed a band of jackrabbit skin, with the head dropping over his left ear. An eagle-down feather was tied to the Dancer's scalplock, pointing backward. A whistle made of eagle-bone was hung around the Dancer's neck.

Meanwhile, the Fasters opened their medicine bundles, burned incense, painted themselves, and adorned themselves as they were taught by their elders and Guardian Spirits. Those having no medicine smeared themselves completely with white paint. Each Faster had an eagle-bone whistle hung from his neck and carried a shield and a lance.

The Singer painted himself and placed raven feathers in his hair. He arranged himself in front of the buffalo skin suspended from the sun-pole. He extended his arms toward it, rubbing his body as if receiving some special power from the buffalo.

Medicine-men arranged themselves south of the entrance to the Sun-Lodge. The old women of the tribe who prepared the spot for the Sun Dance, together with the medicine-women, sat on the north side. All come to pray and to fast. The relatives of the young male Fasters entered, carrying food. Each Faster took a bowlful of the food to a clansman of his father.

Then came the challenge to the Fasters' bravery. They approached the Priest and the Singer. Two small slits were cut in the shoulder skin of each young man presenting himself. Through the slotted skin, a leather thong was threaded with a wooden pin attached to the end, preventing the thong from pulling out of the slotted skin.

The other ends of these thongs were attached to the top of the sun-pole (similar to a Maypole). The Priest and Singer twirled each Faster four times, his feet barely touching the ground. Then the Faster swung free, twisting and circling around the sun-pole. But he dared not touch the thong with his hands. Any attempt to break the taboos was frowned upon by all his people as a lack of courage and endurance.

When the Faster finally broke loose from the sun-pole, he fell to the ground. Priest and Singer placed him gently on his bed of healing sage. There he remained and fasted from two to four days.

Any Dancer must first have been a Faster in an earlier Sun Dance. The Dancer danced back and forth continuously toward the sun-pole in the circle as long as a Faster was attached to the sun-pole. The Dancer sprang from the ground with his legs rigid and his feet together, his eyes fixed upon the buffalo head, and blew his eagle-bone whistle in rhythm with the beating drum.

The Dancer's mind was intent upon his desire to win his secret wish, the Chief's daughter, and to become a strong leader of his tribe. During his dance he prayed silently for those visions. He continued his dance until he fell from exhaustion. There he stayed until his visions appeared, or until the fourth day of the fast, if necessary.

The young Fasters lay upon their beds of sage. They have dreams and visions, which they related to the Priest. If they were sufficient, the Faster left the Sun-Lodge, because his supplications were answered by the Sun-God.

Near the doorway, the medicine-men still fasted and sought visions. Some of the younger boys of the tribe dragged buffalo heads through the village for fun.

If it was seen that a Faster cannot break away from the sun-pole and might be in danger, he was cut loose honorably. At the end of the fourth day, only a few Fasters still seeking visions remained.

The exhausted Dancer was taken to his lodge. If he or any Fasters wished to continue the Sun Dance, the Sun-Lodge was permitted to stand for them. Otherwise, it was torn down. Only the sun-pole with the buffalo head on top was left to mark the spot of the traditional Sun Dance.

The Dancer and all of the Fasters recovered honorably from their sacred experience.

In due time, the Chief of the Hidatsa tribe declared that the Dancer had won his daughter in marriage.

The Dancer went to the high ground, and in gratitude prayed and praised the Sun-God for the many blessings bestowed upon him and his beloved wife, and upon his tribe.

Curtis, *The North American Indian*, vol. iv, 152-155.

■

THE CORN CEREMONY

Hidatsa

The Corn Ceremony was held in the spring or early summer as a prayer to the spirits to grant bountiful harvests and strength to the tribe.

■

A man who in the preceding autumn had witnessed the ceremony in a dream, climbed to the top of his lodge. There he made a vow to the Corn Spirit, whose name, *Kadhutetash* means "Old Woman Who Never Dies."

"Hear me, Old Woman Who Never Dies," the man said in a loud voice. "I shall give a great feast in your honor for four reasons. I want to live to see another season. I want my people to become strong and

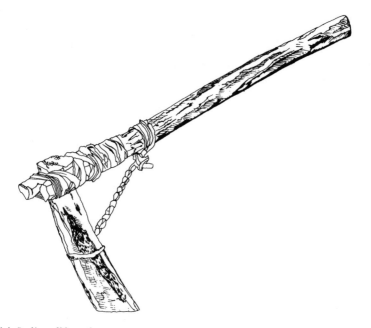

Prairie Indian elkhorn hoe
Hidatsa

prosperous. I want our harvest to be bountiful. And I want our children to become as abundant as the flowers in the spring."

All of his people would hear him, and he would hear a murmur of approval throughout all the village. He then began to collect robes, clothing, horses, and other things of value, to be given away as presents or exchanged as medicine bundles.

When everything was in readiness, he took a gift and a pipe to a man whom, he believed, had greater supernatural strength than himself. He requested this man to act as priest in the Corn Ceremony. If the man accepted the invitation and smoked the pipe, he became the Medicine Maker, the chief medicine man of the ceremony. The Medicine Maker soon went to the lodge of the Singer, who knew all the songs and secrets of the ceremony. When the Medicine Maker offered him a robe and invited him to participate in the Corn Ceremony, the Singer gladly accepted. They then smoked the pipe together.

When the Medicine Maker had left the lodge, the Singer dressed and painted himself. Taking a piece of charcoal, he made three motions, as if he were painting his face. The fourth time, he drew a mark across his face as he sang:

"I am walking. I am walking."

The words meant that he was still following the instructions that the Old Woman Who Never Dies gave to the first priests of the first Corn Ceremony. He then placed a necklace of corn ears about his neck as he sang, "Yellow, Yellow," meaning "corn." Taking an ear of corn in his hand, he chanted:

"I am standing. I am walking."

Putting on a cap of the head-skin of his medicine animal—the kit-fox, for example—he sang:

"Kit-fox is walking. Kit-fox is walking."

When he was ready to depart, he addressed Old Woman Who Never Dies by singing:

"Young Woman, your fire-smoke I see;
I am coming. It is here."

The Singer then went to the lodge of the Medicine Maker, where those who were to participate in the ceremony were seated. They had been invited because their medicines were various birds that were thought to be the children of Old Woman Who Never Dies, and were therefore particularly appropriate for this ceremony. Their medicine bundles were laid in the center of the lodge.

The Medicine Maker burned incense, and then all started for the lodge of the man who had made the vow. He was called the *votary*. The Medicine Maker led the group, carrying the head of a deer. The others followed, with the Singer in the center.

As they approached his lodge, the votary came forth with a pipe, which he offered to the Medicine Maker. He took a few whiffs and then returned the pipe. This stopping and smoking occurred four times before the group reached the votary's lodge.

In the place of honor in his lodge, a very fine buffalo skin had been spread as an altar. Upon it the Medicine Maker placed the deer's head he had carried. The Singer sat behind it, and at his right sat the Medicine Maker, the votary and his wife, and the other participants. Buffalo robes had been spread in front of the positions taken by the assisting medicine men. Each of them placed his medicine bundle upon his particular robe.

The Medicine Maker raised the deer's head and touched the body of the votary's wife with it. Then each of the medicine men touched her body with his bundle and laid it in front of the altar, on robes that had been spread out for that purpose. This part of the ceremony was to give to the woman the strength and the power contained in the medicine bundles.

The votary and his wife then seated themselves on the side of the lodge at the left of the Singer. The Singer said to the votary, "Bring a live coal from the fire in the center of the lodge and lay it on an earthen bowl."

Near it was a special bowl that was considered a symbol of Old Woman Who Never Dies. From it, the Singer took a handful of sage. After making a slow motion toward each of the Four Winds, the Singer lowered the sage to the hot coal, made four circles over it, and let the handful of sage fall.

The Medicine Maker waved a large bundle of sage over the smoke. Everyone was silent. The Singer took up the bowl in which the incense burned and passed it back and forth over the medicine bundles. As he passed it, he sang, again and again:

> Sage is good.
> Sage is good.

When he had set the bowl down, all the people stretched their hands toward it and rubbed themselves as if they were receiving its power. The votary filled a pipe and handed it to the medicine man at the end of the row. After inhaling a puff or two, he passed it to the one seated at his left.

When all had smoked, the Singer raised one of the medicine bundles, perhaps the raven, and sang as its owner came forward:

> Raven is walking. Raven is walking.
> *Pedhifska didahuft.*
> Raven is walking.

The Raven man took the bundle from the Singer's hands and danced backward and forward between the altar and the fireplace. He held the bundle in his hands and swung it back and forth and from side to side. As he danced, he and the Singer chanted:

> Raven is dancing back and forth.
> Raven is dancing back and forth.

The Medicine Maker brought choice bits of meat and pretended to feed the Raven bundle! The votary then gave it back to him, and he returned to his seat. His wife gathered up the presents offered to his medicine by the votary.

The Singer thus called, in the correct order, each of the medicine men, and learned the songs as he had learned the Raven songs. When all these songs had been repeated, the votary and his wife brought food and placed it before the altar. The Singer chanted the prayer to The One Who First Made All Things:

> *Madhidift, Ifdihkawahidith.*
> I am walking in your path.

The votary brought a dish of choice parts of meat and laid it before the Singer. He sang:

> "Old Woman Who Never Dies, I am walking in your path."

Lifting the dish, he extended it to the Four Winds and then threw the meat among the medicine men while he sang:

> I take; I offer; it is done.

This was allegorical of the feeding of her birds by Old Woman Who Never Dies. The people scrambled for the food, chirping like blackbirds, ravens, and chickadees. The votary and his wife distributed the remainder of the food among the participants and the spectators. When the feast was finished, the owners of the medicine bundles advanced to receive them, while the Singer chanted:

I am walking; I have finished.
The land is green,
The land is yellow,
The land is gray.

The Medicine Maker took a bundle of sage and waved it toward the Four Winds and toward the door, as if to rid the lodge of evil spirits. The Singer brushed himself with sage, removed his cap and his necklace of corn ears, and then washed his face with water brought by the votary. His last song was this:

Kadhakowift; huft—
It is done; come—.

This song meant that the vow had been fulfilled and asked the Corn Spirit to answer the prayers for a bountiful harvest.

Curtis, *The North American Indian, vol. iv, 149-152.*

■

AN ADDRESS TO MOTHER CORN
Arikara

The Arikaras came from the south, many years ago, to the Missouri River in what is now North Dakota and the Fort Berthold Reservation in South Dakota, where they live today. With them, they brought not only reliance on corn as their most important agricultural crop, but also their appreciation of it as a divine gift. The Great Spirit Above gave them corn and they show their gratitude every year in their ceremonies.

■

In these religious ceremonies, corn was honored and referred to in the endearing and also the highly respectful title of "Mother Corn." At a certain time in the ritual, one of the leaders of the tribe made an address to Mother Corn in the following words, or in words with similar effect.

"In ancient time the Great Spirit Above sent Mother Corn to our people to be their friend and helper, to give them support and health and strength. She has walked with our people on the long and difficult

Cooking pot
Arikara

path that they have traveled from the faraway past, and now she marches with us toward the future.

"In the dim, distant past days, Mother Corn gave food to our ancestors. As she gave it to them, she now gives it to us. And as she was faithful and bountiful to our forefathers and to us, so will she be faithful and bountiful to our children. Now and in all time to come, she will give to us the blessings for which we have prayed.

"Mother Corn leads us as she led our fathers and our mothers down through the ages. The path of Mother Corn lies ahead, and we walk with her, day by day. We go forward with hope and confidence in the future, just as our ancestors did during all the past ages. When the lonely prairie stretched wide and fearful before us, we were doubtful and afraid. But Mother Corn strengthened and encouraged us.

"Now Mother Corn's return makes our hearts glad. Give thanks! Give thanks to Mother Corn! She brings us a blessing. She brings us peace and plenty. She comes from the Great Spirit Above, who has brought us good things."

Throughout the address and the elaborate ceremony that preceded and followed it, a stalk of corn stood before the altar, representing the spirit of Mother Corn.

About sunset, the staff of corn was dressed like a woman and carried at the head of a religious procession to the brink of the nearby river. White people call it the Missouri River; the Arikaras always called it the Mysterious Waters. With reverence, they placed the stalk in the water so that it might float along as a symbol of their affection for Mother Corn.

Gilmore, *Prairie Smoke*, 172-174.

■

THE BUFFALO DANCE
Mandan

Since 1700 the Mandan tribe maintained their camp in North Dakota, where they belonged to the Siouan linguistic family. Mandans lived at a strategic point on the Missouri River between Heart River and the Little Missouri Rivers, N.D. Their traditions resemble those of more eastern tribes. They became historically famous when Captains Lewis and Clark chose the site of Mandan settlement to build their first winter camp of 1804-05. There Captain Lewis hired Sacagawea and her husband Charbonneau to join the expedition as interpreters. Sacagawea was Shoshone and was able to get horses from the Shoshones to cross the Rocky Mountains. Later, in 1806, the explorers arrived at the Mandan village on their return from the Pacific Ocean. In 1837, the Mandans were nearly wiped out by smallpox, and later moved to Fort Berthold, N.D.

■

Not too long ago, the buffalo was the principal source of food and clothing for the Mandan Indian tribe.

For these reasons, each year their tribe held a feastival to honor the buffalo. It became the chief celebration, a feast for all, marking the time for the buffalo's return. The buffalo-hunting season followed.

The most exciting event of the festival was the Buffalo Dance. Eight men participated, wearing buffalo skins on their backs and painting themselves black, red, and white. Dancers endeavored to imitate the buffalo on the prairie.

Each dancer held a rattle in his right hand, and in his left a six-foot rod. On his head, he wore a bunch of green willow boughs. The season for the return of the buffalo coincided with the willow trees in full leaf.

Another dance required only four tribesmen, representing the four main directions of the compass from which the buffalo might come. With a canoe in the center, two dancers, dressed as grizzly bears who might attack the hunters, took their places on each side. They growled and threatened to spring upon anyone who might interfere with the ceremony.

Onlookers tried to appease the grizzlies by tossing food to them. The two dancers would pounce upon the food, carrying it away to the prairie as possible lures for the coming of the buffaloes.

During the ceremony, the old men of the tribe beat upon drums and chanted prayers for successful buffalo hunting.

By the end of the fourth day of the Buffalo Dance, a man entered the camp disguised as the evil spirit of famine. Immediately he was driven away by shouts and stone-throwing from the younger Mandans, who waited excitedly to participate in the ceremony.

When the demon of famine was successfully driven away, the entire tribe joined in the bountiful thanksgiving feast, symbolic of the early return of buffalo to the Mandan hunting-grounds.

Spence, *Myths of North American Indians*, 134-135.

■

SUN DANCE MOUNTAIN
Dakota-Sioux

The Sun Dance was an important religious ceremony performed by many North American Indian tribes. It was of most importance and most spectacular among the Plains Indians. "It reached its fullest development among the Teton band of Dakota Sioux, who regarded the sun as the greatest manifestation of the mysterious, all-pervading power *waka taka*....The ceremony was held usually during the summer solstice."

■

Near the northwest corner of the Black Hills of South Dakota stands Sun Dance Mountain. Its forbidding cliffs look tall against the western sky. At the foot of this strange mountain, the Dakota-Sioux Indians of the area held their annual dance in honor of their sacred Sun God.

Many, many years ago, a wise old warrior said to a beautiful maiden, "If you will marry a brave that is pleasing to the Sun God, you will bring good fortune to yourself and to all of our people."

The beautiful maiden had many wooers, and knew many young men who had ponies and gold and who would like to marry her. But she really favored one who had nothing to offer her except his love. She promised him that when he had the blessing of the sun, she would marry him.

So the young brave started forth to seek the Sun and get his blessing. After many months of search and difficulties, he found the Sun God and

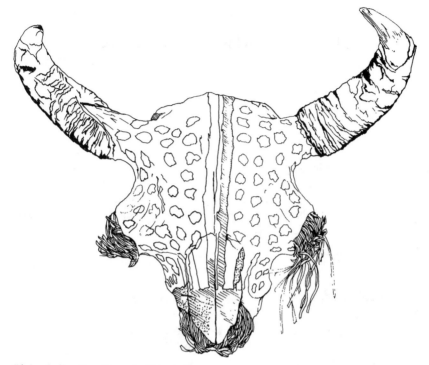

Plains Indian Sun Dance buffalo skull
Dakota-Sioux

received his blessing. He then returned to his beloved, and they were married.

After the marriage ceremony, the people of the young brave held dance at the foot of the mountain. Many different kinds of dances were performed, including the Sun Dance. The Sun Dancers danced all the day under the scorching sun. Some of them had no food and no water all day. Some pierced their ears, so that they would bleed while they danced.

They made these sacrifices in order to obtain the favor of the Great Spirit Above. This dance, honoring the marriage of the beautiful maiden to the young brave who had been blessed by the Sun, became an annual affair.

The dances that were held at the base of Sun Dance Mountain were revered by the Indians for a long, long time.

Kurath, *Standard Dictionary of Folklore, Mythology, and Legend*, vol. 2, 1088-1089
Price, *Black Hills: Land of Legend*, 42-43.

■

ORIGIN OF THE PRAIRIE ROSE
Dakota-Sioux

■

Long, long ago, when the world was young and people had not come out yet, no flowers bloomed on the prairie. Only grasses and dull, greenish gray shrubs grew there. Earth felt very sad because her robe lacked brightness and beauty.

"I have many beautiful flowers in my heart," Earth said to herself. "I wish they were on my robe. Blue flowers like the clear sky in fair weather, white flowers like the snow of winter, brilliant yellow ones like the sun at midday, pink ones like the dawn of a spring day—all these are in my heart. I am sad when I look on my dull robe, all gray and brown."

A sweet little pink flower heard Earth's sad talking. "Do not be sad, Mother Earth. I will go upon your robe and beautify it."

So the little pink flower came up from the heart of the Earth Mother to beautify the prairies. But when the Wind Demon saw her, he growled, "I will not have that pretty flower on my playground."

He rushed at her, shouting and roaring, and blew out her life. But her spirit returned to the heart of Mother Earth.

When other flowers gained courage to go forth, one after another, Wind Demon killed them also. And their spirits returned to the heart of Mother Earth.

At last Prairie Rose offered to go. "Yes, sweet child," said Earth Mother, "I will let you go. You are so lovely and your breath so fragrant that surely the Wind Demon will be charmed by you. Surely he will let you stay on the prairie."

So Prairie Rose made the long journey up through the dark ground and came out on the drab prairie. As she went, Mother Earth said in her heart, "Oh, I do hope that Wind Demon will let her live."

When Wind Demon saw her, he rushed toward her, shouting: "She is pretty, but I will not allow her on my playground. I will blow out her life."

So he rushed on, roaring and drawing his breath in strong gusts. As he came closer, he caught the fragrance of Prairie Rose.

"Oh—how sweet!" he said to himself. "I do not have it in my heart to blow out the life of such a beautiful maiden with so sweet a breath. She must stay here with me. I must make my voice gentle, and I must sing sweet songs. I must not frighten her away with my awful noise."

Bone beads
Sioux

So Wind Demon changed. He became quiet. He sent gentle breezes over the prairie grasses. He whispered and hummed little songs of gladness. He was no longer a demon.

Then other flowers came up from the heart of the Earth Mother, up through the dark ground. They made her robe, the prairie, bright and joyous. Even Wind came to love the blossoms growing among the grasses of the prairie. And so the robe of Mother Earth became beautiful because of the loveliness, the sweetness, and the courage of the Prairie Rose.

Sometimes Wind forgets his gentle songs and becomes loud and noisy. But his loudness does not last long. And he does not harm a person whose robe is the color of Prairie Rose.

Gilmore, *Prairie Smoke: A Collection of Lore of the Prairies*, 48-49, 200-203.

■

THE HERMIT, OR THE GIFT OF CORN
Dakota-Sioux

Corn entered widely into the mythology and religious practices of North American Indian tribes of the Southwest, Southeast, Plains, and Eastern woodlands. Corn gods in different regions are personified as Corn Mother, Corn Maidens, and even Corn Grandfathers as in this story of the hermit. Various parts of the corn plant are used ritually such as husks, pollen, kernels, and whole ears. Major tribal ceremonies are held prior to corn planting and after the harvest.

■

Alone in a deep forest, far from the village of his people, lived a hermit. His tent was made of buffalo skins, and his robe was made of deerskin. Far from the haunts of any human being, this old hermit was content to spend his many years.

All day long, he wandered through the forest, studying the different plants and collecting roots. The roots he used as food and as medicine. At long intervals some warrior would arrive at his tent and get medicinal roots from him for the tribe. The old hermit's medicine was considered far superior to all others.

One day, after a long ramble in the woods, the hermit came home so tired that, immediately after eating, he lay down on his bed. Just as he was dozing off to sleep, he felt something rub against his feet. Awakening with a start, he noticed a dark object. It extended an arm toward him. In its hand was a flint-pointed arrow.

"This must be a spirit," thought the hermit, "for there is no human being here but me."

A voice then said, "Hermit, I have come to invite you to my home."

"I will come," the old hermit replied. So he arose, wrapped his robe around him, and started toward the voice.

Outside his door, he looked around, but he could see no sign of the dark object.

"Whatever you are, or wherever you be," said the hermit, "wait for me. I do not know where to go to find your house."

He received no answer, nor did he hear any sound of someone walking through the brush. Reentering his tent, he lay down and was soon fast asleep.

The next night he again heard the voice say, "Hermit, I have come to invite you to my home." The hermit walked out of his tent to find the person with that voice, but again he found no one. This time he was angry, because he thought that someone was making sport of him. He determined to find out who was disturbing his night's rest.

The next evening he cut a hole in the tent large enough to stick an arrow through. Then he stood by the door, watching. Soon the dark object came, stopped outside the door, and said, "Grandfather, I came to——" But he never finished his sentence. The old hermit had shot his

Plains Indian ladle
Dakota-Sioux

arrow. He heard it strike something that produced a sound as though he had shot into a sack of pebbles.

Early the next morning the hermit went out and looked at the spot near where he thought his arrow had struck some object. There on the ground lay a little heap of corn, and from this little heap a small line of corn lay scattered along a path. The old hermit followed this path into the woods.

When he reached a small mound, the trail ended. At its end was a large circle from which the grass had been scraped off clean.

"The corn trail stops at the edge of this circle," the old man said to himself. "So this must be the home of whatever invited me."

He took his big bone axe and knife and proceeded to dig down into the center of the circle. When he got as far down as he could reach, he came to a sack of dried meat. Next, he found a sack of turnips, then a sack of dried cherries, and then a sack of corn.

Last of all was another sack, empty except for one cup of corn. In the other corner was a hole where the hermit's arrow had pierced the sack. From this hole the corn had been scattered along the trail, which had guided the old man to the hiding place.

From this experience the hermit taught his people how to keep their provisions while they were traveling.

"Dig a pit," he explained to them, "put your provisions into it, and cover them with earth."

By this method, the Sioux used to keep provisions all summer. When fall came, they would return to their hiding place. When they opened it, they would find all their provisions as fresh as they were the day they had been placed there.

The people thanked the old hermit for his discovery of this method of preserving their food. And they thanked him for his discovery of corn, the first they had seen. It became one of the most important foods the Indians knew.

McLaughlin, *Myths and Legends of the Sioux*, 101-103.

■

THE LEGEND OF STANDING ROCK

Dakota-Sioux

The Dakota-Sioux are one of the most famous tribes in North America. They belong to the Siouan linguistic family, known since about 1600. They spread from Mississippi to Minnesota, Wisconsin, Iowa, North and South Dakota, Montana, Nebraska, and Wyoming. Gold discoveries in the Black Hills caused a rush of miners to the region, who existed in warlike conflict with the Dakota-Sioux, leading to General Custer's defeat at Little Big Horn, June 25, 1876.

■

Years ago, a man from the Dakota-Sioux tribe married a girl from the Arikara tribe. After they had one child, the man brought another wife to their home. The first wife pouted because she was jealous. When time came for their people to break camp, she refused to move from her place. After their tent was taken down, she sat there, on the ground, with her baby on her back. Her husband and the rest of their people moved on.

At noon, her husband stopped the line of people and said to his two brothers, "Go back to your sister-in-law. Tell her to come on. We will wait for you here. But hurry! I fear that she may become desperate and kill herself."

The two rode off and in the evening arrived at their last camping place. The woman still sat on the ground. The elder brother said to her, "Sister-in-law, we have come to get you. The camp is waiting for you. Get up and join us."

When she did not answer, brother-in-law put out his hand and touched her lightly on her head. She had turned into stone!

The two brothers lashed their ponies and rode back to camp. They told their story, but were not believed. "She has killed herself," said her husband, "and my brothers will not tell me."

The whole village broke camp and returned to the place where they had left the woman. There she sat, a block of stone in the form of a woman. Her husband's people were very excited. They chose a pony, a handsome one, made a new travois, and placed the stone in its carrying net. Pony and travois were beautifully painted and then decorated with streamers of various colors. The stone was considered holy, and was given a place of honor in the center of the camp.

Whenever the people moved and made a new camp, the stone and travois were taken with them. For years the stone woman traveled with that group. It stands today in front of the Standing Rock Indian Agency in South Dakota.

McLaughlin, *Myths and Legends of the Sioux*, 40-41.

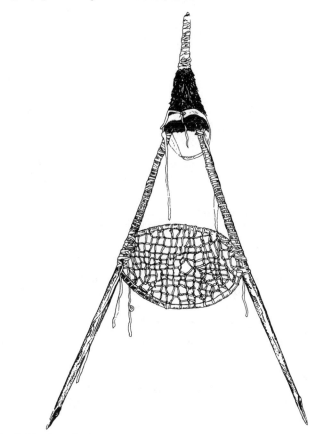

Plains Indian travois
Dakota-Sioux

■

THE MYSTERIOUS BUTTE
Dakota-Sioux

■

One time, long ago, when a young man was out hunting, he came to a steep hill. Its east side suddenly dropped off in a precipitous bank. As he stood on that bank he noticed, at the base, a small opening. Examining it closely after going down the slope, he found that the opening was really large enough for a horse or a buffalo to walk through. On each side of this opening he was surprised to see figures of several different animals carved in the wall.

When he entered, he was amazed to see scattered on the floor before him many pipes, bracelets, and other things that people use as ornaments. They seemed to have been offerings to some great spirit.

Passing through this first room, he entered the second and found it so dark that he could not see his hands in front of him. He was frightened. He hurriedly left the place, returned home, and told what he had seen.

The Chief, hearing the young man's story, immediately selected four of his most daring warriors to go with the young man to find out whether or not he was telling the truth. When they reached the place, the young man refused to go inside because on each side of the entrance, the carved figures had been changed!

The four who entered saw that in the first room everything was exactly as the young man had described it. So was their first glimpse of the second room—so dark that they could not see anything. But they continued walking, feeling their way along the walls. At last they found another entrance—or exit. This one was so narrow that they had to squeeze through it sideways. Again they found their way along the walls until they found another opening. This one was so low that they had to crawl on their hands and knees in order to go into the next room.

It was the last one. Entering it, they were surprised by a very sweet odor coming from the opposite direction. Crawling on their hands and knees, and feeling around with their fingers, they found a hole in the ground. Through that hole came the sweet odor. The four warriors hurriedly held a council and decided to return at once to the camp and report what they had learned.

When they reached the first chamber, one young man said, "I am going to take these bracelets to show that we are telling the truth."

"No!" the other three exclaimed promptly. "You are in the abode of some Great Spirit. Some accident may happen to you for taking something that is not yours."

"Aw! You fellows are like old women!" He took a beautiful bracelet and placed it on his left wrist.

When the men reached the village, they reported what they had seen. The one wearing the bracelet shows it, to prove that they had told the truth.

In a short time, these four men were out preparing traps for wolves. As usual, they raised one end of a heavy log and placed a stick under it to hold it up. About five feet from the log, they placed a large piece of meat and covered the space between meat and log with poles and willows. At the spot where they placed the stick, they left a hole large enough to admit the body of a wolf. A wolf would smell the meat and be unable to reach it and because of the poles and willows, the men felt sure, would crowd itself into the hole. Then it would work itself forward in order to get the meat. When its movement pushed down the stick, the log would trap the wolf under its weight.

When the young man wearing the bracelet followed this procedure with a large piece of meat, the log caught the wrist on which he wore the bracelet. Unable to release himself, he called loud and long for help. Hearing his call, his companions hurried to assist him. When they lifted the log, they found that the man's wrist had been broken.

"Now you have been punished," they said. "You have been punished for taking the bracelet out of the chamber of this mysterious butte."

Some time later, a young man who went to the butte saw engraved on the wall the figure of a woman holding a pole in her hand. With it she was holding up a large amount of meat that had been laid across another pole. It had been broken in two from the weight of so much meat. On the wall, on all sides of the figure of the woman, were the footprints of buffalo.

The next day an enormous herd of buffalo came near the village, and a great many were killed. The women were very busy cutting up and drying the meat. More buffalo meat was at one camp than was at any other. When one of the women was hanging meat upon a long tent pole, the pole broke in two. So she had to hold the meat up with another pole, just as in the engraving the young man had seen on that mysterious butte.

Even after that, the people paid weekly visits to this butte, and would read there the signs that would govern their plans. The butte has been considered the prophet of the band of Sioux who told this story for generations and generations.

McLaughlin, *Myths and Legends of the Sioux*, 104-107.

■

ORIGIN OF THE SIOUX PEACE PIPE
Dakota-Sioux

■

Long, long ago, two young and handsome Sioux were chosen by their band to find out where the buffalo were. While the men were riding in the buffalo country, they saw someone in the distance walking toward them.

As always they were on the watch for any enemy. So they hid in some bushes and waited. At last the figure came up the slope. To their surprise, the figure walking toward them was a woman.

When she came closer, she stopped and looked at them. They knew that she could see them, even in their hiding place. On her left arm she carried what looked like a stick in a bundle of sagebrush. Her face was beautiful.

One of the men said, "She is more beautiful than anyone I have ever seen. I want her for my wife."

But the other man replied, "How dare you have such a thought? She is wondrously beautiful and holy—far above ordinary people."

Though still at a distance, the woman heard them talking. She laid down her bundle and spoke to them. "Come. What is it you wish?"

The man who had spoken first went up to her and laid his hands on her as if to claim her. At once, from somewhere above, there came a whirlwind. Then there came a mist, which hid the man and the woman. When the mist cleared, the other man saw the woman with the bundle again on her arm. But his friend was a pile of bones at her feet.

The man stood silent in wonder and awe. Then the beautiful woman spoke to him. "I am on a journey to your people. Among them is a good man whose name is Bull Walking Upright. I am coming to see him especially.

"Go on ahead of me and tell your people that I am on my way. Ask them to move camp and to pitch their tents in a circle. Ask them to leave an opening in the circle, facing the north. In the center of the circle, make a large tepee, also facing the north. There I will meet Bull Walking Upright and his people."

The man saw to it that all her directions were followed. When she reached the camp, she removed the sagebrush from the gift she was carrying. The gift was a small pipe made of red stone. On it was carved the tiny outline of a buffalo calf.

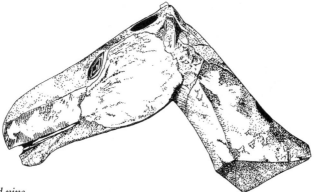

Horsehead pipe
Sioux

The pipe she gave to Bull Walking Upright, and then she taught him the prayers he should pray to the Strong One Above. "When you pray to the Strong One Above, you must use this pipe in the ceremony. When you are hungry, unwrap the pipe and lay it bare in the air. Then the buffalo will come where the men can easily hunt and kill them. So the children, the men, and the women will have food and be happy."

The beautiful woman also told him how the people should behave in order to live peacefully together. She taught them the prayers they should say when praying to their Mother Earth. She told him how they should decorate themselves for ceremonies.

"The earth," she said, "is your mother. So, for special ceremonies, you will decorate yourselves as your mother does—in black and red, in brown and white. These are the colors of the buffalo also.

"Above all else, remember that this is a peace pipe that I have given you. You will smoke it before all ceremonies. You will smoke it before making treaties. It will bring peaceful thoughts into your minds. If you will use it when you pray to the Strong One above and to Mother Earth, you will be sure to receive the blessings that you ask."

When the woman had completed her message, she turned and slowly walked away. All the people watched her in awe. Outside the opening of the circle, she stopped for an instant and then lay down on the ground. She rose again in the form of a black buffalo cow. Again she lay down, and then arose in the form of a red buffalo cow. A third time she lay down, and arose as a brown buffalo cow. The fourth and last time she had the form of a spotlessly white buffalo cow. Then she walked toward the north into the distance and finally disappeared over a far-off hill.

Bull Walking Upright kept the peace pipe carefully wrapped most of the time. Every little while he called all his people together, untied the bundle, and repeated the lessons he had been taught by the beautiful woman. And he used it in prayers and other ceremonies until he was more than one hundred years old.

When he became feeble, he held a great feast. There he gave the pipe and the lessons to Sunrise, a worthy man. In a similar way the pipe was passed down from generation to generation. "As long as the pipe is used," the beautiful woman had said, "Your people will live and will be happy. As soon as it is forgotten, the people will perish."

McLaughlin, *Myths and Legends of the Sioux*, 72- 74.

■

LEGEND OF THE THUNDER GOD

Dakota-Sioux

The Black Hills of South Dakota, "with more than a thousand square miles of mysterious, haze-shrouded peaks, peaceful flowering valleys, turbulent streams and gold-ribbed cliffs, have been aptly termed 'the Happy Hunting Ground of the Dakotas.'"

■

When the Thunder God spoke among the people of the Black Hills, the Medicine Man called together the frightened warriors. They were huddled in the lodges of their camp along the Belle Fourche River. He told them this story:

"You who now listen will not be harmed. It is said that the Evil Spirit once became so angry at the Red People that he caused the mountains to vomit fire and hot stones to terrify them. Their lodges and their children were destroyed. The Great Spirit had compassion, put out the fire, and chased the Evil Spirit away.

"But when they returned to their wickedness, the Great Spirit permitted the Evil Spirit to return to the mountains and again vomit forth fire. When again the Red People became good and made sacrifices to the Great Spirit, He chased away the Evil Spirit and kept him from disturbing the people.

"For forty snows, they were undisturbed, except occasionally. Sometimes the Great Spirit would warn them, through thunder, that if they should return to their wickedness He would have them punished. Again He would have the mountains vomit forth fire and hot stones, and thus destroy them. Even today He occasionally warns us.

"So return now to your lodges, and do not be afraid. The Red People now will come to no harm."

Price, *Black Hills: Land of Legend*, 44.

■

A TETON GHOST STORY
Dakota-Sioux

Long ago there was a large band of Dakota-Sioux Indians who had spread to a village in the present Jackson Hole Basin of Grand Teton National Park in Wyoming.

■

The Teton band flourished, and its people were healthy and strong because they ate plenty of buffalo meat. Usually when they camped for the night, a crier would go among the lodges and call:

"There will be many buffalo tomorrow. Be on the alert!"

One day after the Tetons returned to their camp from a hard buffalo hunt, a young man announced that he wished to marry the most beautiful girl in the tribe, the Chief's daughter.

Her father said, "I will not give you my permission until you bring me many horses." So the young Indian set out in search of many wild horses, hoping to please the Chief and win his beautiful daughter for his bride.

While the young brave was away, his tribe abandoned their regular campsite and moved elsewhere. Later, the young Indian returned to the deserted camp with several captured horses. As it was late in the day, he thought he would take shelter nearby in a solitary lodge.

At first, he could not find a doorway into the lodge, because the sides were covered halfway up with sod. Finally, he managed to make an entrance. Inside were four high posts that had been driven into the ground.

The posts supported a kind of burial bed. On the bed lay a woman whose clothes were ornamented with elk's teeth. She turned her head, looking down at the young Teton brave. He immediately recognized her as a member of his tribe—but now she was a Woman Ghost! They stayed there for a long time and she became his wife.

One day he said to himself, "I think I will go on a buffalo hunt." Although he did not speak aloud, the Ghost Woman knew his thoughts and said, "You are hungry for buffalo meat? Mount your horse and ride back to the bluffs.

"When you come to the buffalo herd, rush into the center of them and shoot the fattest one. Bring home the hide and buffalo meat. Roast the meat and bring me a share before you eat yours."

The young Teton Indian brave left and followed Ghost Woman's instructions. When he reached the valley, he came to a large herd of buffalo. He charged his horse at full speed into the middle of them and shot the fattest one. He skinned it and cut up the meat, carrying the robe and meat upon his packhorse. He skewered a large piece of meat and roasted it until it was cooked enough, then he took it to Ghost Woman, who was standing in the center of the lodge.

Her husband was startled to see her standing there. Rows and rows of beautiful beadwork decorated her leather clothing. Already knowing what the young brave was thinking she said, "Please do not be afraid of me!"

Wooden horse effigy
Sioux

From that time on, they talked freely and planned what they would like to do. The young Indian brave said, "Why don't we begin our life together like our parents did when they were first married?"

But the Ghost Woman replied, "No, no, that would never do, because we will need to pitch our tent during the day and travel by night." The young brave wondered about this arrangement.

That is how it happened that they traveled at night. Ghost Woman walked ahead with her head covered, never saying a word to her husband as they traveled. Her legs were invisible. She made no noise as she floated along, ghostlike.

Whenever the young Teton Indian brave thought about anything, Ghost Woman already knew what it was that he had in his mind. Is this why the Teton Indians say, "Beware of Ghosts because Ghosts know all things."

They say Ghosts know when the winds blow and which ones. Ghosts know when there will be snow. Ghosts know when there will be thunder and lightning. Ghosts are glad when the winds blow, because they can float along more swiftly as they travel from place to place.

This is the way Teton Ghost Woman and the young Teton brave lived. Their tribal people never found them again. The Chief's daughter wondered why her young brave never returned to her.

Finally, the young brave also became a Teton Ghost, floating along with the Teton Ghost Woman, every night, forever.

J. O. Dorsey, "Teton Ghost Story," 71-72.

■

How Medicine Man Resurrected Buffalo

Arapaho

The Arapaho tribe were unusual as they occupied many different regions while migrating westward. They lived for some time in the Red River Valley of Minnesota and North Dakota territories before they crossed the Missouri River and settled in Wyoming. There they divided into the Northern Arapaho and Southern Arapaho. The latter settled on a reservation in Oklahoma, while the Northern Arapaho joined the Shoshones on the Wind River Reservation in Wyoming. In the early 1800s, the Arapaho were famous for raiding other tribes and white settlements on the Great Plains.

■

At one time an Arapaho Medicine Man named Black-Robe wanted very much to be able to make magic because his people were very hungry. How could he lure the buffaloes back to the Arapaho hunting grounds? Buffalo meat was their principal food.

Black-Robe decided to ask Cedar-Tree for his help. "Go west and hunt buffalo for our people. Try very hard to find at least one buffalo."

Cedar-Tree hunted hard as he was asked to do. After a long time, he saw some black objects at a distance. "Could they be buffaloes?" he wondered.

Encouraged, he walked faster, but as he drew closer he was less sure the black objects were buffaloes. Suddenly, he saw the black things fly toward the sky. By then, Cedar-Tree seemed certain the objects were oversized ravens.

Disappointed, he returned to his village, reporting to Black-Robe what he had seen. The Medicine Man scolded him for not believing that what he had seen were buffaloes.

"If you had only believed strong enough, the buffaloes would not have changed to ravens," said Black Robe.

By now the Arapahoes were desperately hungry. One woman on the verge of starving made soup from the soles of her moccasins. The next day her uncle, Trying-Bear, set out early to hunt for anything edible. He had no weapons. Fortunately, on the way he met Black-Robe who loaned him a bow and some arrows.

"Tomorrow morning, I will come to your tent to learn of your success," said Black-Robe. "You must even try to find a dried buffalo, if not a live one."

After hunting a long time to the northwest, Trying-Bear finally found a dried buffalo. He ran home swiftly to tell his people. Black-Robe painted his white pony black and wrapped a black buffalo robe about himself. He stuck his lucky eagle-feather in his hair, mounted his black pony, and took off in a rush to find the dried buffalo.

"Follow me, Trying Bear," Black-Robe called.

Because he wanted to see what Black-Robe would do with the dried buffalo, Trying-Bear followed rapidly. Medicine Man arrived about midday at the place of the dead buffalo. He dismounted, took aim with his magic eagle-feather, and threw it straight at the carcass. Immediately, a live buffalo jumped to its feet!

Black-Robe turned and saw Trying-Bear. "Shoot it!" commanded Medicine Man. Trying-Bear shot it dead.

"Let's skin it and carry everything eatable back to our people," said Black-Robe.

A feast of thanksgiving and rejoicing followed. Black-Robe had saved his people from starvation. Arapahoes still love to tell this story of how their Medicine Man resurrected the dead buffalo with his magic eagle-feather-medicine!

Voth, "How Medicine Man Resurrected Buffalo," 44.

■

THE BUFFALO ROCK

Blackfeet

The buffalo rock, as called by the Blackfeet Indians, was usually a fossil shell of some kind, picked up on the prairie. Whoever found one was considered fortunate, for it was thought to give a person great power over buffalo. The owner put the stone in his lodge, near the fire, and prayed over it. This story reveals not only the use of such a rock, but also a common method of hunting buffalo before the Indians had horses.

■

There was once a very poor woman, the second wife of a Blackfeet. Her buffalo robe was old and full of holes; her buffalo moccasins were worn and ripped. She and her people were camped not far from a cliff that would be a good place for a buffalo drive. They were very much in need of buffalo, for they were not only ragged but starving.

One day while this poor woman was gathering wood, she heard a voice singing. Looking around, she found that the song was coming from a buffalo rock. It sang, "Take me. Take me. I have great power."

So the woman took the buffalo rock. When she returned to her lodge, she said to her husband, "Call all the men and have them sing to bring the buffalo."

"Are you in earnest?" her husband asked.

"Yes, I am," the woman replied. "Call the men, and also get a small piece of the back of a buffalo from the Bear Medicine man. Ask some of the men to bring the four rattles they use."

The husband did as his wife directed. Then she showed him how to arrange the inside of the lodge in a kind of square box with some sagebrush and buffalo chips. Though it was the custom for the first wife to sit next to her husband, the man directed his second wife to put on the dress of the other woman and to sit beside him. When everything was ready, the men who had been summoned sat down in the lodge beside the woman and her husband. Then the buffalo rock began to sing, "The buffalo will all drift back. The buffalo will all drift back."

Hearing this song, the woman asked one of the young men to go outside and put a great many buffalo chips in line. "After you have them in place, wave at them with a buffalo robe four times, and shout at them in a singsong. At the fourth time, all the buffalo chips will turn into buffaloes and go over the cliff."

The young man followed her directions, and the chips became buffaloes. At the same time, the woman led the people in the lodge in the singing of songs. One song was about the buffalo that would lead the others in the drive. While the people were chanting it, a cow took the lead and all the herd followed her. They plunged over the cliff and were killed.

Then the woman sang,

> More than a hundred buffalo
> Have fallen over the cliff.
> I have made them fall.
> And the man above the earth hears me singing.
> More than a hundred buffalo
> Have fallen over the cliff.

And so the people learned that the rock was very powerful. Ever since that time, they have taken care of the buffalo rock and have prayed to it.

Michelson, "Piegan Tales," 246-247.

■

THE WISE MAN OF CHIEF MOUNTAIN
Blackfeet

Chief of the Mountains is grim, rugged, and majestic. Indeed, these are very good reasons for the Blackfeet Indians to have named the awesome peak, Chief Mountain. It is located in Montana, in the northeastern corner of Glacier National Park.

Tribal historian Yellow Wolfe of the Blackfeet tribe always enjoyed telling the following story about Chief Mountain and the people who once lived in its shadow.

■

Two members of the Blackfeet tribe were Wise Man and his wife. Their people called him Wise Man because he always seemed to know how to do everything right.

At that time, the Blackfeet wore the plainest kinds of clothes. Wise Man thought about this for a long time. One day he said to his wife, "Let

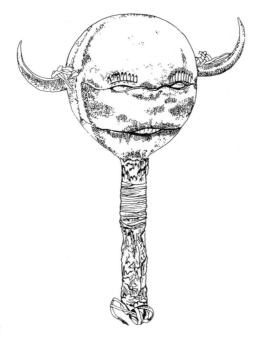

Rawhide rattle
Blackfeet

us go away for a while. I wish to make some things that I have been planning for a long time."

Wise Man and his wife packed their travois, which was drawn by dogs, and moved to the base of the Inside Lakes. There they made their camp. He hunted and killed enough game for him and his wife and their dogs before beginning work on his plan.

First, he climbed to the high ridge between the lakes and Little River, where he dug an eagle trap. Beside the pit, he laid a deer and slashed its body to attract an eagle. When all was ready, Wise Man jumped into the pit and covered it with willow sticks and grass to make a blind. He waited for an eagle to come. Several eagles, with their wings swishing the air, sailed down upon the deer.

While the eagles ate at the deer, Wise Man reached up cautiously, snatched the legs of an eagle, and pulled it down into the pit. By repeating this method, he caught a large number of eagles. These he tied together, dragging them to his camp. There, he removed their tail feathers, their fluffy plume feathers, and other useful feathers that would help his plan.

As winter arrived, weasels appeared, and Wise Man hunted them. This was more difficult than trapping eagles but he set many snares and caught about a hundred weasels.

Eagle headdress
Blackfeet

Wise Man made himself an eagle headdress and hung white weasel fur skins upon it. Along the seams of his shirt sleeves and leggings, he hung more weasel skins. Adorned with his newly decorated clothes, he presented himself to his wife.

"Oh, you look brave and handsome!" she said. "Your new clothes with feathers and furs are the most beautiful ones I have ever seen!"

"I'm glad you like them," he replied. "Now I want to make something special for you."

Wise Man put away his new clothes, and dressed for hunting. He started out to look for elk. From these animals, he collected the skins, tusks, and teeth. He sewed them in decorative rows on the front and back of his wife's new dress. Both of them thought it most attractive.

"Now we have a fine new appearance," she said. "Shall we go home to Chief Mountain and show our people what you have accomplished?"

"Not yet," answered Wise Man. "Something is lacking, and I must discover what it is. I shall ask the Great Spirit to show me what more I must do."

On the very next day, when Wise Man walked through the timber, he found a dead porcupine. Its quills were scattered around on the ground. He examined them, thinking how he could dye the quills different colors. If he could, his wife's new dress would be even more beautiful, he thought. He shot another porcupine for its quills, and carried the animal home to cook.

"I know the yellow moss growing on pine trees will stain anything yellow," his wife suggested. "The color will not fade or wash off. I'm sure you can find other dyes for different colors, too."

He found green in another wood, and red in the juice of a certain plant. So Wise Man dyed the quills three colors—yellow, green, and red. He flattened the quills somewhat and sewed them side by side on the leather clothes, making different designs. He took a long time with his work. Finally, he had enough for his shirt and leggings, as well as for the neck, the front, and the back of his wife's new dress.

Each of them were so pleased with the colorful and charming appearance of the other that they hugged and danced together for joy.

At last, Wise Man felt satisfied with the way his plan had developed. They broke camp and started home to their people near Chief Mountain. When they came within sight of their tribe, they put on their newly decorated clothes.

When their friends saw them approaching they did not at first believe they were Wise Man and his wife. But when they came closer, their people recognized them. All of the tribe crowded about Wise Man and his wife, staring, touching, and asking many questions about how their clothes were made.

Wise Man showed all of the people at Chief Mountain how he created the new ornaments. Immediately, the people began to gather the materials to make decorated clothes for themselves.

Since that time, the Blackfeet Indians have become very well known for their handsome and colorful dress. Wise Man became a strong leader in his tribe. He was acclaimed for discovering how to make everything more beautiful. This is why his people loved him and always called him Chief Wise Man of the Blackfeet tribe.

Schultz, *Blackfeet Tales of Glacier National Park*, 235.

Porcupine quill medicine wheel
Blackfeet

■

ORIGIN OF THE SWEAT LODGE
Piegan

The Piegan tribe was southernmost at the headwaters of the Missouri River in Montana, a subtribe belonging to the Siksika Indians of North Saskatchewan in Canada. Piegans were of the Algonquian linguistic family, but warlike toward most of their neighboring tribes, since they had horses for raiding and were supplied with guns and ammunition by their Canadian sources. Piegans also displayed hostility toward explorers and traders. Several smallpox epidemics decimated their population. Now they are gathered on reservations on both sides of the border.

■

A girl of great beauty, the Chief's daughter, was worshipped by many young handsome men of the Piegan tribe. But she would not have any one of them for her husband.

One young tribesman was very poor and his face was marked with an ugly scar. Although he saw rich and handsome men of his tribe rejected by the Chief's daughter, he decided to find out if she would have him for her husband. When she laughed at him for even asking, he ran away toward the south in shame.

After traveling several days, he dropped to the ground, weary and hungry, and fell asleep. From the heavens, Morning-Star looked down and pitied the young unfortunate youth, knowing his trouble.

To Sun and Moon, his parents, Morning-Star said, "There is a poor young man lying on the ground with no one to help him. I want to go after him for a companion."

"Go and get him," said his parents.

Morning-Star carried the young man, Scarface, into the sky. Sun said, "Do not bring him into my lodge yet, for he smells ill. Build four sweat lodges."

When this was done, Sun led Scarface into the first sweat lodge. He asked Morning-Star to bring a hot coal on a forked stick. Sun then broke off a bit of sweet grass and placed it upon the hot coal. As the incense arose Sun began to sing, "Old Man is coming in with his body; it is sacred," repeating it four times.

Sun passed his hands back and forth through the smoke and rubbed them over the face, left arm, and side of Scarface. Sun repeated the ceremony on the boy's right side, purifying him and removing the odors of earthly people.

Sun took Scarface into the other three sweat lodges, performing the same healing ceremony. The body of Scarface changed color and he shone like a yellow light.

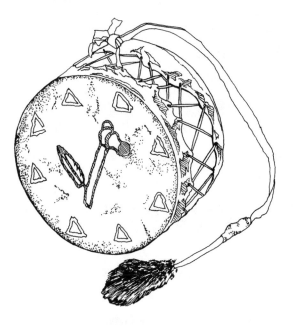

Drum
Piegan

Using a soft feather, Sun brushed it over the youth's face, magically wiping away the scar. With a final touch to the young man's long, yellow hair, Sun caused him to look exactly like Morning-Star. The two young men were led by Sun into his own lodge and placed side by side in the position of honor.

"Old Woman," called the father. "Which is your son?"

Moon pointed to Scarface, "That one is our son."

"You do not know your own child," answered Sun.

"He is not our son. We will call him Mistaken-for-Morning-Star," as they all laughed heartily at the mistake.

The two boys were together constantly and became close companions. One day, they were on an adventure when Morning-Star pointed out some large birds with very long, sharp beaks.

"Foster-Brother, I warn you not to go near those dangerous creatures," said Morning-Star. "They killed my other brothers with their beaks."

Suddenly the birds chased the two boys. Morning-Star fled toward his home, but Foster-Brother stopped, picking up a club and one by one struck the birds dead.

Upon reaching home, Morning-Star excitedly reported to his father what had happened. Sun made a victory song honoring the young hero. In gratitude for saving Morning-Star's life, Sun gave him the forked stick for lifting hot embers and a braid of sweet grass to make incense. These sacred elements necessary for making the sweat lodge ceremony were a gift of trust.

"And this my sweat lodge I give to you," said the Sun. Mistaken-for-Morning-Star observed very carefully how it was constructed, in his mind preparing himself to one day returning to earth.

When Scarface did arrive at his tribal village, all of his people gathered to see the handsome young man in their midst. At first, they did not recognize him as Scarface.

"I have been in the sky," he told them. "Behold me, Morning-Star looks just like this. The Sun gave me these things used in the sweat lodge healing ceremony. That is how I lost my ugly scar."

Scarface explained how the forked stick and sweet grass were used. Then he set to work showing his people how to make the sweat lodge. This is how the first medicine sweat lodge was built upon earth by the Piegan tribe.

Now that Scarface was so very handsome and brought such a great blessing of healing to his tribe, the Chief's beautiful daughter became his wife.

In remembrance of Sun's gift to Scarface and his tribe, the Piegans always make the sweat lodge healing ceremony an important part of their annual Sun Dance Celebration.

Curtis, *The North American Indian*, vol. vi, 59-60.

■

PUMA AND THE BEAR

Ute

A series of Ute legends was collected by A. L. Kroeber in 1900 from the Uintah Utes in Northeastern Utah. These oral recordings were made from English-speaking native Americans. Similar stories seem widespread among various tribes. For example, "Rolling Rock" was told almost everywhere, while "Bungling Host" drew on mythological ideas from other North American Indians. Most of the specific Ute tales seem original with perhaps only slight resemblance to those of other tribes.

■

One day Puma took his son hunting with him. The Bear came to Puma's tent and saw his wife there, and immediately fell in love with her. "I wish to have her for my wife," he thought. Then he went in to where she was sitting. In only a short time, he proposed that she run away with him. She consented and ran away with the Bear.

When Puma returned, he could not find his wife. "I wonder if she could have eloped with that Bear?" he mused. At first he and his son saw no tracks, but eventually they picked up the couple's trail. Angry by now, Puma followed the Bear tracks.

A high wind began to blow, obliterating most of the tracks. The next day Puma found them again and followed on. "Perhaps they are in that

Tipi
Ute

cedar wood," he thought. As he moved closer, he heard voices and recognized his wife's and the Bear's.

He sent his son to circle the wood, approaching from the other side of the wood to force the Bear out toward Puma. The woman said "Puma is very strong." "But I am stronger," said the Bear, seizing a cedar tree and pulling it from the ground. "He is stronger than that," said the woman.

The Bear had his moccasins off when Puma's son attacked. Quickly the Bear put on his moccasins, but in his haste he put them on the wrong feet. Then, not knowing who was coming behind him, he ran forward into Puma. The two grappled and Puma threw the Bear to the ground. The Bear rose up again and charged at Puma, who thrust the Bear down against a rock and broke the Bear's back.

Then Puma sent his wife away into the woods, letting her know that he did not want her for his wife again. Puma and his son left on another hunting trip to find a new wife and home for themselves.

Kroeber, "Puma and the Bear," 252, 274.

■

PORCUPINE HUNTS BUFFALO

Ute

■

In olden days when mostly animals roamed this earth, a Porcupine set out to track some buffalo. He asked the buffalo chips, "How long have you been here on this trail?" He kept on asking, until finally one answered, "Only lately have I been here."

From there Porcupine followed the same path. The farther he went, the fresher the tracks. He continued until he came to a river; there he saw a buffalo herd that had crossed the ford onto the other side.

"What shall I do now?" thought Porcupine as he sat down. He called out, "Carry me across!" One of the buffalo replied, "Do you mean me?" Porcupine called again, "No, I want a different buffalo." Thus he rejected each member of the herd, one after another, as each asked. "Do you mean me?"

Finally the last and best one in the herd said, "I will carry you across the river." The buffalo crossed the river and said to porcupine, "Climb on my back." Porcupine said, "No, I'm afraid I will fall off into the water." Buffalo said, "Then climb up and ride between my horns." "No," replied Porcupine. "I'm sure I'll slide off into the river."

Buffalo suggested many other ways to carry him, but Porcupine protested. "Perhaps you'd rather ride inside of me?" offered the buffalo. "Yes," said Porcupine, and let himself be swallowed by the buffalo.

"Where are we now?" asked Porcupine. "In the middle of the river," said the buffalo, After a little while, Porcupine asked again. "We have nearly crossed," said the buffalo. "Now we have emerged from the water; come out of me!" Porcupine said, "No, not yet, go a little farther."

Soon the buffalo stopped and said, "We have gone far enough, so come out." Then Porcupine hit the buffalo's heart with his heavy tail. The buffalo started to run, but fell down and died right there. Porcupine had killed him. Others in the herd tried to hook Porcupine, but he sat under the buffalo's ribs, where he could not be hooked. Soon the herd tired and ran on their way.

Porcupine came out and said aloud, "I wish I had something to butcher this nice big buffalo with." Now, Coyote was sleeping nearby, and woke up and heard him. Coyote went to Porcupine and said, "Here is my knife for butchering." So they went together to the side of the buffalo.

"Let him butcher who can jump over it," said Coyote. Porcupine ran and jumped, but only partway over the buffalo. Coyote jumped over it without touching the dead animal, so he began to butcher, cutting up the buffalo.

After a little time, he handed the paunch to Porcupine and said, "Go wash it in the river, but don't eat it yet." Porcupine took it to the river, washed it, then he bit off a piece. When Coyote saw what Porcupine had done, he became very angry with him and went after him, "I told you not to eat any of the paunch." Coyote picked up a club and killed Porcupine and placed him beside the buffalo, and went to his home. Then he told his family, "I have killed a buffalo and I have killed a porcupine. Let us go and carry them home."

Before Porcupine had come out of the buffalo, he said magic words, "Let a red pine grow here fast." Then at once red pine began to grow under the meat and under Porcupine. It grew very tall and fast. All of the meat and Porcupine rested at the top of the red pine tree, high in the air, Porcupine magically coming alive again.

Coyote and his family arrived and were surprised that all of the meat was gone. They began to hunt for it. "I wish they would look up," said Porcupine. Then the smallest child looked up and said "Oh!" The family looked up and saw Porcupine sitting on top of the meat in the tall red pine tree.

Coyote said, "Throw down a piece of the neck, we are very hungry."

"Yes," said Porcupine. "Place that youngest child a little farther away. "Yes," they responded and took him to one side.

"Now make a ring and all hold hands upward," said Porcupine. So the family joined hands and held them up. Porcupine threw down several pieces of the buffalo meat, killing Coyote and those in the ring. Porcupine then threw down the rest of the buffalo meat, and climbed down the tree.

He took charge of the young coyote and fed him all the meat he desired. Porcupine took all the meat he could carry to his home. He and the young coyote became good friends and helped each other hunt buffalo together for a long, long time.

Kroeber, "Porcupine Hunts Buffalo," 270-272.

■

COYOTE VS. DUCK
Ute

■

Coyote became disturbed because he had a sick daughter. He thought Duck had done something against his children in order to make them sick. So Coyote determined to bring harm to Duck. He met Duck at a certain place and ordered that Duck should run to a point with his eyes closed. This Duck did. When he opened them again, he found himself in the hole of a big rock, a little cave high on the face of a cliff. There was no way out for Duck.

Coyote took Duck's wife and children, whom he treated badly. In time, Coyote had more children from this woman, and these he took good care of.

Duck tried constantly to get out of the cave, without success. At last Bat camped nearby, and every day, when he went to hunt rabbits, his children could hear someone crying. They told Bat, and he flew upward to look. On his way he killed rabbits and hung them on his belt. Finally he found Duck, who was very weak from lack of food.

"Who is there?" asked Bat. "I am Duck." Bat asked, "How did you come up here?" Duck said, "Coyote caused me to lose my way with my eyes closed. He got rid of me in order to steal my wife." Then Bat said "Throw yourself down." Duck was afraid to try. So Bat told him, "Throw down a small rock." This Duck did and Bat caught it on his back. He said, "That is exactly the way I will catch you. You will not be hurt."

Duck still feared that Bat would not catch him. Bat continued to urge him to let himself fall. Several times Duck almost let himself go, but drew back. At least he thought, "Suppose I am killed; I shall die here anyway; I am as good as dead now."

Duck closed his eyes as Bat commanded, and let himself fall. Bat caught him gently and put Duck safely on the ground. Bat then took Duck to his home and said, "Do not use the fire-sticks that are near my fireplace, but use those stuck behind the tent poles, at the sides of the tent."

Then he entered, and Duck saw the sticks at the sides of the tent, but only thought them to be fine canes, too handsome for stirring the fire. He saw a number of sticks laying around that were charred on the ends. He took one of these and stirred the embers. Oh, how the sticks cried. All the other sticks called out, "Duck has burned our younger brother."

These sticks were Bat's children, and they all ran away. Duck became frightened at what he had done, and went out and hid in the brush. Bat came and called to him, "Come back! You have done no harm."

For a long time Duck seemed afraid that Bat would punish him. Then he thought, "I've already been as good as dead, so I have nothing more to fear, even if they should kill me." Duck went back into the tent. But Bat did not hurt him and gave him plenty of rabbit meat to eat. Soon Duck was strong again.

Duck said to Bat, "Coyote took my wife and children; I think I shall go and look for them." Believing him to be strong enough, Bat encouraged him to go. Duck went to his old camp, but he found it deserted. He followed tracks leading from it, and after a while found some tracks other than his own children's.

"I think Coyote has got children from my wife," he thought, and he became very angry. Coyote came along with Duck's wife. She was carrying a very large basket. Inside were Coyote's children, well kept; but Duck's children sat on the outer edge of the basket. Nearly falling off. These were dirty and miserable.

Duck caught the basket with a finger and pulled it back. "What are you doing, children?" the woman said. "Don't do that; you must not catch hold of something and hold me back." Duck continued to pull at the basket. At last she turned to look at the children and saw Duck. He said to her, "Why do you take care of Coyote's children, while my children are dirty and uncared for? Why do you not treat my children properly?"

The woman was ashamed and did not answer. Then he asked her, "Where will you camp now?" When she told him, he said to her, "Go to the place where Coyote told you to camp, but when you put up the shelter, make the grass very thin on one side and very thick on the side on which you are, so I can reach Coyote."

The woman arrived at the camping place. Coyote asked, "To whom have you been talking now?" She replied, "I have not met nor talked with anyone. Why do you always ask me that?" She then put up the shelter as Duck had directed her. Immediately Duck began to blow. He blew softly, but again, again, and again, until he made it freezing cold.

Coyote could not sleep. He thrust his spear through the sides of the shelter in all directions and nearly speared the Duck. Coyote said to his wife, "I knew that you met someone. It must have been Duck, who is making it so cold." Duck continued to blow and blow. At last Coyote burrowed himself down into the fireplace ashes, hoping to warm himself there. But it was of no use. Coyote froze to death before morning.

Duck let all of Coyote's children go free where they wished. Then he took his wife and his children back to their old home, where they had lived before all of the disruption began.

Kroeber, "Coyote vs. Duck," 272-274.

■

TWO FAWNS AND A RABBIT
Ute

■

Two young Fawns sat on the ground talking about their condition. They were two boys without a mother. "We used to have a deer for our mother," they said. Rabbit came to them and said "I'm hungry. I've traveled without eating, and I've come a long way."

The Fawns said, "We have nothing to eat here; our food is not here." Where is it?" asked Rabbit. "It is not here, I say to you again," said one Fawn.

Rabbit said, "Tell me where it is, I am hungry and I want to eat." He continued talking about the Fawns' food for a long time. But they concealed from him how they obtained it.

Then Rabbit said, "I think you both are too lazy to get the food. Show me the path and I will go after it; I will cut off enough for all of us and bring it here."

"But we never eat here," the Fawns said. Rabbit said, "You boys do not know me. I am your grandfather. You did not recognize me; that is why you hid your food from me." The one boy nudged the other and whispered to him, "I think he is our grandfather; I will tell him where we eat."

For a while, the other boy said nothing. Then he spoke up and said, "What we eat is not on the ground; our food is far up in the sky; and we eat at a certain time. When we ask for our food, something always comes down from the sky; it is white like a cloud. At the end of the cloud it's like a person; it has an eye, a mouth, and it watches us. It comes only at a certain time. If we ask before time, it will think someone else wants our food. But when it's time for us to ask for it, we will hide you out of sight." Then they hid him.

One ran toward the East, the other toward the West; then they ran toward each other. When they met, they cried like young animals at play. They circled about, met each other again, crying, and gradually came nearer to the tent. Something white came down from the sky. Rabbit saw it coming. It looked like a cloud with a face above it; like a man sitting on their food.

The boys took up dull knives, and when the food arrived, they cut off a piece. They cut more than usual, so there would be enough for their grandfather. Then the cloud flew upward as fast as lightning.

The Fawn boys cut up their food and called Rabbit to come out and eat with them. The food tasted good and sweet, and Rabbit wanted more and asked the boys to make the thing come again. The Fawns said, "But it only comes at set times." Rabbit replied, "I will live with you, for your food is very good." He made a burrow in the brush nearby and watched.

The food did come down again. The person riding on it looked around like an antelope watching. Rabbit took a bow and arrow from his quiver. Just before the cloud came low enough for the boys to cut off another piece of food, Rabbit shot at the manlike object on the cloud. The white object fell down in a heap.

"I thought that was what it would do," said the older brother to the younger, as if blaming him. Rabbit said to them, "Well, my grandchildren, I will leave you now. You have something to eat and it will last you a long time. After you have consumed all of it, you will go to the mountains and eat grass and become Deer."

Kroeber, "Two Fawns and a Rabbit," 275-276.

■

TWO GRANDSONS
Ute

■

A man lived on a large rock with his two grandsons. "You had better go hunting and bring home something for us to eat. I am hungry. Go to the hills, sit on top, and watch in all directions; then you may find something," Grandfather said.

The two grandsons went off and watched in the brush. An elk came directly at them. One boy said, "I see an elk, let's kill it." The other said, "My older brother, let us run away. I am afraid." The older said, "No. Sit still. It is an elk. I shall shoot it as our grandfather directed." The other said, "No. I am afraid."

When the older was about ready to shoot, his younger brother fled, crying, "Let's run away. I am frightened." Then the elk started back. The older one said, "What is it? Are you crazy? I was nearly ready to shoot that elk." The younger still said, "I was frightened; but I understand now it is an elk. Let us go after it; it cannot have gone far."

When they neared the elk again, the younger brother wanted to turn to shoot at it. The older brother wanted him to stay behind, but did not persuade him. When ready to shoot, the younger again ran off shouting, and the elk escaped. The older brother scolded him harshly. The younger one said, "I was afraid that it would jump on me. I became too frightened."

The younger brother begged the older boy not to send him back home, as the older brother wished. When they approached the elk another time, he again asked his older brother to allow him a shot, saying, if he missed, the other could be ready and still try to kill the elk. But the same thing happened as before.

The older brother became very angry with his younger brother. It was not yet sunset, but the younger persuaded the older to again go after the elk; so they went around ahead of it. Older brother tied the arms, legs, and mouth of his brother. The elk came close. Younger one tried to scream. At the same time the older brother shot and killed the elk.

Younger brother tossed and thrashed about, trying to scream and flee. "Are you crazy? I have killed the elk," said the older. "Have you truly?" asked the younger. Then the older loosened his brother and showed him the dead elk. "What kind of Deer is it?" asked the younger. "It's an elk," replied the older one. "Hurry! Get some brush for a fire. Let's skin it and go home quickly. There may be bad persons coming about here."

"I'll get some brush presently," said the younger. "Make the fire quickly," said his brother. "I want to roast some meat and eat it, then go home. Be quick." "No, I want to rest now," said the younger. He would not help his older brother. So the older one alone skinned the game and cooked some of the meat. Then he said, "Let's go home now. There may be some bad things about. I am frightened."

"No, I am afraid to go. I cannot go home. Let us stay here all night; there is nothing bad about," said the younger. Then the older urged him no more and said, "Let us sleep in a cedar tree. Make a bed there." The younger agreed and made a bed in the top of the cedar after they had buried the meat for safekeeping. Then they slept.

In the middle of the night the younger one said, "I am hungry. I will go down and eat." The older one awoke and said, "What in the world is the matter with you? Sleep now, eat tomorrow." But the younger one insisted on going down to eat. Finally the older one said, "Very well." So, the younger brother went down, made a large fire, and cooked a whole shoulder of the elk. He began to eat and enjoy himself. He heard cries from far-off in all directions. The younger brother said, "What is it? Is someone approaching? Come here then and eat with me." The older brother remained in the cedar tree.

Someone came to the opposite side of the fire. It was a large man. The younger brother said, "Come, friend, eat; I have good food; sit down there." No answer came from the man. "Here is something to eat," said the boy, holding elk meat out to the man. He did not take it. He did not answer even when he was repeatedly spoken to. Then the boy hit him on the head and knocked him down. When he went closer until he stood by the man's head, suddenly the man reached out and caught him in a violent grip.

"Oh, Oh! Let me go!" cried the boy. The man continued to hold his legs in a tight grip. "Let me go! Older brother, come and help me, this stranger is holding me down." But the older brother was angry at being disturbed so he did not come down from the tree.

The man squeezed the younger boy harder, then picked him up and carried him away. The older brother, half-awake, heard his brother's cries grow weaker and weaker as the distance grew greater. Then there were no more cries.

In the morning the older brother came down from the cedar tree. Crying aloud for his brother, he followed the tracks. They led him to a lake and right down into the water. He could go no farther. He went back, dug up the elk meat, and went home, telling the whole experience to his grandfather.

His grandfather said, "Tomorrow we will go and see that place." The older son went with his grandfather to the lake and watched it. Grandfather said, "Wait here while I go down. I will follow the tracks."

He did not come back until noon, then emerged carrying a dead man, and laid him down.

"Is this the man who killed your brother? Deep in the water I found him. I am going back again, wait here," said the grandfather. He did not return until sunset and said, "This is another man. I entered his house and killed him. Now open his mouth and look between his teeth."

The boy saw a little meat between the teeth. His grandfather said to him, "Take a stick and pick out the meat from his teeth. The boy did so and made a little pile of it. Then the old man told him to cut open the dead man. When the boy had done so, his grandfather asked, "Do you see any bones or other parts? Pick them out."

The boy did as he was told, and then did the same to the other man. They put the meat and bones into a hollow stone and carried them home. They left it standing outside, at a short distance from the tent. Then they slept.

Early in the morning his grandfather called, "He is shouting, Wuwuwuwu! Do you hear him?"

"Yes," said the older brother. They both answered with a loud shout. Then younger brother came walking from the woods, saying, "Grandfather, older brother, I have risen from the meat!"

All three clasped each other warmly, happy to be together again—grandfather and his two grandsons.

Kroeber, "The Two Grandsons," 278-280.

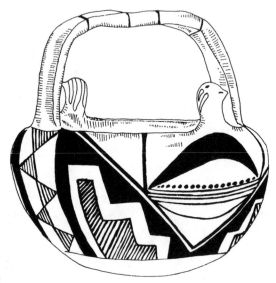

Pueblo pottery
Acoma

■

THE ORIGIN OF SUMMER AND WINTER
Acoma

The oldest tradition of the Acoma and Laguna people indicates they lived on some island off the California Coast. Their homes were destroyed by high waves, earthquakes, and red-hot stones from the sky. They escaped and landed on a swampy part of the coast. From there they migrated inland to the north. Wherever they made a longer stay, they built a traditional White City, made of white-washed mud and straw adobe brick, surrounded by white-washed adobe walls. Their fifth White City was built in southern Colorado, near northern New Mexico. The people were finally obliged to leave there on account of cold, drought, and famine.

■

The Acoma chief had a daughter named Co-chin-ne-na-ko, called Co-chin for short, who was the wife of Shakok, the Spirit of Winter. After he came to live with the Acomas, the seasons grew colder and colder. Snow and ice stayed longer each year. Corn no longer matured. The people soon had to live on cactus leaves and other wild plants.

One day Co-chin went out to gather cactus leaves and burn off the thorns so she could carry them home for food. She was eating a singed leaf when she saw a young man coming toward her. He wore a yellow shirt woven of corn silk, a belt, and a tall pointed hat; green leggings made of green moss that grows near springs and ponds; and moccasins beautifully embroidered with flowers and butterflies.

In his hand he carried an ear of green corn with which he saluted her. She returned the salute with her cactus leaf. He asked, "What are you eating?" She told him, "Our people are starving because no corn will grow, and we are compelled to live on these cactus leaves."

"Here, eat this ear of corn, and I will go bring you an armful for you to take home with you," said the young man. He left and quickly disappeared from sight, going south. In a very short time, however, he returned, bringing a large bundle of green corn that he laid at her feet.

"Where did you find so much corn?" Co-chin asked.

"I brought it from my home far to the south," he replied. "There the corn grows abundantly and flowers bloom all year."

"Oh, how I would like to see your lovely country. Will you take me with you to your home?" she asked.

"Your husband, Shakok, the Spirit of Winter, would be angry if I should take you away," he said.

"But I do not love him, he is so cold. Ever since he came to our village, no corn has grown, no flowers have bloomed. The people are compelled to live on these prickly pear leaves," she said.

"Well," he said. "Take this bundle of corn with you and do not throw away the husks outside of your door. Then come tomorrow and I will bring you more. I will meet you here." He said good-bye and left for his home in the south.

Co-chin started home with the bundle of corn and met her sisters, who had come out to look for her. They were very surprised to see the corn instead of cactus leaves. Co-chin told them how the young man had brought her the corn from his home in the south. They helped her carry it home.

When they arrived, their father and mother were wonderfully surprised with the corn. Co-chin minutely described in detail the young man and where he was from. She would go back the next day to get more corn from him, as he asked her to meet him there, and he would accompany her home.

"It is Miochin," said her father. "It is Miochin," said her mother. "Bring him home with you."

The next day, Co-chin-ne-na-ko went to the place and met Miochin, for he really was Miochin, the Spirit of Summer. He was waiting for her and had brought big bundles of corn.

Between them they carried the corn to the Acoma village. There was enough to feed all of the people. Miochin was welcome at the home of the Chief. In the evening, as was his custom, Shakok, the Spirit of Winter and Co-chin's husband, returned from the north. All day he had been playing with the north wind, snow, sleet, and hail.

Upon reaching the Acoma village, he knew Miochin must be there and called out to him, "Ha, Miochin, are you here?" Miochin came out to meet him. "Ha, Miochin, now I will destroy you."

"Ha, Shakok, I will destroy you," replied Miochin, advancing toward him, melting the snow and hail and turning the fierce wind into a summer breeze. The icicles dropped off and Shakok's clothing was revealed to be made of dry, bleached rushes.

Shakok said, "I will not fight you now, but will meet you here in four days and fight you till one of us is beaten. The victor will win Co-chin-ne-na-ko."

Shakok left in a rage, as the wind roared and shook the walls of White City. But the people were warm in their houses because Miochin was there. The next day he left for his own home in the south to make preparations to meet shakok in combat.

First he sent an eagle to his friend Yat-Moot, who lived in the west, asking him to come help him in his fight with Shakok. Second, he called all the birds, insects, and four-legged animals that live in summer lands to help him. The bat was his advance guard and shield, as his tough skin could best withstand the sleet and hail that Shakok would throw at him.

On the third day Yat-Moot kindled his fires, heating the thin, flat stones he was named after. Big black clouds of smoke rolled up from the south and covered the sky.

Shakok was in the north and called to him all the winter birds and four-legged animals of winter lands to come and help him. The magpie was his shield and advance guard.

On the fourth morning, the two enemies could be seen rapidly approaching the Acoma village. In the north, black storm clouds of winter with snow, sleet, and hail brought Shakok to the battle. In the south, Yat-Moot piled more wood on his fires and great puffs of steam and smoke arose and formed massive clouds. They were bringing Miochin, the Spirit of Summer, to the battlefront. All of his animals were blackened from the smoke. Forked blazes of lightning shot forth from the clouds.

At last the combatants reached White City. Flashes from the clouds singed the hair and feathers of Shakok's animals and birds. Shakok and Miochin were now close together. Shakok threw snow, sleet, and hail that hissed through the air of a blinding storm. Yat-Moot's fires and smoke melted Shakok's weapons, and he was forced to fall back. Finally he called a truce. Miochin agreed, and the winds stopped, and snow and rain ceased falling.

They met at the White Wall of Acoma. Shakok said, "I am defeated, you Miochin are the winner. Co-chin-ne-na-ko is now yours forever." Then the men each agreed to rule one-half of the year, Shakok for winter and Miochin for summer, and that neither would trouble the other thereafter. That is why we have a cold season for one-half of the year, and a warm season for the other.

Pradt, "Shakok and Miochin, The Origin of Summer and Winter," 88-90.

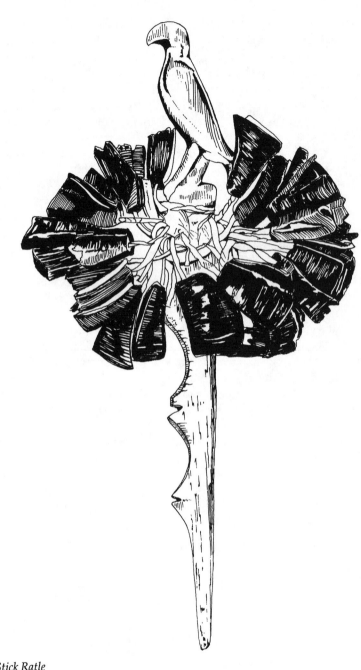

Stick Ratle
Chippewa

PART FOUR

FROM THE CENTRAL REGION

Homelands for these tribal stories were chiefly states of the Middle West. But a series of treaties in the 1790s and early 1800s culminated in the loss of many Indian lands to the whites. Tribes then moved westward and northward. Chippewa and Illini occupied Wisconsin, Illinois, and northern Michigan.

Ottawa, meaning "to trade," were known as the middlemen in transactions between those living in northern Michigan and those in southern Canada, whose principal city was named Ottawa in 1854. In 1858, Ottawa was selected as the capital city of Canada by Queen Victoria. Most famous of the Ottawa was Chief Pontiac.

Winnebago, meaning "people of the filthy water," lived on the south side of Green Bay in Wisconsin. They were the mother tribe of the Chippewas and Iowas, whose names mean "sleepy ones" and "dusty noses." The Iowas stayed mostly in their own territory, now the state of Iowa. A large group of Chippewas came from the East to Mackinaw in northern Michigan and to the shores of lake Superior; they drove out the Dakotas and then spread over northern Minnesota. Chippewa also means "roast until puckered up," referring to the way the seams of their moccasins pucker when held too close to fire.

Illini lived in the Illinois village of Michigamea, meaning "Big Water." When driven out by the Chickasaw, they settled in northern Arkansas on a large lake now called Big Lake. In Nebraska lived the Pawnee, known for wearing elk bone on their heads, a mark of hunters. Helpful to the United States Army, they served as scouts. While horse hunting in about 1541, they aided Francisco Coronado's exploration of the Southwest when he also encountered the Wichitas in Kansas territory.

■

ARCH ROCK ON MACKINAC ISLAND

Ottawa

Arch Rock is a natural rock bridge above the eastern shoreline of Mackinac Island in northern Michigan. From certain angles, the arch, which is about 150 feet above the lake, appears to be suspended in the air. This mythical explanation of its origin was recorded in 1850.

■

Many, many winters ago, the sun descended into an immense hole every evening, as soon as the stars appeared in the sky. This hole was thought to be somewhere off in the distant west.

One time a chief of the Ottawa nation committed a shameful act. It was so shameful that the Master of Life was greatly offended and angered. In punishment, he sent a powerful wind upon the earth. The rocky hills trembled because of the wind, and the waters surrounding the hills roared with a dreadful roar.

For one whole day this turmoil lasted. Even the sun was disturbed. It shot through the heavens with an unsteady motion, and when it reached the center of the sky, it stood still. It seemed to be astonished at the wickedness of the chief.

All the people of the Ottawa nation were greatly alarmed. While they stood gazing at the sun, they saw it gradually change to the color of blood. Then they were horrified to see it fall from the sky. With a terrifying noise, it struck the eastern shore of Mackinac Island.

When the frightened Indians dared to look again, they saw that some rocks had been hollowed out so as to make an arch. It hung high above the waters of the lake. The sun had gone through the opening and on down below the surface of the earth. Next morning it came out of the earth in the east, and then made its usual journey across the heavens.

Many winters have passed since that awful day when the sun stood still and fell from the sky. But even now, not even the bravest Ottawa people will walk over that arched rock. Indeed, they seldom dare to approach the place.

Lanman, "Indian Legends," 115-116.

■

THE GREAT SERPENT AND THE GREAT FLOOD

Chippewa-Ojibwa

From Maine and Nova Scotia to the Rocky Mountains, Indians told stories about the Great Serpent. The man who recorded this story more than a century ago considered the serpent to be "a genuine spirit of evil." Some version of the story of the Great Flood of long ago, as recounted here, is told around the world.

Nanabozho (Nunà-bōzō, accented on bozo) was the hero of many stories told by the Chippewa Indians. They used to be a large tribe living on the shares of Lake Superior, in what are now the states of Minnesota and Wisconsin and the province of Ontario.

■

One day when Nanabozho returned to his lodge after a long journey, he missed his young cousin who lived with him. He called the cousin's name but heard no answer. Looking around on the sand for tracks, Nanabozho was startled by the trail of the Great Serpent. He then knew that his cousin had been seized by his enemy.

Nanabozho picked up his bow and arrows and followed the track of the serpent. He passed the great river, climbed mountains, and crossed over valleys until he came to the shores of a deep and gloomy lake. It is now called Manitou Lake, Spirit Lake, and also the Lake of Devils. The trail of the Great Serpent led to the edge of the water.

Nanabozho could see, at the bottom of the lake, the house of the Great Serpent. It was filled with evil spirits, who were his servants and his companions. Their forms were monstrous and terrible. Most of them, like their master, resembled spirits. In the center of this horrible group was the Great Serpent himself, coiling his terrifying length around the cousin of Nanabozho.

The head of the Serpent was red as blood. His fierce eyes glowed like fire. His entire body was armed with hard and glistening scales of every color and shade.

Looking down on these twisting spirits of evil, Nanabozho made up his mind that he would get revenge on them for the death of his cousin.

He said to the clouds, "Disappear!"

And the clouds went out of sight.

"Winds, be still at once!" And the winds became still.

When the air over the lake of evil spirits had become stagnant, Nanabozho said to the sun, "Shine over the lake with all the fierceness you can. Make the water boil."

In these ways, thought Nanabozho, he would force the Great Serpent to seek the cool shade of the trees growing on the shores of the lake. There he would seize the enemy and get revenge.

After giving his orders, Nanabozho took his bow and arrows and placed himself near the spot where he thought the serpents would come to enjoy the shade. Then he changed himself into the broken stump of a withered tree.

The winds became still, the air stagnant, and the sun shot hot rays from a cloudless sky. In time, the water of the lake became troubled, and bubbles rose to the surface. The rays of the sun had penetrated to the home of the serpents. As the water bubbled and foamed, a serpent lifted his head above the center of the lake and gazed around the shores. Soon another serpent came to the surface. Both listened for the footsteps of Nanabozho, but they heard him nowhere.

"Nanabozho is sleeping," they said to one another.

And then they plunged beneath the waters, which seemed to hiss as they closed over the evil spirits.

Not long after, the lake became more troubled. Its water boiled from its very depths, and the hot waves dashed wildly against the rocks on its banks. Soon the Great Serpent came slowly to the surface of the water and moved toward the shore. His bloodred crest glowed. The reflection from his scales was blinding—as blinding as the glitter of a sleet-covered forest beneath the winter sun. He was followed by all the evil spirits. So great was their number that they soon covered the shores of the lake.

When they saw the broken stump of the withered tree, they suspected that it might be one of the disguises of Nanabozho. They knew his cunning. One of the serpents approached the stump, wound his tail around it, and tried to drag it down into the lake. Nanabozho could hardly keep from crying aloud, for the tail of the monster prickled his sides. But he stood firm and was silent.

The evil spirits moved on. The Great Serpent glided into the forest and wound his many coils around the trees. His companions also found shade—all but one. One remained near the shore to listen for the footsteps of Nanabozho.

From the stump, Nanabozho watched until all the serpents were asleep and the guard was intently looking in another direction. Then he silently drew an arrow from his quiver, placed it in his bow, and aimed it at the heart of the Great Serpent. It reached its mark. With a howl that shook the mountains and startled the wild beasts in their caves, the

Wigwam
Chippewa

monster awoke. Followed by its terrified companions, which also were howling with rage and terror, the Great Serpent plunged into the water.

At the bottom of the lake there still lay the body of Nanabozho's cousin. In their fury the serpents tore it into a thousand pieces. His shredded lungs rose to the surface and coveed the lake with whiteness.

The Great Serpent soon knew that he would die from his wound, but he and his companions were determined to destroy Nanabozho. They caused the water of the lake to swell upward and to pound against the shore with the sound of many thunders. Madly the flood rolled over the land, over the tracks of Nanabozho, carrying with it rocks and trees. High on the crest of the highest wave floated the wounded Great Serpent. His eyes glared around him, and his hot breath mingled with the hot breath of his many companions.

Nanabozho, fleeing before the angry waters, thought of his Indian children. He ran through their villages, shouting, "Run to the mountain-tops! The Great Serpent is angry and is flooding the earth! Run! Run!"

The Indians caught up their children and found safety on the mountains. Nanabozho continued his flight along the base of the western hills, and then up a high mountain beyond Lake Superior, far to the north. There he found many men and animals that had escaped from the flood that was already covering the valleys and plains and even the highest hills. Still the waters continued to rise. Soon all the mountains were under the flood, except the high one on which stood Nanabozho.

There he gathered together timber and made a raft. Upon it the men and women and animals with him placed themselves. Almost immediately the mountaintop disappeared from their view, and they floated along on the face of the waters. For many days they floated. At long last, the flood began to subside. Soon the people on the raft saw the trees on the tops of the mountains. Then they saw the mountains and hills, then the plains and the valleys.

When the water disappeared from the land, the people who survived learned that the Great Serpent was dead and that his companions had returned to the bottom of the lake of spirits. There they remain to this day. For fear of Nanabozho, they have never dared to come forth again.

Squier, "Nanabozho and the Great Serpent," 392

■

The Forsaken Brother
Chippewa

The Chippewa tribe's traditional significance of its name in their own language, "to roast until puckered up," refers to the puckering in seams of moccasins when held too close or too long toward a fire. They were also called Ojibwa, as the band preferred. The Chippewa are one of the two largest divisions of the Algonquin linguistic family. Originally from the Sault Sainte Marie region, they extended along the entire shore of Lake Huron and on both shores of Lake Superior, as well as into the northern interior of North Dakota after separating into Chippewa, Ottawa, and Potawatomi. During the 19th century they gradually gathered upon reservations in the United States and Canada. In 1650, the Chippewa population stood at 35,000. In 1764 at 25,000. They scattered into many states in the Central and Plains regions.

■

One summer evening, scarcely an hour before sunset, the father of a family lay in his lodge, dying. Weeping beside him were his wife and three children. Two of them were almost grown up; the youngest was but a small child. These were the only human beings near the dying man, for the lodge stood on a little green mound away from all others of the tribe.

A breeze from the lake gave the sick man a brief return of strength. He raised himself a little and addressed his family.

"I know that I will leave you soon. Your mother, my partner of many years, will not stay long behind. She will soon join me in the pleasant land of spirits. But, O my children, my poor children! You have just begun life. All unkindness and other wickednesses are still before you.

"I have contented myself with the company of your mother and yourselves for many years, in order to keep you from evil example. I will die content, my children, if you will promise me to love each other. Promise me that on no account will you forsake your youngest brother. I leave him in your charge. Love him and hold him dear."

The effort to speak exhausted the sick man. But taking a hand of each of his older children, he continued his plea. "My daughter, never forsake your little brother! My son, never forsake your little brother!"

"Never, never!" they both exclaimed.

"Never, never!" repeated the father. And then he died, happily sure that his command would be obeyed.

Time wore heavily away. Five long moons passed, and when the sxith moon was nearly full, the mother also died. In her last moments, she reminded the two older children of their promise to their father. Willingly they renewed their promise to take care of their little brother. They were still free from any selfishness.

The winter passed away, and spring came. The girl, the oldest, directed her brothers. She seemed to feel an especially tender and sisterly affection for the youngest, who was sickly and delicate. The older boy, however, already showed signs of selfishness. One day he spoke sharply to his sister.

"My sister, are we always to live as if there were no other human beings in the world? Must I never associate with other men? I am going to visit the villages of my tribe. I have made up my mind, and you cannot prevent me."

"My brother," replied his sister, "I do not say no to what you wish. We were not forbidden to associate with others, but we were commanded never to forsake each other. If we separate to follow our own selfish desires, will we not be compelled to forsake our young brother? Both of us have promised to take care of him."

Making no reply, the young man picked up his bow and arrows, left the wigwam, and returned no more.

For many moons the girl took kindly care of her little brother. At last, however, she too began to weary of their solitude and wished to escape from her duty. Her strength and her ability to provide food and clothing had increased through the years, but so had her desire for company. Her solitude troubled her more and more, as the years went slowly by. At last, thinking only of herself, she decided to forsake her little brother, as the older brother had already done.

One day, she placed in the lodge all the food she had gathered. After bringing a pile of wood to the door, she said to her young brother, "Do not stray far from the lodge while I am gone. I am going to look for our brother. I shall soon be back."

Then taking her bundle, she set off for the villages. She found a pleasant one on the shore of a lake. Soon she became so much occupied with the pleasures of her new life that her affection for her brother gradually left her heart. In time, she was married. For a long time, she did not even think of the sickly little brother she had left in the woods.

In the meantime the older brother had settled in a village on the same lake, not far from the graves of their parents and the solitary home of the little brother.

As soon as the little fellow had eaten all the food left by his sister, he had to pick berries and dig roots. Winter came on, and the poor child was exposed to its cold winds. Snow covered the earth. Forced to leave the lodge in search of food, he strayed far without shelter. Sometimes he passed the night in the crotch of an old tree and ate the fragments left by wolves.

Soon he had to depend for his food entirely on what the wolves did not eat. He became so fearless that he would sit close to them while they devoured the animals they had killed. His condition aroused the pity of the animals, and they always left something for him. Thus he lived on the kindness of the wolves until spring came. As soon as the lake was free from ice, he followed his new friends and companions to the shore.

Now it happened that his brother was fishing in his canoe, far out on the same lake, when he thought he heard the cry of a child. "How can any child live on this bleak shore?" he said to himself. He listened again, and he thought he heard the cry repeated. Paddling toward the shore as quickly as possible, he saw and recognized his brother. The young one was singing,

> My brother, my brother!
> I am now turning into a wolf.
> I am turning into a wolf!

At the end of his song, he howled like a wolf. His brother, approaching, was shocked to find him half a wolf and half a human being. Leaping to the shore, the older brother tried to catch him in his arms. Soothingly he said, "My brother, my brother, come to me!"

But the boy fled, still singing as he ran, "I am turning into a wolf! I am turning into a wolf!" And at the end of his song he howled a terrifying howl.

Conscience-stricken, feeling his love return to his heart, his brother called to him, "My brother, O my brother! Come back to me!"

But the nearer he came to the child, the more rapidly the change to a wolf took place. Still the younger brother sang his song, and still he howled. Sometimes he called on his brother, and sometimes he called on his sister. When the change was complete, he ran toward the wood. He knew that he was a wolf. "I am a wolf! I am a wolf!" he cried, as he bounded out of sight.

The older brother, all the rest of his life, felt a gnawing sense of guilt. And the sister, when she heard what had happened to her little brother, remembered with grief the promise she had solemnly made to their father. She wept many tears and never ceased to mourn until her death.

Jameson, *Winter Studies and Summer Rambles in Canada*, 160-165.

■

FATHER OF INDIAN CORN
Chippewa-Ojibwa

■

In the long, long ago, a poor Ojibwa Indian lived with his wife and children in a remote part of the present state of Wisconsin. Because he was such a poor hunter, he was not very expert in providing food and supplies for his family.

His children were too young to give him much help. But he was a good man with a kind and contented disposition. He always was thankful to Chief of the Sky Spirits for everything he received to share with his family.

His good disposition was inherited by his eldest son, who had just reached the age when he wanted to pursue his Guardian Spirit Quest. Each young Indian boy looked forward to the time of finding the secret Spirit that would be his guide through his life. Each boy sought to learn his spirit name and what special power would be given him by his Guardian Spirit.

Eldest son had been obedient since early childhood. He seemed pensive, thoughtful of others, mild in manner, and always a joy to his family and to his tribe. At the first indication of spring, tradition told

Crooked knife
Ojibwa

him to build a hut somewhere in an isolated place. There, he would not be disturbed during his dream quest. He prepared his hut and himself and went immediately to begin his fast for seven days.

For the first few days, he amused himself walking in the woods and over the mountain trails. He examined trees, plants, and flowers. This kind of physical effort in the outdoors prepared him for a night of sound sleep. His observations of the day filled his mind with pleasant ideas and dreams.

More and more he desired to know how the trees, plants, flowers, and berries grew. Seemingly they grew wild without much help from the Indians. He wondered why some species were good to eat, while others contained poisonous juices. These thoughts came back to him many times as he retreated to his lodge at night. He secretly wished for a dream that would reveal what he could do to benefit his family and his tribe.

"I believe the Chief of Sky Spirits guides all things and it is to him I owe all things," he thought to himself. "I wonder if Chief Sky Spirit can make it easier for all Indians to acquire enough food without hunting animals every day to eat."

"I must try to find a way in my dreams," he pondered. He stayed on his bed the third day of fasting, because he felt weak and faint. Sometimes he thought that he was going to die. He dreamed that he saw a strong, handsome young man coming down from the sky, advancing toward him. He was richly dressed in green and yellow colors. He wore a plume of waving feathers on his head. His every movement was graceful.

"I have been sent to you," said the sky-visitor. "The Sky Chief who made all things in the sky and upon the earth intends for me to be your Guardian Spirit and I have come to test you.

"Sky Chief has observed all that you have done to prepare yourself for your Quest. He understands the kind and worthy secret wish of your heart. He knows that you desire a way to benefit your family and your tribe. He is pleased that you do not seek strength to make war. I have come to show you how to obtain your greatest wish. First, your spirit name shall be Wunzh."

The stranger then told Wunzh to arise and wrestle with him. This was the only way for him to achieve his sacred wish. As weak as he was from fasting, Wunzh wondered how he could ever wrestle the stranger.

He rose to the challenge—determined in his heart to die in the effort if he must. The two wrestled. After some time when Wunzh felt nearly exhausted, the Sky Stranger said, "It is enough for today. I will come again tomorrow to test you some more." Smiling, the visitor ascended in the same direction from which he came.

Next day at the same time, the stranger appeared. Again the two wrestled. While Wunzh felt weaker than the day before, he set his mind and heart to his task. His courage seemed to increase, however, in reverse proportion to his waning physical strength. The stranger stopped just in time before Wunzh dropped to the ground.

"Tomorrow will be your last chance. I urge you to be strong, my friend, as this is the only way for you to achieve your heart's sacred wish," said the sky-visitor.

Wunzh took to his bed with his last ounce of energy. He prayed to the Sky Chief for wisdom and enough strength to endure to the end of his Quest.

The third time they wrestled, Wunzh was so weak that his arms and legs felt like rubber. But his inner determination drove him forward with the kind of endurance necessary to win. The same length of time passed as in the first two wrestling bouts. Suddenly the stranger stopped and declared himself conquered by Wunzh!

Then the sky-visitor entered the lodge for the first time. He sat down beside Wunzh to instruct him in the way he should now proceed to achieve his secret wish.

"Great Sky Chief has granted your desire. You have wrestled manfully. Tomorrow will be your seventh day of fasting. Your father will come to see you and bring you food. As it is the last day of your fast, you will be able to succeed.

"Now I will tell you what you must do to achieve your final victory. Tomorrow we will wrestle once more. When you have prevailed over me for the last time, then throw me down and strip off my clothes. You must clean the earth of roots and weeds and make the ground soft. Then bury me in that very spot, covering me with my yellow and green clothes and then with earth.

"When you have done this, leave my body in the earth. Do not disturb it. Come occasionally to see if I have come to life. Be careful to see that no grass or weeds cover my grave. Once a month, cover me with fresh earth. If you follow what I have told you, you will succeed in your Guardian Spirit Quest. You will help your family and all the Indians by teaching them what I have now taught you," the Sky Stranger concluded as they shook hands and the visitor left.

On the seventh morning, Wunzh's father came with some food.

"My son, how do you feel? You have fasted long enough. It is seven days since you have eaten food. You must not sacrifice your life. The Great Spirit does not require that of you."

"My father, thank you for coming and for the food. Let me stay here alone until the sun goes down. I have my own special reasons."

"Very well. I shall wait for you at home until the hour of the setting-sun," replied the father as he departed.

The Sky Stranger returned at the same hour as before. The final wrestling match began. Wunzh had not eaten the food his father brought. But already he felt a new inner power that had somehow been given to him. Was it Spirit Power from his Guardian Spirit?

Wunzh grasped his opponent with supernatural strength and threw him to the ground. Wunzh removed the beautiful clothes and the plume. Then he discovered his friend was dead.

He remembered the instructions in every detail and buried his Guardian Spirit on the very spot where he had fallen. Wunzh followed every direction minutely, believing his friend would come to life again.

Wunzh returned to his father's lodge at sundown. He ate sparingly of the meal his mother prepared for him. Never for a moment could he forget the grave of his friend. Throughout the spring and into summer he visited the grave regularly. He carefully kept the area clean of grass and weeds. He carefully kept the ground soft and pliable. Soon he saw the tops of green plumes emerging through the earth. He noticed that the more care he gave the plants, the faster the green plumes seemed to grow.

Wunzh concealed his activity from his father. Days and weeks passed. Summer was drawing to a close. Then one day, Wunzh invited his father to follow him to the site of his Quest. He showed his father the graceful-looking plants growing there. They were topped with yellow silken hair and waving green plumes. Gold and green clusters of fruit adorned each side of the stalks.

"Father, these plants are from my dream friend," explained Wunzh. "He is my Guardian Spirit, a friend to all mankind, named Mon- daw-min, meaning 'corn for all Indians.' This is the answer to my Quest, my secret heart's wish. No longer will we need to hunt animals every day for our food. As long as we take care of our corn gift, the earth will give us good food for our living."

Wunzh pulled off the first ear of corn and give it to his father.

"See, my father. This corn is what I fasted for. The Chief of Sky Spirits has granted my Quest. He has sent us this wonderful new food of corn. From now on our people need not depend entirely upon hunting and fishing to survive."

Wunzh talked with his father, giving him all of the instructions he had received from his Guardian Spirit. He showed his father how the corn husks should be pulled off the stalks, and how the first seed must be saved for future plantings. He explained how the ears of corn should be held before the fire only long enough for the outer leaves to turn brown, so that the inside kernels remained sweet and juicy.

The entire family gathered for Wunzh's feast of corn. The father led a prayer of thanksgiving for the bountiful and good gift from the Chief of Sky Spirits. Wunzh felt happy that his Guardian Spirit Quest was successfully completed.

This is how Wunzh became known as the father of Indian corn by the Chippewa and Ojibwa Indian tribes.

Schoolcraft, *North American Indian Legends*, 99.

■

LEGEND OF THE WHITE PLUME
Iowa

The Iowa tribe belonged to the Siouan linguistic family. While the Iowa seemed to move often they generally remained within the boundaries of the state that still bears their name. In their early history, they located on a western tributary of the Mississippi River, and later moved into the northwestern/Iowa Okoboji Lake district as far as the Red Pipestone Quarry, even to the Big Sioux River. The Red Pipestone Quarry was across the Iowa line in southwest Minnesota. Indians from the entire region traveled to obtain the red stone for their pipes, giving name to the surrounding area and the future site of Pipestone National Monument. In the nineteenth century, they encountered the Dakota warriors and were defeated by Black Hawk in 1821. In about 1850, an Oklahoma tract held by the Iowa was granted to them in severalty. Other Iowans were allotted lands extending from the Platte River of Missouri through western Iowa up to Dakota country.

■

Long ago, near what is now Iowa City, lived a flourishing Iowa Indian tribe. The Chief of the Iowas was very proud of his two beautiful daughters. He was secretly hoping for one of them to marry the handsome hero White Plume, so called because he always wore one in his black hair.

One day, the Chief smeared his daughters' faces with charcoal and took them into the woods for them to fast and pray that one of them might attract the White Plume. The girls were most unhappy, crying until all the animals heard them and came running to find out what was the matter.

Each animal in turn asked, "Am I the one you are looking for?"

Catlinite pipe bowl
Iowa

"What do you do for a living?" they asked. "What animals do you kill for your food?" In this way they learned the nature of the animals. When the girls said, "No, you are not the one," that animal ran away.

On another day, a man came wearing a white plume. He announced, "Surely I am the one you are seeking. I hunt for deer, elk, bear, turkey, and all the other good things you like to eat."

Without hesitation, Older Sister decided to marry the man who-wore-the-white-plume. Next morning, Younger Sister said, "You have married the wrong man. Today the real White Plume will come." Older Sister was very cross and declared emphatically that she was certain she had married the true hero, White Plume.

In the middle of that day, birds began to chatter and sing, "White Plume is coming! White Plume is coming!" Even the meadowlarks, whom the Iowas say are really persons in disguise, were broadcasting loudly, "White Plume! White Plume!" Finally White Plume arrived.

"I believe that I am the one you have been seeking," he said to the two sisters.

Older Sister did not believe him, but Younger Sister welcomed him warmly. That same day, the two men each claiming to be White Plume went hunting. The real White Plume killed bear and deer, soon returning with his game.

The other hunter brought back only a few rabbits. Again and again the two men hunted, each returning with the same kind of game as before.

In a few days, the Chief of the Iowas came to visit his daughters. When he judged the results of the hunt, he was convinced that the first man who married Older Sister was an imposter. The Chief believed that the man who was the good provider was the real hero, White Plume.

Older sister began to have some doubts about her husband, and asked, "Why do you not kill larger game for us?" Her husband gave a poor excuse, "I do not think the larger game provide such good meat."

Again the two men hunted together, arriving in a valley where they saw a raccoon. The imposter tricked White Plume into chasing the raccoon into a bog. Now it happened that the imposter had the power to change people; so he changed White Plume into a dog.

Later, when the imposter returned to his lodge with the dog following him, he announced, "I found this dog in the woods. White Plume must have hunted in a different direction."

That night the dog slept in the lodge of Younger Sister. She fed him and made a comfortable place for him to sleep. Next day she took the dog with her into the woods to look for White Plume.

The dog soon killed a sleeping bear and other animals. Together the girl and dog hunted many times, always with success. One day when they were alone in the woods, the dog said to Younger Sister, "Take me to a hollow log and put me in it, then help pull me out at the other end." This she did. From the other end of the log she pulled out the real White Plume!

When the two of them returned to the lodge, the imposter said to the real White Plume, "You must have been lost in the woods." White Plume's answer was casual but pleasant. Later he told his wife, "Sometime, I will even the score."

In a few days, the two hunters started out for more game. White Plume killed a buffalo. They built a campfire, intending to camp there for the night. A sudden snowstorm came upon them. "Watch yourself," said the imposter. "This kind of a moon will burn your clothes."

That evening, they told many stories at the campfire, after which they prepared their blankets for a good night's sleep. Later in the night, White Plume called out to the imposter, but hearing no response, he quietly exchanged his own clothes, which he used for a pillow, with those of the imposter.

Much later in the night, the imposter awoke and stole the clothes from under White Plume's head and tossed them into the fire.

Next morning was bitter cold. White Plume grabbed for his clothes but they were not under his pillow. "Brother, my clothes are gone," he shouted, shivering with cold.

"Did I not tell you that this is the moon that burns your clothes?" said the imposter. Then he reached for his own clothes, only to discover that they were White Plume's clothes! The imposter had burned his own clothes!

Soon they started for home, with White Plume in the lead dragging the frozen buffalo. Somewhere along the way, the imposter must have frozen to death.

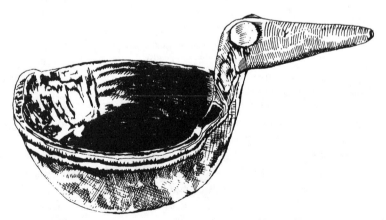

Effigy bowl
Winnebago

White Plume returned to his wife and Older Sister. He supplied them well with plenty of meat for the entire winter. Then he told them and the Chief of the Iowas that he was really an eagle.

"When your supplies run low, I shall return. When your Iowa hunters wish plenty of game, always they should wear an eagle's white plume in their hair," said White Plume with this parting blessing. Instantly he became a beautiful large eagle and flew far away.

Skinner, "The Legend of the White Plume," vol. 38, 458.

■

BOY STOLEN BY THUNDERBIRD
Winnebago

Winnebago were called "people of the filthy water" and even the English called them Stinkards. They belonged to the Siouan family, related to some Iowa, Oto, and Missouri bands, Winnebago of ancient times lived on Green Bay in Wisconsin territory, extending inland to Lake Winnebago. Though they generally maintained peaceful relations with surrounding tribes, in 1671 they were nearly destroyed by Illinois tribe raiders, but recovered from the surprise attack. Winnebagoes thrived upon a delicious native grass they named wild-rice, which grew abundantly in lakes, ponds, and streambeds. These plants, self-seeding in spring and summer and harvested from canoes and barges in fall, maintained their people in good health. They also hunted much game for meat and furs. By treaty in 1825 and 1830 they ceded all of their lands to the federal government in return for a large reservation on the west side of the Mississippi River above the Iowa River. Later, Winnebago moved to another reservation in Minnesota, then to Nebraska where they remain. Winnebago are known as a mother tribe of Siouan linguistic families.

■

Many, many years ago, a young Winnebago Indian orphan boy lived in a small village with his grandmother. He found a friend about his own age. One day, they hunted for hickory wood to make bird arrows, which they used for hunting hawks. Orphan-Boy captured a young pigeon hawk and took it home. Soon, it became his pet bird.

Some time later, Orphan-Boy put a little tobacco in a bundle and tied it around the hawk's neck. It disappeared for a few days, then returned without the tobacco bundle. Again, Orphan-Boy tied another bundle of tobacco around his pet's neck. It disappeared again, but returned to Orphan-Boy as it had before.

When the pet hawk became fully grown, Orphan-Boy suggested that it might want to go away and make a life for itself. So he tied another tobacco bundle around the pigeon hawk's neck, thanking him for staying with him for so long a time. Immediately, the bird flew away and never returned to Orphan-Boy.

Another day, Orphan-Boy and his friend hunted for dogwood to make pointed arrows. They accidentally became separated in a low fog. From above, however, a bad Thunderbird saw Orphan-Boy and swooped down, seizing him in his claws. The huge bird carried him away to its home in the high mountains.

For a long, long time the friend looked for Orphan-Boy. Finally, he gave up searching far and wide. But every day, he faithfully returned to the place where Orphan-Boy had disappeared, mourning still for his lost companion.

When the bad Thunderbird reached its mountainous home, he and his friends tied Orphan-Boy down to the floor. Their purpose was to hold him there until nothing remained in his stomach. Then they planned to devour him.

Little pigeon hawk decided to go and have a look at Thunderbird's prisoner. Imagine his surprise to find that Orphan-Boy, his kind friend, was the prisoner.

Little pigeon hawk left and decided to hunt for some young birds and roast them. Later, he returned, putting some of the meat under his wings and secretly dropping it into Orphan-Boy's mouth. Every day little pigeon hawk brought meat for Orphan-Boy, until the thunderbirds became suspicious of pigeon hawk.

The next day, the bad thunderbirds decided to exclude little pigeon hawk when he came to visit Orphan-Boy. One thunderbird pushed him toward the door, but little pigeon hawk accidentally on purpose fell close to the fire and scorched some of his feathers. He made a great noise and commotion, running to his big brother, Big Black-Hawk, who was Chief of the Thunderbirds.

"What can the matter be, little brother?" asked the Chief. Little pigeon hawk told his big brother the whole story from the beginning. When the Chief heard all, he became very angry.

Immediately, he went to the place where Orphan-Boy was still held down to the floor. The Chief scolded the bad thunderbirds for their wrongdoing. Because they had pushed little pigeon hawk too close to the fire, the Chief announced they could no longer keep Orphan-Boy as their prisoner. Chief Big Black-Hawk cut the ropes and took the freed young boy home with him.

Every day, little pigeon hawk brought roasted bird meat for his friend Orphan-Boy, helping him to regain his strength. Later, Orphan-Boy made a bow and some arrows and took little pigeon hawk hunting with him.

Before winter weather arrived, Chief Big Black-Hawk informed his little brother that it would be better for Orphan-Boy to return to his own people.

"He does not belong up here with the Thunder Spirits, and I do not think Mother Earth Spirit will approve of it," said the Chief.

Little pigeon-hawk took Orphan-Boy back to the very place from where he had disappeared a long time ago. That evening, Orphan-Boy's old faithful friend came as usual to that place and found Orphan-Boy had returned! How surprised and delighted both boys were to see each other again. Orphan-Boy told his old friend everything that had happened to him since he had been kidnapped by the Thunderbird.

A thanksgiving feast was prepared by the grandmother for both families to celebrate the happy homecoming of the boy stolen by the Thunderbird. From that time foreward, Orphan-Boy and his faithful friend had many happy hunting times together, trying never to be separated again.

Radin, "Boy Stolen by Thunderbird," vol. 22, 300.

■

HOLY SONG (MEDICINE SONG)
Winnebago

■

Long ago, before the Winnebagoes left their homes by the Great Water in Wisconsin, a young man went into the hills to fast. He fasted for twelve days, and then a spirit came to him in a vision and talked with him. The Earth-Maker, called *Ma-o-na* by the Winnebagoes, had sent a spirit to teach the young man. The spirit gave him knowledge and also taught him wonderful words that brought him health, well-being, and long life.

Wise was the young man when he left the hills, for he brought with him the teachings of the spirit and the power of the holy words. When he came back to his people, he sang a special song, and this song was the beginning of one kind of medicine ceremony.

The words he had learned from the spirit were so holy that the man lived a long time without any sickness. Nor did he die of any sickness. At the end of his long life, all the joints of his body fell apart from mere old age, and of old age alone the man died.

The song that he created, with the wonderful words learned from the spirit, has always been cherished by the Winnebagoes because of its great power.

The song was created long ago when our language was different from what it is now. Today, our people do not use such words in common speech. Indeed, no one knows the exact meaning of the wonderful words. The song is still sung in some of the medicine ceremonies, but only the Medicine Men, the Holy Men, understand its meaning.

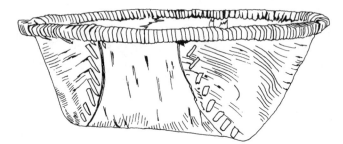

Great Lakes Indian birch-bark dish
Winnebago

The Medicine Ceremony of the Winnebagoes lasts four days and four nights. Holy songs are sung, and there is a spoken ritual. In the ritual, the Holy Man gives commandments and teaches our people the ways of goodness. Now and then, in order that we may not become tired and drowsy, the ceremony is given life by dancing. So the slow part of the Holy Song is followed by the quick part, which is the music of the dance.

In the olden times, the Medicine Ceremony was very solemn and sacred. And its mysteries were known only to the Medicine Men, the Holy Men. White people called it the "medicine religion of the Winnebagoes." Here is one of the Holy songs:

Saith the spirit,
"Dream, oh, dream again,
And tell of me,
Dream thou!
Into solitude went I
And wisdom was revealed to me.

Saith the spirit,
  "Dream, oh, dream again,
  And tell of me,
    Dream thou!"
Let the whole world hear me,
Wise am I!
  Now saith the spirit,
  "Tell of me
    Dream thou!"
All was revealed to me;
From the beginning
Know I all, hear me!
All was revealed to me
  Now saith the spirit
  "Tell of me
    Dream thou!"

Burlin, *The Indians' Book*, 254-255.

■

SOME ADVENTURES OF "THE LITTLE HARE"

Winnebago

"In the summer of 1950, on an Indian reservation along the coast of Washington, I had an experience that I think I shall never forget. I sat on the platform of an old warehouse with three elderly Indians and heard two of them tell some of the old stories they entertained themselves with almost every day.

"The unique feature of most of these tales was the chants. When the storyteller began a chant, the other two joined him. No one translated the words, but the singing was delightful. The Indian words in clear tones must have gone through the entire village. The chants, the gestures, the changes of voice and of facial expressions for the different characters in the tales—all dramatized the story and made the morning one to be remembered."

The songs in the following stories are from the Winnebago Indians, who now live in Nebraska. The Winnebagoes told many tales about *Wash-ching-geka*, "the Little Hare." In many tribes, it has been said, there were "legends to account for the remains for prehistoric animals."

■

While the Little Hare was doing his work, he lived with his grandmother. She was the Earth, and she was very wise. She cooked for the Little Hare, and she took good care of him.

At that time, a great, big elephant lived near them. He devoured people by reaching out for them with his long tongue and then swallowing them. The elephant looked like a large hill all covered with grass. The Little Hare went out to kill the huge elephant, because he devoured so many of the people. First, the Little Hare sprinkled himself all over with small pieces of flint. Then he sat down in front of the elephant and sang this song:

> You, who reach with your tongue,
> Great One, you draw them in.
> So I have heard it told.
> Gather me in!
> Gather me in!

The elephant saw the Little Hare's ears sticking up in the grass, and he thought that they were feathers on somebody's head. So he reached out his tongue and swallowed the Little Hare. Inside the elephant all was dark and vast. There were starving people there, some dead and some dying, for they had no wood to cook with.

Shaman's bone tube
Winnebago

Then the Little Hare said to a young woman who was inside, "Look in my fur and see if you can find a piece of flint."

The woman searched through his fur and found a little piece of flint. The Little Hare struck his hand upon the flint and said, "Grow bigger!" And it became bigger. Four times he struck thus, and each time the flint grew bigger. Then he struck it again and said, "Be a knife!" And it became a knife. Then he struck out again and said, "Be a big knife!" And it became a great big knife.

The Little Hare felt along the ribs of the elephant until he found a soft place between two rib bones. There he cut a hole like a door, and through it he sent out all the people. Then he ran forward to the elephant's heart, and with one blow of his knife he split the heart in two. Like the people inside the elephant, the Little Hare then jumped out through the hole. On his way he caught up the elephant's young ones. When he reached the outside world, he threw the little elephants clear across the water. That is why the elephant now lives only on the other side of the water.

SONG OF THE HARE
You, who reach with your tongue,
Great One, you draw them in.
So I have heard it told.
Gather me in!
Gather me in!

While running here and there over the earth, to see what other work he should do, the Little Hare found a pass or trail where some huge thing had gone by.

"I must find out what this is," he said to himself. "Maybe it is some huge animal that will run over the people and kill them."

So he blocked up the pass with trees and stones. But when he came there again, lo! the huge thing had burst through them! Then he went to his grandmother and told her what had happened. She made a net for him to spread across the pass. Next day he hears someone crying aloud and singing this song:

Wash-ching-geka, let me loose, I cry.
Wash-ching-geka, let me loose, I cry!
Your uncle and your aunts
Oh, whatever will they do,
Whatever, whatever will they do!
Wash-ching-geka, let me loose, I cry.
Wash-ching-geka, let me loose, I cry!

Who was it that the Little Hare had caught? Who but the Sun! The Sun used to go through that pass every day, but this time he had been caught in the Little Hare's net.

"You go and set him loose!" commanded the grandmother. She scolded the Little Hare and beat him with her cane. "What will all your little-fathers and your little-mothers do without the Sun? So! Set him loose!"

So Wash-ching-geka tried to untie the net, but the Sun was so hot that the Little Hare could not face him. He could only back up, turning away his head. And thus the hind parts of the Little Hare were so scorched that, to this day, the skin of the hare's hind quarters is tender and easily broken.

> SONG OF THE SUN
> Wash-ching-geka, let me loose, I cry.
> Wash-ching-geka, let me loose, I cry!
> Your uncle and your aunts
> Oh, whatever will they do,
> Whatever, whatever will they do!
> Wash-ching-geka, let me loose, I cry.
> Wash-ching-geka, let me loose, I cry!

The Little Hare had another adventure with a monster. This monster was shaped like a living ant, with a big body and legs but with a very, very small middle part. At his waist, he was scarcely thicker than a hair. He lived behind a hill. Whenever he left home, he carried a very big tree and pounded the ground with it while singing a song. If elk and other animals came near, he threw the tree down upon them and killed them.

The Little Hare thought that because the Ant-Man was very thin at the waist, he could blow him in two. So the Little Hare blew "Soo! Soo!" But instead of blowing Ant-Man in two, he himself got killed. The Ant-Man threw his tree and crushed the Little Hare. When the Ant-Man lifted his tree, he found only a very small, flattened thing, he picked it up by the ears, said, "No good to eat," and threw away the little dead body.

That evening, when the Little Hare did not return home, his grandmother knew that he had been killed. The next morning she rose and ate, gathered her dress above her knees so that she could run faster, took one of the Little Hare's elkhorn clubs, and started out to find him. The old grandmother, able to run fast like Little Hare, ran over the whole earth until she heard the Ant-Man pounding and singing.

When he lifted up his tree to throw at her, she said, "Brother, better not do that!" So he stayed his hand and talked with her.

In a very short time, he admitted, "I did kill something very small yesterday. It was no good for eating, and so I threw it away. You go down there and look at it."

Finding that the little creature was her Little Hare, she picked him up by the ears and said, "You sleep here too long! Wake up and go to work!"

He went home with her. Next morning he started forth to find a big tree that would protect him from Ant-Man and his big fir tree. The Little Hare went away to the very edge of the earth, where the biggest pine trees grow. There he spoke to Wa-zi- chunk, the tallest tree in the world.

"Big tree," said he, "I plan to use you. I will pull you out of the ground, but when I have finished with you, I will put you back again."

He laid hold of the tree, pulled it out, and carried it to the place where he had been killed. He climbed the hill at one end while Ant-Man climbed it at the other end, singing and pounding with his tree. The Little Hare also sang and pounded with his tree. Then the two danced toward the other, each one singing and pounding with his tree.

Soon big Ant-Man walked more and more slowly. He could hardly keep on his feet because the Little Hare made the ground shake by pounding it with the tallest tree in the world. Slowly the two came nearer and nearer to the other. When the Little Hare reached the tall Ant-Man, he took the tallest tree in the world and crushed the monster.

A swarm of flying ants came out of the monster's body, and the Little Hare said to the dead body, "You can never again kill anything. And you little ants will have to creep on the ground, but sometimes you may fly."

And then the Little Hare carried the tall tree back to the edge of the earth and set it in its place.

Burlin, *The Indians' Book*, 247-253.

■

MAKING THE SACRED BUNDLE
Pawnee

At one time the Pawnee Indians lived largely in what is now Nebraska. From the beginning they grew corn, beans, pumpkins, and fruit, and they harvested a perennial plant of grassy cereal-like grain found in wet or swampy areas, called "wild oats" by the French, and similar to wild rice of today, and hunted for their game and fish. Their women were skillful weavers and pottery makers. Elaborate forms of religious ceremonies were presided over by a strong tribal priesthood. Primarily, the Pawnees were nature worshippers.

■

Long ago, a young Pawnee named Eagle Feather was very proud of the way he looked. He wore the best clothes and the richest ornaments he could find. Always when he hunted, he wore a magic downy eagle feather in his hair. He was not married, though many of the young Indian girls admired his handsome appearance.

One day while hunting with his companions, Eagle Feather became separated from the others, but continued to follow some buffaloes for a long distance. All of the animals escaped him except one young buffalo-cow, which had become stuck in a mudhole. When Eagle Feather aimed his arrow to shoot, the buffalo-cow suddenly vanished and in its place stood a pretty young woman.

Eagle Feather was astonished. He could not understand where the buffalo had gone, or from where the girl had come. They talked together and became friends. She did not want to return with him to his tribe when he asked her to marry him. Eagle Feather agreed to remain there with her and she became his wife. For a wedding gift, he gave her a blue and white string of beads, which she always wore around her neck.

They made a camp there and were very happy together. One day, Eagle Feather returned from hunting to find that his camp had disappeared, his wife was missing, and marks of many buffalo hooves covered his campsite. Since he could not find his wife anywhere, Eagle Feather returned to his Pawnee tribe.

After a few years passed, one summer morning Eagle Feather and his friends were playing stick ball. A little Indian boy came toward them, wearing around his neck a string of blue and white beads.

"Father," he said to Eagle Feather. "Mother wants you to follow me and I will take you to her."

"Go away," replied Eagle Feather. "I am not your father."

When the little Indian boy ran back to the woods, Eagle Feather's compansions laughed at the boy calling him father. They thought Eagle Feather had never married.

In a little while, the boy returned from the woods. Again, he was told to go away, but one of the men said to Eagle Feather, "Maybe you had better go with the child and see what he wants."

All of this time, Eagle Feather had been wondering, "Where have I seen those blue and white beads before?" Suddenly, in his mind's eye, he saw a buffalo-cow and a calf running across a prairie. He then remembered the blue and white beads he had given the buffalo-maiden for a wedding present.

Taking his bow and arrows with him, he followed the two buffaloes that he now believed were his wife and child. A long and weary chase followed, because the woman was angry that first he had denied the boy's request. As she ran, she magically dried up every creek they passed. Eagle Feather thought he was going to die of thirst. But his son secretly left some food and water for him along the way, until they arrived at the home of the buffaloes.

The big buffalo-bulls were the herd leaders. They became angry with Eagle Feather for marrying the buffalo-cow. They wanted to kill him. But first they would test him. Six buffalo-cows were lined up in a row, all looking exactly alike. Eagle Feather was to point out his wife. His son helped him secretly, and Eagle Feather correctly chose his wife.

Surprised, the old bulls gave Eagle Feather another test. This time, several calves were placed in a row, and Eagle Feather was to choose his son. Again the child secretly helped his father point out the right one. Then the bulls decided that Eagle Feather must run a race against the fastest buffaloes.

On the day set for the race, a freeze occurred and the buffaloes could not run well on the slippery ground. Eagle Feather ran swiftly and won the race.

Now the chief bulls grew angrier and they determined to kill Eagle Feather. He was told to sit down on the ground in the center of a circle surrounded by buffalo-bulls. Upon a signal from the Chief, the buffaloes charged Eagle Feather. His magic feather was seen floating above the confusion that followed.

When the Chief called a halt to the charge, he expected to see Eagle Feather trampled to death. The bulls withdrew and there sat Eagle Feather in the center of the ring with his magic feather still in his hair.

A second charge of the buffalo-bulls ended with the same result as the first. Deciding that Eagle Feather possessed powerful magic-protection, the Chief welcomed him into their camp on one condition: that he bring them gifts from the Pawnee tribe. This, Eagle Feather agreed to do.

When he returned to his tribal village with his wife and son in human form, he found his people without food. But his wife had brought some buffalo meat under her robe, and, magically, every one of the Pawnees had enough to eat. Later, when Eagle Feather and his family took gifts to the buffalo leaders, they were greatly pleased.

In return, the leaders offered some of their old bulls to help the Pawnees secure more food. The young son of Eagle Feather returned with the herd in the form of a yellow calf, while his parents went ahead in human form.

"Do not kill the yellow calf," warned Eagle Feather. "When you hunt, always save the yellow calf, because it will always bring back more buffaloes to the Pawnee tribe."

Consequently, they had an abundance of food for a long time. Then one day, the son of Eagle Feather said to his father, "No more will I visit you as a boy. No longer should the hunters spare the yellow calf. They should kill it and sacrifice it to the Great Spirit. They should tan its yellow hide and make a bundle containing an ear of corn and other sacred objects wrapped within. This will be your tribal sacred bundle.

"Every year, you must look for another yellow calf leading the buffalo herd to the Pawnees. Each year you must sacrifice it and keep a piece of its fat, adding it to your sacred bundle.

"Then if food ever should become scarce, your chiefs should gather in council and pay a friendly visit to a young buffalo. He will tell of your need to the Great Spirit, so that another yellow calf might be sent to lead a buffalo herd to the Pawnees."

When he had finished speaking, the boy left the camp. In the future of the Pawnee tribe, everything happened as he said it would. Food was plentiful, Eagle Feather became a great Chief, respected and loved by his tribe. His buffalo-wife, however, was almost forgotten, and one night she vanished forever.

Chief Eagle Feather felt great remorse when he came to realize his neglect of her. He never recovered fully from the loss of his wife. In time, he withered away and died. His magic eagle feather was added to the sacred bundle of the Pawnee tribe.

The Pawnees' sacred bundle has long been preserved by the tribal shaman for its magic charms, which always bring back the buffaloes. The Pawnees knew that in a time of great need, the sacred bundle could be opened by the tribal priest in a proper solemn ceremony, imploring the help of the Great Spirit.

Spence, *Myths and Legends of the Pawnees*, 304- 308.

■

LEGEND OF THE PIASA

Illini

After exploring the Mississippi River in 1673, Louis Joliet and Father Marquette returned by way of the Illinois River. Just above its mouth, they saw a painted, carved creature in the cliffside that resembled more than anything else a flying reptilian dragon. Because of its vicious appearance, Marquette named the creature *Piasa*, meaning "Destroyer." Unfortunately, a zealous land developer excavated the rock sculpture in 1876. It is now considered a lost heritage of another age.

However, Squire Russell of Bluffdale, Illinois, later reported:

"I used to climb the rocks to look at the *Piasa* when I was a young boy. I have been within about sixty feet of it. The colors were always affected by dampness, being very distinct after a rain...:

"The picture was cut into the rock a half inch or more, and was originally painted red, black, and blue. It had the head of a bear, large disproportioned teeth, the horns of an elk, the scaly body of a large fish, and a bear's legs ending with eagle's claws. The tail was at least fifty feet long, wound three times around the body, and tipped with a spearhead thrust backward through its hind legs.

"The upper horns were painted red, the lower portion and head were painted black. The wings expanded to the right and left of its head, and the *Piasa's* body was at least sixteen feet long. Its head and neck were covered with a whiskery mane, and its body...covered with the three colors...In 1820, Captain Gideon Spencer came up the Mississippi River and saw the same picture on the rock. He asked the nearby Indians what it was. They told him it was the Stormbird or Thunderer, and that it had been carved there by an Indian tribe long ago."

"The Mesozoic age of reptiles extended over a hundred million years," said Arthur Loveridge of Harvard University. "Frequently bizarre-looking animals evolved, such as flying saurians (pterosaurs) with combined batlike and dragonlike features, measuring up to twenty feet between wing tips."

U.S. geologist F. V. Hayden stated, "Professor Marsh discovered remains of flying saurians in Kansas Chalk with eighteen to twenty feet between wing tips."

The earth has preserved its record of ancient flying saurians (flying reptiles) and since the beginning of recorded history man has been fascinated with these creatures.

Was there a real *Piasa*—a flying saurian— hanging by its claws in the cliffs along the Illinois River? The Illini Indian tribe has handed down the following legend.

■

Long, long ago, when only animals walked the earth, Storm-bird lived in a cave by the river. His cave was lined with the bones of buffalo victims. He would swoop down upon a buffalo herd and drive his terrible claws into the fattest one, carrying it off to his cave.

After our people arrived upon the earth, Storm-bird captured one of our warriors. From that day on, he was a threat to our whole tribe—men, women, and children. A loud roar and a flapping sound signaled that Storm-bird was coming out of his cave. Everyone agreed that something must be done to destroy the monster, but what?

Ortega was our great Chief of the Illinis. He announced to our people that he was determined to find a way to kill the beast. As part of their

Wooden bowl in beaver form
Illini

tribal ritual, he withdrew in solitude to fast and seek a vision. He prayed to the Great Spirit to reveal a way to conquer the Storm-bird.

When Chief Ortega returned, he directed all of our people to hide in their tepees. He then dispatched his chosen warriors to the brush surrounding an exposed point of land, directly opposite the cave of the Storm-bird.

Dressed in his Chief's warbonnet, Ortega took his stand upon the point of land, without weapons. Storm-bird could see the Chief. It began to roar! Eyeing our Chief with clenched teeth, it opened its huge weblike wings and charged at the Chief!

Ortega stood his ground, chanting his death song! Instantly, the hidden warriors let go their arrows with sharp, pointed flints. The Storm-bird was struck from all sides with a hundred arrows and fell dead!

To honor Chief Ortega and in remembrance of the event, a sculpture of the flying Storm-bird was carved into the cliffside and painted by the Illini tribe a long time ago, an exact replica of the terrible beast.

Cunningham, *Lower Illinois Valley Sketches of Long Ago*, 22.

TWO BROTHERS WHO BECAME STARS
Wichita

There was one Wichita tribe with two chiefs. Their village was divided by a road, so that each chief had his half of the village. Each chief had a child. The west village chief had a son. The child of the chief living in the east was a girl. Both remained single and were not acquainted with each other.

In those times, children of prominent families were shown the same respect as their parents, and they were always protected from danger. The chief's son had a sort of scaffold for his bed, which was so high that he had to use a ladder to get to it. When he came down from his bed, the ladder was removed.

One night the young man set out to visit the young woman, as he was curious to see how she looked. At that very same time, the girl set out to visit the young man. They both came into the divided road when they saw each other. The girl asked the young man where he was going. He replied that he was going to see the chief's daughter, and asked where she was going. She replied, to see the chief's son. He said that he was the chief's son, and the girl said that she was the chief's daughter. They both enjoyed a quiet laugh together there on the division road.

They were undecided whether to go to her lodge or to his home. They decided to go to the young man's home. The next morning his parents wondered why he was not up early as usual. Their family custom was to rise early and sit up late, as their people called at all hours. His grandmother was sent to tap on his ladder to wake him. She found her grandson sleeping with another person. She reported to the others about it. Again she went back to request him to come down for breakfast. The family then learned that the son's companion was the other chief's daughter.

Meanwhile, the other chief wondered why his daughter was late for breakfast. In the village lived Coyote. Since the chief could not find his daughter, he sent his tribal warriors in search of her. Coyote searched both sides of the village, where he found the girl living with the other chief's son.

He returned immediately to the girl's father and alerted him to where his daughter could be found. Her father was angry and sent word that she was never to return home again. Neither did the other chief like the way his son had behaved.

Grass lodge
Wichita

A day came when the young couple decided to leave the village. They gathered together what they would need for a trip, and started south at midnight. They traveled a long way before they rested and fell asleep. On the next day they moved onward in search of a new home. In three days they found a good place with water and timber and a good hunting area, where the husband went daily to supply the meat they needed. His wife arranged their grass lodge nicely, and they resided there for a long while.

Before the man started out to hunt, he cut a stick and put some meat on it, then stuck it into the ground in front of the fire to cook. He told his wife that the meat was for someone who might come to visit, but she must never look at him. If she heard someone talk, she should hurry to her bed and cover her head.

Later, she heard someone say that he was coming to get some food. She ran to her bed and covered her head with her robe. The visitor took the meat and ate it. Before leaving, he spoke and said, "I have eaten the meat and will go back to my home." When he had gone, the woman got up and went about her work.

That evening when her husband returned from hunting, she reported to him what had happened. From then on, her husband always prepared meat to cook before the fire, and always warned her not to look at the stranger, but go to her bed and cover her head. While the stranger ate, the woman always thought she heard two people speaking.

One morning after her husband had left, the woman made a hole in her robe and took a piece of straw with a hole in it. When the visitor appeared, she jumped into her bed and covered her head with the hole over one eye, and the peeking straw ready.

When he started to leave, she looked through the straw in the hole in the robe and saw a two-faced person—with a face in front and a face in back of his head. As she looked at him, the visitor told the woman that she had disobeyed her husband's orders and would be killed.

The double-faced man took hold of the woman and cut her open, taking out a child, which he wrapped with a piece of the robe onto a piece of board. He covered the woman again with her robe, and threw her stomach into a river.

When the husband returned, he found his young wife dead. "You have done wrong, and disobeyed my orders. You made up your own mind to look and see who was the visitor." The young husband took her body south, laid it on the ground, and covered it with buffalo robes.

Upon his return, he heard a baby crying. He looked inside and outside the grass lodge, then finally traced the crying to one of the lodge poles, where the cradleboard was hanging with the baby. He cooked some rare meat and held it for the baby to suck the juice. In this way he nourished his child.

He stayed most of the time with the baby, caring for it, and only hunting when he was out of meat. He carried the baby on his back when he did go out for food. The baby was a boy, and the father was proud to have him and to care for him. The child grew strong and soon was able to walk. When old enough the father made bows and arrows for him to play with.

One day when the boy had been left, he heard someone calling, "My brother, come out and let us play an arrow game." When he turned around he saw another boy about his size standing at the entrance to the grass lodge. The little boy ran outside to see his little visitor, who said they were brothers. The double-faced man had used a poker-stick to thrust into his mother's stomach and throw it into the water.

The same stick was still fastened in the stranger-boy's body, and he had always wondered what it was for. He promised not to tell their father about his winning all the arrows, and the other boy promised not to tell that he had had company all day. When the visiting-boy left, he ran toward the river and jumped into the water.

When the father came home, he asked his son where the arrows were. His son told him he had lost a lot of arrows shooting birds. His father told him to go where he had been shooting and find the arrows, but the boy said he could not find them. So the father made many more arrows for his son to shoot. As soon as his father left, the visiting-boy appeared for another arrow-shooting game. They played all day until the visiting-boy won all of the arrows, then ran to his river home.

When the man came back from his hunting trip, again he found his son had lost all of his arrows, and the boy refused to go look for them, saying the arrows could not be found. Again the father made more arrows for his son's sport and protection.

A long time later, the son told his father of his brother's visits. The father wanted to capture the lost brother to live with their family. The father decided to turn himself into a poker-stick and leave it inside the lodge. His son invited his brother to come inside and have something to eat before they played.

When the visiting-boy looked inside and saw the stick, he became suspicious and thought it must be the old man, so he went away. The father stayed still all day, but could not capture the other brother. There was no hunting the next day, as the father hid himself behind the side of the entrance and turned himself into a piece of straw.

When the other brother called, he was invited inside again. He looked all around inside and saw nothing different this time, so he entered and ate with his brother. The father had coached his son to look for lice in the other boy's hair, and when he had a good grasp of hair to call for his father to come and hold the other brother. The visiting-boy dragged his brother a distance before their father reached them.

The father took hold of the scalp lock, but the visiting-boy was so strong that he dragged father and brother toward the river. The father begged him to stop. They released visiting-boy in time, as he jumped into the water and came up with an armful of arrows. Father and son started for their home with the arrows. The boy was named Other-Boy.

From that time forward both boys lived with their father. When he went hunting, the boys would shoot birds for sport and food, besides decorative feathers. One day their father forbid them to go to four certain places: On the north, where lived an old woman; on the east, where lived the Thunderbird in a nest of a very high tree; on the south, where lived the double-faced man. The father made the boys a hoop and also forbade them to roll it to the west.

Some time passed before the boys decided to expand their territory during their father's absence. They agreed to visit the place to the north. On their way they shot a few birds and carried them along. When they arrived at the place, they saw smoke.

The old woman who lived there asked the little boys to come into her lodge. They gave her the birds, which pleased her. She told the boys she needed to boil water to cook them before eating. She gave them a bucket to go to the creek for water. She hung the potful of water over the fire to boil. But instead of the birds, she snatched the two boys in their place.

Other-Boy was on the side, bubbling the hardest. He told his brother to make a quick leap, while he did the same. They escaped from the kettle and poured the hot water on the old woman and killed her. They hurried home before their father could arrive, but they hastened to tell him about their experience with the old woman of the north. He reminded them of his warning to stay away from the Little-Old-Spider-Woman of the north.

The next day, the brothers started east to visit the Thunderbird. They came to the high tree, which held the nest of the Thunderbird family. Other-Boy said to his brother, "Take my arrows and I will climb the tree and see what young ones these Thunderbirds have."

He began to climb when all of a sudden he heard thundering and saw lightning bolts, which struck him and made his left leg disappear. He called down to his brother to look for his leg while he kept on climbing. When he climbed higher, Thunderbird came again, and lightning took off his left arm. He still climbed, anxious to see inside the nest.

He was near the top when his right leg disappeared, so only his right arm remained as he reached the nest. Now the Thunderbirds did not bother him any more. He picked up one little one and asked whose child he was. He replied, "The child of Weather- Followed-by-Hard-Winds." The boy threw the bird down to the ground, saying he was not the right kind of child.

He picked up another and asked the same question, and the child replied, "Clear-Weather-with-Sun-Rising-Slowly." He put the bird back in the nest, saying he was a good child. He took up another and asked again the question, and the child replied "Cold-Weather-Following-Wind-and-Snow." The boy dropped him down to the ground, saying it was a bad creature.

The boy picked up the last bird. It answered that it was of "Foggy-Day-Followed-by-Small-Showers." This he put back in the nest, telling it that it was the right kind of child. Then, with one arm, he started to climb down the tree.

He finally reached the ground where his brother put on his right leg and he hopped around to see if it felt secure. When his brother put on his right arm, then his left leg, he ran and hopped around and waved his arms wildly.

The two boys returned home before their father came back from the hunt. They greeted him with their Thunderbird adventure of the day. The father began to think Other-Boy must have great powers, and he did not say much more to the boys about their choice of dangerous places to visit.

Some time later, the boys went out again and came to the place where their mother was put to death. They saw a stone in the shape of a human being, and they both lay down on the stone. When they started to get up, they were stuck to the stone, so they took it home with them for their father.

When they reached home, he said they should take the stone back to where they had found it. He told them the stone was like a monument of their mother, as she had turned to stone after her death. The brothers took the stone back to its special place.

Another day, the two brothers decided to go to the forbidden place where double-faced man lived, the man who had killed their mother. He lived in a cave. The boys went in it to see what they could find. Double-faced man's children came forward and scratched the boys. Other-Boy took his bow and slew the children. He caught double-faced man and tied the bow string around his neck, and half-led and half-choked him, taking the man back to their father, who did not want the bad one. He commanded the two brothers to take him away and kill him, and they obeyed.

Every day the boys played as before, shooting birds, and rolling their hoop. "Let's roll the hoop toward the west and see what will happen," said Other-Boy. They rolled and rolled it toward the west, and the hoop began rolling faster and faster. The boys kept running faster and faster, until they could not stop. They landed in the water where the hoop had rolled, then into the mouth of a giant water-monster called Kidiar-kat that swallowed them completely.

Inside, the boys thought it looked like a tepee, as the ribs of the monster reminded them of the tepee poles. "How can we ever escape?" they wondered. Other-Boy stretched out his bowstring and swung it round and round, which disturbed the monster slightly. A second time he swung it faster, and the monster moved a little more. A third time he swung even faster, which moved the monster more and more. The next time around, the monster gave such a high jump that he leapt out of the water and onto dry land.

When the monster opened its mouth wide, the boys ran out as fast as they could and all the way home. No one was at their lodge. Their father had gone somewhere, but they could not find him. The two brothers looked everywhere for a trail, but no trace of him was visible. At last they grew weary and decided to rest for a while.

Later, when darkness overtook them, they found a trail and followed it until it stopped. Other-Boy called for his brother to shoot an arrow straight up toward the sky. They waited for a while, and finally a drop of blood came down from above. It was the blood of their father.

When the boys were so late in returning from their adventure, their father gave up all hope of seeing them again, so he disappeared into the sky and became a star. The boys were certain the blood came as a message from their father to let them know where he had gone.

They decided to shoot two arrows upward and then caught hold of them and flew up into the sky with their arrows. Now the two brothers stand side by side with their father in the sky—as three stars.

Dorsey, G., "The Two Boys Who Became Stars," 153-160.

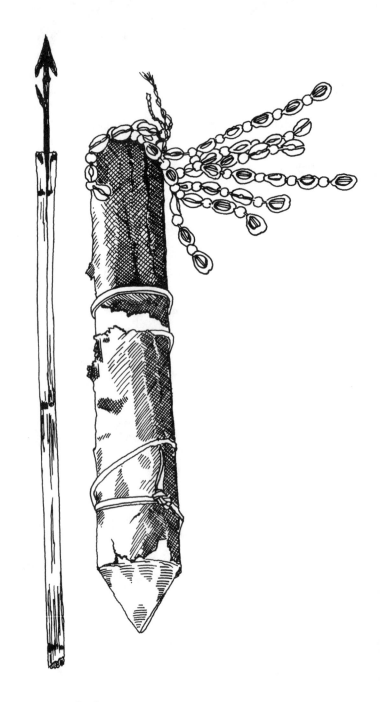

Southeast Indian harpoon and quiver
Cherokee

PART FIVE

FROM THE SOUTHEAST

All South Atlantic Coast states and West Virginia, Tennessee, Mississippi, and Alabama are represented in these stories.

The Creek Nation, a confederation of many tribes, reigned as the principal political element in Georgia, Alabama, and Florida. They confronted Hernando de Soto's explorers as far back as 1540. Seminole, meaning "one who has camped out from town," left the Creek villages and settled in Florida.   .

Yuchi, meaning "far away," spread over the southern states and as far west as St. Louis. Tuskegee, meaning "warrior," located mainly in Georgia and Tennessee. Alabama, meaning "to camp," stayed in their homeland, for which the state of Alabama is named.

The Natchez tribe in Mississippi, east of the present city of that name, welcomed the explorer René La Salle in 1682. Shawnee, the "Southerners," lived chiefly in South Carolina, then later scattered into other states, as far west as Ohio.

Cherokees, "people of a different speech," belonged to the Iroquois language family and lived in North Carolina and Tennessee. The most famous Cherokee was Sequoya, son of a mixed-breed Cherokee woman and a white man.

In 1821, Sequoya submitted his Cherokee alphabet to the Chief's Council. He was the first Indian known to have created an alphabet. Upon approval, Cherokees of all ages began to learn it; in a few months many of them could read and write. The next year, Sequoya went west to teach the western Cherokees and he remained there permanently. His name was given to Sequoia National Park.

■

THE ORIGIN OF EARTH
Tuskegee

■

Before the beginning, water was everywhere. But no people, animals, or earth were visible.

There were birds, however, who held a council to decide if it might be best to have all land or all water. "Let us have land, so we can have more food," said some of the birds. Others said, "Let's have all water, because we like it this way."

Subsequently, they appointed Eagle as their Chief who was to decide one way or the other. Eagle decided upon land and asked, "Who will go and search for land?"

Dove volunteered first and flew away. In four days he completed his hunt and returned, reporting, "I could not find land anywhere."

Crawfish came swimming along and was asked by the council to help search for land. He disappeared under the water for four days. When he arose to the surface again, he held some dirt in his claws. He had found some land deep in the water.

Crawfish made a ball of the dirt and handed it to Chief Eagle, who then flew away with it. Four days later he returned and said to the council, "Now there is land, an island has been formed— follow me!"

The whole bird colony flew after Eagle to see the new land, though it was a very small island. Gradually, the land began to grow larger and larger as the water became lower and lower. More islands appeared and these grew together, creating larger islands into one earth.

Tuskegee Indians say they were chosen by the Great Spirit to be the first people to live upon the new earth, a long, long time ago.

Swanton, "Creation," 487.

■

IN THE BEGINNING
Yuchi

Southeastern Indian traditions indicated their belief in an Upper World, a Lower World, and This World, where they, the animals and plants, lived and thrived. Early on in This World, some extraordinary humans and animals came down to visit from Upper World. Later, they returned to their previous world, where they felt more comfortable. Mankind of This World in time learned to resolve frictions and to maintain some order between themselves and the other two worlds. They became mostly villagers and agriculturists with more permanent tribal homes, since they were not nomadic by nature. Their tribes enlarged and prospered as hunters, fishermen, builders, and skilled craftsmen, including the women's abilities in weaving, basketry, and herbal medicines; the latter maintaining the good health of their people.

■

In the beginning, water covered everything. Wind asked, "Who will make the land? Who will make the land appear?"

Lock-chew, the Crawfish, said, "I will make the land appear."

So he went down to the bottom of the water and began to stir up the mud with his tail and his claws. He brought up some mud to a certain place and piled it up until it made a mound.

The owners of the land at the bottom of the water said, "Who is disturbing our land?" They kept careful watch and discovered it was Crawfish. When they started toward him, Crawfish stirred up the mud so much with his tail that they could not see him.

Lock-chew continued to pile up mud, until it came out on top of the surface of the great water. This is how land first appeared. It was so soft that Wind said, "Who will spread the land to make it dry and hard?"

Hawk and Buzzard appeared. Because Buzzard's wings were larger, he tried first. He flew, fanning the soft earth and spreading it all about. When he flapped his wings, hills and valleys were formed.

"Who will make the light?" Wind asked. It was very dark.

Yo-hah, the Star, said, "I will make light." It was agreed. The Star shone forth, but its light only remained close to the Star.

"Who will make more light?" Wind asked.

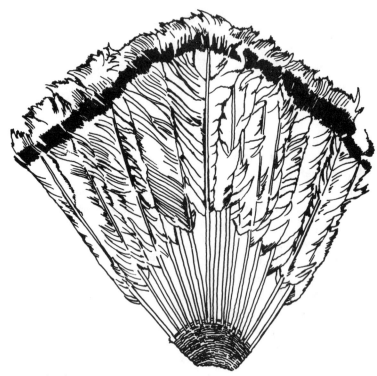

Dance feather fan
Yuchi

Shar-pah, the Moon, said, "I will make enough light for all my children and I will shine forever." But the world was still too dark.

T-cho, the Sun, said, "Leave it to me to make enough light for everyone everywhere."

Sun went to the East and suddenly enough light was everywhere. As Sun traveled over the earth, a drop of blood fell from the sky to the ground. From this spot sprang the first people, the children of the Sun they were called, the Yu-chis.

The Yu-chis wished to find their medicine since a large monster had destroyed some of their people. The Yu-chis cut off its head, but the next day its head and body were together again. They killed the monster a second time. Again, its head grew back on its body.

A third time, they cut off its head. They placed the head on top of a tall tree, so the body could not reach the head. The next morning, the tree was dead and the head had rejoined the monster's body. They killed it once more, putting its head at the top of a cedar tree. The next morning the cedar tree was still alive, but covered with blood from the head. The monster remained dead.

This is how the Yu-chis found their great medicine, the Cedar Tree. Fire was soon discovered by boring a stick into some hard, dry weeds.

The Yu-chis selected a second medicine, as each one made a picture of the Sun upon their door.

In the beginning, all of the animals could talk with one another. All animals and people were at peace. The deer lived in a cave watched over by a Yu-chis keeper. When the Yu-chis became hungry, the keeper selected a deer and killed it for their food. Finally, all of the deer were set free with the other anima l s, and a name was given to every animal upon the earth.

This is how it was in the beginning with the first people, the Yu-chis Indian tribe.

Swanton, "In the Beginning," 84-85.

■

THE FIRST FIRE
Cherokee

Almost every North American Indian tribe told some story about the origin of fire. So did other early peoples. Here is a fire myth that the Cherokee Indians of North Carolina used to tell.

■

In the beginning of the world, there was no fire. The naimal people were often cold. Only the Thunders, who lived in the world beyond the sky arch, had fire. At last they sent Lightning down to an island. Lightning put fire into the bottom of a hollow sycamore tree.

The animal people knew that the fire was there, because they could see smoke rising from the top of the tree. But they could not get to it on account of the water. So they held a council to decide what to do.

Everyone that could fly or could swim was eager to go after the fire. Raven said, "Let me go. I am large and strong."

At that time Raven was white. He flew high and far across the water and reached the top of the sycamore tree. While he sat there wondering what to do, the heat scorched all his feathers black. The frightened Raven flew home without the fire, and his feathers have been black ever since.

Then the council sent Screech Owl. He flew to the island. But while he was looking down into the hollow tree, a blast of hot air came up and nearly burned out his eyes. He flew home and to this day, Screech Owl's eyes are red.

Then Hooting Owl and Horned Owl were sent to the island together. But the smoke nearly blinded them, and the ashes carried up by the wind made white rings about their eyes. They had to come home, and were never able to get rid of the white rings.

Then Little Snake swam across to the island, crawled through the grass to the tree, and entered it through a small hole at the bottom. But the smoke and the heat were too much for him, too. He escaped alive, but his body had been scorched black. And it was so twisted that he doubled on his track as if always trying to escape from a small space.

Big Snake, the climber, offered to go for fire, but he fell into the burning stump and became as black as Little Snake. He has been the great blacksnake ever since.

At last Water Spider said that she would go. Water Spider has black downy hair and red stripes on her body. She could run on top of water and she could dive to the bottom. She would have no trouble in getting to the island.

"But you are so little, how will you carry enough fire?" the council asked.

"I'll manage all right," answered Water Spider. "I can spin a web." so she spun a thread from her body and wove it into a little bowl and fastened the little bowl on her back. Then she crossed over to the island and through the grass. She put one little coal of fire into her bowl and brought it across to the people.

Every since, we have had fire. And the Water Spider still has her little bowl on her back.

Mooney, "Myths of the Cherokee," "The First Fire," 290.

■

THE ORIGIN OF GAME AND OF CORN
Cherokee

The first explorers of the Southeast discovered the most talented Indians north of Mexico. Builders, agriculturists, artisans, fishermen, and hunters epitomized especially the Cherokees' varied skills. Knowledgeable in herb culture, they developed useful medicines from them that are still used today. They also developed environmental concepts about ecological thought and survival. We are blessed by the legacies of Cherokee oral traditions, providing ethnologists with opportunities for cultural interpretations: legends about man, animals, supernatural deities, witches, and other evil influences. Their most famous Sequoya, believing literacy provided power to the white man, alone developed the Cherokee alphabet, and became immortalized when his name was given to Sequoia National Park in California.

∎

Long ages ago, soon after the world was made, Kenati, a Cherokee Indian hunter and his wife Selu, lived on Looking-glass Mountain in North Carolina. They had a little son named Good Boy.

Whenever Kenati hunted in the woods, he always brought back all the game his family needed. His wife cut up the meat and washed it in the river not far from their lodge. Good Boy played near the river almost every day. One day his parents thought they heard laughing in the bushes, as if there were two children playing there.

That evening Kenati asked his son, "Who were you playing with today down by the river?"

"He is a boy who comes out of the water and calls himself my elder brother," replied Good Boy.

When Selu washed game in the river agian, the parents throught the water boy must grow from the animal blood. She never saw the water boy, because as she approached he disappeared.

One evening, Kenati said to his son, "Tomorrow when your playmate comes out of the water, wrestle with him and hold him down and call me, so we can come and see him." Good Boy promised to do as his father asked.

Next day a wrestling match took place between the two boys. Kenati and Selu were not far away, and at the first call from their son, they ran to see the boy from the river. Compared with Good boy, the other one looked wild.

"Let me go! Let me go!" he cried out. Good Boy held him down until his parents arrived. They took the water boy home with them.

The family kept the wild one in the house form some time, trying to tame him. But he was always disagreeable in his disposition and tried to lead Good Boy into mischief. The family discovered that wild one possessed some magic powers, so they decided to keep him. They named him Wild Boy.

Always Kenati came home from hunting with a large fat deer on his back. Always he was lucky with game. One day Wild Boy said to his brother, "I wonder where our father finds so much game? Let's follow him next time."

In a few days, Kenati took his bow and arrows and went hunting. Shortly afterward the boys followed. Staying out of sight, they saw their father go into a swamp where some strong reeds were growing. With these, hunters usually made arrow shafts. Wild Boy changed himself into a puff of bird's down. A little wind carried him up and onto Kenati's shoulder. There he watched where Kenati went and what he did. The father was not aware of Wild Boy's presence on his shoulder as he gathered reeds and fitted them with feathers.

"I wonder what those things are for?" thought Wild Boy to himself. Kenati came out of the swamp and went on his way into the woods. The wind carried the down off Kenati's shoulders and soon Wild Boy was his normal self again. Still keeping out of sight of their father, the two brothers followed him into the mountains.

When Kenati reached a certain place, he stopped and lifted a large rock. At once, a large buck deer came running out of the hole. Kenati shot it and lifted it upon his back, starting home with his prize.

Reed shaft blowgun and darts
Cherokee

"Oho!" said the boys. "He keeps the wild animals shut up inside a cave until he needs them. He then kills the game with those things he made in the swamp." They hurried to reach home before their father arrived with his heavy load.

The very next day, the boys wanted to see if they could do as their father had done. First, they went to the swamp and made some arrows. When they came to the big rock, they lifted the cover and instantly a deer ran out, but they forgot to replace the cover.

As they made ready to shoot the deer, another deer came out of the hole, then another, and another--the boys became so confused they forgot what to do next.

Long ago, a deer's tail stuck straight out from his body. When Wild Boy struck at a deer's tail with an arrow, the tail stood straight up. The boys throught it great fun. As another deer ran by, Good Boy swung at it with an arrow so hard that the tail curled over the deer's back. Since that time most deers' tails curl at the end.

All of the deer in the cave came out and disappeared into the forest. Following them were raccoons, rabbits, and all the other four-footed animals. Last came turkeys, partridges, pigeons, and other winged creatures. They darkened the air as they flew away. Such a noise arose that Kenati heard it at his lodge. To himself he said, "I must go to see what trouble my boys have stirred up."

Kenati went to the mountain, to the place of the large rock. There stood the two boys, but all the animals and birds were gone. Kenati was furious with them, but said nothing. He went into the cave and kicked off the covers of four large jars that stood in the back corner.

Out of the jars swarmed bedbugs, lice, and gants that attached the two boys. they screamed from terror as they tried to beat off the insects. Bitten and stung, the boys dropped to the ground from exhaustion.

When Kenati thought they had learned their lesson, he brushed away the pests. "Now you rascals," he scolded them. "You have always had plenty to eat without working for it. When we needed game, all I had to do was to come up here and take home just what we needed. Now you have let all of the game escape. From now on when you are hungry, you will have to hunt throughout the woods and mountains and then not find enough game."

The two boys went home and asked their mother for something to eat.

"There is no more meat," said Selu. "I will go to the storehouse and try to find something."

She took her basket and went to the two-story provision house set upon poles high above the ground, out of reach of most animals.

Every day before the evening meal, Selu climbed the ladder to the one opening. She always came back with her basket full of beans and corn.

"Let's go and see where she gets the corn and beans," urged Wild Boy to his brother. They followed Selu and climbed up in back of the storehouse. They removed a piece of mud from between the logs and looked through the crack. There stood Selu in the middle of the room with her basket on the floor. When she rubbed her stomach, the basket was half-filled with corn. When she rubbed her legs, the basket was full to the top with beans. Wild Boy said, "Our mother is a witch. Maybe her food will poison us."

When Selu came back to the house, she seemed to know what the boys were thinking. "You think I am a witch?"

"Yes, we think you are a witch," Wild Boy replied.

"When I die, I want you boys to clear a large piece of ground in front of our lodge. Then drag all of my clothes seven times around the inside of the circle. If you stay up all night and watch, next morning you will be rewarded with plenty of corn."

Booger mask
Cherokee

Soon thereafter Selu became ill and died suddenly. The boys set to work clearing the ground as she had said. But instead of the whole piece of ground in front of the lodge, they only cleared seven small spots. This is why corn does not grow everywhere in the world.

Instead of dragging Selu's clothing seven times, they only went around the circle twice, outside and inside the circle. The brothers watched all night, and in the morning there were fully grown beans and corn, but only in the seven small spots.

Kenati came home from a long hunting trip. He looked for Selu but could not find her. When the boys came home, he asked them, "Where is your mother?"

"She turned into a witch and then she died," they reported. Kenati was saddened by the news.

"I cannot stay here with you any longer. I will go and live with the Wolf people," he said.

He started on his journey. Wild Boy changed himself into a tuft of bird's down and settled upon Kenati's shoulder to learn where he was going.

When Kenati reached the settlement of the Wolf people, they were having a council in their town-house. He went in and sat down with the tuft upon his shoulder. Wolf Chief asked Kenati what was his business.

"At home I have two bad boys. In seven days, I want you to go and play a game of ball with them."

The Wolf people knew that Kenati wanted them to punish the boys and promised to go in seven days. At that moment the down blew off of Kenati's shoulder and the smoke carried it up and through the smoke hole in the roof. It came down to the ground outside, where Wild Boy resumed his own shape and ran home fast to tell his brother. Kenati did not return but went on to visit another tribe.

The two brothers prepared for the coming of the wolves. Wild Boy the magician told his brother what to do. Together they made a path around the house, leaving an opening on one side for the wolves to enter.

Next, they made four large bundles of arrows. These they placed at four different points on the outside of the circle. Then they hid themselves in the woods nearby and waited for the wolves.

At the appointed time, a whole army of wolves surrounded the house. They came in the entrance the boys had made. When all were within, Wild Boy magically made the pathway become a high fence, trapping the wolves inside.

The two boys on the outside began shooting arrows at the wolves. Since the fence was too high for the wolves to jump over, they were trapped and most were killed.

Only a few escaped through the entrance and made their way into a nearby swamp. Three or four wolves eventually survived. These were the only wolves left alive in the world.

Soon thereafter, some strangers came from a great distance to learn about the brothers' good grain for eating and making bread. Only Selu and her family had the corn secret.

The two brothers told the strangers how to care for the corn and gave them seven kernels to plant the next night on their way home. They were advised that they must watch throughout the night, then the following morning they would have seven ears of corn. This they should do each night, and by the time they reached home, they should have enough corn for all their people to plant.

The strangers lived seven days' distance. Each night they did as the brothers had instructed them. On the last night of the journey, they were so tired that they fell asleep and were unable to continue the whole night's watch. Next morning, the corn had not sprouted and grown as on the previous six nights.

Upon arriving in their own village, they shared all the corn they still had left with their people. They explained how the two brothers told them the way to make the corn prosper. They watched over the planting with care and attention. A splendid crop of corn resulted. Since then, however, the Cherokee Indians needed to tend their corn only half the year to supply their people.

Kenati never came back to his home. The two brothers decided to search for him. Wild Boy sailed a magic disk to the northwind and it returned. He sailed it to the southwind and it returned, but it did not return from the eastwind. They knew that was where their father was living. They walked a long, long time and finally came upon Kenati with a dog walking by his side.

"You bad boys," rebuked Kenati. "Why have you followed me here?"

"We are men now," they replied. "We plan to accomplish what we set out to do." Wild Boy knew that the dog was the magic disk that had not returned, and had become a dog only a few days ago.

Kenati's trail led to Selu, waiting for him at the end of the world where the sun comes up. All seemed glad to be reunited for the present.

Their parents told the two brothers that they must go to live where the sun goes down. In seven days, the two boys left for the Land of the Setting-Sun. There they still live, overseeing the planting and the care of corn.

The brothers still talk about how Selu brought forth the first corn from her seed. Since that time, the Cherokee tribe refer to her as the "Corn Woman."

Mooney, "The Origin of Game and of Corn," 97-108.

THE BALL GAME OF THE BIRDS AND THE ANIMALS

Cherokee

The following myth explains the origin of a custom of the Cherokee Indians of North Carolina. They used to prepare for a popular ball game by holding a dance the night before. While the drummers beat on their drums, the rest of the people chanted songs. Before the game, each player asked the help of the bat and of the flying squirrel. For good luck, each player tied a small piece of bat's wing to the stick he would hit the ball with.

■

Long ago, the animals sent a message to the birds. "Let us have a big ball game. We will defeat you in a big ball game."

The birds answered, "We will meet you. We will defeat *you* in a big ball game."

So the plans were made. The day was set. At a certain place, all the animals gathered, ready to throw the ball to the birds in the trees. On the side of the animals were the bear, the deer, and the terrapin or turtle. The bear was heavier than the other animals. He was heavier than all the birds put together. The deer could run faster than the other animals could. The turtle had a very thick shell. So the animals felt sure that they would win the game.

The birds, too, felt sure that they would win. On their side were the eagle, the hawk, and the great raven. All three could fly swiftly. All three had farseeing eyes. All three were strong and had sharp beaks that could tear.

Lacrosse stick
Cherokee

In the treetops the birds smoothed their feathers. Then they watched every movement of the animals on the ground below them. As they watched, two small creatures climbed up the tree toward the leader of the birds. These two creatures were but a little bigger than mice.

"Will you let us join in the game?" they asked the leader of the birds.

The leader looked at them for a moment. He saw that they had four feet.

"Why don't you join the animals?" he asked them. "Because you have four feet, you really belong on the other side."

"We asked to play the game on their side," the tiny creatures answered. "But they laughed at us because we are so small. They do not want us."

The leader of the birds felt sorry for them. So did the eagle, the hawk, and the other birds.

"But how can they join us when they have no wings?" the birds asked each other.

"Let us make wings for the little fellows," one of the birds suggested.

"We can make wings from the head of the drum," another bird suggested.

The drum had been used in the dance the night before. Its head was the skin of a groundhog. The birds cut two pieces of leather from it, shaped them like wings, and fastened them to the legs of one of the little fellows. Thus they made the first bat.

The leader gave directions. He said to the bat, "When I toss the ball, you catch it. Don't let it touch the ground.

The bat caught it. He dodged and circled. He zigzagged very fast. He kept t he ball always in motion, never letting it touch the ground. The birds were glad they had made wings for him.

"What shall we do with the other little fellow?" asked the leader of the birds. "We have used up all our leather in making the wings for the bat."

The birds thought and thought. At last one of them had an idea.

"Let us make wings for him by stretching his skin," suggested the eagle.

So eagle and hawk, two of the biggest birds, seized the little fellow. With their strong bills they tugged and pulled at his fur. In a few minutes they stretched the skin between his front feet and his hind feet. His own fur made wings. Thus they made the first flying squirrel.

When the leader tossed the ball, flying squirrel caught it and carried it to another tree. From there he threw it to the eagle. Eagle caught it and threw it to another bird. The birds kept the ball in the air for some time, but at last they dropped it. Just before it reached the ground, the bat seized it. Dodging and circling and zigzagging, he kept out of the way of the deer and other swift animals. At last bat threw the ball in at the goal. And so he won the game for the birds.

Mooney, "Myths of the Cherokee," 286-287.

———, "The Cherokee Ball Play," 575-586.

■

THE ORIGIN OF MEDICINE
Cherokee

■

At one time, animals and people lived together peaceably and talked with each other. But when mankind began to multiply rapidly, the animals were crowded into forests and deserts.

Man began to destroy animals wholesale for their skins and furs, not just for needed food. Animals became angry at such treatment by their former friends, resolving they must punish mankind.

The bear tribe met in council, presided over by Old White Bear, their Chief. After several bears had spoken against mankind for their blood-thirsty ways, war was unanimously agreed upon. But what kinds of weapons should the bears use?

Chief Old White Bear suggested that man's weapon, the bow and arrow, should be turned against him. All of the council agreed. While the bears worked and made bows and arrows, they wondered what to do about bowstrings. One of the bears sacrificed himself to provide the strings, while the others searched for good arrow-wood.

When the first bow was completed and tried, the bear's claws could not release the strings to shoot the arrow. One bear offered to cut his claws, but Chief Old White Bear would not allow him to do that, because without claws he could not climb trees for food and safety. He might starve.

The deer tribe called together its council led by Chief Little Deer. They decided that any Indian hunters, who killed deer without asking pardon in a suitable manner, should be afflicted with painful rheumatism in their joints.

After this decision, Chief Little Deer sent a messenger to their nearest neighbors, the Cherokee Indians.

"From now on, your hunters must first offer a prayer to the deer before killing him," said the messenger. "You must ask his pardon, stating you are forced only by the hunger needs of your tribe to kill the deer. Otherwise, a terrible disease will come to the hunter."

When a deer is slain by an Indian hunter, Chief Little Deer will run to the spot and ask the slain deer's spirit, "Did you hear the hunter's prayer for pardon?"

If the reply is yes, then all is well and Chief Little Deer returns to his cave. But if the answer is no, then the Chief tracks the hunter to his lodge and strikes him with the terrible disease of rheumatism, making him a helpless cripple unable to hunt again.

All the fishes and reptiles then held a council and decided they would haunt those Cherokee Indians, who tormented them, by telling them hideous dreams of serpents twining around them and eating them alive. These snake and fish dreams occurred often among the Cherokees. To get relief, the Cherokees pleaded with their Shaman to banish their frightening dreams if they no longer tormented the snakes and fish.

Now when the friendly plants heard what the animals had decided against mankind, they planned a countermove of their own. Each tree, shrub, herb, grass, and moss agreed to furnish a cure for one of the diseases named by the animals and insects.

Thereafter, when the Cherokee Indians visited their Shaman about their ailments and if the medicine man was in doubt, he communed with the spirits of the plants. They always suggested a proper remedy for mankind's diseases.

This was the beginning of plant medicine from nature among the Cherokee Indian tribe a long, long time ago.

Spence, *Myths of the American Indians*, 249-251.

■

THE HERO WITH THE HORNED SNAKES
Cherokee

■

In ancient times, there lived some very large snakes that glittered nearly as bright as the sun. They had two horns on their heads, and they possessed a magic power of attraction. To see one of these snakes was always a bad omen. Whoever tried to escape from one instead ran directly toward the snake and was devoured.

Only a highly skilled medicine man or hunter could kill a two-horned snake. It required a very special medicine or power. The hunter had to shoot his arrow into the seventh stripe of the snake's skin.

One day a Shawnee Indian youth was held captive by the Cherokees. He was promised his freedom if he could find and kill a horned snake. He hunted for many, many days in caves, over wild mountains, and at last found one high in the Tennessee Mountains.

The Shawnee youth made a large circle of fire by burning pinecones. Then he walked toward the two-horned snake. When it saw the hunter, the snake slowly raised its head. The Shawnee youth shouted, "Freedom or death!"

He then aimed carefully and shot his arrow through the seventh stripe of the horned snake's skin. Turning quickly, he jumped into the center of the ring of fire, where he felt safe from the snake.

A stream of poison flowed from the snake, but was stopped by the fire. Because of the Shawnee youth's bravery, the grateful Cherokees granted him his freedom as they had promised.

Four days later, some of the Cherokees went to the spot where the youth had killed the horned snake. They gathered fragments of snake bones and skin, tying them into a sacred bundle. These they kept carefully for their children and grandchildren, because they believed the sacred bundle would bring good fortune to their tribe.

Also on the same spot, a small lake formed containing black water. Into this water the Cherokee women dipped their twigs used in their basketmaking. This is how they learned to dye their baskets black, along with other colors.

Kate, "The Hero With the Horned Snake," 55.

■

THE GREEN CORN FESTIVAL

Shawnee

Prior to the Green Corn Festival was the Ceremony held when the first green corn shoots appeared. For the Festival, chanting shamans and warriors circled a cooking fire, carrying cornstalks. These first ears were boiled, removed from the pot, and tied to four tepeelike poles above the fire, as a sacred offering to the Great Spirit. The first ashes were buried, then a large new fire was kindled, cooking corn for the entire village to share in the ensuing feast and dance.

■

No one of the Shawnee people was allowed to eat any corn, even from his own field, until the proper authority was given. When some corn was ready to be eaten, the one who had the authority announced the date for the Corn Feast and Dance.

Strap-handled and incised pot
Shawnee

On this occasion, great numbers of roasting ears were prepared, and all the people ate as freely as they desired. After this feast, everyone could have what he wished from that particular field.

This was probably the most highly esteemed Peace Festival among the Shawnees and other corn-growing tribes. It might properly be called the First Fruits Festival, similar to the First Roots Festival and the First Berries Festival held annually by many tribes.

Another Corn Feast was held in the fall, but not so universally as the one when the first corn was ready to be eaten. The first one of each year was held at planting time. It was a feast to secure the blessing of the Great Spirit, so that they might have a bountiful crop.

All of these were religious festivals, and all were accompanied by chants and dancing.

Spencer, "Shawnee Folklore," 319-326.

■

THE WALNUT-CRACKER
Creek

Creeks became a combined Creek Confederacy of most tribes of the southeastern states who thrived as early as de Soto's time in the early 1500s. Two strong geographical groups, the Upper Creeks and Lower Creeks, each possessed many interesting tribes that gradually increased in size and spread throughout Georgia, Alabama, Florida, Louisiana, Mississippi, and the Carolinas. As whites spread southward along coastal areas, Creeks were driven to the interior areas, especially along the Chattahoochee and Ocmulgee rivers. In the 1700s and 1800s bands of Creek tribes migrated northward, infiltrating tribes of the central, plains, and southwestern areas.

■

A long time ago in western Georgia, among the Southeastern Creek-Hitchiti Indians, lived Walnut-Cracker. His name was given him because he spent most of his time gathering, cracking, and eating walnuts in the same spot.

He always placed walnuts on a large stone and cracked them open, using a smaller stone. For the rest of the day and evening he ate walnuts. This was how Walnut-Cracker lived for many years. When he died, his people buried him at the place where the walnuts grew.

Some time later, a Creek hunter passed that very place and found a large mound of walnuts. As he was hungry, he cracked some and ate the good meat. Later that same evening the hunter returned. He sat down and cracked many walnuts on the large stone.

While the hunter was busy cracking and eating walnuts, a man came out of his nearby lodge. He heard someone at the place where Walnut-Cracker had lived. He listened and plainly heard the cracking noise. Looking closely through the darkness, he saw what looked like a person sitting where Walnut-Cracker always sat.

The man went back into his lodge announcing, "Walnut-Cracker, who died and was buried, now sits at his same place, cracking walnuts on the large stone! Do you think it is his ghost?"

All of the man's family came outside quietly, looking toward Walnut-Cracker's place. There they saw someone cracking walnuts on the large stone, who surely looked like Walnut-Cracker himself.

One of the family was a Lame Man, a good friend of Walnut-Cracker.

"Take me along on your back," he pleaded. "I want to see him again." So he was carried on the back of another who walked quietly toward the ghost.

That is what they thought, and they stopped in fear. But Lame Man whispered, "Please, take me a little farther." His companion took him a little way, then stopped. The hunter did not hear them, because he was cracking walnuts.

"Please take me a little farther," again asked Lame Man. The hunter looked up and saw the people through the shadows. He jumped up, seized his bow and arrows, and ran away!

When the ghost moved, the people ran back to their lodge. The one carrying the Lame Man became frightened and dropped him and left, running back to the lodge. Lame Man, too, jumped up and ran to his people. He was no longer a lame man!

Tribal storytellers say, "He outran the others, beating them to the lodge. He walked perfectly ever after."

As for Walnut-Cracker, no one saw his ghost again!

Swanton, "The Walnut Cracker," 115-116

■

How Rabbit Fooled Alligator
Creek

Long ago, the Creek tribe lived mostly in the area of Georgia and Florida. Tribal storytellers loved to relate the following legend over and over to their young people, who loved to hear it again and again.

■

When the animals talked with each other just like people do today, a very handsome alligator lay sunning himself luxuriously on a log in which we now call the Florida Everglades. Then along came Mr. Rabbit, who said to him, "Mr. Handsome Alligator, have you ever seen the devil?"

"No, Mr. Rabbit, but I am not afraid of the devil. Are you?" replied Mr. Alligator.

"Well now, Mr. A., I did see the devil. Do you know what he said about you?" asked Rabbit.

"Now, just what did the devil have to say about me?" Alligator replied.

"The devil said that you are afraid of him," said Rabbit. "Besides, he said you would not even look at him."

"Rubbish," said Alligator. "I know that I am not afraid of the devil, and I am not afraid to look at him. Please tell him so for me the next time you see him."

"I do not think you are willing to crawl up the hill the day after tomorrow and allow me to introduce you to the devil himself," said Rabbit.

"Oh, yes, I am willing and ready to go with you," replied Alligator. "Let us go tomorrow."

"That is just fine with me," replied Rabbit. "But Mr. A., when you see some smoke rising somewhere, do not be afraid. It is a sign that the devil is moving about and will soon be on his way."

"You do not have to worry about me," said Alligator. "I told you I am not afraid of the devil."

"When you see the friendly birds flying about, and the deer running at a gallop, do not be afraid," said Rabbit.

"Don't you be concerned, because I will not be afraid," repeated Alligator.

"If you hear some fire crackling and its comes closer to you, do not be scared," said Rabbit. "If the grasses near you begin to smoke, do not be scared. The devil is only wandering about. Then is the time for you to get a good look at him when the heat is hottest."

After Rabbit's final words of wisdom, he left Alligator sunning himself.

Next day, Rabbit returned and asked Alligator to crawl up the hill, following him. Rabbit led him to the very top and directed him to lie in the tallest grass. Then Rabbit left Alligator, laughing to himself all the way down the hill, because he had led Alligator to the farthest place away from his home in the water.

On his way, Rabbit came to a smoldering stump. He picked up a piece, carrying it back to the high grass, where he made a fire so the wind blew it toward Alligator.

Soon the fire surrounded the place, burning closer and closer to Alligator. Rabbit then ran to a sandy knoll and sat down to watch the fun, chuckling over the trick he had played on Mr. Alligator.

Only a short time passed when the smoke rose in thick spirals, and the birds flew upward and away. Other animals ran for their lives across the field.

Alligator cried out, "Oh, Mr. Rabbit, where are you?"

"You just lie there quietly," replied Rabbit. "It's only the devil prowling about."

The fire began to roar and spread rapidly. "Oh, Mr. Rabbit, what is that I hear?" asked Alligator.

Southeast Indian alligator basket
Creek

"That's just the devil breathing hard," replied Rabbit. "Do not be scared. You will see him soon!"

Rabbit became so amused that he rolled and rolled on the sandy knoll and kicked his heels up in the air with glee.

Soon the grass surrounding Alligator caught fire and began to burn beneath him. Alligator rolled and twisted with pain from his burns.

"Do not be afraid now, Mr. Alligator," called Rabbit. "Just be quiet for a little while longer, and the devil will be there for you to get a firsthand look at him."

Alligator could not stand any more toasting! He started to crawl as fast as he could down the hillside toward the water. He wriggled through the burning grass, snapping his jaws, rolling in pain, and choking from the smoke.

Rabbit, upon his sandy knoll, laughed and laughed, jumping up and down with delight at the trick he had played on Alligator.

"Wait a minute, Mr. A. Don't be in such a hurry. You said you were not afraid of the devil," called Rabbit.

By that time Alligator had reached his home in the water, tumbling in to stop the pain of his roasted skin.

Never again did Mr. Handsome Alligator trust that trickster, Mr. Rabbit, or any of his family, ever!

Swanton, "How Rabbit Fooled Alligator," 52-53.

■

THE CELESTIAL CANOE
Alabama

The Alabama tribe was recognized as early as the 1500s in the chronicles of the Spanish explorer Hernando de Soto, and their relationship with the French dates as far back as the establishment of Fort Toulouse in Alabama in 1717. The tribe's long history was recognized when the state of Alabama took its name and called its principle river the Alabama.

■

Many eons ago, a magic canoe descended from the sky and touched earth near where the Alabama Indian tribe had its camp. Several young women came out of the canoe, singing and laughing. They ran everywhere, enjoying their freedom and playing a game of bounce-ball and catch with each other.

When they tired, they climbed back into their magic canoe, still signing and laughing, and sailed back up to the sky. Another day, they came again the same way as before, singing and dancing, and playing ball. They repeated this performance many times, and always the canoe returned to the same place on earth.

One day, an Alabama Indian youth watched from behind some bushes as the magic canoe descended. During a game, the ball was thrown toward him. A young woman came running after it. When she was near enough, the youth grabbed her hand. The others were frightened and took off in their magic canoe and disappeared into the sky.

The captured woman from the sky became the wife of that same Alabama Indian, and in time they had several children. The father made a large canoe for his family and a smaller canoe for himself.

"Father, we would like to have some fresh meat," the children said one day. "Will you please hunt a deer for us?" The father started through the woods to hunt deer. But in a short time he returned without any game.

The mother said to her children, "Ask your father to go farther away and hunt for a big fat deer this time." Again the children asked their father, and again he went hunting.

While he was away, the mother put the children in the larger canoe with herself, singing the magic song. They rose toward the sky. But the father came running back just in time to pull the canoe down to the ground.

Another time when the father was away, the mother put the children in the large canoe and herself in the small canoe, singing as they rose. At that moment the father came running home, pulling down the large canoe with his children. The mother, singing continuously, disappeared into the sky.

After many weeks, the father missed his wife and the children became lonesome for their mother. Finally, all of them climbed into the large canoe and sang the magic flight song. They sailed upward and away to the sky and through the clouds.

When they arrived in the sky, they came to an old grandmother sitting beside her lodge. The father said to her, "Grandmother, we have come because my children want to see their mother."

"She is yonder, dancing and singing all the time," answered the old grandmother. "If you will please sit down in my lodge, I will cook you some squashes."

When she placed the food before them, they thought to themselves, "This will not be enough." But when they ate one little squash, a larger one magically took its place! They were very hungry and ate for a long time. When they finished, more food was left than when they started to eat. The old grandmother broke an ear of corn and gave the pieces to the children.

The father took his children to another person's house and inquired of their mother. "She stays here, dancing all the time," was the reply. Suddenly the mother danced by, but she did not recognize her family. The next time she danced by, the children threw pieces of corn to attract her attention.

"I smell something earthy," she said. But she danced by on the run again. When she returned, dancing, to the same spot, a small piece of corn hit her feet and she exclaimed, "My children must be here!"

She ran back to them, hugging her entire family. The father then loaded all of them into his canoe and brought his entire family back to earth.

When the family was nicely settled, the father again went hunting. This time the mother took all of her children back to the sky in the magic canoe, singing her song that carried them away. The father never saw his family again, because they became sky people forever.

The father returned to the camp of his Alabama tribe, where he chose another wife, an Indian maiden, whom he felt assured would remain with him on earth.

Swanton, "The Celestial Canoe," 138.

■

THE MILKY WAY
Seminole

These Seminole stories were told to their people by Josie Billie,
an old Seminole raised in the Big Cypress Swamp of the Everglades.
These beliefs he learned from the ancients of his tribe, when he was
very young, and later he became the Seminole tribal historian.

■

Ever so long ago, the Breathmaker blew his breath toward the sky and
created the Milky Way. This broad pathway in the night sky leads to the
City of the West. There is where the souls of good Indians go when they
die.

Bad Indian souls stay in the ground where they are buried. When the
Seminole Indians walk through the woods and step where a bad person
has been buried, they become fearful. Even though the grave is covered
with brush, they always seem to know that a bad person is buried there.

The Seminoles say the Milky Way shines brightest following the death
of one of their tribe. They believe this is so that the path to the City in
the Sky will be lighted brightly for the traveling Seminole.

For a good Indian to be able to walk over the Milky Way, he must first
be one whom everyone likes. He cannot be one who talks in an evil
manner, or lies and steals. He must be brave at all times and an honor
to the Seminoles.

In the Seminole language, *so-lo-pi he-ni* means "spirit way" or "the
Milky Way for human souls." And *if-i he-ni* means "dog way" and is the
sky-path for the souls of dogs and other animals that die. Spirits never
return to earth from the City in the Sky. Seminoles do not believe that
ghostly visitors ever come back and visit their people again.

Along the Milky Way lives Rain and Rainbow. The Seminole word
for Rainbow means stop-the-rain, and that is what the Rainbow does
when it appears.

When the Sun is eclipsed, Seminoles say that toad-frog has come
along and taken a bite out of the Sun. Toad-frog continues eating at the
Sun until the Sun disappears. Seminole hunters shoot arrows at toad-
frogs whenever they see one, preventing eclipses of the Sun or Moon.
Seminole hunters like to make a loud clamor to scare the toad-frogs away
when they do appear.

Along the Milky Way is Big Dipper, which seems like a boat to the
Seminoles. They say it is used to carry the souls of good Seminoles along

the Milky Way to the City in the Sky. The Seminole tribe calls the Morning Star the Tomorrow Star, and the Evening Star is known to them as the Red Star.

Greenlee, "The Milky Way," 138-140.

■

MEN VISIT THE SKY
Seminole

■

Near the beginning of time, five Seminole Indian men wanted to visit the sky to see the Great Spirit.

They traveled to the East, walking for about a month. Finally, they arrived at land's end. They tossed their baggage over the end and they, too, disappeared beyond earth's edge.

Down, down, down the Indians dropped for a while, before starting upward again toward the sky. For a long time they traveled westward. At last, they came to a lodge where lived an old, old woman.

"Tell me, for whom are you looking?" she asked feebly.

"We are on our way to see the Great Spirit Above," they replied.

"It is not possible to see him now," she said. "You must stay here for a while first."

That night the five Seminole Indian men strolled a little distance from the old woman's lodge, where they encountered a group of angels robed in white and wearing wings. They were playing a ball game the men recognized as one played by the Seminoles.

Two of the men decided they would like to remain and become angels. The other three preferred to return to earth. Then to their surprise, the Great Spirit appeared and said, "So be it!"

A large cooking pot was placed on the fire. When the water was boiling, the two Seminoles who wished to stay were cooked! When only their bones were left, the Great Spirit removed them from the pot, and put their bones back together again. He then draped them with a white cloth and touched them with his magic wand. The Great Spirit brought the two Seminole men back to life! They wore beautiful white wings and were called men-angels.

"What do you three men wish to do?" asked the Great Spirit.

"If we may, we prefer to return to our Seminole camp on earth," replied the three Seminoles.

Chickee
Seminole

"Gather your baggage together and go to sleep at once," directed the Great Spirit.

Later, when the three Seminole men opened their eyes, they found themselves safe at home again in their own Indian camp.

"We are happy to return and stay earthbound. We hope never to venture skyward again in search of other mysteries," they reported to the Chief of the Seminoles.

Greenlee, "Men Visit the Sky to See God," 143.

■

ADOPTION OF THE HUMAN RACE

Natchez

Before Europeans arrived in the Great Southeast, between the Atlantic Ocean and the Mississippi River, there were one to two million tribal Indians gathered in their fertile homeland, speaking a variety of languages. The Natchez tribe, on the Gulf Coast, developed skills in contriving numerous kinds of fishing equipment to catch the tremendous quantities and types of fish available to them in fresh and salt waters. Their people had an abundance for themselves and for sale or trade with others.

■

In the very beginning, Moon, Sun, Wind, Rainbow, Thunder, Fire, and Water once met a very old man. This wise old man turned out to be Chief of the Sky Spirits. Thunder asked him, "Can you make the people of the world my children?"

"No, no, no!" Wise Old Man replied. "They cannot be your children, but they can be your grandchildren."

Sun asked Old Man, "Can you make the people of the world my children?"

"No, they cannot be your children" answered Old Man. "But they can be your friends and grandchildren. Your main purpose is to give plenty of light."

Moon asked, "Can you make the people of the world my children?"

"No, no, I cannot do that," Old Man replied. "The people of the world can be your nephews and friends."

Fire asked that the people of the world be made his children.

Wise Old Man replied, "No, I cannot give them to you to be your children, but the people of the world can be your grandchildren. You can be their warmth and give them fire to cook their food."

Wind asked the same question as the others. Wise Old Man told Wind, "No, no, the people of the world cannot be your children, but they can be your grandchildren. You can remove the bad air and all kinds of diseases from the people, and keep them healthy."

Rainbow wanted the people to be his children. "No, they cannot be your children," Wise Old Man explained. "You will always be busy preventing too much rain and floods upon the earth."

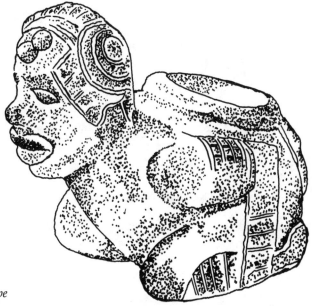

Effigy pipe
Natchez

Water asked that human beings be made his children, but Wise Old Man answered, "No, the people of the world can never be your children. When they get dirty, you must always be available to wash them clean. You shall give them long life."

Wise Old Man continued, "I have now told all of you the best ways to guide yourselves and what you can do to help the people of the world. You must always remember that these children of the human race are my children."

Swanton, "Adoption of the Human Race," 240.

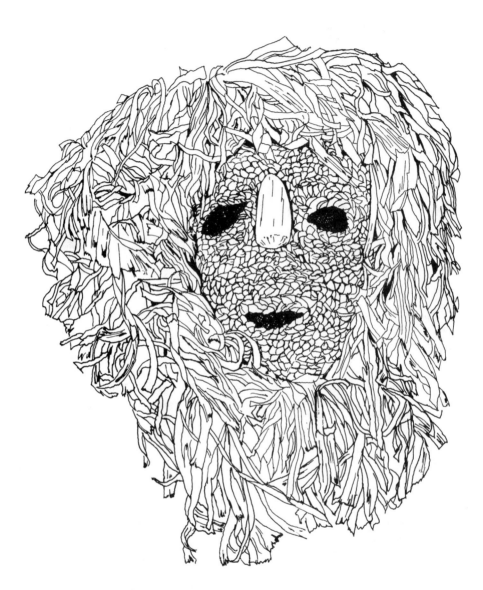

Corn husk mask
Seneca

PART SIX

FROM THE NORTHEAST

Abnaki or Wabanaki, meaning "those living at the sunrise," was the farthest northeastern Maine tribe. Belonging to the Algonquian linguistic family, they were believed to have immigrated from the South. It is possible that they saw their first white men in 1498 when John Cabot explored the Abnaki territory along the northeast coast.

Penobscot and Passamaquoddy tribes were closely related to the Abnaki. When the boundary line between the United States and Canada was established, the Penobscot and Passamaquoddy settled on the southern side. Some of their relatives still lived in Canada. Each of these tribes have a representative in the Maine legislature to speak only on tribal concerns.

Iroquois, meaning "we are of the extended house" or "longhouse people," consisted of five strong tribes in the New York State area. The Cayuga, Mohawk, Oneida, Onondaga, and Senecas united to form the large and powerful Iroquois Confederacy in about 1390. The Tuscaroras joined the league in 1715. Influence of the Iroquois League of United Nations spread to other tribes from the eastern shore of Maine to the Mississippi River.

■

THE FIRST PEOPLE AND THE FIRST CORN
Penobscot-Passamaquoddy

This legend was written by a Penobscot Indian, Joseph Nicolar,
and was published in 1893. The Passamaquoddy of Maine, as well
as the Micmac and Malecite of Nova Scotia, also told this story.

■

Long ago, Klos-kur-beh, the Great Teacher, lived in the land where
no people lived. One day at noon, a young man came to him and called
him "Mother's brother."

Standing before Klos-kur-beh, he said, "I was born of the foam of the
waters. The wind blew, and the waves quickened into foam. The sun
shone on the foam and warmed it, and the warmth made life, and the
life was I. See—I am young and swift, and I have come to abide with
you and to help in all that you do."

Again on a day at noon, a maiden came, stood before the two, and
called them "my children." "My children, I have come to abide with you
and have brought with me love. I will give it to you, and if you will love
me and will grant my wish, all the world will love me, even the very
beasts. Strength is mine, and I give it to whosoever may get me. Comfort
also is mine, for though I am young, my strength shall be felt over all the
earth. I was born of the beautiful plant of the earth. For the dew fell on
the leaf, and the sun warmed the dew, and the warmth was life, and that
life is I."

Then Klos-kur-beh lifted up his hands toward the sun and praised the
Great Spirit. Afterward, the young man and the maiden became man
and wife, and she became the first mother. Klos-kur-beh taught their
children and did great works for them. When his works were finished,
he went away to live in the Northland until it should be time for him to
come again.

The people increased until they were numerous. When a famine
came among them, the first mother grew more and more sorrowful.
Every day at noon she left her husband's lodge and stayed away from
him until the shadows were long. Her husband, who dearly loved her,
was sad because of her sorrow. One day he followed her trail as far as
the ford of the river, and there he waited for her to return.

When she came, she sang as she began to ford the river, and as long
as her feet were in the water she seemed glad. The man saw something
that trailed behind her right foot, like a long green blade. When she came

Longhouse
Iroquois

out of the water, she stooped and cast off the blade. Then she appeared sorrowful.

The husband followed her home as the sun was setting, and he bade her come out and look at the beautiful sun. While they stood side by side, there came seven little children. They stood in front of the couple, looked into the woman's face, and spoke: "We are hungry, and the night will soon be here. Where is the food?"

Tears ran down the woman's face as she said, "Be quiet, little ones. In seven moons you shall be filled and shall hunger no more."

Her husband reached out, wiped away her tears, and asked, "My wife, what can I do to make you happy?"

"Nothing else," she said. "Nothing else will make me happy."

Then the husband went away to the Northland to ask Klos-kur-beh for counsel. With the rising of the seventh sun, he returned and said, "O wife, Klos-kur-beh has told me to do what you asked."

The woman was pleased and said, "When you have slain me, let two men take hold of my hair and draw my body all the way around a field. When they have come to the middle of it, let them bury my bones. Then they must come away. When seven months have passed, let them go again to the field and gather all that they find. Tell them to eat it. It is my flesh. You must save a part of it to put in the ground again. My bones you cannot eat, but you may burn them. The smoke will bring peace to you and your children."

The next day, when the sun was rising, the man slew his wife. Following her orders, two men drew her body over an open field until her flesh was worn away. In the middle of the field, they buried her bones.

Basket
Penobscot

When seven moons had passed by and the husband came again to that place, he saw it all filled with beautiful tall plants. He tasted the fruit of the plant and found it sweet. He called it *Skar- mu-nal*—"corn." And on the place where his wife's bones were buried, he saw a plant with broad leaves, bitter to the taste. He called it *Utar-mur-wa-yeh*—"tobacco."

Then the people were glad in their hearts, and they came to the harvest. But when the fruits were all gathered, the man did not know how to divide them. So he sent to the great teacher, Klos- kur-beh, for counsel. When Klos-kur-beh came and saw the great harvest, he said, "Now have the first words of the first mother come to pass, for she said she was born of the leaf of the beautiful plant. She said also that her power should be felt over the whole world and that all men should love her.

"And now that she has gone into this substance, take care that the second seed of the first mother be always with you, for it is her flesh. Her bones also have been given for your good. Burn them, and the smoke will bring freshness to the mind. And since these things came from the goodness of a woman's heart, see that you hold her always in memory. Remember her when you eat. Remember her when the smoke of her bones rises before you. And because you are all brothers, divide among you her flesh and her bones. Let all share alike, for so will the love of the first mother have been fulfilled."

Burlin, *The Indians' Book*, 3-6.

■

THE ORIGIN OF THE THUNDERBIRD
Passamaquoddy

This tribe, primarily fishermen, was surrounded by lakes, bays, rivers, streams, and the ocean. Passamaquoddies were an old, old tribe, related distantly to the Abnaki and Penobscot. Even today, they still have a representative in the Maine legislature; however, they can speak only on concerns of the tribe.

Passamaquaddy Indians are believers in a power by which a song or chant in one place can be heard in another area many miles away. This power is thought to be the work of *m'toulin* or magic, an important part of their belief. One example gives a strange account of an Indian so affected that he left his home and traveled north to find a cold place. Although barefooted and lightly clothed, he complained he was still too hot. He continued northward seeking colder comfort. One is led to believe that the man must have been insane. To these Indians, insanity is simply the result of magic.

A belief in the magic of the Thunderbird is held by the Passamaquoddy Indians, because he can tame the winds alternating between calm and storms.

■

This is a legend of long, long ago times. Two Indians desired to find the origin of thunder. They traveled north and came to a high mountain. These mountains performed magically. They drew apart, back and forth, then closed together very quickly.

One Indian said, "I will leap through the cleft before it closes. If I am caught, you continue to find the origin of thunder." The first one succeeded in going through the cleft before it closed, but the second one was caught and squashed.

On the other side, the first Indian saw a large plain with a group of wigwams, and a number of Indians playing a ball game. After a little while, these players said to each other, "It is time to go." They disappeared into their wigwams to put on wings, and came out with their bows and arrows and flew away over the mountains to the south. This was how the Passamaquoddy Indian discovered the homes of the thunderbirds.

The remaining old men of that tribe asked the Passamaquoddy Indian, "What do you want? Who are you?" He replied with the story of his mission. The old men deliberated how they could help him.

They decided to put the lone Indian into a large mortar, and they pounded him until all of his bones were broken. They molded him into a new body with wings like thunderbird, and gave him a bow and some arrows and sent him away in flight. They warned him not to fly close to trees, as he would fly so fast he could not stop in time to avoid them, and he would be killed.

The lone Indian could not reach his home because the huge enemy bird, Wochowsen, at that time made such a damaging wind. Thunderbird is an Indian and he or his lightning would never harm another Indian. But Wochowsen, great bird from the south, tried hard to rival Thunderbird. So Passamaquoddies feared Wochowsen, whose wings Glooscap once had broken, because he used too much power.

A result was that for a long time air became stagnant, the sea was full of slime, and all of the fish died. But Glooscap saw what was happening to his people and repaired the wings of Wochowsen to the extent of controlling and alternating strong winds with calm.

Legend tells us this is how the new Passamaquoddy thunderbird, the lone Indian who passed through the cleft, in time became the great and powerfurl Thunderbird, who always has kept a watchful eye upon the good Indians.

Fewkes, "The Origin of the Thunderbird," 265-266.

■

THE FLYING CANOE

Passamaquoddy

This story was printed in 1901—two years before the Wright brothers traveled by air for 59 seconds. It was told by the Passamaquoddy Indians in the eastern part of the state of Maine and in the province of New Brunswick.

■

Beside a beautiful lake not far from the sea, there lived three brothers. They were young rivals, each trying to do everything better than the others.

Sometimes they were visited by an old woman. She was nearly blind, so crippled that she could hardly walk, and always hungry. But when she had eaten some food, she could do wonderful things, and she could give remarkable power to a person she liked.

Joseph, the youngest of the three young men, treated her very well. Whenever he gave her food, she was grateful. One day after he had fed her, she said to him, "Take your axe and make some moccasins for yourself—some wooden ones. In them you will be able to run as fast as a bird."

Wabanaki "type" canoe (birchbark)

And so Joseph made for himself a pair of wooden moccasins. When he wore them, he could run very fast. In fact, he could run faster than the swiftest animals. He caught game animals and brought home much meat.

His two brothers were jealous because the youngest was a more skillful hunter. They wondered what he had been doing, and they watched him continually. One day they saw him open his birch-bark box and take out his wooden moccasins. Then he disappeared.

The brothers had already noticed certain curious chips where Joseph had been working. So they were very glad when they saw what he took from his box. They gathered together all the wood chips and made moccasins for themselves. In their wooden moccasins they could run even faster than Joseph.

Then Joseph knew that they had learned his secret.

The next time the old woman came for food, he fed her as usual. This time she said, as she thanked him, "Make for yourself a dugout canoe. Then you shall soar across the water like a bird."

So Joseph made a dugout canoe. Using it on the lake, he caught big fish and many birds. Again his brothers were jealous, and again they watched him in all that he did. Finding some chips after he had made his boat, the two older brothers gathered them and built a canoe for themselves. Working together, they made it better than Joseph's. It was a wonderful canoe. In it they went out to sea and speared many whales.

This time Joseph was angry. He called the old woman and fed her well, giving her more food than ever before.

"Now you will make another canoe," she said when she had eaten. "This one will fly in the air. You will really fly like a bird."

And so Joseph made another dugout. When he had finished making it, he carefully picked up all the chips and burned them. Then he took leave of his brothers and sailed off in the air.

He saw many strange lands and many strange people below him. He passed over high mountains and rivers and lakes. He passed over oceans. At last, after much journeying through the air, and after many adventures in other lands, Joseph returned home. There he lived in peace.

Prince, "Notes on Passamaquoddy Literature," vol. XXIII, 381-385 ... and vol. XI, 369-375.

■

THE LOYAL SWEETHEART
Passamaquoddy

■

Long ago, in a village beside a river, there lived a beautiful girl whom many a young man wished to marry. But she smiled on all alike and encouraged no one. Her name was Blue Flower.

Among her admirers was a young man who was especially skilled in hunting. For many moons he looked upon the girl with longing, but without any hope that he could win her favor.

At last, one autumn, she gave him reason to hope. And so he dared to consult the old woman of the village who carried proposals of marriage. He wanted to know his chances before he departed on the winter's hunt.

To the young man's great joy, the marriage-maker brought back a favorable reply from both the girl and her father. The message made him determined to win even greater fame as a hunter. He wanted to prove to the girl's father that he was indeed worthy of so beautiful a daughter.

"Will you wait for me until we return from he winter's hunt?" he asked her.

The girl gave her consent to his plan and her promise to remain true to him, whatever happened. She added the promise, "If you do not return, I will remain a maiden all my life. I will never marry any other man."

So the young man completed his plans to join the others of the village on the long winter's hunt. On the evening before their departure, he and the girl had a final canoe ride on the river. Then he sang his farewell in this love song of his people:

> Often on a lonely day, my love,
> You look on the beautiful river
> And down the shining stream.
>
> When last I looked upon you,
> How beautiful was the stream,
> How beautiful was the moon,
> And how happy were we!
> Since that night, my fair one,
> I have thought of you always.
>
> Often on a lonely day, my love,
> You look on the beautiful river
> And down the shining stream.
>
> When we paddled the canoe together
> On that beautiful water,
> How fair the mountains looked,
> How beautiful the red leaves
> As the gentle wind whirled them!
>
> After the winter snows,
> When spring has come once more,
> We will paddle again together.
> Then the leaves will be green,
> The mountains fresh and fair.
>
> Often on a lonely day, my love,
> Look on the beautiful river,
> Down the shining stream,
> And know that spring will come.

Next day, the hunters departed. The old men, the women, and the children settled down to finish the autumn's work of preparing for the winter.

Not many days afterward, a war party attacked the village and destroyed it. They carried away as prisoners all the young girls. Among them was the promised bride of the hunter. When the warriors reached their home territory, they persuaded, or forced, many of the young

women to become their wives. But Blue Flower refused to submit. The
warriors threatened to burn her alive. Still she refused. She preferred
death to breaking her promise to her sweetheart.

The warriors complained to their chief and asked that she be burned
at the stake. But he would not listen to the cruel counsel of his men.
Instead, he gave the girl a longer time in which to make up her mind.
Her bravery greatly impressed him. He would save her life now, he
thought, and marry her later to one of his best warriors, in order that
their children might become a race of heroes.

Weeks passed, and the hunters returned. When they found their
village in ashes, they knew which war party had struck. The young
hunter, singing his vengeance song, gathered a host of warriors and
started northward. They surprised the largest village of their enemy,
killed many people, and took others as prisoners.

When the fighting was over, the victors and their friends who had
been held captive by the enemy were reunited. There was great rejoicing. Perhaps happiest of all were the young hunter-warrior and Blue
Flower, who had remained true to him in spite of threats and promises.

The young man, still thirsting for revenge, wanted to torture and burn
the enemy that had been taken prisoners. But his sweetheart stopped
him. She reminded him that they had not treated her cruelly.

She was a gentle and peace-loving girl, as well as a loyal sweetheart.
In a short time, she became a loyal wife.

Prince, "The Passamaquoddy Wampum Records," 479-495.

■

ORIGIN OF THE MEDICINE MAN

Passamaquoddy

The first part of this legend strongly reminds one of the biblical
story of Moses, which may have been due to the influence of early
contacts with Europeans. Note that the mother of the child became
pregnant by eating an herb.

In 1884, the writer Charles G. Leland, determined the Medicine
Man to be Glooscap, the Good-Spirit. Legend has it that the father
of Glooscap is a being who lives under a great waterfall beneath the
earth. His face is half-red, and he has a single all-seeing eye. He can
give to anyone coming to him the medicine he desires. Glooscap is

still busy sharpening his arrows off in a distant place, preparing sometime to return to earth and make war.

Passamaquoddies tell all of their old stories as truth. But of other stories, they speak of them as "what they hear," or hearsay.

■

This is a legend of long, long ago about a Passamaquoddy Indian woman who traveled constantly back and forth and through the woods. From every bush she came to, she bit off a twig, and from one of these she became pregnant. Bigger and bigger she grew, until at last she could not travel, but she built a wigwam near the mouth of a fresh-running stream.

In the night, the woman gave birth to a child. She thought at first that she should kill the child. Finally, she decided to make a bark canoe in which she placed her child. She set it adrift and let it float down the stream. Though the water was rough in places, the child was not harmed, or even wet.

The canoe floated to an Indian village, where it became stranded on the sandy shore near a group of wigwams. One of the women found the baby and brought it to her home. Every morning thereafter, it seemed that a baby of the village died. The villagers did not know what was the matter with their babies.

A neighbor noticed how the rescued child toddled off to the river every night and returned shortly after. She wondered if this could have anything to do with the death of so many babies. Then she saw the child return to its wigwam with a small tongue, roast it, and eat it. Then it lay down to sleep all night.

On the next morning, a report circulated that another child had died. Then the Indian woman was certain she knew who the killer was. She alerted the parents of the dead child and found that the child's tongue had been removed, and the child had bled to death.

Tribal deliberations were held to decide what should be done with the murderer. Some said, cut up the person and throw him into the river. Others said, burn the fragments; this they did after much consultation. They burned the fragments of the wayward child, until nothing but its ashes remained.

Naturally, everyone understood the child was dead. But that night it came back to camp again with a small tongue, which it roasted and ate. The next morning another child was found to have died in the night. The weird child was found sleeping in its usual place, just as before its cremation. He said to everyone that he would never kill any more children, and that now he had become a big boy, in fact.

The big boy announced he would take one of his bones out of his side. This he started to do, and all of his bones spilled out of his body at the same time. He closed his eyes by drawing his fingers over his eyelids, hiding his eyes. He could not move without bones and he began to grow very fat.

He surprised the Passamaquoddies by becoming a great Medicine Man. Anything they desired within reason, he granted. Later, however, his tribe moved away from their old camp. Before they left, they built a fine wigwam for the Medicine Man. So accustomed had they become to call upon his powers that they still returned to make their requests. His tribal members asked him for medicine of all kinds. When he granted their wishes, he asked them, "Turn me over and you will find your medicine beneath me."

A young man came and wished to have the love of a woman, so he asked for a love potion. The Medicine Man said, "Turn me over." The young man turned over the conjurer and found an herb. "You must not give this away or throw it away," said the old man. The young Passamaquoddy went back to his own wigwam.

Soon he was aware that all the young women followed him in the camp, at all times. In fact, he longed to be alone for a change. He did not like to be chased by the women. At last when he became too troubled by the tribal women, he returned to the Medicine Man and gave back the herbal love portion. The young Passamaquoddy left without it.

Another young man went to the conjurer for help. The Medicine Man asked, "What is it you want?" This man said, "I want to live as long as the world shall stand."

"Your request is a hard one to consider, but I will do my best to answer it," replied the Medicine Man. "Now turn me over," and underneath his body was an herb. He said, "Go to a place that is bare of everything, so bare it is destitute of all vegetation, and just stand there." The Medicine Man pointed out this direction for the young man.

The young man went according to the Medicine Man's instructions, but looking back at the conjurer, the standing man saw branches and twigs sprouting all over his own body. He had been changed into a cedar tree, to stand there forever—useless to everyone.

Fewkes, "How a Medicine Man Was Born, and How He Turned a Man into a Tree," 273-275.

■

THE GIANT AND THE FOUR WIND BROTHERS

Penobscot

Penobscots belonged to the Algonquian linguistic family of Abnakis, Passamaquoddies, Malecites, and Pennacooks. They lived on both sides of Penobscot Bay and up and down the whole area of the Penobscot River. They were visited by Samuel de Champlain in 1604 and numerous later explorers for the next 150 years. Penobscots made peace with the colonials and remained in their own country (not withdrawing to Canada). Conjointly with the Passamaquoddies, the Penobscots have a representative at sessions of the Maine legislature, privileged to speak on native American tribal affairs only.

■

There were four brothers in a family that lived in a huge cave on the top of a high mountain in the present state of Maine. One brother was Northwind, one Southwind, another Westwind, and the other one Eastwind. They were the ones who made all of the winds blow.

Westwind was the youngest, Northwind the oldest, Southwind second oldest, and Eastwind second youngest. To cause the winds, they stood up with their heads above the cave hole and blew. The forthcoming wind occurred according to whichever brother performed—North, South, East, or West.

Westwind was very wild when he blew. Northwind chided him, "No, No! Don't do that! You will raise such high winds that you will destroy our good people, the Penobscots."

When Westwind jumped up again to blow, Northwind again told him, "No! No! Stop or you will kill our mother." So lived the Four Wind Brothers, causing and regulating the winds of the world.

Northwind was always the softest wind, Eastwind a little stronger and harsher, Southwind with strong gusts, but not as much as Westwind the youngest. Whenever the Four Wind Brothers blew the winds, they were not satisfied until each performed in his particular style to perfection.

Often they would say to each other as a warning, "We must try to care for our friends, the Penobscots, so we do not destroy any thing or any one of them."

About this same time, a Giant Beaver had this home on the top of a great rock by the shore of Big Lake. This Giant Beaver, about one hundred feet long, had a very large lodge. Near him lived a Giant Penobscot who liked to hunt for the Giant Beaver. But Giant Penobscot lived in fear of a Monster Eagle, who kept watching all the time for the right moment to snatch and carry Giant Penobscot to its nest.

Monster Eagle was so large that he could pick up a giant man like an ordinary eagle would carry a rabbit, even though the giant was as tall as the tallest tree. At last Giant Penobscot's family was out of food, and he was compelled to go out and hunt. He took his long-handled ice chisel and went in search of the Giant Beaver.

Giant Penobscot succeeded in driving the Beaver from his Lodge, and he cornered him and killed him. After packing the Giant Beaver on his back, Giant Penobscot joyfully started homeward with his prize. Monster Eagle had seen Giant Penobscot from a great height. Down swooped the Eagle, picking up both Giant Beaver and Giant Penobscot, as easily as carrying two rabbits.

Far up on a rocky mountainside, Monster Eagle flew with its prey to its nest, which was thousands of feet above the valley. Monster Eagle's nest was enormous, with many young eagles in it. When Monster Eagle deposited his victims in the nest, he began feeding the dead beaver to his eaglets. Monster Eagle kept Giant Penobscot safely to one side, until all of the beaver had been eaten.

Then Monster Eagle prepared to kill the Giant Penobscot. He quickly flew high into the air and turned sharply, diving straight down to strike Giant Penobscot with his beak, wings, and claws. But Giant Penobscot held upright his sharp ice chisel with the butt end braced against a rocky ledge beside him. Monster Eagle descended violently upon the point of the ice chisel and he died instantly.

Now that Giant Penobscot was free, he wondered how he could get down to earth again before being eaten by the eaglets as they grew larger. He thought and thought, finally deciding to cut out the body of Monster Eagle and crawl inside the feathered skin, using Eagle's wings to glide down from the mountain.

Coincidentally, on this same mountain lived the Four Wind Brothers. Northwind saw Monster Eagle destroy himself. He also observed Giant Penobscot preparing to fly down to earth. Northwind called his three brothers to come and see.

"Let us all blow gently beneath Eagle's wings and help the good Penobscot to land softly upon the earth," said Northwind to his Brother Winds.

Inside Monster Eagle's wings, the Giant Penobscot soared off the mountain. Gently the Four Wind Brothers blew beneath his wings, guiding him while he easily floated to the Penobscot village below.

Meanwhile, when Giant Penobscot's family found that he had disappeared, they knew he must have been carried away by some flying giant, because his tracks led to nowhere.

One of the ancient men of the Penobscot tribe said, "We must all help our brother escape with our good thoughts. We must wish for his safe return by Chief of the Sky Spirits."

When Giant Penobscot floated safely back to his tribe and told his people of his adventure, the Ancient One said, "It was the strength of our wishes to Chief Sky Spirit that brought you back to your people. Now let us have a thanksgiving feast and rejoice."

Gently the Four Wind Brothers passed over the Penobscot Indian village on their happy return to their mountaintop cave.

Speck, "The Giant and the Four Wind Brothers," 74.

■

THE ORIGIN OF INDIAN SUMMER
Penobscot

■

Long, long ago, the Penobscot Indians used to say, an old man went to the Chief of the Sky Spirits to ask his help. The man's name was Zuni. In the spring, when all of his people were planting their vegetables, Zuni was too ill to do his usual planting. He was ill all summer. During that summer, his people, as usual, gathered their vegetables and dried them for use in winter. But Zuni had none.

So he went to the Chief of the Sky Spirits and said to him, "I have been sick all through the planting and the harvesting seasons. The winter is coming on, and I have no food ready for it. What am I to do?"

"I will help you," was the prompt reply. "Go ahead now. Plant your vegetables as you have always done in the spring. I will see that you have a crop right away."

Zuni went home and immediately put his seeds into the ground. The weather favored him, and almost as soon as he had finished planting, his crops were ready to harvest. In seven days he had as much as any other man in his tribe had. Then winter came.

The Penobscots gave that warm period in the autumn a name that means Indian summer. White people also call it Indian summer.

Speck, "Penobscot Tales," 95-96.

■

THE WATER FAMINE
Penobscot

In early Penobscot family narrative history, there are a few family groups possessing associated legends as their specific property. In the myth of the water famine, the transformer, Gluskabe, changes certain human beings into aquatic creatures. One of the original families' identity was connected with creatures residing in the water.

■

From this legend we learn of the origin of fish, frogs, and turtles. A long, long time ago, Indians settled up the river. A Monster frog forbade these Indians the use of water. Some died from thirst. Their Spirit Chief, Gluskabe, came to help them. He saw how sickly his people seemed. He asked them, "What is your trouble?"

"The Monster is killing us with thirst. He forbids us water."

"I will make him give you water," Gluskabe replied. The people went with their Chief to see the Monster frog. The Chief said to the Monster, "Why do you abuse our grandchildren? You will be sorry for this treatment of our good people. I will give them water, so all will have an equal share of the water. The benefits should be shared."

Gluskabe suddenly grabbed the Monster frog and broke his back. From thenceforth, all bullfrogs are broken-backed. Even then the Monster did not give up the water. So Gluskabe took an axe and cut down a large yellow birch tree, so that when it fell down, the yellow birch tree killed the Monster frog.

That is how the Penobscot River originated. The water flowed from the Monster frog. All the branches of the yellow birch tree became rivers, and all emptied into the main Penobscot River.

Now, all of the Penobscot Indians were so thirsty, some even near death, that they jumped into the river to enjoy the water inside and outside. Some of them turned into fish; some turned into frogs; some turned into turtles. A few human Penobscots survived. That is the reason they inhabit the whole length of the Penobscot River. This is how they took their family names from all kinds of fish, turtles, and other sea creatures.

Speck, *Penobscot Man, the Life History of a Forest Tribe In Maine.*

■

THE LEGEND OF THE BEAR FAMILY

Penobscot

The story concerning the Bear family was revealed through a descendant of the original hero of the following tale. He owned a very old powder horn bearing an incised representation of his mother, who was a Bear, seated in the bow of a canoe traveling to the hunting grounds with her husband.

■

Many, many generations ago, a Penobscot, his wife, and their little son started out from their village to go to Canada. They were from Penobscot Bay, bound for a great council and dance to be held at the Iroquois village of Caughnawaga. They went upriver to the point where they had to make a 20-mile portage to reach another river that would take them to the St. Lawrence.

The man started ahead with the canoe on his back, leaving his wife to pack part of the luggage to their first overnight campsite. The little boy ran alongside of her. While she was busy arranging her pack, her son ran on ahead to catch up with his father.

The man had gone so far ahead, the boy became lost. The mother assumed the boy was with his father. When she arrived at the campground, they discovered that their son was with neither of them. They began a search immediately, but they could not find him.

The parents returned home to tell their story to their tribe. All of the men turned out for a wide search party, which lasted for several months without success. In March of the next year, the Penobscots found some sharpened sticks near the river. They concluded that the boy must be alive and had been spearing fish. Footprints of bears were seen, and they thought perhaps the boy had been adopted by a bear family.

In the village, there was a lazy man who did not enter into the search, but lay around idly. Everyone asked him, "Why don't you help hunt for the boy? You seem to be good for nothing."

"Very well, I will," he replied. He went right to the bear's den and knocked with his bow on the rocks at the entrance. Inside, a great noise arose where the father, mother, baby bear, and adopted boy lived. The father-bear went to the entrance, holding out a birch-bark vessel. The lazy man shot at it and killed the bear.

The mother-bear says, "Now I will go." She took another vessel, held it out at the entrance, and also was killed. The baby bear did the same and was killed. All of the bears were laid out dead in the cave. Then the lazy man entered and saw the little boy terribly afraid and huddled in a dark corner, crying for his realtives and trying to hide.

The lazy hunter gently carried him home to the village and gave him to his parents. Everyone gave the lazy man presents: two blankets, a canoe, ammunition, and other good things. He became rich overnight.

The boy's parents, however, noticed that their son seemed to be turning into a bear. Bristles were showing on his upper back and shoulders, and his manners had changed. Finally they helped him to become a real person again, and he grew up to be a Penobscot Indian like his father. He married and had children. Forever after he and all of his descendants were called Bears.

They drew pictures of bears on pieces of birch-bark with charcoal and left them at camps wherever they went. All of their descendants seemed to do this and declare, "I am one of the Bear family."

Speck, *Penobscot Man, the Life History of a Forest Tribe In Maine.*

■

THE STRANGE ORIGIN OF CORN

Abnaki

The main body of Abnaki was in western Maine, mostly in the valleys of the Kennebec, Androscoggin, and Sacos rivers, and the neighboring coast. They originally emigrated from the Southwest, having encountered John Cabot in 1498; but the Indians had no other dealings with white people at that time. In 1604, Champlain passed along the coast and visited Abnaki bands. In 1607 and 1608 the Plymouth Company made an unsuccessful effort to form a permanent settlement at the mouth of the Kennebec. Later, the Abnaki withdrew to Canada, settling around St. Francis.

■

A long time ago, when the Indians were first made, one man lived alone, far from any others. He did not know fire, and so he lived on roots, bark, and nuts. This man became very lonely for companionship. He grew tired of digging roots, lost his appetite, and for several days lay dreaming in the sunshine. When he awoke, he saw someone standing near and, at first, was very frightened.

But when he heard the stranger's voice, his heart was glad, and he looked up. He saw a beautiful woman with long *light* hair! "Come to me," he whispered. But she did not, and when he tried to approach her, she moved farther away. He sang to her about his loneliness, and begged her not to leave him.

At last she replied, "If you will do exactly what I tell you to do, I will also be with you."

He promised that he would try his very best. So she led him to a place where there was some very dry grass. "Now get two dry sticks," she told him, "and rub them together fast while you hold them in the grass."

Soon a spark flew out. The grass caught fire, and as swiftly as an arrow takes flight, the ground was burned over. Then the beautiful woman spoke again: "When the sun sets, take me by the hair and drag me over the burned ground."

"Oh, I don't want to do that!" the man exclaimed.

"You must do what I tell you to do," said she. "Wherever you drag me, something like grass will spring up, and you will see something like hair coming from between the leaves. Soon seeds will be ready for your use."

The man followed the beautiful woman's orders. And when the Indians see silk on the cornstalk, they know that the beautiful woman has not forgotten them.

Brown, *The Strange Origin of Corn*, 214.

■

WA-BA-BA-NAL, THE NORTHERN LIGHTS
Wabanaki

Before 1890, Mrs. W. Wallace Brown wrote that folktales among the Wabanaki must have been extensive, for, though these legends were so swiftly dying out, there seemed to be few things in nature for which they had no legend of its life or beginning. They were known as people living at the sunrise in northeastern and northwestern Maine. A large Wabanaki camp was situated in the Kennebec Valley of Maine.

■

Old Chief M'Sartto, Morning Star, had only one son, so different from the other boys of the tribe as to be a worry to Old Chief. The boy would not stay and play with the others, but would take his bow and arrows, and leave home for many days at a time, always going toward the north.

When he came home his family asked, "Where have you been and what did you see?" But he had no reply. At last Old Chief said to his wife, "The boy needs watching. I will follow him when he takes off again."

A few days later, Old Chief followed the boy's trail and they traveled for a long time. Suddenly, Old Chief's eyes closed. He could not hear. A curious feeling came over him. Then he *knew* nothing.

Later, when his eyes opened, he found himself in a strange light country, with no sun, no moon, no stars, but the country was lit by a peculiar brightness. He saw many beings, but all of them different from his own people. They gathered around him and tried to talk, but he did not understand their language.

Old Chief M'Sartto did not know where to go or what to do. He was very well treated by this strange tribe. He watched them play games and became attracted to a wonderful game of ball that he had never seen played before. The game seemed to turn the light into many colors. The players all had lights on their heads and wore very curious kinds of belts, called *Menquan*, or "Rainbow" belts.

In a few days, an old man came and spoke to Old Chief in his own language, asking if he knew where he was. "No," Old Chief replied.

"You are in the country of Wa-ba-ban of the northern lights," the stranger said. "I came here many years ago. I was the only one here

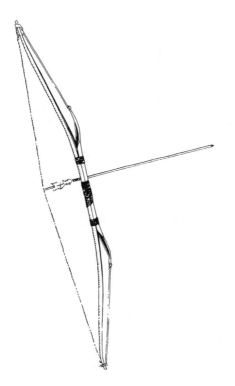

Bow and arrow
Abnaki

from the 'Lower Country,' as we usually call it. But now there is a boy who comes to visit us every few days."

"How did you get here, and what tribe did you come from?" Old Chief asked.

"I follow the path called Spirits' Path, through the Milky Way," said the old man.

"That must be the same path I followed to come here," said Old Chief M'Sartto, Morning Star. "Did you have a queer feeling, as if you lost all sense of knowledge when you traveled here?"

"Yes, exactly that kind of sensation," he replied. "I could neither see nor hear."

"We did come by the same path," Old Chief said. "Can you now tell me how I can go to my home at the Wabanaki camp?"

"Yes, the Chief here can direct you."

"Now can you tell me where I can see my son? He's the boy who comes here to visit you."

"Stay here and watch, you will see him playing ball," said the old man, as he left to visit many wigwams to invite everyone out to a ball game.

Old Chief was very glad to hear the news of his son, and soon the ball game began, and many beautiful colors spread out over the playing field.

"Do you see your son playing?" the old man asked.

"Yes, the boy with the brightest light on his head is my son."

The two men then went to see the Chief of the Northern Lights. The old man spoke up and said to him, "The Chief Morning Star of the Lower Country wants to go home and desires to take his son with him."

Chief of Northern Lights called all of his people together to bid good-bye to Old Chief morning Star and his son. Then he ordered two great birds to carry them to their home. When they traveled the Milky Way, Old Chief again felt the same strange feelings he had experienced when going there.

When Old Chief came to his senses again, he found himself near his home. His wife was very glad to see him. Her son had arrived first and told her that his father was safe and would come soon. She paid little notice to that announcement for she had thought that her husband had lost his way.

Now her wigwam was filled with joy again at the sight of her son and Old Chief M'Sartto, Morning Star, returned to Wabanaki.

Brown, "Wa-Ba-Ba-Nal, Northern Lights," 213-214.

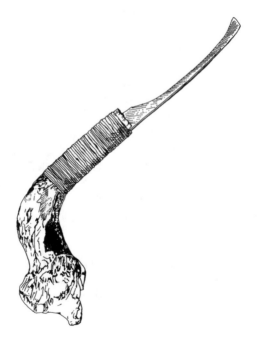

Crooked knife
Abnaki

■

INDIANS AT NIAGARA FALLS
Seneca

The Seneca tribe became one of the five strong tribes of the Iroquois linguistic family in central New York state, forming the Iroquois Nation as early as 1390. Later they obtained guns from the Dutch, giving them a dominating influence over the entire northeast. Senecas lived between Lake Seneca and the Genesee River, about in the middle of the region. Reservations were given to the Iroquois tribes in New York, but later movements of these tribes to Oklahoma were encouraged by the government. The Iroquois Nation attained the highest form of governmental organization reached by any native American tribe.

■

A powerful Seneca Indian tribe lived near Niagara Falls on the Canadian side. For several years, they experienced crop failure from frost. An epidemic followed, killing many of their tribe.

One day a young Seneca girl went into a little cave above the falls to bathe. Suddenly a large rattlesnake attacked her. When she tried to escape, she fell into the rapids, which swept her onto the cataract. By a miracle, the water swirled her into the Cave-of-the-Winds, behind the falls.

There lived the Good Spirit of Thunder and Lightning. It was he who created the mist, which ascended toward the heavens and formed clouds, out of which came the Lightning. Good Spirit told the young girl that also under the waterfall lived Evil Spirit of Famine and Starvation. It was he who caused the crops to fail.

Evil Spirit also controlled a huge Water Serpent that lived in the Niagara River and Lake Erie. Often the Serpent came to the little bay of the river, just above the falls. He cleaned himself there, poisoning the water, which the Senecas used for drinking and cooking.

"Your water is poisoned," said Good Spirit to the girl. "Because of that many of your tribe have died. I want you to return to your people and report to your Chief what I now tell you.

"Your whole tribe must move at once. Your people must pack all of their property and load their canoes. They must go from the Chippewa River up the Niagara River and make a new settlement on Buffalo Creek. There they will grow good crops and enjoy themselves again.

"I know the Evil Spirit will send his Water Serpent after you. Tell your Chief that I will follow the Senecas in a dark cloud. I will send lightning and a thunderbolt upon Water Serpent and kill him, if he does follow you."

Immediately, the young girl went to the Chief of the Senecas and repeated all that Good Spirit had said. The tribe packed and moved as they were directed. Water Serpent followed the canoes.

The Senecas arrived at their new landing site and heard a loud thunderbolt when a lightning flash struck the monster. It thrashed in the water with great force, scooping out a broad basin in Buffalo Creek, which formed the now-famous "horseshoe" of Niagara Falls, according to Seneca storytellers.

After the Senecas had set up a temporary camp, the young girl said, "Can we now send our chiefs to visit Good Spirit and honor him for his kindness to us?"

When the tribal chiefs reached the little bay below Buffalo Creek, they saw the dead Water Serpent. In the village, they saw the Evil Spirit of Famine and Starvation hanging from a high pole. The chiefs thanked the Good Spirit of Thunder and Lightning for the safety of the Seneca Tribe.

Good health and fine crops always have been theirs ever since Chief of the Senecas obeyed the Good Spirit by moving his tribe as directed.

Dow, *Anthology and Bibliography of Niagara Falls*, vol. II, 380-381.

■

THE SACRIFICE AT NIAGARA FALLS

Seneca

■

Nee-ah-gah-rah, meaning "Thundering Waters," is the Iroquois Indian pronunciation of *Niagara*. They believed that the sound of the cataract was the voice of a mighty spirit that dwelt in the waters. In the years gone by, they offered to it a sacrifice every year.

The sacrifice was a maiden of the tribe who was sent over the cataract in a white canoe decorated with fruits and flowers. To be chosen for the sacrifice was considered such a great honor that girls contended for it. In the spirit world, the happy hunting grounds, were special gifts for such a person.

Corn paddle
Seneca

Probably the last sacrifice at Niagara Falls was made in 1679, when Lela-wala, the beautiful daughter of Chief Eagle Eye, was chosen for the honor of the sacrifice. That year, the French explorer La Salle was in the area. He had been trying to convert the Senecas to Christianity, and he protested against their plan for the sacrifice.

His Protests were answered by one of the tribal leaders: "Your words witness against you. You say that Christ set us an example. We will follow it. Why should one sacrifice be great and our sacrifice be horrible?"

The maiden's father was a brave warrior and a noble chief. His wife was dead. The only member of his family left was the beautiful Lela-wala, very dear and precious to him. But he showed no sign of the grief he felt and made no protest against the choice of her for the sacrifice.

On the day set for the sacrifice, the tribe gathered on the bank of the river. They enjoyed the games, the singing, and the dancing that always took place on special occasions. Everyone became quiet when the little white canoe came into sight, covered with fruits and flowers given to their chief's daughter.

Shortly after her canoe entered the current, another white canoe darted out from under the trees along the bank of the river. Chief Eagle Eye's grief was so great that he was on his way to join his daughter. With swift and strong movements through the rapids, he was soon beside her.

The two looked at each other once. The crowd lost their calmness and shouted at them, some with frantic despair and some with admiration. Side by side, the canoes plunged over the cataract. The brave maiden and the brave chief were beyond rescue.

"After their death, they were changed into pure spirits of strength and goodness. They live so far beneath the falls that the roaring is music to them." He is the ruler of the cataract; she is the maiden of the mist.

Skinner, *Myths and Legends of Our Land*, vol. I, 61-62.

■

THREE BROTHERS WHO FOLLOWED THE SUN

Seneca

The Iroquois Nation tribes still retain vestiges of their former adoration of the Sun. They continue to observe certain rites, such as the Sun Dances, which are survivals of more elaborate sun ceremonies of long, long ago.

Among the most popular sun dances of many tribes and bands of Iroquois Indians were the Ostowa-gowa, or the Great Feather Dance. This became a prime religious dance of the Gai'wiu religion of Handsome Lake, the Seneca Prophet. He revolutionized the religious system of the Iroquois of New York and Ontario.

Few of the early folk-beliefs have survived the taboo of the Prophet. These beliefs are difficult to trace, unless one has the Gai'wiu religion of Handsome lake and the Code of Dekanawida, the founder of the Iroquois Confederacy.

The Seneca Sun Ceremony of Thanksgiving is called by any tribal member who dreams that the rite is necessary for the welfare of the community. The ceremony begins promptly at high noon, when three arrows or three musket shots are fired heavenward to notify the Sun of their intention to address him.

After each volley, the people shout their war cries to the Sun—for the Sun loves war. A ceremonial fire is built. In ancient times, fire was started by a pump drill, and more recently by striking a match. The tribal Sun-Priest chants his thanksgiving song while he casts from a husk basket handfuls of native tobacco upon the flames to carry his words upward to the Sun.

The ceremony begins outside of the Long House, where the rising smoke lifts everyone's thoughts and songs to the sun. Immediately after this beginning, the entire assemblage enters the Long House, where costumed Feather Dancers begin their ritualized Sun Dance. The New York Iroquois tribes do not carry effigies of the Sun in their preparation for or in their dance, according to their traditions.

The following Seneca legend was related by Edward Cornplanter, the recognized head preacher of the Gai'wiu of the

Handsome Lake. Cornplanter was a Seneca Indian and a descendant of Gaiant Waka, the Prophet's brother.

In the following legend, there seem to be some modern features, stated Cornplanter. He asserted, however, that the portion relating to the sky and sun are very, very old traditions. He said that he had always heard the upper world described as told in this legend. He then added that the Sun loved the sound of war, and would linger in his morning journey to observe battle activities anywhere, but after he reached midheaven, the Sun traveled on at his usual speed.

■

This legend developed in olden times, when not many people were about. Three brothers who were not married spent their lives hunting. When young they enjoyed the excitement of hunting, but as they grew older they seemed to lose the pleasure of the sport. Youngest brother suggested that for a new experience they walk to the edge of the earth, where the sky comes down and touches the big sea of salt water. At the western side of the salt water, this world is an island.

The other brothers thought the plan sounded like a good one. When everything was ready, they started on their journey. For a good many years they kept going and many things happened to them; however, they always continued straight westward.

Finally, the brothers came to a place where the sun goes under the sky's edge. The sky bends down there, and sinks into the water. For a month, they camped and watched the things that were happening. They noticed just how the sun got under the rim of the sky and disappeared quickly. They saw some men trying to get under the edge of the sky, but it descended too quickly for them, and they were crushed.

The brothers noticed when the sky came up, the water sank lower; and when the sky went into the water, the water rose higher. Youngest brother said he wanted to try to pass under the rim of the sky when the sun slipped under on its sun-road. But eldest brother said he thought the happenings were too evilly mysterious, and he was afraid for them to try.

Without waiting for anyone's opinion, youngest brother ran very quickly under the sky's rim, and found the rim very thick. Second brother followed youngest brother like a flash. They kept on the sun-road with the water on each side of them. Eldest brother watched, and when he saw nothing had injured his brothers, he began to run after them.

The younger brothers turned from their safe place to encourage him, but at that moment the sky came down on the sun-road and crushed

Headdress
Seneca

eldest brother. But they did see his spirit shoot by them quickly. The two remaining brothers felt very, very sad.

They discovered that, on the other side of the sky, everything was different. Before them loomed a large hill, which they ascended, and they saw a very large village in the distance. A man came running toward them. As he approached them he called out, "Come!" They realized he was their eldest brother.

"How did you arrive here so quickly, brother?" they asked. "We did not see you come."

"I was too late, and passed by on a spirit road," he replied.

They noticed an old man walking toward them. He was youthful and strong in body, but his hair was long and white. He seemed like a very old man. His face showed wisdom and he bore himself like a chief. "I am the father of the people in the Above-the-Sky-Place," he said.

"Haweni'u is my son. I wish to advise you, because I have lived here a long time. I have always lived here, but Haweni'u was born of the woman on the island. When you see my son, call quickly, 'Nia'we 'ska'no!' If you fail to speak first, he will say, 'You are mine,' and you will be spirits as your brother is."

The three brothers proceeded and came to a high house made of white bark. They walked up the path to the door. A tall man stepped out quickly, and the brothers said the magic words. The great man said, "Doges' I have been watching you for a long time." The brothers entered the house. When inside, the tall man said, "In what condition are your bodies?"

"We have fine bodies," they replied.

"You do not speak the truth," the great man answered. "I am Haweni'u and I know all about your bodies. One of you must lie down, and I will purify him and then the other."

One brother lay down, and Haweni'u placed a small shell to his own lips, and put it on the brother's mouth. He also tapped him on the neck, and sealed the shell with clay. Haweni'u began to skin the brother. He took apart the muscles, and then scraped the bones. He took out the organs and washed them. Then he built the man again. He loosened the clay and rubbed his neck. He did this with both brothers, and they sat up and said, "It seems as if we had slept." Haweni'u said, "Every power of your bodies has been renewed. I'll test you."

The brothers followed Haweni'u to a fine grove of trees surrounded by a thick hedge. All kinds of flowers were blooming outside. "My deer are here," said Haweni'u.

A large buck with wide antlers ran toward them. "He is the swiftest of my runners. Try and catch him," said Haweni'u.

The men ran after the deer and rapidly overtook him. "He has given us good speed," the brothers said. They soon discovered they had many other superior abilities, and the great man tested them all on that day.

They returned to the white lodge, and the brothers saw a messenger running toward them. Upon his wide chest was a great bright ball of light. It was very brilliant. In some unknown language he shouted to Haweni'u and dashed on.

"Do you understand his words, or do you know that man?" asked Haweni'u. "He is the Sun, my messenger. Each day he brings me news. Nothing from east to west escapes his eye. He has just told me of a great war raging between your people and another nation. Let us look down on the earth and see what is happening."

He led them to a high hill in the middle of the country, and looked down through a hole where a tree had been uprooted. They saw two struggling bands of people and all the houses burning. They could hear people crying and shouting their war-cries.

"Men will always do this," said Haweni'u, and then they came back down the hill.

The brothers stayed a very long time in the upper world, and learned so much they could never tell it all at one time. Sometimes they looked down on the earth and saw villages in which no one lived. They seemed to be waiting for people to be born and live there. In the upper world they saw villages, likewise, awaiting the coming of people from below.

Haweni'u told them a good many things, and after a time asked a messenger to lead the brothers to the path that the Sun took when he came out on the earth in the morning. They followed the messenger and came out on the earth. They waited until the Sun had gone over the earth to the west. Again they went under the edge of the sky in the east, and came out in their own country again.

It was night and they slept on the ground. In the morning they saw their village, and it was overgrown with trees. They followed a familar path through the woods, and came upon another village. Their own people were living there. They went into a council-house and talked. They told their story, but no one recognized them except their sister, who was an aged woman by then.

She said, "The war of which you speak took place fifty years ago."

The brothers did not care too much for the earth now, but wished themselves back in the upper world. They were not like the other men, because they never grew tired. They were very strong and could chase animals and kill them with their hands. Nothing could kill the brothers, neither arrow nor disease. After a long time, they were struck by lightning, and they were both killed. Presumably, they were granted their wish, and joined eldest brother in the Above World.

Parker, "Three Brothers Who Followed the Sun," 473-478.

■

SEEK YOUR FATHER

Seneca

Mrs. Asher Wright served as a Christian missionary to the Senecas for fifty years. She spoke their language perfectly, and recorded these two legends that were related to her by Esquire Johnson, an old Seneca Chief. He described the origin of the twins Good and Evil, and said the Sun was made by the Good-minded twin out of the face of his dead mother, the first earth-woman, who was the daughter of the Sky-woman.

Another version of this Seneca legend, dated 1876, tells practically the same story, but names the Sky-woman as having borne first a daughter, who, without any knowledge of a man, became that earth-mother of the twins Good and Evil. That daughter died giving birth to the twins, and she was buried by her mother, the Sky-woman.

■

Sky-woman said to her grandson the good-mined-spirit, "Now you must go and seek your father. When you find him, you must ask him to give you power."

She pointed to the East and said to him, "He lives in that direction. You must go on and on, until you reach the limits of this huge island. Then continue onward, as you must paddle upon the waters, until you come to a high mountain, which rises straight up out of the water. You must climb this mountain to the summit. There you will see a wonderful being, sitting on the highest peak. You must say to him, 'I am your son.'

"Your father is the Sun, and through you, he is also the father of mankind, because of your earthly origin from my daughter."

Parker, "Seek Your Father," 474-478.

■

A MASHPEE GHOST STORY

Wampanoag

Nauset or Cape Cod Indians, from the exposed position on the Cape, included the Mashpees of the Wampanoag tribe. Their entire territory came under the observation of many early explorers to the "New World," including Samuel Champlain in 1606, and the English Captain Thomas Hunt in 1614-1615. Hunt kidnapped 27 Wampanoag Indians, all of whom were sold into slavery, a just cause perhaps why five years later the Pilgrims landed and first were met by wary, unfriendly Wampanoags. Later, their Chief Massasoit officially welcomed the Pilgrims at Plymouth and signed a treaty of friendship dated 1621.

This area had escaped a great smallpox epidemic of 1617. The Nausets increased in population as tribal members were driven from their original villages by whites toward 1700. Mashpee village became the principal location of Wampanoags, also referred to as Massasoits after their famous Chief Massasoit. Later, his second son succeeded him and was called King Philip, establishing a strong Indian confederacy. King Philip's war against the whites, 1675-1676, in which the Chief was killed, resulted in the loss of central power of the New England tribes. Long established tribes on Martha's Vineyard also belonged to this Group, derived from the Algonquian linguistic family.

■

One night on Cape Cod at Gay Head, a Mashpee woman and her children were alone in their wigwam. The children were sound asleep in their blankets and their mother sat knitting beside her central fire-pit. As customary, her door-flap was wide open. Suddenly she became aware of someone approaching her doorway, and went to see who it might be.

A sailor stood outside. She asked him, "What do you want?" He replied, "I'd like to come inside and warm myself by your fire, because my clothes are wet and I feel chilled to the bone."

She invited him inside and offered a place for him to sit beside the fire to dry out and warm himself. She placed another log on her fire, then resumed her knitting. As she watched the fire, she noticed that she could see the fire right through the sailor's legs, which were stretched out between her and the fire—as if he were a ghost!

Her fear of him increased, but since she was a brave woman, she kept on with her knitting while keeping a suspicious eye toward the visitor. Finally the sailor turned to the Indian woman and said, "Do you want any money?"

Her first thought was not to answer his question. Then he repeated, "Do you want any money?" She replied, "Yes."

The sailor explained, "If you really want a large amount of money, all you have to do is go outdoors behind your wigwam. Beside a rock there you will find buried a kettle full of money. I thank you for your hospitality. Good night." He went away.

The Mashpee woman did not go outdoors immediately, as she wanted to think about the sailor's proposal. She sat and knitted and thought for a while longer. Still, she felt frightened from the evening's experience and was reluctant to leave her wigwam. More knitting time elapsed. Then she thought, "I might as well go out and see if the sailor spoke the truth—to see if there really is a kettle of money out there."

She took her hoe and went outside to the back of her wigwam, and easily saw the place described by the sailor. She began to dig with her hoe. She realized that every time she struck her hoe into the ground, she heard her children cry out loudly, as if in great pain. She rushed indoors to see what was their trouble. They were soundly sleeping in their blankets.

Again and again she dug with her hoe; each time her children cried out loudly to her; each time she rushed in to comfort them, only to find them soundly asleep as she had left them.

After these episodes had occurred several times, the mother decided to give up digging for the night. She thought she would try again early next morning after bright daylight and her children were awake.

Morning came, but she wondered if she had only dreamed last night's happenings. Her children were eating their breakfast when she went out to the digging place. There was her hoe, standing where she had left it. But she could see that someone else had been there in the meantime, and had finished digging while she slept.

Before her, she saw a big round hole. She knew someone had dug up the hidden treasure. She was too late for the pot of gold promised by the ghostly sailor. But again she thought and wondered, "But was I really too late?"

Again she thought, "That sailor may have been the Evil Spirit in disguise—or even a real ghost. Perhaps he was tempting me to see whether I cared more for my children, or more for the gold?"

Nevertheless, the Mashpee woman and her children continued to live in their village for a long, long time, even without the benefit of the ghost's kettle of gold.

Knight, "Mashpee Ghost Story," 136-137.

■

RABBIT AND OTTER, THE BUNGLING HOST
Micmac

Many native American tribes have legends in which various animals display their ways and means of obtaining food from others, sometimes using trickster methods. They return meal invitations and even attempt to provide food of a similar nature and in the manner of the previous host. Sometimes, this leads to trouble.

■

There were two wigwams. Otter lived in one with his grandmother, and Rabbit lived with his grandmother in the other. One day Rabbit started out and wandered over to visit Otter in his camp. When Rabbit entered Otter's wigwam, Otter asked if he had anything to eat at home. "No," replied Rabbit. So Otter asked his grandmother if she would cook something for Rabbit, but she told him she had nothing to cook.

So Otter went out to the pond directly in front of his camp, jumped in, and caught a nice long string of eels. Meanwhile, Rabbit was looking to see how Otter would catch his food. With Otter's great success, Rabbit thought he could do the same.

Rabbit then invited Otter to come over to his camp the next day. His grandmother had already told him that she had nothing to cook for their meal, but asked him to go out and find something. Then Rabbit went out to the same pond where Otter had found the string of eels; but he could get nothing, not one fish, as he could not dive no matter how hard he tried.

In the meantime, his grandmother was waiting. She sent Otter out to find Rabbit, who searched and finally found him at the same pond, soaked and with nothing to show for his efforts.

"What's the matter with you?" he asked.

"I'm trying hard to get us some food," he replied.

So friendly Otter jumped into the pond and again caught a string of fish, this time for Rabbit's grandmother to cook for their dinner. Then Otter went home.

The next day, Rabbit started out to visit Woodpecker. When he reached Woodpecker's wigwam, Rabbit found him at home with his grandmother. She got out her large pot to cook a meal, but said, "We have nothing to cook in the pot." So Woodpecker went out front to a dry tree-trunk, from which he picked a quantity of meal. This he took to his grandmother, and she made a good dinner for them.

Rabbit had watched how Woodpecker obtained his meal, so he invited Woodpecker over to visit him. The very next day Woodpecker arrived at Rabbit's wigwam for a visit. Rabbit asked his grandmother to hang up her pot and cook them some dinner.

"But we have nothing to cook," she replied. So Rabbit went outside with his birch-bark vessel to fill it with meal. He tried to dig out the meal with his nose, as he had seen Woodpecker do. Soon Woodpecker came out to see what caused the delay.

Quilled box
Micmac

Poor Rabbit was hurt, with his nose flattened out and split in the middle from trying to break into the wood. Woodpecker left to return to his own wigwam without any dinner. Ever since then, Rabbit has had to carry around his split nose.

Another day, desperate for food, Rabbit thought he would go and steal some of Otter's eels. He got into the habit of doing this every second night. Toward spring, Otter began to wonder where his eels had gone, as his barrel was getting low.

Otter thought he would keep watch and soon found Rabbit's foot tracks, and said to himself, "For that, I am going to kill Rabbit." Now Rabbit knew what was going on in Otter's mind, and when Otter reached Rabbit's camp, he fled.

Otter asked Rabbit's grandmother, "Where has Rabbit gone?"

"I don't know," she replied. "Last night he brought home some eels, then he went away."

"He has been stealing my eels," said Otter. "Now, I'm going to kill him."

So began Otter's search for Rabbit, who guessed Otter would be trailing him. Otter began to gain on Rabbit, who picked up a small chip and asked it to become a wigwam. Immediately, the chip became a wigwam and Rabbit became an old man sitting inside.

When Otter came along and saw the wigwam, he also saw the gray-headed old man sitting inside. He pretended to be blind. Otter did not know that this was Rabbit himself. Out of pity for him, Otter gathered some firewood for the old man and asked if he had heard Rabbit passing by. "No, I have not heard any one today." So Otter continued his search.

Later, Rabbit left his wigwam and started out on another road. Otter could not pick up Rabbit's trail, so he returned to the wigwam. Not only was it empty, but gone entirely. Only a chip remained in its place.

Otter then saw Rabbit's tracks where he had jumped out of the wigwam. This trick made Otter very angry and he cried out, "You won't fool me again." Otter followed the new trail.

When Rabbit sensed Otter was closing in on him, he picked up another chip and wished it to become a house, and there was the house, ready to live in. Otter came along and was supicious as soon as he saw the house with a veranda across the front, and a big gentleman walking back and forth all dressed in white, reading a paper.

This, of course, was Rabbit himself, but Otter did not know it. He asked the big gentleman, "Have you seen Rabbit go this way?" The man appeared not to hear. So Otter asked again. The gentleman replied in Pidgin English a phrase that meant, "Never saw Rabbit." But Otter looked hard at him and noticed the man's feet, which were Rabbit feet. So Otter felt certain this was his prey.

The big gentleman gave Otter some bread and wine, and Otter left hurriedly to again track Rabbit back to the house. He came to the place, but the house was not there. Otter could see the tracks where Rabbit started running away.

"He'll never have a chance to trick me again, that's his last time!" declared Otter.

Rabbit soon came to the head of a bay where there was a very small island, so small that a person could almost jump over it. He jumped onto the island and wished it to become a man-of-war.

Otter came to the same shore and saw the big ship anchored there, and the big gentleman in a white suit walking the deck. Otter called to him, "You can't trick me now! You're the man I want."

Then Otter swam out toward the ship, to board it and to kill Rabbit. But the big gentleman sang out to this sailors, "Shoot him! His skin is worth a lot of money in France."

Speck, *Micmac Tales of Cape Breton Island*, vol. VI, 64-66.

■

THE ORIGIN OF THE IROQUOIS NATIONS
Iroquois

About 1390, today's State of New York became the stronghold of five powerful Indian tribes. They were later joined by another great tribe, the Tuscaroras from the south. Eventually the Iroquois, Mohawks, Oneidas, Onondagas, and Cayugas joined together to form the great Iroquois Nation. In 1715, the Tuscaroras were accepted into the Iroquois Nation.

■

The Five Nations

Long, long ago, one of the Spirits of the Sky World came down and looked at the earth. As he traveled over it, he found it beautiful, and so he created people to live on it. Before returning to the sky, he gave them names, called the people all together, and spoke his parting words:

"To the Mohawks, I give corn," he said. "To the patient Oneidas, I give the nuts and the fruit of many trees. To the industrious Senecas, I give beans. To the friendly Cayugas, I give the roots of plants to be eaten. To the wise and eloquent Onondagas, I give grapes and squashes to eat and tobacco to smoke at the camp fires."

Many other things he told the new people. Then he wrapped himself in a bright cloud and went like a swift arrow to the Sun. There his return caused his Brother Sky Spirits to rejoice.

The Six Nations

Long, long ago, in the great past, there were no people on the earth. All of it was covered by deep water. Birds, flying, filled the air, and many huge monsters possessed the waters.

One day the birds saw a beautiful woman falling from the sky. Immediately the huge ducks held a council.

"How can we prevent her from falling into the water?" they asked.

After some discussion, they decided to spread out their wings and thus break the force of her fall. Each duck spread out its wings until it touched the wings of other ducks. So the beautiful woman reached them safely.

Then the monsters of the deep held a council, to decide how they could protect the beautiful being from the terror of the waters. One after

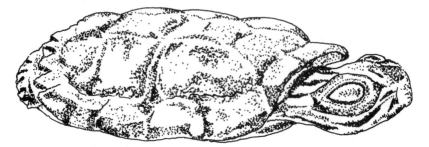

Soapstone turtle
Iroquios

another, the monsters decided that they were not able to protect her, that only Giant Tortoise was big enough to bear her weight. He volunteered, and she was gently placed upon his back. Giant Tortoise magically increased in size and soon became a large island.

After a time, the Celestial Woman gave birth to twin boys. One of them was the Spirit of Good. He made all the good things on the earth and caused the corn, the fruits, and the tobacco to grow.

The other twin was the Spirit of Evil. He created the weeds and also the worms and the bugs and all the other creatures that do evil to the good animals and birds.

All the time, Giant Tortoise continued to stretch himself. And so the world became larger and larger. Sometimes Giant Tortoise moved himself in such a way as to make the earth quake.

After many, many years had passed by, the Sky-Holder, whom Indians called *Ta-rhu-hia-wah-ku*, decided to create some people. He wanted them to surpass all others in beauty, strength, and bravery. So from the bosom of the island where they had been living on moles, the Sky-Holder brought forth six pairs of people.

The first pair were left near a great river, now called the Mohawk. So they are called the Mohawk Indians. The second pair were told to move their home beside a large stone. Their descendants have been called the Oneidas. Many of them lived on the south side of Oneida Lake and others in the valleys of Oneida Creek. A third pair were left on a high hill and have always been called the Onondagas.

The fourth pair became the parents of the Cayugas, and the fifth pair the parents of the Senecas. Both were placed in some part of what is now known as the State of New York. But the Tuscororas were taken up the Roanoke River into what is now known as North Carolina. There the Sky-Holder made his home while he taught these people and their descendants many useful arts and crafts.

The Tuscaroras claim that his presence with them made them superior to the other Iroquois nations. But each of the other five will tell you,

"Ours was the favored tribe with whom Sky-Holder made his home while he was on the earth."

The Onondagas say, "We have the council fire. That means that we are the chosen people."

As the years passed by, the numerous Iroquois families became scattered over the state, and also in what is now Pennsylvania, the Middle West and southeastern Canada. Some lived in areas where bear was their principal game. So these people were called the Bear Clan. Others lived where beavers were plentiful. So they were called the Beaver Clan. For similar reasons, the Deer, Wolf, Snipe and Tortoise clans received their names.

Erminnie Smith, *Origin of the Iroquois Nation*, 47.

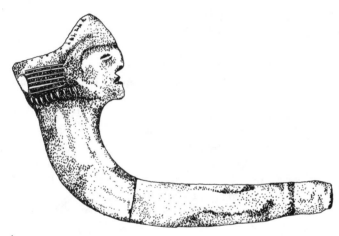

Clay pipe
Iroquois

DE-KA-NAH-WI-DA AND HIAWATHA
Iroquois

The Hiawatha in this story is the historic person of the late fourteenth century. He should not be confused with the character in Henry Wadsworth Longfellow's poem, *The Song of Hiawatha*.

In the late nineteenth century, the Iroquois Six Nations Council asked their six hereditary Chiefs to write in English for the first time the traditional oral history of the formation of the League of Five nations. It was formed about 1390, 100 years before Columbus discovered America. (The Tuscaroras joined the League conditionally in 1715.)

The traditional history was dictated by the six ceremonial Chiefs, one from each of these tribes: the Mohawks, Oneidas, Cayugas, Senecas, Onondagas, and the Tuscaroras. Two subchiefs were appointed secretaries, and the typewritten report was prepared by an Indian. On July 3, 1900, the completed history was approved by the Council of the Confederacy.

■

About 1390, an Iroquois mother living near the Bay of Quinte had a very special dream: A messenger came to her and revealed that her maiden daughter, who lived at home, would soon give birth to a son. She would call him De-ka-nah-wi-da (De-käh-a-wēē-dà). When a grown man, he would bring to all people the good Tidings of Peace and Power from the Chief of the Sky Spirits.

De-ka-nah-wi-da was born, as the dream foretold. He grew rapidly. One day he said to his mother and grandmother, "The time has come for me to perform my duty in the world. I will now build my canoe."

When it was completed, and with the help of his mother and grandmother, he dragged the canoe to the edge of the water. The canoe was made of white stone. He got into it, waved good-bye, and paddled swiftly away to the East. A group of Seneca hunters on the far side of the bay saw the canoe coming toward them. De- ka-nah-wi-da stepped ashore and asked, "Why are you here?"

The first man replied, "We are hunting game for our living."

A second man said, "There is strife in our village."

"When you go back," De-ka-nah-wi-da told them, "you will find that peace prevails, because the good Tidings of Peace and Power have come to the people. You will find strife removed. Tell your Chief that De-ka-nah-wi-da has brought the good news. I am now going eastward."

The men on the lakeshore wondered, because the swift canoe was made of white stone. When they returned to their village and reported to their Chief, they found that peace prevailed.

After leaving his canoe on the east shore, De-ka-nah-wi-da traveled overland to another tribal settlement and asked the Chief, "Have you heard that Peace and Power have come to earth?"

"Yes, I have heard," answered the Chief. "I have been thinking about it so much that I have been unable to sleep."

De-ka-nah-wi-da then explained, "That which caused your wakefulness is now before you. Henceforth, you will be called Chief Hiawatha. You shall help me promote peace among all the tribes, so that the shedding of blood may cease among your people."

"Wait," said Hiawatha. "I will summon my people to hear you speak." All assembled quickly.

"I have brought the good tidings of Peace and Power from the Chief of the Sky Spirits to all people on earth. Bloodshed must cease in the land. The Good Spirit never intended that blood should flow between human beings."

Chief Hiawatha asked his tribe for their answer. One man asked, "What will happend to us if hostile tribes are on either side of us?"

"Those nations have already accepted the good news that I have brought them," replied De-ka-nah-wi-da. Hiawatha's tribe then also accepted the new plan of peace.

When the Messenger departed, Hiawatha walked with him for a short distance. "There is one I wish to warn you about because he may do evil to you," confided De-ka-nah-wi-da. "He is a wizard and lives high above Lake Onondaga. He causes storms to capsize boats and is a mischief-maker. I go on to the East."

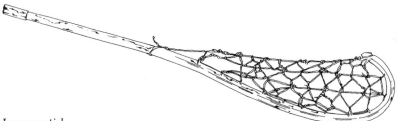

Lacrosse stick
Iroquois

Hiawatha had three daughters. The eldest became ill and died. Not long afterward, the second daughter died. All of the tribe gathered to console Hiawatha and to help him forget his great sorrow. One of the warriors suggested a game of lacrosse.

During the game, the last of Hiawatha's daughters went to the spring for water. Halfway there, she saw a beautiful high-flying bird of many bright colors. She called for the people to look at the bird. Then the huge creature swooped down toward her. In fear, she started to run back to her lodge. At the same time, the people came running to see the bird. Hiawatha's daughter was knocked down in the confusion. They did not see her and she was trampled to death.

"Has the wizard sent that bird and caused the death of my daughter?" wondered Hiawatha. Deeper in sorrow, he decided to leave his tribe and go away.

A few days later, he met De-ka-nah-wi-da, who commissioned him a Peacemaker. Henceforth, Hiawatha would spend his time going from village to village and spread the good Tidings of Peace and Power, so that the children of the future would live in peace.

The Mohawk Nation was the first to accept the peace plan, and they invited Hiawatha to make his home with them. One night De-ka-nah-wi-da appeared outside Hiawatha's sleeping room. "It is now urgent," he said softly, "that you come with me. We must go at once to another settlement. I have been there before and I promised to return."

On their way, they came to a large lake. De-ka-nah-wi-da asked Hiawatha to choose between paddling across the rough water and flying over it. Remembering the warning about the wizard, he chose to fly over the lake. De-ka-nah-wi-da used his supernatural power and turned both of them into high-flying birds.

When they reached the opposite shore, they resumed their natural bodies. Then they journeyed to the top of a very high hill to see the one chief, the great wizard, who had not yet accepted the good news of peace. Upon seeing him, Hiawatha was startled—the wizard's head was a mass of writhing snakes. His hands and feet were clawlike and twisted. He used his power to persecute others.

After a long time of discussion and gentle persuasion, Hiawatha noticed that the wizard began to smile! He exclaimed, "I do want to accept your plan of Peace and Power."

At once the wizard began to change. His hands and feet straightened. Hiawatha combed the snakes from his hair. Soon other chiefs arrived to help in the wizard's regeneration.

De-ka-nah-wi-da then asked all the chiefs and their chief warriors and assistants to meet on the shores of Lake Onondaga for a Council. Hiawatha, Chief of the Mohawks, asked the Oneida, Seneca, and Cayuga chiefs to bow their heads with him before the reformed wizard, who was the Onondaga Chief Atotarho (A-tä-tär'-ho). This was their way of showing their acceptance of him and their willingness to follow his leadership when called upon.

The Messenger stood before the Council and explained a plan for the Constitution of the Iroquois League of Peace:

"Let us now give thanks to the Great Chief of the Sky Spirits, for our power is now complete. 'Yo-Hen, Yo-Hen,'" he said, meaning praise and thanksgiving.

The Great Spirit created man, the animals, earth, and all the growing things. I appoint you, Atotarho, Chief of the Onondagas, to be Fire-

Keeper of your new Confederacy Council of the Five United Iroquois Nations.

"Chief Warrior and Chief Mother will now place upon your head the horns of a buck deer, a sign of your authority.

"Hiawatha shall be the Chief Spokesman for the Council. He will be the first to consider a subject and to give his opinion. He shall then ask the Senecas, Oneidas, and the Cayugas for their opinions, in that order. If not unanimous, Atotarho's opinion will be considered next. Hiawatha shall continue the debate until a unanimous decision is reached. If not accomplished within a reasonable time, the subject shall be dropped.

"Let us now make a great white Wampum of shell beads strung on deer sinews. Each bead will signify an event and create a design of memory. We shall place it on the ground before the Fire-Keeper. Beside it we shall lay a large White Wing. With it, he can brush away any dust or spot—symbolic of destroying any evil that might cause trouble.

"We shall give the Fire-Keeper a rod to remove any creeping thing that might appear to harm the White Wampum or your grandchildren. If he should ever need help, he shall call out in his thunderous voice for the other Nations of the Confederacy to come to his aid.

"Each Chief shall organize his own tribe in the same way for the peace, happiness, and contentment of all his people. Each Chief shall sit at the head of his own Council and matters shall be referred to him for final decision.

"In the future, your Annual Confederacy Council Fire shall be held here at the Onondaga village of Chief Atotarho. It will be your Seat of Government.

"Let us now plant a symbolic tree of long leaves destined to grow tall and strong. It will represent your unity and strength. When other nations wish to accept the good Tidings of Peace and Power, they shall be seated within the Confederacy Council. Atop the tall tree will proudly sit an all-seeing eagle to watch and warn you of any danger.

"Let each Chief now bring one arrow to form a bundle of arrows. Tie them together so tightly that they cannot be bent or broken apart. Place the bundle of arrows beside the Council Fire as another symbol of your unity and strength.

"Let us join hands firmly, binding ourselves together in a circle. If a tree should fall upon the circle, your circle cannot be broken. Your people can thus be assured of your unity and peace.

"If a Council Chief should ever want to remove himself as Chief, then his Horns of Authority shall be placed upon the head of his hereditary successor.

"You Chiefs must now decide what you will do with your war weapons," said De-ka-nah-wi-da.

Hiawatha wampum belt

Hiawatha then led the thoughtful discussion of the subject. The men agreed to dig a deep chasm where there was a rushing river beneath. Into this river the chiefs and their chief warriors threw all of their armaments of war. Then they closed the chasm forever.

De-ka-nah-wi-da reconvened the Council and stated:

"I charge you never to disagree seriously among yourselves. If you do, you might cause the loss of any rights of your grandchildren, or reduce them to poverty and shame. Your skin must be seven hands thick to stand for what is right in your heart. Exercise great patience and goodwill toward each other in your deliberations. Never, never disgrace yourselves by becoming angry. Let the good Tidings of Peace and Power and righteousness be your guide in all your Council Fires. Cultivate good feelings of friendship, love, and honor for each other always.

"In the future, vacancies shall be filled from the same hereditary tribes and clans from which the first Chiefs were chosen. The Chief Mother will control the chiefship titles and appoint hereditary successors. New Chiefs shall be confirmed by the Confederacy Council before the Condolence Ceremony. At that time, the Horns of Authority shall be placed upon the head of the new Chief.

"All hunting grounds are to be in common. All tribes shall have co-equal rights within your common boundaries. I now proclaim the formation of the League of the Five Iroquois Nations completed. I leave in your hands these principles I have received from the Chief of the Sky Spirits. In the future you will have the power to add any necessary rules for the safety and well-being of the Confederacy.

"My mission is now fulfilled. May your Confederacy continue from generation to generation—as long as the sun will shine, the grass will grow, the water will run. I go to cover myself with bark. I will have no successor and no one shall be called by my name." De-ka-nah-wi-da departed from the Council Fire.

Chief Spokesman and Lawgiver Hiawatha arose before the Council and stated, "Hereafter, when opening and closing the Council Fire, the Fire-Keeper shall pick up the White Wampum strings and hold them high to honor all that has gone before. He will offer praise and thanksgiving to the Great Spirit. In Annual Council, the Chiefs will smoke the Pipe of Great Peace.

"If a chief stubbornly opposes matters of decision before the Council, displaying disrespect for his brother Chiefs, he shall be admonished by the Chief Mother to stop such behavior and to act in harmony. If he continues to refuse, he shall be deposed.

"If a family or clan should become extinct, the Chief's title shall be given to another chosen family within his Nation, and the hereditary title will remain within that family."

All of the Chiefs of that first Council Fire agreed with Hiawatha's plan as a part of their new Constitution.

Chief Fire-Keeper Atotarho arose before the Council with his arms outstretched, holding the White Wampum strings high in praise and thanksgiving to the Holder of the Heavens. Herewith, he closed the historic first Confederacy Council Fire of the Iroquois League of Five Nations. "Yo-Hen, Yo-Hen!" he solemnly concluded, "thank you."

The Five Chiefs then smoked the Pipe of Great Peace!

Scott, *Royal Academy of Canada, Proceedings and Transactions*, 194-246.

Wallace, *White Roots of Peace*.

Glossary

Adobe Sun-baked mud and straw bricks used by Southwestern Indians to make pueblos.

Adz A woodworking tool with an arched axlike blade at right angles to the handle.

Balil A four-piece folding wand.

Bidarka A large skin boat.

Barrabara Native home of Aleuts.

Dine or Dinneh People.

Hogan An Indian dwelling constructed of a log and stick frame covered with mud or sod. It traditionally faces east.

Kiva An underground ceremonial chamber or men's clubhouse. Typical of Southwest Indians.

Language family A term used in linguistics to describe languages spoken by other tribes but with elements in common.

Maize Indian corn.

Parfleche A leather storage bag.

Parka Native dress or coat.

Pipestone A type of red clay used to make pipes. Also called "catlinite" after the frontier painter George Catlin, who wrote about the pipestone quarry in Minnesota.

Plochgo A sling.

Pitistchi Glittering grains of mineral.

Pueblo Term used for a particular type of architecture common among Southwest Indians—apartment-like, up to five stories high, interconnected by ladders, made from stone or adobe bricks.

Sachem The chief of a tribe.

Shaman A tribe member who keeps tribal lore and rituals, and interprets and attempts to control the supernatural. Also called "medicine man."

Torbarsars Native shoes.

Travois A wooden-framed device used for transporting people and posessions behind dogs.

Tule A marsh reed common to the Southwest region, used to make rafts, sandals, and other items.

Tepee A conical tent home typical of the Plains Indians.

Sweat lodge A grass and mud hut with a central fire pit for sweating, a ritual purification through exposure to heat.

Scared bundle Personal items wrapped for ceremonials and prayers.

Wampum Strings or belts of small shell beads originally used as tribal records that became a form of money after the arrival of Europeans.

Wigwam A domed or conical dwelling with a pole frame overlaid with bark or animal skin.

Weewish Corn meal mush.

Yucca root Makes good suds.

Yukelah Dried salmon.

Bibliography

Abbreviations used: BAE=*Bureau of American Ethnology*; JAFL=*Journal of American Folklore*; OHQ=*Oregon Historical Quarterly*. NOTE: Legends from *JAFL* are reproduced by permission of the American Folklore Society.

Books and Periodicals

Bell, James Mackintosh. "The Legend of the Big Bird." *JAFL* 16 (1903): 73, 77.

———. "The Legend of the White Bear." *JAFL* 16 (1903): 78.

Brindze, Ruth. *The Story of the Totem Pole*. New York: The Vanguard Press, 1951.

Brown, Wallace. "The Strange Origin of Corn." *JAFL* 3 (1890): 213-214.

Burlin, Natalie Curtis. *The Indian's Book*. New York: Harper & Bros., 1907.

Clark, Ella E. "Warm Wind Brothers vs. Cold Wind Brothers." Oregon Folklore Bulletin. (Winter 1962).

Clark, Ella E., ed. *In the Beginning*. Billings: Montana Council for Indian Education, 1977.

Coolidge, Mary Roberts. *The Rain Makers*. Reprint. New York: AMS Press.

Cunningham, Eileen Smith. *Lower Illinois Valley Local Sketches of Long Ago*, 1980.

Curtis, Caroline. *Life in Old Hawaii*. Honolulu: Bishop Museum Press, 1970.

Curtis, Edward S. *The North American Indian*. 20 vols. Orig. pub. 1907-1930. Reprint. New York:Johnson Reprint Corp.

Cushing, Frank H. "How the Hopi Indians Reached Their Country." *JAFL* 36 (1923): 12.

———. "Origin Myths from Oraibi." *JAFL* 36 (1923): 163-169.

Dixon, Roland. "The Origin of Mount Shasta Eruptions." *JAFL* 13 (1910): 27-29.

Dorsey, J. Owen. "Teton Ghost Story." *JAFL* 1 (1888): 71-72.

Dorsey, George A. "The Two Boys Who Became Stars." *JAFL* 17 (1904): 153-160.

Dow, Charles Mason. "Indians at Niagara Falls." *Anthology and Bibliography of Niagara Falls* 2 (1921): 380-381.

Du Bois, Constance Goddard. "The Story of Creation." *JAFL* 14 (1901): 181.

———. "The Fly at the Council." *JAFL* 14 (1901): 183.

———. "Impiety of Frog." *JAFL* 14 (1901): 183-184.

———. "Fiesta Tu-Chai-Pai." *JAFL* 14 (1901): 184-185.

Gifford, Edward W. and Gwendoline H. Block. *California Indian Nights Entertainment*. Orig. pub. Reprint. New York: AMS Press.

Fewkes, J. Walter. *"How a Medicine Man Was Born, and How He Turned Man Into a Tree." JAFL* 3 (1884): 273-275.

———. "Origin of Thunderbird." *JAFL* 3 (1884): 265-266.

Gilliland, Hap. *The Flood* . Billings: Montana Council for Indian Education, 1972.

Gilmore, Melvin. *Prairie Smoke*. Bismarck, N. Dak.: Bismarck Tribune Co., 1922.

Golder, F.A. "Raven and His Grandmother." *JAFL* 16 (1903): 16-9.

———. "The White Faced Bear." *JAFL* (1907): 296-299.

———. "Two Inquisitive Men." *JAFL* (1903): 19.

———. "The Girl Searches for Her Lover." *JAFL* (1903): 26.

———. "Girl Who Married the Moon." *JAFL* (1903): 28-31.

———. "Kodiak Island Legends." *JAFL* (1907): 16-19, 26.

Gray, Ralph. *America's Wonderlands*. Washington, D.C.: National Geographic Society, 1959.

Greenlee, R. F. "The Milky Way." *JAFL* 58 (1945): 138-40.

———. "Men Visit the Sky." *JAFL* 58 (1945): 143.

Grinnell, George Bird. "How Buffalo Hunt Began." *Scribner*. 1892 and 1920. Reprints.

———. "Eagle War Feathers." *JAFL* 13 (1900): 163.

———. "Enough is Enough." *JAFL* 13 (1900): 169.

———. "Falling-Star," *JAFL* 34 (1921): 308-312.

Hudson, J. W. "Legend of the San Joaquin Valley." *JAFL* 15 (1902): 104-105.

Hutchings, J. M. *In the Heart of the Sierras, the Yosemite Valley.* Oakland and San Francisco: Pacific Press Publishing House, 1886.

James, Harry C. *Haliksai: A Book of Hopi Legends.* El Centro, Calif.: Desert Magazine, 1940.

Jameson, Anna. *Winter Studies and Summer Rambles in Canada,* vol. 2. New York: Wiley and Putnams, 1839.

Jones, Louis Thomas. *So Say the Indians.* San Antonio, Texas, The Naylor Co.: 1970.

Kate, Dr. H. "The Hero with the Horned Snake." *JAFL* 2 (1889): 55.

Knight, Mabel Frances. "A Mashpee Ghost Story." *JAFL* 38 (1926): 136.

Kroeber, A. L. "Puma and the Bear." *JAFL* 14 (1901): 252; 274.

———. "Porcupine Hunts Buffalo." *JAFL* 14 (1920): 270.

———. "Coyote vs. Duck." *JAFL* 14 (1920): 272.

———. "Two Fawns and a Rabbit." *JAFL* 14 (1920): 275.

———. "Two Grandsons." *JAFL* 14 (1920): 278.

Kurath, Gertrude P. ed. *Standard Dictionary of Folklore, Mythology and Legend.* vol. 2. New York: Funk & Wagnalls, 1950.

Lauman, Charles, "Arch Rock on Mackinac Island." *Magazine of History,* 3 (1906): 115-6; 192-3.

McDermott, Louisa. "Coyote's Adventures in Idaho." *JAFL* 14 (1901): 240-251.

McLaughlin, Marie. *Myths and Legends of the Sioux.* Bismarck, N. Dak.: 1916.

McWhorter, Lucullus V. *Papers.* Pullman, Wa.: Washington State University.

Michelson, Truman. "Piegan Tales." *JAFL* 24 (1911): 246-247.

Mooney, James. "The Ball Game of the Birds and the Animals." *19th Annual Report BAE (part 1, 1900): 286-287.*

———. "The Cherokee Play Ball." 24th Annual Report, BAE (1907): 575-586.

———. "The First Fire." BAE (1900).

———. "The Origin of Game and of Corn." *JAFL* 1 (1887): 97-108.

Nequatewa, Edmund. *Truth of a Hopi: Stories Relating to the Myths and Clan Histories of the Hopi.* Flagstaff, Ariz.: Northland Press, 1967.

Nusbaum, Aileen. *Zuni Indian Tales.* New York, 1926.

Palmer, William R. *Pahute Indian Legends.* Salt Lake City: Desert Book Co., 1946.

Parker, Arthur C. "Three Brothers Who Followed the Sun." *JAFL* 23 (1910): 473-474.

———. "Seek Your Father." *JAFL* 23 (1910): 474-478.

Potts, William John. "A California Creation Myth." *JAFL* 5 (1892): 73-74.

Powers, Stephen. *Tribes of California.* Washington D.C., Government Printing Office, Department of Interior, 1877. Reprint. New York: AMS Press, 1976.

Pradt, George H. "The Origin of Winter and Summer." *JAFL* 15 (1902): 88-90.

Price, Samuel. *Black Hills: The Land of Legend.* Los Angeles, Calif.: DeVorse & Co., 1935.

Prince, John. "The Passamaquoddy Wampum Records." *Proceedings of the American Philosophical Society.* 23 (1897): 479-95.

———. "Notes on Passamaquoddy Literature." *Annals of the New York Academy of Science.* 23 (1901): 381-85; 11 (1898): 369-75.

Radin, Paul. "Boy Stolen by Thunderbird." *JAFL* 22 (1909): p. 300.

Ray, Verne. "Coyote Introduces Salmon." *JAFL* (1932): 167-71.

———. "Sanpoil Folk Tales." *JAFL* (1932): 152-53.

Russell, Frank. "The Origin of Animals." *JAFL* 11 (1898) p. 259.

———. "The Origin of Fire." *JAFL* 11 (1898): 261-2.

———. "An Apache Medicine Dance." *American Anthropologist.* December 1898: 367-72.

Sampson, Martin, and Rosalie Whitney. *Swinomish Totem Pole Tribal Legends.* Bellingham, Wash.: Union Printing Co., 1938.

Schoolcraft, Henry R. *North American Indian Legends.* Philadelphia: Lippincott & Co., 1856. Reprint.

Schultz, James Willard. *Blackfeet Tales of Glacier National Park.* New York: Gordon Press, 1977.

Scott, Duncan C. "De-Ka-Nah-Wi-Deh and Hiawatha." *Royal Society of Canada Transactions,* vol. 5, Section 2 (1911): 194.

Skinner, Alanson. "The Legend of the White Plume." *JAFL* 38 (1925): 458.

Skinner, Charles. *Myths and Legends of Our Own Land.* 3 vols. Philadelphia: J. B. Lippincott Co., 1896. Reprint. Singing Tree Press, 1969.

Smith, Bertha H. *Yosemite Legends.* San Francisco: Paul Elder & Co., 1904.

Smith, Erminnie. "Origin of the Iroqouis Nation." *Second Annual Report, BAE* (1880-1881): 47.

Speck, Frank G. "The Giant and the Four Wind Brothers." *JAFL* 28 (1915): 74.

———. "Micmac Tales of Cape Breton Island." *JAFL* 6: 660.

———. "Penobscot Tales." *JAFL* 48 (1935): 95-6.

————. *The Penobscot Man: Life History of a Forest Tribe in Maine.* Philadelphia: University of Penn. Press, 1940.

Spence, Lewis. *Myths and Legends of the Pawnees.* London: George G. Harrap, 1914. Reprint: Krause, 1972.

————. *Myths of North American Indians.* Orig. pub. 1930. Reprint. Krauss.

Spencer, J. "Shawnee Folklore." *JAFL* 22 (1909): 319.

Squier, Ephraim. "Nanabozho and the Great Flood." American Whig Review 8 (October 1848): 392-93. Reprint. New York: AMS Press, 1965.

Steele, Richard F. The History of Northern Washington. Chicago: Western Historical Publishing Co., 1904.

Swan, James. "The Indians of Cape Flattery." Smithsonian Contribution to Knowledge #220 (1869-70): 64-5.

Swanton, John R. "The Walnut Cracker." BAE Bulletin 88 (1929): 115-6.

————. "How Rabbit Fooled Alligator." BAE Bulletin 42 (1924-1925): 52-3.

————. "In the Beginning." BAE Bulletin 42 (1924-1925): 84-5.

————. "The Celestial Canoe." BAE Bulletin 42 (1924-1925)

————. "Adoption of the Human Race." BAE Bulletin 42 (1924-1925): 240.

————. "Creation." BAE Bulletin 42 (1924-1925): 487.

Voth, H. R. "How Medicine Man Resurrected Buffalo," "The Origin of the Buffalo." *JAFL* 25 (1912): 44, 45.

Wallace, Paul A. W. *The White Roots of Peace.* Philadelphia: University of Penn. Press, 1946. Reprint. Chauncy Press.

Wilson, Maggie. "Spider Rock." Arizona Highways (March 1977): 44.

Wright, Harold Bell. *Long Ago Told (HUH-KEW-AU-KAH) Legends of the Papago Indians.* New York: D. Appleton Co., 1929.

Transcripts

Office of Indian Affairs. "Buffalo and Eagle Wing." Bulletin 17 (1922).

A personal collection of legends and myths recorded mostly by Ella E. Clark from Indians in five northwestern states, 1950-55:

"Coyote and the Monsters of Bitteroot Valley," recorded by E.E.C. "Coyote and Multnomah Falls," told by a Wasco woman to her husband, Henry Charley, a Nez Perce; recorded from him by Clara Moore of Hood River, Oregon, transcribed by E.E.C.

INDEX